INDIAN SHAKERS

A *messianic cult*

of the

Pacific Northwest

H. G. BARNETT

SOUTHERN ILLINOIS UNIVERSITY PRESS

Carbondale and Edwardsville

FEFFER & SIMONS, INC.

London and Amsterdam

Library of Congress Cataloging in Publication Data

Barnett, Homer Garner, 1906-
    Indian Shakers.
    (Arcturus books edition)
    1.   Indian Shaker Church.   2.   Indians of North
America—Northwest, Pacific.
[E78.N77B3 1972]   299'.7   72-5482
ISBN 0-8093-0595-X

ARCT
URUS
BOOKS ®

First published November 1957
Arcturus Books Edition September 1972
This edition printed by offset lithography in the
United States of America

CONTENTS

Introduction 3

I In the Beginning 11

II Adding Converts 45

III The Opposition 86

IV Internal Troubles 107

V Doctrine 141

VI Faith 176

VII Ritual Elements 204

VIII Ceremonies 243

IX John Slocum's Religion 285

X Later Accretions 308

XI Turmoil and Prophecy 337

Notes 355

Bibliography 365

Index 371

LIST OF ILLUSTRATIONS

	FACING PAGE
John Slocum's Relatives	26
Shaker Church near White Swan, Washington	218
Dining Hall next to the Church	218
Interior of the Church	218
Altar of the Church	250
Shaker Church at Tulalip, Washington	250
A Shaker Cemetery	314
Interior of a Shaker Home	314

INDIAN SHAKERS

INTRODUCTION

MANKIND has never lacked its visionaries who claim supernatural power to alleviate its ills. Societies everywhere have produced seers and clairvoyants who draw upon their mystic insight to allay the anxieties of petitioners beset with doubts and dilemmas beyond human power to resolve. More spectacular, but answering the same need for security, are the messiahs or prophets who cry out against the afflictions of their people and proclaim a divinely inspired formula for mass relief from frustration and oppression. Such dedicated men with self-appointed missions to admonish and lead their fellowmen have emerged on numberless occasions throughout history and in all parts of the world. Few of them survive the indifference of their contemporaries; still fewer are remembered after their passing; and only rarely do the names of the few come to the attention of men who write books. Still they continue to appear, regardless of their reception, for they are impelled by the conviction that they are the chosen instruments of some divine purpose.

Prophets are seldom honored among a people who feel that they are masters of their own destiny. A social atmosphere which stimulates a spirit of self-confidence is not one to encourage reliance upon superhuman forces. It is only when the shocks and perils of existence are overwhelming that the individual feels the need for something to support his mortal weaknesses. Prolonged frictions and failures can accomplish this demoralization, and the effect is magnified when a whole society is so affected. Intense deprivation keeps the individual in an emotional turmoil, and his inability to command or even to comprehend the sources of his frustration makes it appear to him that it is humanly impossible to reduce the confusion and doubt that engulfs him and others about him. Under such circumstances the way is prepared for the messiah. For in this extremity of despair men have no recourse save supernatural help, and frequently they have been ready to place their trust in the insights and the promises of a self-anointed vehicle of the almighty.

Subjugated peoples suffering from the oppression of their masters have often reached this desperate decision. So have nations, tribes, and communities of people who, while not reduced to ignominious bondage, have lost the initiative to establish their own patterns of existence. Still others have brought catastrophe and impotence upon themselves through wars of attrition, fratricidal cleavages, and prolonged dynastic struggles. Whatever the far cause of the helplessness of such people, the immediate cause of their disquiet is the collapse of a valued way of life and their failure to find a satisfying substitute for it.

The Indians living around Puget Sound, in Washington State, like many other native groups overrun by the expansion of western civilization, reached this impasse by cumulative steps through the relinquishment of their independence to alien standards and controls. In 1855 the several bands occupying the area formally abandoned to the United States government all title to land formerly claimed by them with the exception of a few square miles of territory incorporated in reservations set aside for their exclusive use. In return for this peaceful cession they were guaranteed certain compensations, mostly in the form of services designed to bring them within the orbit of western ideas and practices. They were, for example, to receive assistance in farming and in other aspects of the settled life as well as formal schoolroom instruction in academic subjects. At the same time certain restraints were placed upon them. They were required to live peaceably in accordance with standards of conduct determined by federal laws and regulations. In order to ensure their rights and to hold them to their obligations a representative of the government, a reservation superintendent, was assigned to administer their affairs. In the prosecution of his duties the agent inevitably frowned upon or explicitly forbad the continuance of certain native customs and, in varying degrees and according to his lights, insisted upon the acceptance of the white man's ideals.

In the process of becoming civilized the Indian became a ward of the government and gradually lost the initiative to set his own goals and to follow his own inclination. His community and family life were disrupted and his religious convictions were shaken. The white man's rules were obscure and came to be feared rather than to be supported. Many of the promised rewards held out for good behavior failed to materialize or were disillusioning in their realization. Further complications arose in some localities with the introduction of liquor, gambling, and other enticements for the unsophisticated. There were also bewildering sectarian struggles for Indian converts among the Christian mission agencies in the area. The turmoil was further intensified in some communities in the 1870's by rumors of government plans to dispossess the Indian of his land, an agitation that was doubtless relished if not inspired by unscrupulous whites who coveted the land and were willing to abet the demoralization of the Indian in any way possible in order to dispose of the obstacle and the nuisance that he presented.

John Slocum was one of the many Indians who were caught in the cross currents of these troublous times. He belonged to the Squaxin band, a small group formerly concentrated along the shores of a southern branch of Puget Sound. During his lifetime, however, most of this homeland was ceded to the government and his people were scattered and reduced in numbers in their efforts to adjust to changed conditions and new demands. Not much is known of Slocum's early life. It is reported that he received some instruction in the Catholic faith from the missionaries who arrived in this area about 1840. He married Mary Thompson and fathered thirteen children, several of whom died in infancy. Only two daughters, it seems, lived to raise families of their own. By his own admission Slocum was not industrious or provident; as a young man he had a weakness for whisky, betting on horse races, and other white man's vices. In these respects he was not unlike many of his contemporaries. There was, in fact, nothing remarkable about him during most of his life. He was "about 5 feet 8 inches high ... rather stoop shouldered, with a scattering beard, a shock of long black hair, a flat head (fashionably flat, and produced by pressure while a baby), bright eyes, but in all rather a common expression of countenance." [1]

Slocum first attracted public attention in 1881 when he was about forty years of age. At that time he lived with his family on an isolated homestead on Skookum Chuck, not far from Olympia, where he worked at logging. In the fall of that year he fell sick and apparently died. His friends were summoned and preparations were made for his funeral. But during the long wake that was held and while the mourners were waiting for his coffin to arrive, Slocum revived in view of his wife and others assembled around the room in which his body lay covered with a sheet. His resurrection was in itself an awful sight, but the words that he soon began to speak were even more wonderful. He confirmed his death and related that his soul had left his body and gone to the judgment place of God where it had been confronted by an angel who turned it away from the promised land. The error of his sinful life was revealed to him, and he was instructed to return to earth to bear witness to his transformation and to lead other sinners into the Christian way of life. It was, he said, for the purpose of carrying out this mission among the Indian people that he was granted a brief stay of ultimate death. He announced that a church must be built for him immediately and that he would begin his preaching at a stipulated time in the near future.

Slocum's account of his experience made a profound impression on those who heard him. A church was soon built, and many local Indians came to hear him proclaim the need for their regeneration and to learn what they must do to accomplish it. Excitement ran high for a time, and out of it came a number of conversions. Slocum was not a colorful figure or a vigorous proselytizer, however, and gradually the dramatic appeal of his death and resurrection was dulled by his unimaginative leadership. Also, it appears that he, too, began to lose conviction in his mission or felt defeated by its requirements. At any rate, after a few months, he began to grow indifferent to his own admonitions and slipped into the rut of his old vices. It is probable that the whole episode of his translation might have faded out of memory had not another spectacular event precipitated a second crisis in his life and that of his faithful wife, Mary. That event was his second serious illness.

Slocum again fell ill about a year after his presumed death. He was expected to die, this time without promise of a reprieve. Mary had remained a devoted adherent of her husband's teachings, and the impending catastrophe of his death disturbed her profoundly. The crisis induced in her a hysterical seizure in the course of which she approached Slocum's prostrate body praying, sobbing, and trembling uncontrollably. When her convulsion had passed it was observed that Slocum had recovered slightly. This improvement Mary attributed to her seizure, which she interpreted as a manifestation of divine power. That was the beginning of "shaking." The incident also provoked a renewal of interest in Slocum's message and marked its rebirth as the Indian Shaker religion.

With the revitalization of the cult that came with Mary's inspiration, news of it spread far beyond the Squaxin and their immediate neighbors. Within a short time Indians on all the adjoining reservations were informed of the miracle of shaking, and many converged on Skookum Chuck and Mud Bay to witness and experience its effects for themselves. Converts and local congregations soon made their appearance among the Skokomish, Chehalis, Puyallup, Nisqually, Clallam, and other Indian groups in Washington. The movement was given considerable impetus in 1892 through the guidance and assistance of an attorney in Olympia; and a few years later it was consolidated as a religious body with legal sanction through the efforts of another sympathetic white man in the same city. With these encouragements the cult continued to spread in all directions and ultimately gained followers on most of the reservations of Washington and Oregon and spilled over into southern British Columbia and northwestern California. The vigor of the various congregations has fluctuated over the years, but at the present time there are active Shakers in all these localities.

The Shaker religion, like many other messianic cults, is a compound of native and Christian forms. Yet, in their reworking of these ingredients, the Shakers have created a unique system of belief and behavior. Frequently they have accepted an alien interpretation in the beginning, and then proceeded to build upon this foundation with a minimum of reference to the original nature or meaning of the borrowed idea. Many Christian elements were incorporated and manipulated within the cult framework in this fashion. In other instances, as with most of the ideas associated with the practices of Indian medicine men or shamans, there has been a spontaneous and perhaps an unwitting absorption of alien ideology. In any event, the cult soon repudiated its heritage, refused to accept the status of an affiliate of the established religions, developed inspiration and sanction of its own, and evolved a pattern of internal development peculiarly its own. Persecution by outsiders had certain negative effects, but it also acted as a powerful stimulus for the consolidation and intensification of belief. The particular historical circumstances surrounding the origin and growth of the cult have given it content and emphasis; but there is, nonetheless, much about it that it has in common with other religious movements. From the standpoint of theology as well as history it is an interesting phenomenon.

The cult has undergone numerous changes since its inception in 1881. Its history is, in fact, marked by constant flux of ritual and belief. In part, this characteristic is due to the fact that the movement has diffused through several Indian groups with quite different cultural backgrounds. At the geographical extremes, the Indians of Vancouver Island have little in common in point of language and general pattern of living with the Yurok of northwestern California, and the Squaxin differed in important respects from both. Under such circumstances, numerous local remodelings and infusions were inevitable as one tribe after another became acquainted with shaking and the relief that it promised.

There is, however, an even more fundamental reason for the dynamic quality of the religion. That is its sanction of individualism. Cult doctrine exhibits a remarkable tolerance toward individual interpretation and the extension of its forms and meanings. Private convictions, based on alleged supernatural sanctions called "teachings" or "gifts," have always been regarded as the true sources of doctrine and procedure; and while conflicts of personalities and ideas have inevitably resulted, the basic tenet granting the truth of individual inspiration has never been questioned.

Individual reactions to situations have been fluid and spontaneous, a circumstance which has given the cult an effervescent, unpredictable aspect that can be disturbing to those accustomed to the orthodoxy of Christian denominations. The Shaker ideal encourages individual deviation. New ideas and departures from past routines have not been without limit—they never are—but it remains true that the Shaker religion affords an outstanding instance of the effects of placing a premium on the imagination.

The individual Shaker is free in still another respect: there are very few rigid standards which demand his conformance. A member of the church, even an officer, has few obligations and restraints placed on him. The degree to which he submits to the pronouncements of others or to the recognized ethical, ritual, or ideological standards is primarily a matter of conscience and personal conviction. Whether and to what extent he participates in Shaker activities, whether he prays, confesses his sins, fears God, loves his fellowmen, shakes, cures—all these things are left to his decision. Certain compulsions and strictures are operative, but they are not immutable. In the last analysis, the individual generally does what he pleases, takes what he likes and leaves the rest.

There can be no complete account of a movement still in progress. As with the history of any living, growing thing, so with the history of the Shaker cult. Any record of its development must select an arbitrary segment for study. The historical segment considered in the following chapters comprises the evolution of the cult from its beginnings in John Slocum's mystical experience to the stage of elaboration it has now reached. The included data embody the results of direct observation and inquiry in Shaker communities over a five year period as well as library research on the reports of other observers. For the most part and for better or worse, the Shakers themselves have here told their story. They at any rate are recognized as the primary and ultimate sources of information about their religion.

✠

✠

THE ORIGINS of most human institutions remain unknown despite our interest in them and our efforts to uncover them. Our ignorance in this respect is due not simply to the fact that many customs are ancient and their beginnings have been forgotten. Neither is it due solely to the difficulty of setting one particular turn of events apart from all that preceded it and saying, "That was precisely when and how it began." Equally important is the fact that no human being can with certainty assess the social significance of his experiences; hence he frequently ignores or belittles events which in retrospect turn out to be the beginnings of important developments. John Slocum's death and resurrection made slight impression on his contemporaries, and of those who heard about it only a few intimate friends viewed the mystery with more than a passing interest. Contemporary written accounts of this episode in the life of an obscure Indian are therefore practically nonexistent, and for a knowledge of it we must resort to hearsay, speculation, and faulty memory records.

While everyone thinks that he knows a fact from a fancy, it is often difficult or impossible to get agreement on what is one and not the other. Even eyewitnesses to an event can violently disagree on its true character; and the occurrence takes on new aspects with each retelling as one interested

11

reporter passes his interpretation along to another. These divergences are magnified with the passage of time and the fading of memory, so that in the end, when the event is long passed, it becomes impossible to reconcile essential differences; and the "truth" is, again, a matter of evaluation and interpretation. Thus it is with the beginnings of the Shaker cult, and doubly so because all knowledge of it has been carried in the minds of an illiterate people.

The brief account of the origin of the cult given in the Introduction is a generalized sketch abstracted from the specific statements offered by a number of Shakers. It is as accurate as such a synthesized narrative can be, and it would probably be endorsed by most Shakers; but it does not tell the story of John and Mary Slocum as any particular Shaker has related it. The individual accounts are illuminating in their variations and in the points of their convergence, in addition to revealing the meaning that the religion has for its adherents.

The first statement of this nature that I encountered was among the Yurok Indians in 1938. It was given to me reluctantly by Jimmy Jack, the introducer of the cult among this group of Indians at Requa, California, at the mouth of the Klamath River. He was so diffident and apologetic that at first it was difficult to get him to talk about it, a circumstance that was understandable in part as a result of the attitude which most outsiders, especially white people, have taken toward the cult, but even more so on account of his personality, about which more will be said later. He gradually warmed to those aspects of the subject within his personal experience, but it was evident that he knew little about the historical antecedents of the religion which he had first heard about at Siletz, Oregon, in 1926. His knowledge of, and his interest in, the history of the church of which he at the time was a minister were confined mainly to events that had taken place during the previous twelve years within a circuit of Indian communities extending from Siletz, Oregon

to Eureka, California, on the coast and to the Klamath
Reservation in the south central part of Oregon in the interior.

He knew that the religion had been started a long time ago
by John Slocum in Washington. Slocum had died and come
back to life to teach the Indians to be good so that they
could go to heaven. Jack was unable to fill in any details surrounding the alleged death and resurrection, and when inquiry was made about Slocum's moral teachings he said that
members of the church must love one another and must not
drink or smoke. Pressed further, he brought out two typewritten sheets of paper and a picture. The latter was the
same picture which appears in James Mooney's account of
the Ghost Dance,[1] and was inscribed on the back: "John Slocum who died in 1882 and returned to life in the living fire
of God for 14 years. Mud Bay Louie the first Bishop of the
Shaker Church." The typewritten material was entitled "The
Rules and By-laws of the Shaker Church," and "The Papers
of Incorporation of the Shaker Church." More will be said
of these documents later. It is probable that Jack, although
unable to read, knew or had at one time known the import
of the documents, but it was evident that their particulars
had left no lasting imprint upon his mind. He did not trust
himself to discuss or expand upon the contents of the papers
after showing them. They were for him a shield and a warrant rather than a source of doctrine and inspiration.

On the Hupa Reservation shortly after this interview, the
question was broached to a prominent Indian there. This
man was not himself a Shaker, but he had befriended the
first converts who visited the Hupa six years before. He was
a leader in the traditional Hupa ceremonies; but he had a
reputation for being lax and irregular in the performance of
his ritual obligations. He was amiable and indifferent about
most things. When the group of Shakers appeared they had
no place to hold their meetings so he offered them his house
"if they wouldn't get drunk and make too much noise."

They claimed later to have cured him of an illness, but he did not admit this. He had heard the story of John Slocum from one of the visiting Yurok Shakers.

According to this informant Slocum was a Washington Indian who had died and gone to hell. There he saw people drinking, dancing, gambling, smoking, and disporting themselves in all manner of reckless and rowdy fun. Then he was given just a peek into heaven, which was solemn and restful. God promised Slocum this more serene future existence if he would go back to the Indians and teach them to be good and be good himself. He was also given the promise of some new kind of "medicine" to heal the sick. With that Slocum came to life. He told the people what God had said. His wife had been crying over his dead body for so long that her head and arms began to tremble uncontrollably. Later, when she heard what John said, she claimed that her "shaking" was the medicine that God had promised.

An ex-minister of the Hupa church was more explicit. In addition to being willing and able to discuss the subject he, as well as the other Hupa Shakers, had recently had occasion to be reinformed and reflect upon various aspects of it. The month before, in August of 1938, a convention had been held at the local church with the Shaker bishop from Tulalip, Washington, and other visitors in attendance. The meetings were enlivened by a renewal of the controversy between the fundamentalist element in the membership who reject the Bible as a source of inspiration and the progressive Bible-reading faction. There had been no public review of church history, nor any announced question of precedent or original sanction; but no doubt some of these issues came up in conversations outside the meetings.

In any event, the former minister, who was a mild but a very sincere Shaker, had some knowledge of the details of John Slocum's death and the advent of shaking. Slocum died, he said, about fifty-two to fifty-five years ago (1938), at Mud Bay in Washington. It was no longer than that, because Peter

Heck, who was still living up there, had known him. He had been a sinful man all his life, gambling and betting on race horses, until one morning at four o'clock he died. He went to heaven and there saw God who showed him seven churches, now represented by seven candles on the Shaker altar, from which he was to choose one to take back to the Indian people. He took the one that called for the use of bells, candles, and singing, because he knew that the Indians would like those things. And while he lay dead his wife wept over him. Finally, still sobbing, she went outside their house and down to the beach. There her whole body began to tremble and, coming back inside, she continued to shake over her husband's corpse. God's power was in her because Slocum came back to life. This was at four o'clock in the afternoon of the same day.

There was some confusion when Slocum returned to life because he did not like his wife's interpretation of her shaking and did not think that God had inspired it. She, however, was stronger and the people believed her when she said that it had brought Slocum back to life. Two other men, Mud Bay Louis and Mud Bay Sam, became the leaders of this new religion. They were put in jail because of it, but they would not give it up. Finally, they were asked to appear before a Presbyterian minister to be questioned about their beliefs. They told the minister the same things that are in the Bible, although neither of them could read. After that no one bothered the Shakers; and now their church is incorporated, and if anyone disturbs their meetings he can be arrested. The incorporation took place in 1910.

The account of another former Hupa minister was less extended but in its details it contained some significant differences from the others. This individual was not illiterate, as were the others, but he sided with those who belittle the importance of the Bible for Shakers and emphasize direct revelation. He had been the minister of the local church for two years, but his constant condemnation of Bible reading in the services created so much trouble that he resigned. During the convention he took the same stand and vigorously opposed the bishop on this issue. He was one of the most aggressive of the local members.

According to him, John Slocum died several years ago in Washington. He had lived a sinful life and so could not enter heaven. He was required to go back to earth and teach the Indian people to be good. Jesus showed him seven churches to choose from, and he took the Shaker religion because in it nobody needed to read the Bible. This was good for the Indians, and the Shaker religion is an Indian religion. By following John Slocum's teaching Indians know what is in the Bible without having to read it. Jesus also promised Slocum some medicine for the sick. After this he came to life and began preaching what Jesus had told him. Later on he fell sick and his wife thought that he was to die again. She cried a lot as he lay ill, and while still weeping she went out of the house and sat by a creek. Finally, she began to wash her face in the water of the creek, and as she did so she started to shake. She came back into the house, unable to stop. Slocum was afraid of her and said, "What is the matter with you? Are you crazy?" And then it came to him that this was the medicine that he had been promised.

A few years later, in 1942, the inquiry into the origin of the cult was continued in Washington. One of the first individuals to offer an explanation there was a phlegmatic Yakima Indian who was not a Shaker. Several years previous, perhaps around 1920, the Shakers had "worked on" him when he was sick for two nights, and they claimed to have cured him. He said nothing of this, however, in his references to the religion. According to his version, the religion began when a man over on Puget Sound died after leading a bad life. "His name was Louie, I think." He died "maybe about thirty years ago." He was dead six days and nights and came back to life on the seventh day. He began to preach and everybody came to hear him. He could cure people and read what was in their minds. They called him "My Brother." The white preachers did not like for him to start the religion; they wanted him to get a license. Today the Shakers cure each other, and they can find lost articles, too. But they do not charge anything for it. They first came among the Yakima when a man's body was lost in the river. Aiyel, a Cowlitz Indian, and five other Shakers were brought over to look for it. They found it and everybody was surprised. They are good at things like that.

C. J. Johns was one of the most active Shakers on the Yakima Reservation. It cannot be said that he was prominent in church affairs, nor even that his attendance at services was regular. He was not much interested in these matters, nor in anything that had gone before him. He was concerned with the present and he stood apart in his self-assumed capacity as a prominent practitioner of the faith-healing tenets of the religion.

According to him the cult began a long time ago, he did not know just when. He had joined in 1909, and "maybe it started forty or fifty years before that." John Slocum of Mud Bay was the originator. He was a logger, and one day while working a log fell on his neck and broke it. He was dead for three days. Then he came to life and told the people that it was not yet his time to die and if they wanted him to live to come forward and shake hands with him. He did this because one of his enemies was present and Slocum wanted to force a confession from him. When everybody had shaken hands with him he said that he had work to do and that they must build a "little house—he didn't say church—where he would tell them about it." His friends brought lumber from Olympia and began to erect the building, but before they had quite finished the roof Slocum began to preach. They had to cover the hole in the roof with canvas.

Johns did not know just what Slocum told the people, but he supposed that it was all about God. He preached every Sunday for quite a while. "But his wife was the first to receive

the shakes." This happened later on when Slocum again fell
sick. An Indian doctor was called to heal him, and his wife
was sorry about this. She went to the beach to dig clams,
and there received the shake. She came back to the house,
and the shaman was frightened and left. That was the real
beginning of the religion.

Enoch Abraham was a friend of Johns, but intellectually
and temperamentally they were quite different. Abraham
had an inquiring and a reflective mind, and he had given
much thought to Shaker doctrine and ritual. He had been intimately associated with the church since his conversion in
1899, and had served as head elder for thirteen years when
he was forced to retire because of blindness in 1939. He was
perhaps the best informed of anyone upon its activities, and
he remembered an impressive amount of historical detail.
Like Johns, he read the Bible religiously; but, unlike Johns,
he advocated its use in church. He was a practicing Christian,
humble and tolerant, for to him Shakerism was a Christian
religion. His knowledge of many of the facts about it had
come from associating with the early leaders such as Mud Bay
Louis. He had spent the winter of 1899–1900 with Louis,
his brother Sam, Doctor Jim, and two others at their oyster-
ing grounds on Mud Bay. A new convert at the time, Abraham was eager to know about the religion, but he was able
to find out less than might be expected from these close
associates of John Slocum. "They were too busy culling
oysters," and apparently did not talk much about it. Slocum
himself was dead by then.

According to Abraham's information, Doctor Jim was
present when Slocum died the first time. He was the shaman
called to save Slocum's life. Some people say that Slocum
died of tuberculosis, others that a log fell on him. When
he died he was washed and laid out on a board while two
men went to Olympia in a canoe to get a coffin. "Some say
that he was dead for three days, but it must not have been
so long because when he came back to life a man was sent

on horseback to Olympia to tell the others that they did not need to get a coffin." The first thing that he did when he rose up was to say, " 'Anybody who wants me to live, come and shake hands with me.' And that's where the handshaking in Shaker services comes from." One man was present who did not like Slocum, and he was reluctant to shake hands. Then Slocum told the people to build a house for him where he could tell them about what he had seen. They started it, but the roof was unfinished when he began to preach. They had to cover the holes with canvas.

When he talked Slocum told the people that Indian doctors were bad. Indians must give them up and be cured by prayer. "I don't know what else he told them. That was eighteen years before my time, and Mud Bay Louie didn't talk about it. They didn't say how many he healed by faith —I asked that when I became an officer in 1926—because John Slocum was not a Shaker." His wife, Mary Slocum, started this part of the religion about a year later. Slocum was very sick and they thought he was going to die again. Doctor Jim was again called upon to save him and "Mary Slocum was sorry because Slocum had forgotten what he got from heaven." She went out to the beach, crying, and there "the power fell on her." She went back to the house and, turning to the left, circled it three times, shaking all the while. The people inside were afraid when she came in, and some of them left. She touched or brushed her brother Isaac and he started to shake; she touched his wife and a Nisqually man named Sylvester Yucton and they did the same, so that all four were shaking at the same time. Mud Bay Louis was not there, but he heard about it and later on he "got the power." "Seems like Mary Slocum didn't want to let people know about her power, but Louie did." Louis became a leader and gave out many new "teachings."

It was from Abraham that an account of the "teachings" and activities of Louis and several others was obtained, as well as many particulars on church organization and history.

The foregoing, however, sums up practically all that he knew about the origin of the cult.

John Allen, a former treasurer of the Yakima church, was prosperous, progressive, and rather well educated. While not volunteering that he was a member or had had any connections with the organization, he nevertheless praised what it had done for the Indians. It prohibited smoking and drinking, and "if a person gives himself up to it he can be cured by faith." He was not more specific. "The religion began," he said, "over by Olympia. Mud Bay Louie died—no, it was Mud Bay Sam. But before he died he told his wife not to bury him for three days. On the third day he came back to life and began to preach to the Indians, telling them that it was bad to lie, steal, drink, or gamble."

In 1943, John Ike, a Chehalis Indian who was currently active in the church near Oakville, Washington, gave the following odd version: There were two brothers, Jack and John Slocum. John died, but before this he told the people not to bury him for five days. They dressed him and laid him out, but the Indian agent heard about it, and on the fourth day he came to tell them that they must bury him. As he was arguing with them John's body began to move, and gradually he came to life. Then he began to preach. He started the Shaker religion.

A sincere Shaker, Silas Heck took a more mystical view of his religion than anyone else encountered. He was well educated, articulate, and thoughtful. Upon our first meeting in 1943 he showed me a copy of Willkie's *One World* and asked whether I had read it. We talked of that and other things on a more expanded horizon than is ordinarily possible with older Indians. He was seventy-one years old, the brother of a long-time bishop of the church, Peter Heck, and a relative of Mary Slocum through his father. When the question of the Shaker religion came up he said that a man by the name of Mooney had written it up in a large book. Asked whether the account was accurate, he replied that, "It is as accurate as he could get it, because it came straight from Slocum himself. Just a part of the book is about Slocum though, just a few pages; most of it is about the Sun Dance of the Sioux." [2]

Silas Heck had seen John Slocum and heard him preach after his supernatural experience. He did not know him before, because he was not a prominent man and the Heck family lived on the Chehalis Reservation. Seeing him after his presumed death and resurrection Heck remembered him as "a very quiet man. He seldom spoke, but when he did he said something. He was a sorrowful man. He learned a lot by that [his death]; so much that we couldn't understand him."

Despite this recollection—which was probably formed in retrospect—and his intimate connections with the important figures in the cult, Heck, like almost everyone else, had little historical interest in it. He did not, for example, know when John finally passed on or where he was buried; and the circumstances surrounding Slocum's trance were all but unknown to him. He recalled that when John "died" two men were sent to Olympia in a canoe to get a coffin for his body, but while they were away John rose up and began to talk and so another person was dispatched by a shortcut over the land to notify the others that a coffin was not needed. He guessed that John was dead for several hours, but his wife, who was present at our first interview, corrected him. Her mother was present as a mourner, having been one of the attendants who had helped to lay the body out. She affirmed that "John Slocum was cold—dead," and her mother had placed coins on his eyes, with one bandage to hold them on and another under his chin to keep his mouth closed. He was then stretched out on planks raised in the middle of a room in the Slocum house while many women and a few men sat in mourning around the walls. The wake had begun early one evening and continued through one full day and two nights when on the third day John's hand began to move and clutch at the bandages. The women who were present jumped up terrified, and many bolted out. Mrs. Heck's mother was frightened too, but since she had put the bandages on she helped take them off. John was somewhat stiff but alive and well.

At this point, Heck himself took up the story, saying that John's first act was to ask for a bath. His relatives complied by bringing in a bucket of water, but this he rejected. Wet cloths were then offered to him but he refused them too. Finally, he went to the beach and washed himself in salt water, "nature's own way to cleanse him." The second thing that he called for was a "garment," which had to be white. None such was at hand, so a sheet was folded over him after a hole had been cut in it to admit his head. His third request was for a church, "and it had to be built in two weeks, I think." There could be no delay in following his instructions, because he threatened to leave the people, "to die again," if they did not have confidence in him. The church was therefore built, but lumber was scarce and there were not enough split boards for the roof so the holes in it had to be covered with cattail matting.

When the church was thus made ready Slocum called the people into it and began to tell them what had happened to him. His spirit, he said, had left his body and gone to a gate beyond which was a beautiful land. But he could not enter for "he was stopped by a guard that Slocum called an angel." The angel told him to look back, and when he did so he could see his body lying dead. He was told that he could not go through the gate but must go back and teach the Indians about the second coming of Jesus Christ. They must prepare for this by giving up gambling, horse racing, drinking, smoking, and other bad habits. No one knew when Jesus would come again, but it might be soon. Furthermore, if they believed in what he, John Slocum, said, God would send them a new kind of medicine.

The people who came to hear Slocum were afraid that he was going to leave them again. It was because of this that they were so excited when once, while preaching, he fell to the floor unconscious. Several men rushed forward to pick him up. At another time he fell very sick and his wife, Mary, thought that he was going to die. That was when she began to shake, and it was the first time anybody did. That was the medicine that had been promised by God.

"Mud Bay Louie was the promoter of the Shaker religion," Heck said. "I don't know when he got the shakes, but I think that he was going along in a canoe after hearing Slocum preach. Slocum was always looked upon as the head though." Mary died many years ago. She carried on the religion after John died, but she never became a minister—"she refused it." Jack was an older brother of John. John and Mary had two daughters, Jenny and Cora. They both married Krise boys and their descendents live a few miles out of Olympia, near Kamilche.

Heck recalled that when word first began to reach the Chehalis people about the new religion they heard that all those who did not believe in it would be turned into birds and animals. "This was just a rumor," Heck continued. "Slocum did say that unbelievers would be destroyed. He didn't say how. I never heard him talk about hell. Once, though, Mary Slocum did tell a crowd that if they did not believe they would all be put on a mountain of ice and be left to die when the faithful marched off to heaven."

Peter Heck was fourteen years older than his brother Silas. He was not as well educated, and his English was not as good. He knew more facts. He had been the bishop of the Shaker church for almost twenty-five years. He talked freely, and the paragraphs which follow conform very closely, except for the English, to the character and extent of his responses to initiating questions.

John Slocum was living at Skookum Chuck, about twelve miles to the northwest of Olympia, when he "died" in 1881. He was dead for six hours, and during this time he lay in a room in his house covered with a sheet. His two brothers, Jack and Tom, went to Olympia in a canoe to get a coffin;

but before they returned Slocum came back to life, and another man was sent on horseback to stop them. When he first woke up only his father, his mother, and Jack Judson were there. He began to talk in English, and his father, who could not understand him, "thought that he was crazy." He told the people who came in that they must build a church for him in four days. "I don't know what else he said then," Heck continued, "but he began to preach after the church was put up." The roof on it was not finished by the evening of the fourth day, so they had to cover the open places with mats.

A lot of people came to hear what Slocum was going to say. He told them that when he left them ("he didn't say 'died'") he arrived at a gate where he was stopped by angels who told him that it was not time for him to die. "Everybody, when he is born, is given a time to die." The angels told him that he had four more years to live, if he would reform, and maybe more. "He was a bad man before this, drinking, gambling, and betting on racing horses." He was told to look behind him. He did, and there he saw his body laid out like a dead person. The next thing he knew his body was rising up in his house. But before this happened he was told that he must teach his people to be good. They must "clean their hearts, confess their sins," and prepare for the day when Jesus Christ would return to the earth. They were to have "a day and a half to get ready, but they wouldn't know when." Everybody should be prepared and hope for this time because when it arrived "John Slocum said all your dead children, and all your dead relatives would come back to this earth alive. . . . We liked that." It would be a new world then, a Christian world. And there would be so many people living that there would not be enough land for all of them; so the ocean would disappear and only one large river would remain from which to get water. Everybody would know when the time came because they would hear the voices of all the dead people up in the sky coming from a long ways off out of the east. But if a person were unprepared his dead children and other loved ones would pass by him.

John Slocum said that we must feel right in our hearts toward others. We should always be glad to see each other, and when we meet we should shake hands. Otherwise someone might die, and we should be sorry that we had not been able to shake his hand before he "left."

Another thing that John Slocum said was that God ("but he never said he saw God—only angels") was going to send down some kind of "medicine" for the Indians. He did not say what kind, but it was different from the doctoring of the shaman. All this time, from the beginning of the world, the Indians had had to go to shamans when they were sick, and these men were evil because they made people sick and even killed them. Also, a sick person, even if he were poor, had to pay a high price to these men in order to get well. God wanted to change this when he sent the new "medicine" because with it any person could cure, not only others, but himself; and it would be free to everybody. John Slocum did not know it, but when it came "this medicine was the shake." It came about a year after he "died." He was sick again and almost everyone expected him to die. Mary Slocum, his wife, was in despair. Exhausted from weeping, she went out of the house to a creek nearby to wash her face. There she felt something come down from above and flow over her body. "It felt hot," and she began to tremble all over. She came into the house, and when she touched her brother Isaac, he began to shake in the same way. "In those days it was contagious. Now we have to ask for it and get it direct from God." Mary also touched John, but he pushed her away. By the next day, however, he felt better, "and it came to his mind that this was the medicine."

It was an Indian doctor, Heck believed, who was responsible for Slocum's apparent death. Doctors were mean, and in those days they were always "poisoning" someone just to see whether they could do it or to get even for some slight. They did this by shooting their "tamanowus" (guardian spirit) into a person. Just before he died the spirit would begin to talk through the victim's mouth, telling who its master was and why he sent it into his enemy. Then it escaped back to its master. Doctors were killed for this, or they might be forced to pay, or both. John Slocum's relatives believed that Doctor Jim had "poisoned" him, and it was not certain what they were going to do about it. That was why Doctor Jim had two representatives sitting with Slocum's relatives at the wake; they were pleading his case. One of them was Jack Judson. But Doctor Jim did not "poison" Slocum; it was another shaman who was embittered by his gambling losses and envious of his victim's luck.

Doctor Jim was related in some way to Slocum. They addressed each other as "uncle" and "nephew," but they were not so directly related. It was like Heck and Doctor Jim's wife: she was a first cousin of his mother; and the same with Mary Slocum: she was Heck's father's first cousin. Both of these women he called "aunt." Doctor Jim he called "grandfather, but he wasn't a real grandfather."

Big Bill, Heck said, was a logger who got so sick that he couldn't work. Maybe he had tuberculosis. His wife tried to support them by taking in washing from the white people. Bill got so despondent because of this and his condition that he resolved to end his life. He tied two handkerchiefs together and tried to hang himself from the limb of a tree close to his house. When the cord tightened about his neck he saw a blinding light approaching him. It grew brighter and brighter, and then he could see that it was really the reflection from buttons on the shirt of his dead brother. His brother was standing in front of him and remonstrating with him, saying that he must save himself so that he could preach to the people. With that Big Bill began to struggle and make an outcry so that someone came and helped him down. Then he began to hold a kind of church service in his house on Sundays. Many of his neighbors came to hear him preach

FRONT ROW: Jenny Slocum (a daughter of John and Mary), Tom Slocum, Cora Slocum (another daughter of John and Mary), Ellen Slocum (wife of Tom)
BACK ROW: an unidentified woman and Mary Slocum

because they were curious. "They didn't believe him. They thought that he was crazy, talking all about God and sin." But he could see things that others could not. Once, for example, a prostitute came to hear him. He did not know her, but he soon realized her true character and sensed that she was there to flaunt her sins in his face. He shamed her before the others and turned her out. He also made prophesies, the most important of which was that soon "a great power" was going to fall upon some one in this vicinity. The recipient was to be either a Chehalis or a Skokomish Indian but because the songs of the latter were "a little faster" he was more likely to be one of them. And when this man appeared everyone must help him and believe in him, for he would be sent to them by God for their good. John Slocum was this man.

Peter Heck did not know Big Bill personally. He had never heard him preach. He knew no further particulars about his "services," nor about the circumstances surrounding Mary's original shaking experience. He did not know anything in particular about some of the other men intimately linked with the spread of the new gospel. Asked whether they believed in John's message he said, "I guess so. Everybody did. They got scared. They did not know how long that 'day and a half' was going to be. A white man said that a day is the same as seventy years, but nobody knew." Heck did not know what punishment, if any, John predicted for the unbelievers at the millennium. All that Slocum said was that unbelievers were on the left side of God and they were like sick people; when they decided to go to the right side it is just as if they had been cured. Slocum never mentioned hell or death. He said that if you mentioned the devil that made him proud and strong, and he might get you. For the same reason a person while praying or shaking should hold his face up to God, not look down at the floor toward the devil.

Willie Yucton, another Chehalis informant, was eighty-two years old. He was the younger brother of Sylvester, one of the men who was present when Mary began to shake. The father of Willie and Sylvester was a first cousin of Mary's father, and Sylvester Tucton had been living with the Slocums, helping John at logging when the latter became so ill. Willie Yucton knew the Slocums and their daughters well. He very early embraced the new faith and remained steadfast in it. Despite these auspicious circumstances, his knowledge of the background of the cult was fragmentary.

John Slocum, he said, was "killed by a broken bone in his neck," but this was caused by a shaman who "shot his tamanowus" into him. His brothers made a trip to Olympia to get a coffin, going by canoe; but before they could return Slocum revived and another man was sent by land to tell his brothers. The first thing that he wanted after he came back to life was a church. It had to be built in one day. The roof was unfinished when Slocum began to preach, so tent canvas was placed over the holes. He said that people were to shake hands when they met and when they parted; otherwise "they might die." He talked against Indian doctors. He said that the only good "power" comes from up above your head, never from other directions. If you "catch something" in your hands down on the floor, or over in the corner of the room, or outside the door, it is bad—throw it away. But if it comes from above it is good power; it will help you. He also warned against gambling, drinking, and smoking. God told him these things, and God told him to travel around and tell them to all of the Indians. "But he never did. He didn't want to; he was afraid he would be killed. Mud Bay Louie did though."

Some time later, Yucton said, John Slocum got sick again. The same shaman tried to kill him. He was very sick. His father had hired another shaman to cure him. His brother-in-law Isaac, and Sylvester were there. His wife, Mary, "got the shakes first." She was outside the house at a creek washing her face when "the power fell on her." Isaac and Sylvester got it too, and they were all shaking around Slocum when he revived. He did not like it and wanted them to stop. He said that it was the devil's work, but Mary claimed that it came from God. They argued about it later, but Slocum agreed to pray to find out what it was. He learned that it was good.

After this, Isaac, Mary Slocum's brother, took the lead in urging people to join the Shakers. He was a good talker. Sylvester did very little talking, but he had the power to cure sick people. He could see in advance whether a person could be made well or not. Both Isaac and Sylvester supported Mary in her declaration that the creek where the power had come to her must not be defiled by filth. The water could be used only for drinking and for washing the hands and face if they were already clean. Clothes, dishes, and dirty hands must not be washed in it. Mary would know if this happened.

John Slocum, Yucton said, was finally killed by the same shaman who had tried to do it twice before. His Shaker friends wanted to save him with God's power; but he refused, saying that it was time for him "to go now. He wanted to go to the good place."

Two other men in the lower Puget Sound area, both active Shakers, and both about seventy-five years of age, were able to supply only very condensed versions of the origin of the cult. George Bob of Nisqually affirmed that Slocum had been "killed" by a shaman, but that after a while he came to life and preached against whisky, tobacco, and gambling. "People make a mistake," however, when they say that he started the shaking. It was his wife, Mary, who first did this. She was gathering wood in the forest when the trembling came upon her. Slocum was impatient with her and thought that she was crazy. He finally had to admit, though, that it was a good thing.

George Sanders, living at Oakville, Washington, had heard that John Slocum was walking in the woods when he fell down "dead." When he came to, he was shaking. He touched his wife, as God had told him to do, and she began to shake. This shaking was a substitute for the old shaman's power which was used to kill people. Shaking is God's power, he said, and it is used only to cure the sick.

Annie James, a younger sister of Mary Slocum, was still living on the Skokomish Reservation in 1943, a kindly, generous, and sincere woman of about seventy years of age. She had been an adherent of the Shaker faith almost from the day of its inception; and she was the only known living eyewitness to the two most critical events in its formation. She was between eight and eleven years old when John Slocum, her brother-in-law, "died." The year of his "death" is uncertain; but the month was probably November. As she understood it, the ostensible cause was a broken neck, due to a fall in the woods where he was logging. "It was the talk," however, that this was the result of a shaman's machinations. His body was brought to the Slocum home at Skookum Chuck, on Mud Bay. The house was old style and roughly built. It had a dirt floor and was divided into two rooms or sections. The Slocum family lived in one section; in the other John kept his logging oxen. When he was "killed" his body was cleaned, dressed, and placed under a sheet in the middle of the living quarters. His two half-brothers, Tom and Jack, set out for Olympia in a canoe to get a coffin, but they had been gone only a few hours when John's body began to move. Several people were in the room at the time, including Mary, her mother, and young Annie. The three were quite close to the body, but Mary was weeping and her mother was preoccupied with efforts to console her. Annie had just come in to sit by her mother when she saw the movement. She nudged her and whispered, but her mother replied, "Go outside. Don't look at it." Then John stirred noticeably and began to push the sheet away from his face. He then placed his hands on the back of his neck and moved his head from side to side. He stretched his arms upward three times, then wiped his eyes three times. He sat up and looked around. Everybody was terrified. Then he began to speak.

He asked Mary for a clean sheet, and some water with which to wash himself. There was no water in the house, so someone went to bring it from the creek. John, however, went outside, removed his clothes, and washed in the rain barrel. He wrapped the sheet that Mary brought around him and told her to get rid of his clothes and the bedding on which he had been lying—the things associated with his "death." After that he spoke to everyone in the room, asking them to shake hands with him. He asked them to kneel, as he did, while he prayed; then he began to talk to them. He said that he had a message from God; that he had been up above but had been stopped at a gate and told that he must come back to earth. He had been told that he must explain to the people that gambling, drinking, and Indian doctoring were bad; that they must learn to pray before eating or going to bed and after getting up in the morning; that they must cross themselves on all these occasions; that they must confess their sins; and that they must go to church on Thursdays and Sundays. He added that he was to teach them more about these things on those days and would need a place to do it; so they must build a church for him by next Sunday. A man was sent on horseback to tell Tom and Jack that no coffin was needed.

In church Slocum prayed and preached against sin. He said that sometime Jesus was coming to this earth and that everyone must have a clean heart when this happened. That would be the end of the world, and those who did not believe in Jesus "would be destroyed."

"But John Slocum didn't keep his own word," Annie said. With time he grew lax in avoiding the very sins that he warned the others against. He was tempted by his old vices and gradually thought less and less of what God had told him. About a year after his death and resurrection the Skokomish, Nisqually, and other Indians met at Shelton's Prairie as they were accustomed to do for several days of feasting, visiting, and horse racing. Slocum went too, riding his horse. He intended to go just to look on but the temptation was too great. He entered his horse in a race and won his bets. Then, not long after that, a child of one of his relatives died and

he, along with some other men, took the corpse in a canoe
to the cemetery on a nearby island. On the way back the
paddlers of two of the canoes that had attended began to
race. Slocum was in one of them and in the excitement he
joined in the vigorous paddling. His crew won the race to the
mainland, but from the very moment that he touched the
paddle he began to get sick. He grew worse and nothing
seemed to help him. Unable to eat, he wasted away and finally
was "nothing but skin and bones." He was expected to die.

Throughout his illness Mary, his wife, refused to let a
shaman come near him. She was a sincere believer in his
message and had been grieved at his backsliding. She prayed
and cried a great deal. At length, as Slocum became steadily
worse, his father intervened in spite of Mary's opposition. He
hired a female shaman, erected a mat hut for her close to
the Slocum house, and had Slocum brought there for her
to doctor without interference. At the same time he made a
threat: if Slocum died he would kill Mary himself and bury
her body under her husband's coffin.

The distrust which exploded in this display of bitterness
had been smoldering over a number of years. Slocum's father
did not like the Thompson family, to which Mary belonged,
and his dislike had been fanned into hostility by a state of
tension and suspicion over a series of illnesses and deaths in
the two families which were attributed to the activities of
hired shamans. Years before, Henry Isaac Thompson, the
brother of Mary, was supposed to have coveted the wife of
John Kittle, a Slocum relative, and was alleged to have had
him killed by a shaman to secure her. Somewhat later Mary's
father died, and it was believed that Slocum's father had had
him disposed of in a similar fashion out of revenge. Then
when John "died," and when he again was near death, his
father was convinced that this was the work of a shaman acting at the behest and under the pay of the Thompson family. In particular, he suspected Doctor Jim and Sylvester
Yucton's father, both of whom were shamans, and both re-

lated to the Thompsons. Doctor Jim was a "cousin" of Mary's father and the other man was his "nephew." Slocum's father was confirmed in his suspicions when it was apparent that Mary intended to do nothing for her husband except pray, in which nonsense he had no faith.

The climax of these developments, according to Annie, unnerved Mary. When Slocum was taken to the shaman's hut she left the house and began to collect his logging implements, crying all the while. Annie followed her, not understanding what she was doing but worried about her. She showed unnatural strength in handling Slocum's heavy tackle; but as she started to wash her face in the creek near the hut where she could hear the shaman she "fainted." Annie screamed and others came to pick Mary up and carry her into the house. She was trembling and moaning and when she "came to" her head and hands were twitching. In this state she began to demand that Slocum be taken away from the shaman and be brought back in his house. Her strange appearance and her frantic demands unnerved the opposition, and Slocum was carried in and placed on mats on the floor. His nose was bleeding rather freely. He wore only some red underwear. Mary commanded that he be stripped of this, that he be washed, and that everything that had touched him while the shaman worked over him be thrown away. She called for her daughter Maggie, aged thirteen, who was at the time undergoing her puberty seclusion in a hut nearby under the care of an old woman.[3] She had Maggie stand at Slocum's head so that he would not have to face her in her dangerous condition; then she told her mother to stand at his left shoulder, her sister-in-law at his left side, her brother Henry (Isaac) on his right side, while she took her place across from her mother. All except Henry held candles in their hands and extended their arms upward over Slocum's body. Mary gave Henry a hand bell that Slocum used in his religious services and told him to ring it. At first, "he was bashful," but after a while he began to twitch and jump just as Mary was doing. Before long the two other women were doing the same. In the meantime Mary prayed fervently, calling upon God and Jesus to spare her husband's life, and repeating from time to time in a sobbing voice: "He is going to live. He is going to live. Jesus will save him. Jesus will save him." No one knows how long this performance continued; but when it was over Slocum's nose had ceased to bleed. It had stopped miraculously.

This was the beginning of shaking. Slocum at first rejected it as "devil's work." Then he had a relapse. Mary prayed over him again and he felt better. Others present accepted this as proof of God's power in shaking and joined in to help. More came when they heard about it, and the shaking went on for several days and nights. Some who were sick submitted themselves to the cure and attested to its efficacy. "Everybody was shaking before long."

As the first excitement subsided, Friday, Saturday, and Sunday nights became the regular times for curing. "In those days the power was very strong—not like now." Henry lost his bashfulness under its influence and passionately exhorted those who came to hear about it. Sometimes as they listened to him, or to Mary, they began to cry. Some fell to the floor as if they had fainted; then when they got up they jumped around and started to shake spontaneously. "You never had to give the power to them in those days," said Annie. "It just came. It was catching, like the measles."

Each of the foregoing versions represents a single individual's knowledge of the historical events which marked the beginnings of the Shaker faith. In that respect they differ from almost all the published statements on the same subject. There are surprisingly few of the latter. There is only one approximately contemporary record of the events connected with the beginning of the religion and that, by Reverend Myron Eells, is founded more upon rumor than upon impartial observation. The newspapers of the day took no notice of John Slocum's death and resurrection, although it is known from other sources that it created considerable excitement and talk among the citizens of Olympia at the time.

The principal published record of Slocum's experience was made by James Wickersham, legal counsel and public defender of the Shakers, ten years after it took place. He obtained the statement from Slocum himself, through an interpreter, in a form which purports to be his own words. Standing before his congregation, in the presence of Wickersham, Slocum said:

"I was sick about two weeks, and had five Indian doctors. I grew very weak and poor. Dr. Jim was there. He could not cure me. They wanted to save me, but my soul would die two or three hours at a time. At night my breath was out, and I died. All at once I saw a shining light—great light—trying my soul. I looked and saw my body had no soul—looked at my own body—it was dead.

"I came through the first time and told my friends, 'When I die, don't cry,' and then I died again. Before this I shook hands and told my friends I was going to die. Angels told me to look back and see my body. I did, and saw it lying down. When I saw it, it was pretty poor. My soul left body and went up to judgment place of God. I do not know about body after four o'clock.

"I have seen a great light in my soul from that good land; I have understand all Christ wants us to do. Before I came alive I saw I was sinner. Angel in heaven said to me, 'You must go back and turn alive again on earth.' I learned that I must be good Christian man on earth, or will be punished. My soul was told that I must come back and live four days on earth. When I came back, I told my friends, 'There is a God—there is a Christian people. My good friends, be Christian.'

"When I came alive, I tell my friends, 'Good thing in heaven. God is kind to us. If you all try hard and help me we will be better men on earth.' And now we all feel that it is so.

"A good Christian man prayed with me four days. After four days, a voice said to me, 'You shall live on earth four weeks.' My soul was told that they must build a church for me in four weeks. I had lumber for a house, and my friends built church. Had it all done in four weeks but six feet of roof, and spread a mat over that. Soon as the church was finished the people came and filled the house and began to worship God. I felt strong—bigger than today—all these men know this. My friends worked hard, and I am here because they finished the house in four weeks. My soul was told to remain on earth four weeks more. All my friends came and every Saturday we worshipped God. In four weeks more my soul was told that I should live on earth four years if I did right and preached for God. All felt thankful, and people joined the church—about fifty people. I was promised more time if we worshipped God.

"A bad man can't reach heaven. I believe in God. I saw how bad I used to be. God sends us light to see. They know in heaven what we think. When people are sick, we pray to God to cure us. We pray that he take the evil away and leave the good. If man don't be Christian, he will suffer and see what is bad. When we remember Jesus Christ's name, we always felt happy in our hearts. This is good road for us to travel if we hold on. If we do, God's angels are near to our souls. Power from this to help us. When we pray, it helps us lots in our hearts. We don't do good sometimes, because our hearts are not right. When our body and heart feel warm, we do good and sing good songs. As Christ said, he sends power to every believing soul on earth.

"While one man can try to start religion here on earth, it don't do much good; they won't believe him much. That's why we join to worship. Now we are preparing ourselves for judgment. For it is said, it don't make any difference if he prays good and does good. God gives him help and words to speak. Makes no difference if 'Boston' or Indian, if God helps we know it. These things are what we learned. We learn good while we pray—voice says, Do good.

"It is ten years, now, since we began, and we have good things. We all love these things and will follow them all time. We learn to help ourselves when sick. When our friend is sick, we kneel and ask for help to cure him. We learn something once in a while to cure him. Then we do as we know to help him and cure him. If we don't learn to help him, we generally lose him." [4]

Another version that shows evidence of an attempt to give a sympathetic account of the origin of the cult was written by Sarah Endicott Ober, an assistant Presbyterian missionary among the Makah on Neah Bay during the first decade of this century. Her sympathies were, in fact, too pronounced for objective reporting; but her intimate acquaintance with many of the leading Shakers of that period supplied her with bits of information which do not appear elsewhere. Her version alone, of all those printed, gives proper notice to the important part which Mary Slocum played in the cult's history. Even Slocum ignored this in his statement to Wickersham.

"It is within thirty years," wrote Miss Ober, "that the Shaker religion started, having its inception with two Indians, John Slocum and wife, Twana Indians, living on the Big Skookum, near Olympia. They were ignorant, drunken and degraded. They had some religious instruction in the mission of Rev. Myron Eells, but later joined a Catholic church. But they were not saved from their sins. When in November, 1882, the man was sick unto death, he sent for an Indian medicine man. His wife was distressed, and urged him to be faithful to the 'white man's God,' and the religion they had professed, and not revert to heathenism again. But she could not prevail on him, and when the Medicine Man came, with tom-tom, rattles, bells and witch-charms, dancing, howling and performing incantations and hypnotic performances, the poor woman fled to the woods, there for three days and nights pouring out her soul to God for her husband's salvation. Then a vision of the Savior was vouchsafed her, comforting, assuring and cleansing her from all sin. There came with it an ecstacy and a strange tremor, every nerve, muscle and limb shaken in a marvelous manner. This was the first inception of Shakerism, and from this the name is derived.

"The woman returned to her home, shaking, dancing, praising God. She found her husband to all appearance dead, and the Indians wailing over his body, awaiting her return before burial. When the Medicine Man saw her he fled in terror. The Indians assert with all reverence that 'those in whom is the spirit of evil cannot stay in the presence of those in whom is God's spirit.' The strange power came upon the seeming dead man, and he arose shaking, and praising God. He always asserted that his soul had gone into God's presence, and there he realized his sinful and lost condition. That God had given him a new lease of life, entrusting to him a message to his people, that 'Jesus Christ, the Son of God, could save and keep them from sin.' " [5]

Myron Eells, the Congregationalist missionary on the Skokomish Reservation, made a lengthy statement regarding Shakerism in response to a letter of inquiry from James Mooney in 1893. The portion which is relevant at the moment is quoted below. Eells was the resident missionary on the Skokomish Reservation for over twenty-five years, and he knew well the principals in the drama about which he wrote. He maintained an aloofness toward it, however, which had its effects upon his accuracy. His most obvious error is in confusing Slocum's "death" with his subsequent illness. Although he was living and working among the Skokomish at the time—in October or November of 1881—he apparently was not aware that the first of these events had taken place. He became cognizant of the new faith only when shaking became a part of it a year later, and to this date he assigned Slocum's "death." To some extent his error was due to the fact that the Squaxin Reservation was not within his missionizing orbit; it was under the care of Reverend M. G. Mann, whose headquarters were at Puyallup. But Eells's attitude toward the cult was also important. He wrote:

"In the fall of 1882 an Indian named John Slocum, who was living on Skookum Bay, in Mason county, apparently died. Some years previous he had lived on the Skokomish Reservation, where he had attended a Protestant church, and had learned something of the white man's religion, God, Jesus Christ, and the morals inculcated. He had also learned something in his early life of the Catholic religion and its forms and ceremonies. Many Indians were present when he was sick and apparently died. They said his neck was broken, and that he remained dead for about six hours, when he returned to life, jumped up, and ran off a short distance, and soon began to converse with the people. Whether or not it was a case of suspended animation is a question. A white man, a near neighbor of his, who saw him before his apparent death, while he thus lay, and after his resuscitation, said he believed the Indian was 'playing possum.' But the Indians believed that he really died and rose again.

"The Indian stated that he had died and attempted to go to heaven, but could not enter it because he was so wicked. He was there told, however, the way of life, and that he must return to this earth and teach his people the way, and induce them to become Christians. He gained a small band of followers, a church was built for him, and he steadily preached to the people." [6]

Finally, there remains a document, heretofore unpublished, of equal significance with any that have gone before. The original, in typewritten form, is in the possession of Mrs. Mary Bob Krise of the Nisqually Reservation in Washington. Copies have also been deposited in the Washington State Library in Olympia. Its immediate authorship is un-

certain, but its substance has been derived from many sources.
It was written in January, 1940. The primary motivation in
compiling the information which it contains was to establish a quasi-legal foundation for the claims of one faction in
the struggle for church dominance that has been developing
for several years. The concluding portion, which deals with
this issue, has been omitted in the following quotation: [7]

THE INDIAN SHAKER CHURCH

"For, as much as it seems proper for church organizations
to have a written form, to make harmony among the members
of the church in reference to doctrine as well as church government, we, the members of the Indian Shaker Church by prayer
and supplication to God and a firm belief in the rectitude of
our intention, do hereby set forth the simple faith that was
delivered to us by John Slocum, Indian, chosen of the Lord.

The Origin of the Church

"In God's appointed time, and in a manner that was more
than man's invention, God, in great mercy, visited the Indians
of the Puget Sound, and placed a burden on the heart of a man
by the name of Big Bill, of the Skokomish tribe. This humble
unlettered member of the Indian race was used as an instrument in the hands of God to proclaim a message of hope to his
people.

"About the year 1880, Big Bill prophesied that God would
visit the Indian people with a great message. He said that it
would fall either among the Chehalis tribe, or the Skokomish
tribe. And because of the inconvenience of the Chehalis language, it fell among the Skokomish tribe of Indians. Big Bill,
being a member of the Skokomish tribe, urged his people to
be watchful and ready to accept the message when it would
be delivered to the people. (See Heb. 1:1).

"In due time, in the year 1881, God moved upon the heart

of John Slocum, an outstanding member of the Skokomish
tribe. He was unlettered, careless—but very generous to his
people. He was a gambler and a race horse enthusiast, but
earned the money to support his family as a logger. There
were times when the spirit of God brought such heavy conviction upon the heart of John Slocum, that he fell prostrate
upon the skidroads while at his work; but being ignorant of
the will of God, temptations overcame him, and he continued
in the ways that were not convenient.

"One day, however, the spirit of God allowed John Slocum
to fall into the hands of the Indian Medicine Man. He became
very sick; so sick indeed, that after many days of untold suffering, he fell into a trance. His wife and relatives, not knowing the determinate will of God, thought that John Slocum
was dead. They prepared for burial, and had even purchased
a casket for him in the city of Olympia, Washington. Then
John Slocum came back to life where his body lay in state at
his home. A message was sent to inform the party at Olympia,
Washington, not to bring the casket because John Slocum
had become alive again. And all his relatives were called to the
home, as he ordered.

"Then in a clear and unmistakable manner and language,
he told them of his experience with the Lord. To the people
of his tribe he said, 'I was shown many things that I cannot
tell you, but the things that I was instructed to tell, I shall
tell to you. I was taken out of this world because of the things
of this world that would not let me hear the things of God.
I was taken to the gate of Heaven and an angel met me there
and told me to look back to the earth. I looked and saw the
wickedness of gambling and horse racing; I saw the wickedness of the evil medicine men; the use of tobacco and whisky;
and the angel said, "T H O S E things have made Y O U unfit
for the kingdom of Heaven." Those are the things that I saw
and have told you. Each of you in this house, if you believe
all this teaching that I have told you, will show it by passing
before me and shaking my hand.'

"So, all the people rose and shook hands with John Slocum. Then he said, 'This is now four days from the Sabbath. You must make us a church for us to meet in on the Lord's day.'

"The people then went to work and split cedar planks to make the first Indian Shaker Church, where the simple truth of the faith of the Shakers began to be taught to the Indian tribes. Many who began the work on the building became discouraged and left before the work was finished. But a few remained, and for want of sufficient materials for the roof, it was necessary to finish the last tier with a mat of tulie rushes.

"On the morning of the Sabbath, John Slocum entered the church and began to pray. When all the people arrived, they passed before John Slocum and shook hands with him as a symbol of their faith in his message. No mention of time for worship was made, but the services were ever after held at the hour of ten (10) in the morning. John Slocum caused the people to kneel with him in a long sermon of prayer, after which he taught them as follows:

" 'My dear brothers and sisters, we are in great need of the W O R D S of God. We must be willing to listen to them so that our ears may be opened to hear the great truth of God. We must put his words in our hearts so that they will be a power to, and in us, to help us in the sight of God. If we do not listen to the words of God and let them dwell in our hearts, we will be sorry in the last day. For the Lord will cause his children to pass over the face of the earth towards the rising of the S U N on that great day, and every person will hear and see him—even them that are in the graves will hear and see him. But only they who have the word of God with power in their hearts will have the strength to arise and follow him (all scriptural as well as spiritual). For the Lord will lift them up; then the earth will be filled with the wail and knashing of teeth of those who have not listened to the words of God with a true heart, for they will see their loved ones rejoicing in the presence of the L O R D, but they will have no power to follow them. This is the message from God. Hear it and he will give us another message for healing.'

"The ministry of John Slocum was followed by many signs and through the predictions that were fulfilled in the presence of many of his people, many were converted into this faith, following after his teaching.

"God was pleased to place upon the heart of Mary Slocum, wife of John Slocum, the burden of the sick and distressed of the people. So great was the burden that as she lifted up her hands in surrender to the Lord, her whole body trembled and she was given a song to sing and the spirit of the Lord caused her to move lightly on her feet and her eyes were opened to see the afflictions of the people who were suffering in body. A hand bell was given to a brother by the name of Isaac, brother of Mary Slocum to ring in harmony with the songs she uttered by the spirit.

"About this time, an altar was revealed to these brothers. A cross as a symbol of the suffering of the Son of God, with four (4) burning candles as a symbol of the spirit of God (Prov. 20:27). God sent his son to die that man might be redeemed and have the 'light of life; even Jesus Christ himself,' dwelling within our hearts in the person of the Holy Ghost, the third person of the triune God, the gospel of Jesus Christ is four-fold (four sided). Only the redeemed who are seeking to know and obey because they love him, may have this indwelling of this Holy Spirit.

"A brother by the name of Sylvester Yucton was moved to stand by this altar and received by hand clasp all persons seeking healing of their body, or if they desire the power of the word of God.

"At the death of John Slocum, in the year—[?], a man by the name of Mud Bay Louie, succeeded him as the leader of the Shaker faith. Then the brethren of the faith began to be persecuted, and leaders were put in chain and ball and in prison; and through it all they remained faithful to their calling. They prayed and sang in the prisons, and predicted that they would be delivered from the snare of the prison walls; which was accomplished in spite of the determination of their persecutors to hold them there. By the will of God, the Shaker Faith continues today (1940) more so."

TWO ✠ Adding Converts

IT IS CLEAR from the foregoing accounts that the presumed death of John Slocum marked only the initial phase of what came to be known as the Shaker religion. Its effects were in large measure obscured by the second phase, which was initiated by Mary Slocum's shaking. In view of the great tendency of most informants to telescope the two events, it is not easy to determine the range and depth of the appeal of John's message. Certain facts lead to the inference that the story of his experience with death was widely disseminated, and that it provoked considerable interest, but that in spite of all the commotion and talk it led to few real conversions beyond the limited circle of his relatives and close associates.

Although the Squaxin Indians were more isolated than the rest, they nevertheless did not lack occasions to communicate with others around the southern part of Puget Sound. There were annual congregations of all the tribes, from the Skokomish to the Puyallup, to celebrate the Fourth of July or to hold potlatches. In addition there was a great amount of visiting between families on the different reservations who were related by blood or marriage. And above all, work in the hop fields at Puyallup each summer drew great numbers of Indians from all over the Puget Sound area and even beyond from over the mountains. Reverend M. G. Mann, the

Presbyterian missionary stationed at Puyallup, reported that some two thousand Indians were congregated around the fields there in 1881. The circumstances were therefore propitious for the diffusion of news, and it is quite probable that the story of John Slocum was widely told at these gatherings.

Inferentially, the excitement that was stimulated by the report was manifested in a marked increase in religious interest in the winter of 1881 and the spring of 1882. Both Eells and Mann noticed this agitation, and, while assigning no cause to it, found it sufficiently remarkable to comment upon it in their reports to their sponsoring societies. Mann describes an ecstatic meeting which he conducted among the Nisqually in the spring of 1882 which reminded him of the "early apostolic times" on account of the fervency and simple faith of his new converts. At about the same time he paid one of his infrequent visits to his charges on the Squaxin Reservation and was there surprised at the reception which he received. The "chief" welcomed him to his house; and although it was a wet, cold evening, he went out to fetch the other Indians. About forty of them assembled, "and the chief commanded them to shake hands with me." Boxes and boards were set up for seats so that Mann could proceed with a sermon and prayers. He spoke in Chinook jargon, and when he had finished the chief harangued the others at some length in his own language. A lively discussion followed, during which one individual wanted to know by what authority Mann had come to tell them these things about God. Who had sent him? Mann replied that "Hyas Lee Plet, the Secretary of the Board [of Home Missions]" had sent him; but this did not seem to satisfy his questioner.[1]

At the same time Eells was moved to note that the work at Skokomish "was more encouraging than last year. . . . The older Indians are taking more interest than heretofore, asking for extra meetings. . . ." And a few months later he wrote, "There has been considerable religious interest among the Indians. The Indians on other reservations have been more interested than usual, and intercourse with these has caused a similar interest here." And again, "Our little church at Skokomish has swarmed, granting letters to seven of its members who live at Jamestown. . . ." [2]

That the spectacular revival of Slocum, coupled with his testimony of reform, had something to do with this excitement is probable; but the specific data are difficult to assemble in confirmation. Doubtless many Indians came to hear John Slocum, and some were immediately convinced of the truth of his doctrine. Mud Bay Louis was an early convert. His testimony, in fact, would lead us to believe that he was a humble follower of Slocum from the very beginning. In Wickersham's presence he said, "John Slocum came alive, and I remember God and felt frightened. We never heard such a thing as man dying and bring word that there was a God. I became sick for three weeks, four weeks. I hear a voice saying to soul, 'Tomorrow they will be coming to fix you up.' Had just heard about John Slocum, and knew it was punishment for my bad habits. My heart was black— it was a bad thing. Now I have quit swearing—my heart is upside down—it is changed. After I heard the voice I heard another say: 'There it is now—someone to fix you up. Have you prepared your heart? If you don't believe in Christ, you will go into a big fire and burn forever.' I saw a man's hand coming to my heart. That day I got up—was well—talked to my friends, advising them. I will remain a follower of Christ as long as I live." [3] Upon the same occasion Mud Bay Sam testified to his faith in terms which seem to relate his conversion directly and immediately to the preaching of John Slocum: "When I joined this religion, I was told to be good. When John Slocum was preaching, I heard that if I prayed I would have power to be a medicine-man, and could cure the sick. From time John Slocum preached I tried to be a good Christian man. I prayed and was sick—my soul was sick."

Although these two brothers were doubtless sincere at the

time they made these statements, the facts of their conversion and their submission to Slocum's leadership were not quite as they have implied. Louis at first scoffed at what he had heard about his unimportant neighbor over on Skookum Chuck; but in a short time he became ill and his cousin's husband, Big John, came to see him and urge him to repent and pray for salvation. Big John was Mary Slocum's cousin; and, like her, he immediately acknowledged divine sanction for Slocum's inspiration. Louis was more skeptical; and, although he joined the band of adherents and at first accepted the teachings of Slocum as leader, he soon manifested a propensity for revelations of his own which introduced deviant concepts and led eventually to a rupture with Mary.

In addition to these evidences of the appeal of Slocum's message we have his statement that his church was built by the volunteer labor of his friends and that about fifty of them joined him in his services. Some of his listeners, if not converts, came from the Chehalis, Skokomish, and Puyallup reservations, as is evidenced by a number of anecdotes that are told about these Indians' experiences at Slocum's meetings. It is from Myron Eells, however, that information comes of an organized support for the new religion. The stage had already been set for this, and the motivation for it sprang from an opposition to Eells's teachings which had taken shape among a small group of Indians on the Skokomish Reservation. Eells disparagingly called them "the Catholic set."

The leader of this faction was Billy Clams. Like some of the other Indians under Eells's charge, he had had some instruction in Roman Catholicism and may have been baptized in that faith. He had other reasons for opposing the Congregationalist missionary and his brother Edwin, who was the Indian agent there, but he cunningly chose to make the religious issue the justification for his attempts to nettle and frustrate them. The opportunity arose when Big Bill received his revelation and began to preach his doctrine of a messiah before the advent of John Slocum. Big Bill was well connected on the reservation; his brother-in-law, Dick Lewis, was the "head chief" there, and his brother, David Charley, was a "sub-chief." Lewis was also the brother of a former wife of Charley. Nursing old grievances, this nucleus, led by Billy Clams, rallied around Big Bill as an opposition symbol. Big Bill was not himself antagonistic to Eells. He had, in fact, asked to join the Congregational Church and was admitted in May, 1880. But he was not in a position to control the currents of hostility which caught him up and sped him along even if he had willed to do so. When he died in June, 1881, they swept on. Eells says of this event, "They [Clams, Lewis, and Charley] had always given as an excuse for not coming to church that as Big Bill could not come they went to his house for his benefit and held services. But after his death their services did not cease. They kept them up as an opposition, partly professing that they were Catholics, and partly saying that their brother's last words and songs were very precious to them, and they must get together, talk about what he had said and sing his songs. In course of time this proved a great source of trouble—one of the most severe trials which we had." [4]

The death of Big Bill catalyzed the recalcitrant sentiment on the reservation, which was sanctioned by the prestige of the "head chief," and focused it around a set of ritual devotions to his memory. Many were attracted by its appeal. With the advent of John Slocum it received another fillip. The effect was heightened by the fact that only a few months intervened between the two events. Eells makes the interval more than a year. Although evidently unaware at the time that Slocum had "died," Eells recognized later that his opponents made capital of the occasion. In retrospect he wrote of Slocum: "At first his teaching agreed partly with what he had learned from me, partly with the Catholic religion, and partly with neither, but he was soon captured by the Catholics [i.e., Clams, *et al.*], baptized, and made a priest.

There was much intercourse between him and Billy Clams and friends. Their waning church was greatly revived and ours decreased." [5]

Although these facts indicate that the news of Slocum's vision had traveled far, had provoked much popular curiosity, and had even regenerated the spirits of some sinners, its over-all effects were limited spatially and temporally. New life was injected into it, and the real impetus for its dissemination evolved, when the shaking element was introduced. The most pronounced effects of this new development appeared on the Skokomish Reservation where the excitement over it initiated the most intense phase of the struggle between Eells and the "Catholic set." But the climax did not occur until a year after Mary Slocum received her divine inspiration for it. We have no precise knowledge of its immediate consequences during that interval. Indian informants at the present time state that the effects were electric; but it is impossible to estimate how far reaching they were. Particular inquiries suggest the inference that they were rather local for a period of six months or more.

Eells, in his account, is more suggestive than informative. Describing the events of this period he offers the paradox of a missionary plunged into gloom by a resurgence of religious interest among his charges. Torn between thanksgiving for its tentative gropings in the direction of his ministrations, and dispairing over his recognition of its causes, Eells barely weathered the dark days of the winter of 1882–83. He confesses that the blackest hours came in February and that their murk was deep enough to cause him seriously to consider abandoning his labors among the Skokomish. Commenting upon the turmoil and anxiety of these days, he says, "There was one good result from the whole excitement: it kept the subject of religion prominently before the people. It did not die of stagnation, as it had almost seemed to do during some previous years. In my visits I was well treated and was asked many questions on the subject. I was wel-

comed at two or three of the logging-camps during the winter
[of 1882–83] for an evening service, where I talked Bible to
them as plainly as I could. They at least asked me to go to
them, although they would not come to our church. A constant call, too, came for large Bible pictures." [6] Among the
sources of his discouragement, Eells listed the "half-Catholic
movement" led by Billy Clams, the John Slocum affair, and
his dwindling church membership, which, never numbering
more than nineteen Indians, fell away to three school girls
and four adult Indians. He properly saw a significant relationship between the causes for his rejoicing and the roots of
his desperation. He knew that the current of the religious agitation was not of his making, that it was passing him by and
veering out of his control. But he attributed his frustration to
the deviltry of Billy Clams. He viewed the Slocum incident
as a symptom rather than as a cause and Slocum himself
as a dupe of the "Catholic crowd." Indeed, all indications
point to the conclusion that Eells interpolated the Slocum
episode into the context of his woes at a later date and in
retrospect; and he did not know about it or the shaking development until the month of August, 1883.

Beginning with that month a series of events occurred
which brought the whole movement into the limelight, gave
it character, and started it upon its ramifications in a clearly
distinguishable form. At that time the word went out that a
big meeting was to be held at John Slocum's church, near
his logging camp, about twelve miles from the Skokomish
agency. The message created great excitement, as there were
rumors that phenomenal things were to happen and that
those who failed to attend would suffer some dire misfortune. Some of the Chehalis people heard that those who did
not join the religion would be turned into animals. Eells
states that among the Skokomish it was rumored that they
would be lost if they did not attend the meeting and "that
the baptism of those whom I had baptized was good for
nothing, being done with common water, and that they must

go and be baptized again, and that the world was coming to an end in a few days." [7] Furthermore, "that four women would be turned into angels; that persons would die and be raised to life again, and that other wonderful things would be done." [8]

Whatever the true character of the reports and warnings which emanated from Skookum Chuck at this time, and however well they conveyed the intentions of the Shaker leaders there, it is a fact that a large number of Indians did arrive at the meeting.

Two of the four Indian logging camps in the vicinity closed down completely for the occasion in expectation of great things. About one half of the Skokomish people went, and strange events did transpire. Relating what he had heard from others, Eells wrote: "Visions were abundant; four people, it was said, died and were raised to life again; women, professing to be angels, tried to fly around. People went around brushing and striking others until some were made black for a week, the professed intent being to brush off their sins. A shaking took hold of some of them, on the same principle, I thought, that fifty years ago nervous jerks took hold of some people in the South and West at their exciting camp-meetings; and this continued with them afterward until they gained the name of the shaking set. Some acted very much like crazy people, and some indecent things were done. It was reported that they saw myself, Mowitch Man, and others in hell; that I was kept on the reservation to get the lands of the Indians away from them, and that I told lies in church." [9]

A Skokomish man told Silas Heck years ago that he remembered attending this meeting as a child. Some people did indeed attempt to ascend directly and bodily to heaven. His mother was one of them, and he recalled his terror at the prospect. She hopped around the room with one knee on the floor, waving her arms like a bird. He followed her closely, ready to take hold and pull her back if she started to rise.

Writing of subsequent developments, Eells later on informed Mooney: "The followers of this new religion dreamed dreams, saw visions, went through some disgusting ceremonies à la mode the black *tomahnous*, and were taken with a kind of shaking. With their arms at full length, their hands and arms would shake so fast that a common person not under the excitement could hardly shake half as fast. Gazing into the heavens, their heads would also shake very fast, sometimes for a few minutes and sometimes for hours, or half the night. They would also brush each other with their hands, as they said, to brush off their sins, for they said that they were much worse than white people, the latter being bad only in their hearts, while the Indians were so bad that the badness came to the surface of their bodies and the ends of their fingernails, so that it could be picked off. They sometimes brushed each other lightly, and sometimes so roughly that the person brushed was made black for a week, or even sick.

"In connection with this they held church services, prayed to God, believed in Christ as a savior, said much about his death, and used the cross, their services being a combination of Protestant and Catholic services, though at first they almost totally rejected the Bible, for they said they had direct revelations from Christ, and were more fortunate than the whites who had an old, antiquated book." [10]

The meetings at Skookum Chuck in the fall of 1883 lasted about a week. By that time the authorities on the Skokomish Reservation had decided to intervene. The Indians under their jurisdiction returned to their homes under pressure, but the meetings continued. Again, the opposition centered around Billy Clams, firmly supported by Dick Lewis and David Charley. The two brothers-in-law lived in a logging camp about eight miles outside the reservation, but they returned with the rest of the Skokomish to encourage the shaking in the face of authoritative interdicts. Pursuing this course, they maneuvered Eells into contending with them over the possession of a corpse, and of having to co-operate with a shaman in order to frustrate them.

The death of Ellen Charley, the wife of David, precipitated this contest. During the latter part of August she became seriously ill, and her child died, as a result, Eells maintained, of an excess of excitement and neglect. The Shakers wanted to employ their own methods to restore her health. Her sister, a Chehalis woman, refused to allow this and had her taken out of their hands and put under the care of a shaman. Ellen grew steadily worse; and, on the eighth of September, she died. "All of the members of our church," wrote Eells, "Indian doctors, and all who were opposed to the shaking set, now joined company with her sister." The body was placed in the Congregational Church under his protection and he was forced to reject the pleas of Charley and his son for its possession. They wanted to take Ellen's body to their home, lay it out for three days with candles around it, and conduct their own final ceremonies involving prayer and shaking. Eells insisted that they obtain her sister's consent, and when they failed in this they compromised by attending the funeral services performed by him, then holding their own over the grave after his departure.

Eells considered this a victory, and he expected that the disillusionment incident to it would be sufficient to put an end to the "foolishness." In this, however, he was disappointed, for, as he says of his enemies, "Although cast down, they were not destroyed. I was a little surprised to see how strongly they still clung to their religion." They retired from the battle, but only to take up a stronger position out of sight.

Lewis and Charley returned to their logging camp accompanied by Clams and others who had been stimulated to greater resistance by the death of Ellen. There they continued their meetings unmolested and reinforced by others who had stayed on after the assembly in August, and by some who heard the news and came later. The fervor of the sessions was unabated, perhaps even reinvigorated by the frustrations that they had suffered. According to Eells: "They sometimes held meetings from six o'clock in the evening until about midnight, lighting candles and putting them on their heads for a long time. They became very peculiar about making the sign of the cross many times a day, when they began to eat as they asked a blessing, and when they finished their meal and returned thanks; when they shook hands with anyone—and they shook hands very often—when they went to church and prayer meeting on Thursday evening, and at many other times, far more often than the Catholics do." [11]

The series of meetings instigated by Clams and his associates continued until the middle of October. By that time the agent was able to give the matter his personal attention, and he forthwith ordered the individuals belonging to the Skokomish Reservation to return to it and meet him at the agency office. There he made it plain to the assembled Indians that two conflicting religions on one reservation could not be tolerated; they must either accept the missionary's guidance or have no meetings at all. His words and his actions were so vigorous that it appeared that he had broken the spirit of the leaders of the cult. Billy Clams, as their representative, appeared before the missionary a few days later ostensibly to accept the terms laid down by the agent. He confessed his error and, with an air of humility, asked that Eells meet with his friends and hold proper services for their instruction and comfort. This was agreed to, and the missionary marked this down as a final triumph over the disturbing element in the Skokomish community.

There were, however, two or three brief but spectacular flare-ups in other quarters. One of them centered around Big John, who was a relative and a close associate of Louis. He was a Skokomish Indian, who had taken up residence on Mud Bay at his wife's home among the Squaxin. They attended the meeting in August, and Big John was conspicuous as a converter. "He had that gift." When the Skokomish were ordered to break up the meeting and return to their homes, Big

John did not heed the order. Instead he went to Mud Bay and continued to meet with a crowd which had moved over to Louis' house to carry on with their shaking. In the latter part of October he received a startling revelation to the effect that he was Christ Incarnate and that his wife was the Virgin Mary. So intoxicated was he and his auditors with this idea that all of them, to the number of fifty or more, set out for Olympia with the intention of heralding the arrival of the millennium. Followed by the rest, Big John and his wife rode on horseback through the streets of Olympia, he with his arms extended like the crucified Christ. After this disturbance he was again ordered to return to Skokomish, but he did not comply until the following month; and then he came alone, leaving his wife at Mud Bay. There he was so ridiculed by the whites and other Indians for his pretentions that he determined to return to Mud Bay. When he refused to come back, the agent sent policemen after him and had him imprisoned.

The hope for an immediate fulfilment of Christ's promise to return and establish the new order announced by Slocum did not die with Big John's disillusionment. The time was postponed. It was predicted that the day would be the Fourth of July the next year. This again caused considerable excitement, and a large number of believers congregated at Louis' place to welcome the event. When it did not transpire, the date was repeatedly reset. But in time expectancy was dulled; and today one hears nothing of this hope. The younger people do not even know that it is or was a part of Shaker faith.

The firm demands of the agent and the apparent submission of Billy Clams put an end to one phase of the cult's history on the Skokomish Reservation. For several years there were no overt evidences of its existence which could not be ignored by the authorities. But it did not die. Meetings were still held, especially to cure the sick. The participants met either secretly at some distance from the agency or outside the reservation boundaries. It flourished elsewhere, and when

the controls were relaxed it was apparent that the Skokomish
had lost nothing of the spirit in the interval of suppression.

The opportunity for relief came in 1887, but it was not
realized for some years after that. Almost from the beginning
of his administration in 1871, agent Eells had worked dili-
gently to have the reservation surveyed into farm lots for the
purpose of assigning them to individual families in accordance with the treaty made with these Indians in 1855. He was
convinced that the Indians must settle down to a sedentary
life on a secured piece of ground before any real progress
could be made in civilizing them, and it was toward this end
that he had all of the reservations under his superintendency
surveyed, allotted, and their sub-divisions recorded. Certificates of occupancy, and, later, trust patents, were issued to
the allottees protecting their titles from levy, alienation, or
forfeiture. This much had been done for the Nisqually,
Squaxin, Puyallup, Tulalip, Swinomish, and Lummi Indians,
and was under way for the Skokomish and Chehalis when the
Dawes Severalty Act was passed by Congress and became a
law in 1887. By the provisions of this act, Indian tribes everywhere were to be granted lands in severalty at the discretion
of the President. In addition, any individual who received an
allotment under this or any other law or treaty, or who should
take up residence apart from his tribe and adopt the habits of
civilized life, was forthwith to be declared an American citizen and be accorded all of the privileges and immunities belonging to that status.

To agent Eells, as to many another person, the granting of
full citizenship to unprepared applicants seemed a mistake.
Furthermore, it was apparent that in his case the emancipa-
tion, strictly considered, left small scope for the exercise of
controls. Aside from enforcing certain regulations applying
specifically to the Indians, he could legally do little in his
jurisdiction beyond acting as advisor and protector to those
who voluntarily appealed to him. Eells was a conscientious

administrator, and it was thus that he officially interpreted his position. It was a difficult situation, but he made the best of it by continuing to treat the Indians, for their own good as he saw it, very much as he had done without challenging the letter of the law. It was only gradually, and by a series of steps upon particular issues, that the concept of the citizen Indian was defined. Skokomish citizens first began to protest against the compulsory education of their children as an infringement of their rights. Others, at the instigation of unscrupulous white men, soon began to insist upon their privilege of drinking whisky. Gradually it became apparent to them that the agent had no authority to regulate their marriages or to insist upon the abolition of shamanism. The development was accelerated when, in 1889, Washington was admitted into the Union and the citizen Indians, in accordance with the Dawes Act, became citizens of the State and subject to its laws, both civil and criminal. In a short time voting precincts were established on the reservations and constables and justices of the peace were elected. By 1892 the Courts of Indian Offenses, which had been authorized in 1883 to take care of reservation offenders, had become obsolete or were in a dubious position among the Skokomish, Puyallup, and other Indians within Eells's jurisdiction.

The climax came in 1891 with the ruling by a United States District Court that citizens of the State could not be placed under the jurisdiction of an Indian agent. Eells concluded that the Indian Bureau had no further authority over that class of Indians. The following year a case was brought before the District Court in Tacoma involving a white man charged with selling liquor to a Puyallup Indian. The defense was argued by James Wickersham who had been appointed by the court. He became interested upon realizing the implications of the Dawes Act. He won his argument upon the grounds that the Indian was a citizen and hence entitled to be treated like any other. The prisoner was dismissed.

The Shakers came to life immediately. A delegation led by Mud Bay Louis called upon Wickersham to inquire into their rights as members of a religious denomination. He outlined to them the nature of their immunities and confirmed them in their belief that they were free to worship in any peaceful manner that they chose. With these assurances they resolved, with Wickersham's assistance, to organize themselves into a regularly constituted church body. They held, accordingly, a charter meeting on June 6, 1892, and determined upon a course of open defiance of their persecutors. Wickersham relates that this "was too much for the average citizen of Puget Sound," and that at first Shaker meetings were repeatedly disturbed by both whites and Indians. Upon request he issued several impressive-looking documents to intimidate would-be disturbers of the peace of a religious meeting. His vigorous support put the new church upon a firm foundation, and gave it renewed stimulation and hope. Its right to exist, except locally, has not been challenged since. By 1899 a church building was in existence on the Skokomish Reservation and a congregation, led by Dick Lewis and Billy Clams, was flourishing.

In the meantime, the faith was being consolidated and elaborated at its point of origin, which was not on any Indian reservation. The sources of inspiration were still in the same vicinity as at its foundation, but the precise locus of paramount influence had shifted from Skookum Chuck to Mud Bay. Although Louis never denied the leadership of John Slocum, he was inclined to use him and did soon eclipse him in actual importance. Furthermore, and perhaps because of this, Louis very early came into conflict with Mary Slocum. The tension was evident even at the first big convention in August of 1883. While the call was for a meeting at Slocum's, and while it was held there, Louis left it in chagrin at the accusations made of him by some of those present. He immediately went to his own home accompanied by a band of supporters and there proceeded to continue the meeting according to his

understanding of what it should be like. This offshoot became
the most viable and influential spore of the cult, even in the
lifetime of Slocum.

The church built for Slocum at Skookum Chuck fell into
disuse very early, and by 1899 it was no longer standing. By
1885 attention had been shifted to Louis, and he was holding
meetings in a building constructed for that purpose with the
assistance and contributions of the faithful near his home on
Mud Bay. This was to become the fountainhead of inspiration, the "mother church" of the cult. It was rebuilt in 1910
at the time when the Shakers were organizing themselves into
a church body with legal sanctions. This building, however,
was allowed to disintegrate, and eventually it collapsed. Its
undisturbed remains may be seen today beside a more recent
structure, the present Mud Bay church. It is on Louis' old
homestead, which came into the possession of Jack Slocum
when Louis died around 1905. Fearing that the site and the
building would be lost, the Shakers took in contributions
from the congregations on several reservations and bought
two acres of land from Slocum to be set aside as church
property.[12]

Wickersham's support of the Shakers in 1892 gave an impetus to church building. Within a year meeting houses were
erected at Oyster Bay, Puyallup, Longview, and Chehalis. All
of them had a short life, however. Big John built the church
at Oyster Bay, about five miles from Louis' place. For a few
years this was as important as the church on Mud Bay. James
Tobin and Richard Jackson were active among its supporters.
But Big John did not live long after the Shakers were free to
worship as they pleased and his church scarcely survived his
death. By 1899 it was no longer used and it had fallen into
decay. Meetings were still being held in the vicinity, but, as
elsewhere, houses were then being used for that purpose.

The Puyallup church had a similiarly brief history. Among
the early leaders in that region were William (Bill) James,
J. W. Simmons, and John Powers. Around 1892 James set

aside two acres of his allotment upon which to build a church. It functioned for but a few years before he died. His wife then remarried, and his allotment was sold to a white man. The church went with the land, and by 1900 it was no longer in existence. Although the faith spread, and many of the Puyallup and Nisqually became Shakers, their congregations never assumed the leadership that seemed destined for them in the beginning. In 1943 there was no organized ministry in this area.

The Clallam Indians lived to the north of the Skokomish, not on any reservation. In 1880 their principal villages were at Port Gamble,[13] Port Discovery, Jamestown, Port Angeles, Elwha, and Clallam Bay. Jamestown, with 120 residents, was the most populous and the most progressive of these settlements. The leader of this newly founded community in its early years was Lord James Balch, a man for whom Myron Eells had genuine admiration. Christianity received more encouragement there than in any other community ministered to by Eells, and by 1882 he had organized a church there with seven members. It would appear that it was also the first of these northern communities to become acquainted with Shakerism. The date is uncertain. It was somewhat later than for the groups at the southern end of Hood Canal, but before 1900. The occasion for its introduction was a long continued illness of Annie Newton. Some of her friends had heard about the healing faith among the Skokomish; and, when she could get no relief from her sickness by other means, they urged her to send for the Shakers. With her apparent cure to its credit, the cult took a firm hold at Jamestown. Among the early converts there were William Hall, Jacob Hall, David Hunter, and Robert Collier. Hall was a forceful leader, and for many years he was a prominent figure at Shaker meetings and conventions, not only in his own locality, but to the south as well. His church grew to be the most vigorous of any in the north, one reason for this being that Jamestown was not on a reservation. The land for the town was purchased by the Indians, and they were therefore in an independent position, to a great extent free of interference from the agent. Under Hall's leadership the Jamestown church became the source of further impulses in the spread of the cult to other Clallam villages, to the Makah, and into British Columbia.

In 1899 the Jamestown church was one of three left standing and in use. The other two were at Skokomish and at Mud Bay. The latter had holes in the roof and was going to ruin at the time, but it was still being used. Meetings were also being held in dwellings, but the turn of the century seems to have marked a depression in the growth of the cult at its hearth. In the summer of 1899, the year of his conversion, Enoch Abraham met Louis in the hop fields near Yakima. He was invited to spend the winter on Puget Sound, culling oysters. Louis, Sam, Doctor Jim, and two other men owned an oyster bed on Mud Bay, and the prices were good: three dollars a sack delivered in Olympia. Abraham stayed five months, from October to March, and during that time he and Louis went to meetings only five times, and one of these was incidental to another affair. Services were held twice at the dilapidated Mud Bay church, and once at a nearby house on Oyster Bay. At another time there was a big meeting at the Skokomish church. Louis and his friends attended the Sunday services at Skokomish and afterwards conducted a prayer meeting at the house of a sick man by request. Then at Christmas time the Mud Bay people were invited to Port Gamble by Tyhee Jack to participate in a potlatch held in memory of his dead son. There were quite a few Shakers there; and when the potlatch was over, Louis was asked to lead a meeting for them at the home of a member. This was the extent of his religious activities for the winter, a fact that disturbed the new convert Abraham. He remarked in discussing it that, "By 1899 Louis and Sam were forgetting their church. They were too busy culling oysters. They made a mistake, like the rest of us sometimes. I was just a beginner, so I had to do as they did."

The Jamestown church, however, was a center of activity at the time. By 1902 the enthusiasm had spread to the Makah of Neah Bay from this source. It was introduced by Clara Cortesa, who had been sick for several years and who claimed to have been cured on a visit to the Jamestown meetings. Her two brothers, Lans and Jimmy Kalapa, joined with her and became strong advocates of the power of the new faith. Lans assumed leadership of the group and was soon performing such astonishing miracles as raising two children from the dead, restoring the sight of another, and causing water to disappear from a bucket. These were acceptable demonstrations of God's omnipotence; but when Lans attempted to eliminate the cross from Shaker ritual and ideology he met with opposition. His brother and sister refused to follow him, but he gained enough adherents to threaten the unity of the church. By 1903 he and his supporters were practicing a ritual which varied considerably from the orthodox requirements. In that year Enoch Abraham and his cousin, Joe Riddle, of the Yakimas visited Neah Bay. They were asked to stay in the house of Skyler Colfax, a follower of Kalapa. Colfax, his wife, and others of their persuasion refused to shake hands with Abraham and Riddle when the latter crossed themselves in the orthodox manner before extending their hands.

The immediate cause of Kalapa's defection was his conflict with the resident Presbyterian missionary and the Indian agent. A few months before the arrival of Abraham and Riddle these authorities had summoned Kalapa before them and requested him to give up his shaking and miraculous pretensions. Kalapa agreed—ostensibly at least—but went to his home, set up a partition to enclose the back part of it, and there secluded himself. Five days later he emerged with a new version of the religion which conformed in some respects to the demands of the Indian agent. His motivations are not entirely clear, but there is an interesting document which throws some light upon his design. Albert B. Reagan was the school teacher among the Quileute a few years later and knew Kalapa well. He has left what purports to be a deposition given him by Kalapa. It reads as follows:

"Many years ago the government stopped the war dance among the Indians; then the ghost dance, and Sun dance, and all other similar dances and so-called religious ceremonies. Then there came an order to stop potlatches and tomaneous doctoring. This seemed to be the complete overthrow of the old customs. But not. The crafty Indian to the west of the cascades was not to be outdone by his white brother and the orders of the Indian Office. The scheme was to clothe their old performances with a 'veneer' that would give them the protection of the government. Many of the Indians had been educated and now was the time to use their education. The scheme took a religious trend; and by the clothing of the old tomaneous ceremonies and practices with a very thin cloak of christianity, they succeeded in organizing what is now known as the Shaker Church of the Indians.

"The officers of the Indian Department sought to crush this new organization, when in its infancy; but by the aid of Judge Wickersham, now in Alaska, the Indians won on the constitutional ground that every one has a right to worship God according to the dictates of his own conscience.

"The church is incorporated in the state of Washington. Its purpose, set forth in the articles of incorporation, is to spread christianity and to build churches and schools."

Signed   his

Lans **X** *Kalapa* [14]

mark

Doubtless these are not the words of Lans Kalapa. There is also the suspicion that the idea that Shakerism originated and was perpetuated as a great conspiracy to mislead the white authorities was Reagan's rather than Kalapa's. Reagan subscribed to this interpretation, as he indicates in a later portion of his manuscript upon Shaker activities. "The shamans," he writes, "are the leaders of the organization; and, as previously stated, they use it to screen their practices." Kalapa may have given him the idea, or vice versa; but in any event Kalapa's new pronouncements, following close upon his overt submission to the Neah Bay authorities, gives credence to the view that he subscribed to the theory of appeasement and subterfuge to gain Shaker ends.

Kalapa exercised considerable influence among the Makah and the Quileute during the first decade of this century. Writing of the Quileute of this period and a little later, Reagan stated that "at the present time there are two kinds of shakers; the Slocum shakers who use the cross, and the followers of Lans Kalapa of Neah Bay who do not believe in using it. The dance and worship however, is practically the same." More remains to be said upon this subject; for the present it may be noted that the popularity of Kalapa's heterodox forms and beliefs faded with time until scarcely anyone belonged to his sect ten years later. Other Shakers scorned and disavowed him; many say that he was a "coward to sign the paper" when requested by the Indian agent and that he has not been a Shaker since, "only a Presbyterian." Kalapa himself never accepted this stricture, considered himself a good Shaker, and continued to attend their annual meetings.

Johnny Steve and his wife brought word of the new religion to the Tulalip people, again on account of an alleged cure of a lingering illness. The time was somewhere around 1896, but due to the suppression of their activities and the well-organized opposition of the Catholic Church, the cult grew more slowly there than on some of the other reservations. Among the Tulalip leaders were Bob Klickam, Johnny Bowers, and Johnny English. The Tulalip church, dedicated in 1924, was one of the last to be established around Puget Sound. In other communities under the same administration, but less subject to control, a foothold was gained earlier. There were a number of Shakers around Port Gamble in 1900, although they had no building set aside for their meetings. Thirteen years later the Catholic missionary to this group reported that the last Catholic convert had deserted to the Shakers and that very likely the church there would be taken over by them.[15] A church was dedicated at Muckleshoot in the same year, that is, in 1913.

In Canada the Shaker faith has not flourished to the extent that it has in the United States. This has not been due to a lack of communication between the two areas; for years the Canadian Indians on the coast have been accustomed to going to the hop fields of Washington during the harvest season, there to work and visit with friends. Also the Clallam of Washington, from aborginal times onward, have had relatives and cultural congeners in the Indian settlements around Victoria on Vancouver Island, and there has been rather free intercourse between them across Juan de Fuca Strait. Neither is the relatively limited distribution of the cult in Canada due to its late introduction there. Meetings were being held among the Songish and the Clallam Indians around Victoria in 1903; and the Cowichian Indians to the north near Duncan dedicated their church in 1907. A little later another church was built near Koksilah, a small town not far from Duncan. North of this point the faith has never made any appreciable gains, although there are a few Nanaimo Shakers.

The Koksilah church has since burned down and has not been replaced. At present, only three organized bodies of worshippers are to be found on Vancouver Island: there are two churches near Victoria, one on the Songish reserve and one for the Sanetch people on the peninsula by that name (Saanich). The other church is still near Duncan.

The cult has met with even less success on the mainland side of Canada, a fact which the local Shakers attribute to the steadfast opposition by the Catholic Indians. The first church on this side of Georgia Strait was built on the Musquium reserve, on Point Grey, near the city of Vancouver. This is no longer used. For some time a few converts used to meet in a hall or barn on the Squamish reserve at the head of

Howe Sound, but there were not enough of them to build a church or to keep their interest alive. They were too far away from the source of their stimulation and support, namely the congregations at Duncan and Koksilah. The most active Shaker among them was Isaac Jacobs, who later moved to the outskirts of North Vancouver. With very little help from others he proceeded to build a church on his property behind his dwelling. At first it was only a meeting house; later he added a room for cooking and eating so that visiting groups could be provided for. It has, however, been put to little use; there have been few meetings since its completion. There are only three other Shakers in the vicinity, and their interest has flagged in late years. Ordinarily Jacobs and his wife meet alone in the church for their Sunday prayers.

To the south of Puget Sound one of the earliest centers of the cult was among the Chehalis, who lived in the vicinity of what is now Oakville, Washington, about twenty-five miles from Olympia. This became an important point of dispersal for the reservations to the south, east, and west. The leader among these people, and one of their first Shakers, was John Smith. He attended the big convention at Skookum Chuck in August, 1883, and returned with news about it. He had not "received the power" himself, but he bore testimony to its reality.

When the Heck family heard about it, and when rumors reached them that scoffers might be changed into animals, they decided to go to Mud Bay where Louis was continuing the meetings. Mrs. Heck's cousin, the wife of Doctor Jim, lived there and they were fearful of what might happen to her. Silas was in the Chehalis boarding school at the time, and remained behind; but his older sister, and Peter and his wife, accompanied his parents. When they arrived they found that the wife of Doctor Jim was already a confirmed Shaker. Most of the people there were. "Nobody had to talk to get them to join then like they do now. Some people got the power just by shaking hands with another person who had it." The Heck girl and Peter's wife received the power in this way soon after their arrival.

The meetings were being held at Louis' place. There was no church building, so they used the large room of his barn-like house. The Slocums were not there, but Mud Bay Sam and Big John were, the latter taking the lead in exhorting and transferring the power to those who submitted themselves.

On their way home to Oakville, the Hecks met John Smith who was returning to the meetings. Some say that he was "jealous" of the Heck women; he was chagrined that they had received the power before he did. Big John helped to bring the blessing to him, and when he came home he immediately began to hold "shaking parties" at his house. Peter's wife and sister, and a few others including James and Charlie Walker joined them. "The rest of us," said Silas Heck, "thought that they were crazy. They prayed every night before they went to bed and every morning when they got up. They crossed themselves every time they did anything—before they ate, or came through a door, or went outside—because you never know what danger you are going to meet, and with the cross you have the protection of the Lord."

Silas was not converted until years later, in 1895; but Peter followed his wife and sister within a few months. In the early part of 1884 he inaugurated a series of conversion meetings at his house and Mud Bay Louis came down to lead them. Peter renounced his sinful life and yielded to the power upon this occasion; and, according to his testimony, he has remained a steadfast Christian ever since with never any desire to smoke, drink, or gamble. He built the church now in use among the Chehalis on his property in 1911. An earlier building, erected by John Smith on his land, had almost been abandoned by then. It was near the river bottom and was difficult to reach during the flood season.

The Upper Chehalis, around Oakville, were related cultur-

ally and by intermarriage to their neighbors, the Lower Chehalis, who lived around Grays Harbor, and through them to
the Quinault up the coast. There was sufficient traffic and visiting over this route in the decade of 1880 to 1890 for the
coastal people to learn about the new religion and for some of
them to become converted. Our data on this area are scanty.
It is known that three prominent Upper Chehalis members,
John Smith, Ed Smith, and Charlie Walker, made a trip to
the Quinault in 1888 in company with the Presbyterian minister, M. G. Mann; and while this circumstance might have
been unfavorable for spreading the news of John Slocum
among the Quinault upon this occasion, it is certain that
there were other opportunities within a brief span of years
which were not overlooked. Olson reports that two Quinault
men made a trip to Puget Sound sometime between 1885 and
1890 and were there converted. Upon their return "nearly
everyone" in the village joined the Shakers. Later on these
new converts carried the message to the Queets and the Quileute farther north on the coast.[16] By 1902 there were adherents among the last mentioned people, and the spread of
the cult had completed a circuit around the Olympic Peninsula.[17]

Although some Cowlitz Indians lived with the Chehalis
around Oakville, others had never agreed to accept this as a
reservation and remained on scattered farms on the prairies
adjacent to the Cowlitz River. Most of them in the 1880's
were around Longview and Kelso, at the mouth of the river
near its junction with the Columbia. An Indian living in
Kelso, Aiyel Wahuwa, had relatives among the Chehalis. Because of these connections he made an early acquaintance-
ship with the religion and became an important agent for its
dissemination. By 1893 there was a nucleus of adherents
around Kelso and Longview who helped Aiyel build a church
on his homestead. Very shortly, however, Aiyel sold his land
to a white man and the building suffered the same fate as

the one at Puyallup. It no longer existed by 1900; and Aiyel, with his family, had moved to the Yakima Reservation to obtain an allotment there.

For some time before this, the Yakima had heard rumors of the religious excitement over the mountains. One of them, William Zack, had married a woman from Longview; and according to his reports the people over there did wonderful things under the new power: they could cure rheumatism and sore eyes, and they could find lost objects. In 1891 or 1892 a man was drowned in the Yakima River, near Union Gap, and his body was not recovered. There was some mystery about its disappearance, and his relatives, at the suggestion of Zack, sent for the Shakers from Longview with the request that they employ their power to ascertain the location of the corpse. Money was sent for the travel expenses of Aiyel, Johnny Johnson, Lincoln White, and Paddy White. In the presence of a crowd that had gathered for the occasion, Aiyel set up a small table on the bank of the river and put a white cloth and three lighted candles on it. Assisted by the others who rang hand bells, Aiyel's extended arms began to shake. He "let his hands lead him," and the rest of the people followed behind him. They moved up and down the river bank until evening, but without success. The next day, after making a second start, Aiyel revealed that he had located the body across the river in a clump of brush. It was found there or in that general vicinity.

With this success the Shakers gained confidence and an opportunity to further demonstrate their powers. The wife of Homer Hoffer, who came from Siletz, Oregon, was sick at the time, and Aiyel volunteered to make her well. She agreed to give him a chance. She regained her health, but it is doubtful whether she was convinced of the power of the Shakers, for she did not join them. They made their first real conversion in the case of Sarah Lumley. Aiyel and his companions cured her of a lingering illness and convinced her of their claims. She was the first among the Yakimas to receive the power, and she remained a prominent figure in the local church until her death in 1940. She had a cousin, Mabel Teio, whose younger sister had been wasting away to death from attempts on her life by shamans. Mabel and her husband Alex decided to call the Shakers to their home after witnessing the effects of their performance upon Sarah Lumley. Aiyel and his companions, accompanied by their new convert, spent three nights shaking over Mabel Teio's sister, at the end of which time she declared that she felt better. It was then decided that the same treatment might bring relief to another of Mabel's sisters who was troubled by an attack of "spirit sickness." In the course of a prolonged shaking session to rid her of the spirits that were trying to force themselves upon her, all three of the sisters began to shake.

The Yakima men were not so susceptible. David Lumley, the husband of Sarah, tried to get the power, but failed for a year or two. Alex Teio was not so anxious to join for he liked to play the fiddle for square dances and drink and use tobacco, but in time his wife prevailed upon him and he eventually became the minister of the local church and a well known figure in Shaker affairs off the reservation.[18]

After the preliminary conversions in the Lumley and Teio families, Aiyel and his missionary associates returned to Kelso. Three of them, Aiyel, Johnny Johnson, and Lincoln White, came back later to assume an important role in the growth of the cult among the Yakima. For some time there was no church building there. The converts met in their homes and in the homes of others who invited them. But after David Lumley abandoned the Methodist faith and joined the Shakers he built a small church on his allotment in Medicine Valley. Aiyel was its minister. The location was inconvenient because it was in one corner of the reservation, from twenty to thirty miles from the homes of some of the members. So when, in 1899, a prominent Indian called Captain Simpson likewise disavowed Methodism and offered land for a new church more centrally located his offer was accepted. Aiyel continued as minister for a time, then Simpson was chosen; but his death a few years later put matters in an uncertain state. His wife was only doubtfully converted, and taking account of the damage inflicted upon her fields and haystacks by the horses of the Sunday worshippers, she demanded that they remove the church. Fortunately, they were in a position to comply. The members, including Enoch Abraham, who was a carpenter, contributed their labor; a subscription of two hundred dollars was collected for necessary expenses, and a new building was put up on unencumbered land in 1900. This is the place of worship which is in use today. The earlier and smaller building was removed from the Simpson farm and now stands beside the newer structure where it is used as a kitchen and dining room at the time of conventions. Another building on Satus Creek, in the southeastern part of the reservation, is also used for meetings upon occasions. This is an old Methodist church which was gradually relinquished to the Shakers as its congregation diminished through death, disinterest, and reaffiliation.

The main church is in a rather unique position. Much of the credit for this is due Enoch Abraham. As early as 1899, the year of his conversion, he was made to realize the precarious position of a church whose future depends upon the personal whims and fortunes of an individual. In that year, during a visit to the Puget Sound area, he learned what had happened to the churches on private property at Kelso and Puyallup, and later he had seen how nearly the Mud Bay church had come to suffering the same fate. He knew, too, that the Methodists and Catholics on the Yakima Reservation had been confirmed in their occupancy of church lands by the provisions of the Dawes Act. He therefore urged his fellow Shakers to petition the Indian agent for a similar concession to them. His insistence eventually bore fruit. A delegation consisting of Captain Simpson, Lincoln White, Joe Riddle, and Alex Teio appealed to agent Lynch, and they received a favorable hearing. In 1908 they were granted seventy-nine acres of land in the center of the reservation, thus insuring the Yakima congregation of a property right which is not enjoyed by any other Shaker group. With proper management of their affairs they could exercise an important influence upon the future of the cult.

In the past there have been attempts to make the Yakima church self-sustaining. In 1917 its farm land was leased to a white man on shares. The results were auspicious; almost eight hundred dollars was paid into the treasury. The next two years were also profitable, and by 1919 the church had a balance of around one thousand dollars in the bank. This sudden prosperity was too much for most of the congregation. They wanted to spend the money immediately in one way or another. Five hundred dollars was voted for repairs on the church and for a series of feasts. The rest was loaned to members at 10 per cent interest, but without collateral or even an investigation of need or the ability to repay. No machinery was set up for the administration of these financial involvements. A clique of the older members assumed control of the allocations, and they showed little sense of discretion or responsibility. A personal warranty by one of them—who did not thereby become a bondsman—was sufficient for a loan. In consequence none of these assignments has been recovered, and the church treasury is almost empty, if not completely so. In 1935 Abraham signed a new five year contract with the same lessee. The proceeds from this agreement were a few beef cattle and some hay. The hay was sold and the money used on current expenses. The beef was eaten. In 1940, the tenant asked for a renewal of the lease. Abraham brought the matter up before the church congregation only to discover that a prominent member had already made a verbal agreement with the tenant and considered the question settled. Presumably the land is still being rented, but the authority for signing the contract, for determining its conditions, and for enforcing its stipulations is in doubt. There is no accounting system, and neither the congregation nor the leaseholder

knows where they stand. Abraham repeatedly attempted
to organize this chaos; but by 1940 the prospects seemed so
hopeless that he abandoned his efforts.

Like the Yakimas, the Indians of Oregon first became acquainted with the Shaker religion through the intermediation
of Aiyel and his associates around Kelso. The time was probably 1893. The known details are few; but according to available information, knowledge of the new religion was carried
to the Warm Springs bands in north central Oregon by a
Wasco Indian named Hunaitca. With some companions
from the Oregon reservation, he was picking berries during
the summer in the vicinity of Hood River when he saw a
Shaker performance by the Longview people. From there,
at an uncertain date, it is said that word of the cult spread to
the Klamath, on the reservation in southern Oregon. It was
not until sometime later, however, that the record becomes
clear. In 1914 a Klamath man got sick, and word was sent
to the Yakima Shakers requesting them to pay him a visit to
try to cure him. About fifteen of them decided to answer the
call, among them Alex Teio, his son Harry, Joe Riddle, Frank
Gunyer, and Enoch Abraham. There were already some
Shakers among the Klamath, but they had no church. Their
first meetings were therefore in a temporary structure on a
camp ground. Later on, a new convert, Pedro Stanley, turned
a dance hall that he owned over to them. It is said that this
man was white, or part white, and that he urged that the religion be renamed and called the Ann Lee Religion. His argument was that the Shaker religion was "the same as the one
across the ocean," that it was founded in Scotland by Ann
Lee, that she was persecuted and fled to Germany, and then
to America, where she adopted the name Quakers for the
sect. Several converts were made upon the occasion of this
meeting, which lasted for a week or two, and another community was added to the growing list of Shakers congregations. The church which is at Chiloquin has flourished and
developed into a key element in the Oregon-California sector.

The next church to be opened was at Siletz, on the coast of Oregon, in 1923. Reports of the religion had reached this reservation long before this date directly from the north, but it was slow in developing a foothold. Several of the Yakima had relatives at Siletz whom they visited even before the opening of this century. It will be recalled that Homer Hoffer's wife came from Siletz. So did one of his daughters-in-law. When the first wife of his son, Andrew, died, the latter married a Siletz woman and moved to that reservation to live with her. He was a Shaker before 1923, as were some others who had been in contact with the Klamath group. But in that year members from elsewhere were invited to dedicate a new church building and to hold a revival meeting. The leaders among the Yakimas and the Klamath arrived in several automobiles and there was an immediate response to the appeals for converts. A large number of the local Indians joined in the next few years; so many, in fact that their desertion from the other churches alarmed the missionaries. In 1928 Reverend Charles Raymond was appointed to undertake a preaching mission here because of "the deplorable fact that the Catholic Siletz Indians have joined the Shakers and the Four Square churches." [19]

Jimmy Jack, whose home was in the town of Klamath, near the Yurok village of Requa, was living at Siletz at the time of the greatest excitement over the new religion. He had voluntarily exiled himself to this locality in 1919 because of trouble with his family over his infatuation for a Siletz woman whom they did not like. Although he was impressed with the Shaker performances that he saw, he was not converted until early in 1926. Then he resolved to reorder his life, return to Requa, and preach the gospel among the Yurok. He commenced his mission in earnest, first asking the forgiveness of his mother, whom he had treated most inconsiderately, then going from house to house pleading for a hearing. He praised the newly revealed religion, enumerating its benefits and declaring that the acceptance of Jesus Christ had wrought a glorious revolution in his life. He called upon the sick and volunteered his services to prove the divine power of shaking. Realizing the disadvantage of his illiteracy he approached Robert Spott, an outstanding member of the community, with a plan to make him his lieutenant because he could read and write.

In spite of his sincere effort Jack was received with skepticism or indifference by almost everyone. Toward the end of the summer he announced that a meeting would be held in his house and that all were welcome, especially those who were suffering from prolonged illnesses. Seventeen Indians attended out of curiosity. Three chairs were placed in the center of the floor and the sick were asked to come forward and take a seat. None did. But when Jack began to sing, several joined in, "because Indians naturally like to sing." When the meeting was over, there were still no converts. Those who had attended talked it over; some soberly and quietly rejected Jack's religion, others laughed openly at him.

He received some support from his relatives, especially his mother and two female cousins. Toward the end of the year he prevailed upon the two young women and the husband of one to accompany him to Siletz in order to attend the meetings there. The women succumbed to the shaking soon after their arrival, and one of them had visions condemning the Yurok opponents of the cult. Her husband was also converted. Encouraged by these favorable results, Jack invited the Siletz Shakers to a big meeting at Klamath. The Chiloquin people were also notified and asked to lend their support by uniting with an eager group from Siletz. The combined parties arrived at Klamath in several automobiles led by Jackson, the elder of the Siletz church.

A meeting of two weeks duration was announced. The salmon cannery at Requa was in operation at the time, and a large number of Indians from other places were collected in the vicinity for the work that it offered. Many of them were attracted to the meetings by the prospect of their novelty, as were the resident Indians who were scattered along the coast near the mouth of the Klamath River. Sessions were held daily from nine to twelve in the morning and from seven to midnight, or later, depending upon the temper of the crowd. There were some immediate triumphs. On the first evening four members joined the fold. Jack's mother was one of them. Others were added in increasing numbers over the two week period, and the final evening brought a climax which augured the fulfilment of the highest hopes of the proselytizers.

Jackson and his co-workers had set their hearts upon, and directed their greatest efforts toward, the conversion of Robert Spott because of his intelligence, his influence in the community, and his identification with the conservative Yurok element. They offered to make him the head elder of the church, even if he did not receive the power, and tendered other blandishments for his support. Although he attended the meetings and was fascinated by the proceedings there, he resisted all attempts to convert him until the last night. Then, as the enthusiasm rose to a climax, Spott lost control of himself and began to shake with the others. When he recovered his composure, Jackson urged him to acknowledge the irresistible power of God and be converted; but Spott refused to take this step of public admission. The meeting was held over another week for this purpose, but without success. Spott attended the meetings for his benefit and was overcome with shaking upon one other occasion; but this only made him more cautious and resistent. From that time on he passively opposed the movement at Requa.

Some of the other Yurok converts, reconsidering their experience in the light of day, fell by the wayside; but, withal, the 1926 revival meeting was a success. There was enough enthusiasm for regular meetings that Jack decided to build a church on his land on the outskirts of the town of Klamath, a few miles from the Yurok village of Requa. It was completed in the spring of 1927, and Shakers from other places were invited for the dedication. This fell on Easter Sunday, and five automobiles carrying visitors from as far away as Mud Bay arrived for the occasion. Peter Heck, the bishop from Oakville, arrived with George Jack, another ardent Chehalis Shaker; Enoch Abraham, as head elder of the church, came with his cousin and militant co-worker from Yakima, Joe Riddle; Thomas Lang and others from Chiloquin were also present.

A number of the Indians who witnessed some of the first meetings at Klamath and Requa were from places scattered along the coast of northern California from Eureka to the border of Oregon. Several Tolowa, from Smith River, were working at the cannery during the fishing season. None of them accepted the religion at the time; but by 1929 their interest had been sufficiently aroused to cause five or six of them to make a trip to Klamath to learn more about it. Norman George was the leader of this group, and at the Klamath meetings which followed for the benefit of his party, he was the first to get the power. He decided to organize a congregation at Smith River, and arranged with Jimmy Jack and Ery Turner for a series of meetings at his house or wherever the opportunity offered. Several local converts were made in this way, and in the following year the Smith River church was built.

To the south of Klamath there were earlier successes. Five of the southern Yurok who lived around Trinidad and several other individuals whose home was at Blue Lake, and who were therefore presumably Wiyot, were among the group converted by Jackson and his zealous followers during the lengthy meeting in 1926. Upon returning home, they endeavored to hold services of their own in the two places, but since there were so few of them they had to work out a plan for cooperation between themselves and some of the Klamath Shakers. To encourage them, Ery Turner periodically assembled a crowd of Yurok who wanted to make the trip, and the Blue Lake members then met them at the home of a host member at Trinidad. Several meetings would be held there, and then everybody moved on to congregate at an appointed house in Blue Lake for another session. A few years later, after some of the Hupa had joined, the tour was extended to include a few days on their reservation and a few more at Johnson's Landing among the Yurok on the lower Klamath River. By 1933, however, this circuit was broken by the defection of the Trinidad and Blue Lake elements. There were very few Indians in that area, so the opportunities for growth were limited. The small congregation in that locality never acquired a church, and without external stimulation its enthusiasm flagged. With the incorporation of a lively group at Hoopa, this disintegrating focus was bypassed on the revival tours.

Although the Hupa had known of the agitation going on around them for some time, the cult did not get established among them until the fall of 1932. At that time John Charley, suffering from Bright's disease and other complications, had almost abandoned hope of recovery. He had tried everything, including both Indian and white doctors, and had just been released from the hospital, he believed, as a hopeless case. Some of his friends suggested the Shakers, so his wife wrote to Ery Turner asking for help. Without replying, Turner arrived in a few days with fourteen other Shakers from various places, including Jimmy Jack, George Jack from Chehalis, and a Tolowa man from Smith River. They stayed two weeks, holding meetings nightly. They applied themselves to the sick man, and on the third day he was well enough to walk around. Within a week he joined in the shaking along with four other converts, two men and two women. The news spread quickly, the crowd of curious onlookers increased, and others received the power. The sessions were further enlivened by the visions of Turner and his companions. To the Tolowa man it was revealed that an "Indian devil" was lurking about the meeting house and must be driven away. Impelled by the vividness of his vision, he rushed into the darkness in pursuit of the fleeing devil. Most of those who were under the power fol-

lowed close upon his heels, picking up sticks and stones for
the assault. A straggling of fascinated spectators brought up
the rear. An erratic chase led the crowd through a neighboring
field, and ended at the foot of a large oak tree. The Tolowa
man had seen the devil climb the tree, and he continued the
pursuit up the trunk and out on a large limb. At that point
the devil somehow got away. It was said that if his pursuers
had taken thought, they could have trapped him with ropes,
or could have killed him by building a bonfire under the limb.
As it happened, he "shot" the Tolowa man with his "poison"
and made him very sick the next day. But the Shakers worked
over him and cured him. On two other occasions Indian
devils were discovered attempting to poison the Shakers as
they danced, and similar chases followed.

The visiting party was invited to several homes during these
first two weeks by individuals who were too sick to go elsewhere for help. The new members also invited them around
and fed them. Others gave them a chance, but were unconvinced. After their departure, a leader, one of the first two
women to shake, was appointed and regular meetings continued. At the end of their first year the Hupa Shakers could
claim twenty-five faithful members. There were perhaps as
many more who had played with the idea of joining but
whose interest was fitful or lagging.

A church was built a couple of years later by subscription.
Members were expected to contribute five dollars to the
building fund or supply an equivalent in materials. Outsiders,
or those who were believed to have received some benefit
from the religion, were approached and asked to give what
they thought they should. At first the church was not very
large, but in 1937, in anticipation of a convention to be held
at Hoopa, its length was extended by sixteen feet. At present
(1943) this church is the hub of Shaker activities in California and southwestern Oregon. It has eclipsed the churches
at Siletz and Klamath. The Tolowa branch, which grew out
of the Yurok stimulus in 1930, has never been very strong.

Contacts with all these points now radiate from Hoopa and converge upon it. Washington visitors also make the Hupa church their headquarters. Its importance is lessened somewhat by the lack of aggressive leaders. In this respect it is overshadowed by the nearby church at Johnson's Landing, but the small size and inaccessibility of this village, which must be reached by a road through the Hupa Reservation, operates against the extension of its influences into new areas. However, in 1938, one of its leading members initiated a move and was chosen "sub-bishop of California."

The Hupa church was the last Shaker building erected. It brought the total number of existing, specially erected, and recurrently used meeting places to twenty-five. Their locations and the Indian groups which they serve are as follows: Mud Bay (Squaxin), Lynn or Shelton (Skokomish), Tahola (Quinault), La Push (Quileute), Neah Bay (Makah), Elwha (Clallam), Jamestown (Clallam), Port Gamble (Clallam), Auburn (Muckleshoot), Tulalip (Snohomish), La Conner (Swinomish), Concrete (Skagit), Esquimault (Songish), Brentwood (Sanetch), Duncan (Cowichan), Oakville (Chehalis), White Swan (Yakima), Satus (Yakima), Warmspring (Wasco and Tenino), Chiloquin (Klamath), Siletz (Tututuni, Tillamook, etc.), Smith River (Tolowa), Klamath (Yurok), Johnson's Landing (Yurok), Hoopa (Hupa). In addition, there was a small church near Celilo Falls which was used during the summer time by the several bands of Indians who congregated in this vicinity for salmon fishing. Also, the Lummi Indians started to build a church some years ago near Marietta, but having exhausted their funds and enthusiasm, it still remains to be completed. In several other places buildings which once served as churches have collapsed or disappeared. We have already noted this to be the case for churches at Skookum Chuck, Oyster Bay, Puyallup, and Kelso. To the list may be added one burned down at Koksilah, between Victoria and Duncan, Vancouver Island; another destroyed by storm at Georgetown on Grays Harbor; two that became obsolete on the Yakima Reservation, and one which disintegrated at Cowlitz, Washington.

The churches named represent established communities of Shakers. In other localities there have been, and there continue to be, faint glimmerings and tentative approaches toward the consolidation of new units. There are, or were, individual Shakers scattered in many places: a few at Georgetown, Crescent City, and Blue Lake in California; many more among the Puyallup and Nisqually. In 1914, at the time of the opening of the Chiloquin church, a few Achomawi from Pit River in California joined, but they were never able to organize a unit at home. Apparently none of the Karok have, as yet, taken an interest in the activities at nearby Hoopa and Johnson's Landing.

The Umatilla, near Pendleton, Oregon, heard about Aiyel's wonderful clairvoyant powers soon after he had convinced the Yakima. About 1906, a Umatilla man had some property stolen from him, and he decided to apply to the Shakers for assistance in recovering it.[20] The Presbyterians and Catholics were strongly entrenched on that reservation and Aiyel was fearful of a trap, so he took Alex Teio, the Yakima elder, and several other people with him. As in the case of the lost body at Union Gap, Aiyel's hands led him, under power, to the hiding place of the stolen goods and the thief's house. Some of the Umatillas were interested, and later a few came to the Yakima meetings and were converted. But they were never able to attract a following or establish an independent church. With their deaths the movement came to an end, and today there are no Shakers in that locality. The Yakimas attribute this failure to the vigorous opposition of the local Christian churches. In 1912, Enoch Abraham was asked to come to Pendleton by a delegation of Umatilla Indians. He supposed that they wanted him to explain the Shaker faith to them and to offer advice to potential converts. Instead, he found that he had been summoned to an inquisition by the native Presbyterian elders. According to him, they were confounded by his Christian exegesis. No conversions were made however.

The Nez Perce of Lapwai, Idaho, have more recently shown some stirrings of interest in the Yakima Shakers. There has been intermittent contact between the Indians of these two reservations for some time. As early as the final decade of the last century, George Waters and Thomas Pearne, native Methodist preachers among the Yakima, were making missionary trips to Lapwai, apparently not in competition with the established Christian missions there—except possibly the Catholic—for they were welcomed and entertained by the local Presbyterian missionary. In recent days, with better transportation facilities, there have been more occasions for contact between the two groups. Some of the Nez Perce, along with hundreds of other Indians, annually congregate on the Yakima and Moxee hop fields for six weeks during the summer. In 1943 visiting parties in two automobiles appeared at the White Swan church for a Sunday service. They did not participate in the ritual but manifested a respectful interest. The Nez Perce, like the Umatilla, have been deterred by the challenging attitudes of Christian church members. Two or three zealous Nez Perce missionaries belonging to the Presbyterian Church cover these eastern reservations, and in the course of their exhortations they find occasion to anathematize the Shaker religion.

It is almost impossible to arrive at any significant figures upon the number of Shaker adherents. None of the churches keep membership or other written records. It is possible to obtain a person by person enumeration of local members from any one of several individuals in a district who is close to the church. Several such counts have been collected, but it becomes obvious in acquiring them that subjective judgments on the question of what constitutes a Shaker yield great individual variability in the results. Some enumerators will include every person in the count who has actively participated in a meeting, including the backsliders and those who merely attend the meetings and assist the shaking members. Others are more selective, basing their estimates upon any one of several criteria or a combination of them: receipt of the power, testimony of conviction, maintenance of the ethical standards, demonstration of zeal, acceptance or rejection of the Bible as the ultimate source of inspiration. In 1938 one ex-minister at Hoopa counted twenty-one "regular members" of the local church, in addition to several others who were lukewarm, and some who had been helped by the religion but had never made public acknowledgement of it. Another ex-minister was more jealous of what constituted membership; he named only eleven persons who were entitled to be called "true Shakers," and of them only three were "the real John Slocum kind." The whole question is rendered more confusing by self-evaluations of status; that is, there are many individuals who have had the experience of shaking, and may even have believed it to be divinely ordained, but have since denounced it and will have nothing more to do with the church.

In other words, taking a census of Shakers raises many of the same questions as would occur in an attempt to make a reliable count of "Christians"—or of any sect within that category. However, no matter upon what basis the count is made, it is certain that a rather large number of Indians in the northwestern states have at one time or another been significantly affected by the Shaker cult. It is not uncommon to find between one and two hundred individuals from remote parts of these states assembled for the annual conventions and camp meetings at the present time. Eells mentions a "gathering of several hundred" at the Chehalis Reservation on July 4, 1892. Wickersham, whose estimate is as valid as any, noted that in 1893, when there were churches at Mud Bay, Oyster Bay, Chehalis, Puyallup, and Kelso, there were five hundred members. C. J. Johns, less reliably, affirmed that he had seen that many persons convened for meetings at Mud Bay at the turn of the century. In 1903 Enoch Abraham, acting as secretary, made a count of those he considered to be Shakers and arrived at a total of a few over the same number; without having made a count of them, he believes that there are over two thousand today. As an over-all figure, intended to include all those who attend meetings in a sympathetic spirit, this estimate of present Shaker strength is perhaps not far off; but the number who have yielded to the conviction of shaking must be much smaller, probably even less than one-half of the total who hope or believe that this religion is a gift of God.

THREE ✛ The Opposition

AS ONE might suppose, the official representatives of government and established religion were rather
uniformly opposed to the spread of Shaker practices. From
their reports to their superiors and sponsors it is difficult to
determine what their individual reactions were, the reason
being that they rarely mention the matter at all. From a reading of contemporary documentary materials one would not
suspect that anything untoward had occurred among their
charges to disturb their peace of mind; and yet we know, from
later sources, that Shakerism in the first decade of its growth
was a source of considerable anxiety to missionaries and agents
alike.

In his annual reports to the Commissioner of Indian
Affairs, as published, agent Eells of the Skokomish Reservation makes his first reference to the Shakers in 1892,[1] although it must be added that he had previously informed
the Commissioner of the existence of the sect in explanation
of certain repressive measures he had felt himself obliged to
take with respect to some of its leaders.[2] Superintendent
Buchanan of the Tulalip Reservation likewise refrained from
a public acknowledgement of the existence of the cult until
1906, while at the same time stating that he had been personally acquainted with its activities for the preceding twelve
years.[3] A search through the documentary files of the Office

of Indian Affairs now preserved in the National Archives in Washington, D.C., has failed to disclose any mention of the movement or its repercussions upon other affairs of the agencies concerned. While these files are incomplete, and agency records might be more informative, other elements than chance are to be held accountable for the lack of contemporary information upon the development and spread of the cult. It appears that officially the local administrative policy was to ignore the phenomenon.

The same attitude appears upon an examination of the accounts of missionaries close to the Shaker movement. Although it is probable that the representatives of the several Christian sects on the reservations around Puget Sound communicated their early alarms and discouragements to their sponsoring bodies, nothing of it appears in any of the available published sources. Also, the various missionary journals are mostly silent upon this disturbing result of their contributors' efforts to win the Indian to their respective faiths. Although each of the three denominations involved, the Catholic, the Congregational, and the Presbyterian, maintained organs for the dissemination of news from the various areas in which they were interested and published in them frequent letters and reports of trials and successes from their missionaries, references to the Shaker cult are so scanty that one must conclude that there was a deliberate effort to minimize its importance. Of the several missionaries who had to contend with it only Eells, the Congregational minister at Skokomish, saw fit to allude to Slocum's trance and subsequent developments at about the time they were taking place. In two restrained communications he has left us the only approximately contemporary account of the cult in its formative stages.[4] In 1886 he expanded and embodied the data of these letters in the informative story of his experiences after ten years at Skokomish.[5] Thereafter his published statements about the cult are so infrequent and brief as to suggest an inverse correlation with the success of its growth.

It was not until 1884 that Mann, the Presbyterian minister for the area, published his account of the movement.
In a report of his recent activities to the readers of a Presbyterian journal he indicated a tolerant attitude toward the cult
and hinted at attempts to assimilate it. He told of a visit to
Mud Bay where a great many Indians were assembled for
services which "began on Saturday and continued all Sunday,
with very little intermission, till nearly midnight." The services were "partly preaching interspersed with singing, talks
by elders and other enlightened Indians, and [my] answering questions concerning the polity and doctrines of our
church. . . ." He was gratified with the interest he found.
As a result he was able to baptize twelve of the Indians
present and so founded a new church, this being the occasion
for his report. It is perhaps not too much of an assumption
to suppose that the services he witnessed were Shaker ceremonies; but in any event he rightly credited the enthusiasm
at the meetings to the agitation caused by Slocum's experience. Of this he says:

"This movement and earnest inquiry was started about two
years ago, by one of the Squookum Bay Indians' having been
in a trance for some time, and on his coming to, told the relatives and others who were present, and who had come to weep
and lament, believing him dead, that he had been translated
to heaven and seen the Saviour Jesus Christ, who told him
to return to earth and convert his Indian brethren, and that
His second coming was near at hand. The influence of his
eloquent preaching brought Indians from all parts of the
Sound to hear him. Of course the teaching is a mixture of
Roman Catholic ceremonies, heathen superstitions, and evangelical truths acquired by coming in contact with our Christian Indians. The Romish priest at Olympia sought to draw
them all into the Roman Catholic Church, and baptized many;
they are now dissatisfied with the husks of the Roman Catholic
religion, and are eager to hear the Bible taught and expounded.

Peter Stanup, our young native helper, has been to see them at Mud Bay twice, and I have preached at various times, usually in the Chinnook jargon; the effort culminated in the conversion and baptism of twelve adult Indians, including the chief, and the organization of an Indian church." [6]

Seemingly, the Catholics, who had charge of religious instruction within reservations on the northeastern part of the Sound, were even more reluctant to take official recognition of the spread of the cult to their province. Nothing appears upon the subject in the report and correspondence files of the Bureau of Catholic Indian Missions, their sponsoring agency; and it was not until 1913 that some mention of it appeared in the official publication of that organization. [7]

For these failures to accord official notice to Shakerism two reasons are perhaps to be held accountable. It is evident from the writings of Eells and others that upon their first contact with it most officials were inclined to treat the cult as trivial and ephemeral. Guided more by wishful thinking than by a realistic appreciation of the strength and appeal of the movement for the Indian, they tended to regard it as being due to a misunderstanding that could be corrected or as a futile rebellion against authority that could be quashed by a firm hand. In 1886 Eells felt justified in declaring that "at present it seems to be dying." After that the movement spread to most of the reservations of Washington and into British Columbia. Again in 1923 Lindquist concluded that "There would appear to be no elements of permanency in the Shaker churches, and the problem they present can safely be regarded as temporary only." [8] Since then churches have been established on the reservations of coastal Oregon and in northern California, with some stirrings of interest evident in Idaho.

A more personal reason for maintaining silence about the cult lay in the understandable desire of responsible agents to protect their reputations against suspicions of incompe-

tence and neglect of duty. Although such charges are often
unfair, and are frequently made by people who are lacking
in understanding, they none the less have to be guarded
against by persons in authority if they value their official
lives. Many critics would probably agree with Lindquist when
he says that "Shakerism can be laid at the door of the
Church's neglect in not adequately providing wholesome ave-
nues of religious expression for these northwestern tribes." [9]
It is safer to attempt to manage the local difficulties within
one's jurisdiction quietly than to report them and thereby
invite such criticism or an investigation; and doubtless this
accounts in large part for the gaps in the official record of the
Shaker cult and for the depreciatory and paternalistic tone
of the references when they occur.

It is to unofficial sources that we must look for the real
attitudes of missionaries and government employees on the
reservations. Principally these are the Indians themselves,
but Myron Eells has left a frank account of the forceful
measures employed on the Skokomish Reservation to suppress and discourage the first upsurge of the movement. He
was the brother of Edwin, the Indian agent there. They were
the sons of Cushing Eells, the pioneer missionary in this region, and they saw the matter in the same light. To them it
was nonsense that was not to be indulged. Myron always
wisely refrained from interfering in administrative affairs but
gave his assistance and his moral support to his brother's
decisions. In the beginning both men took an unqualified
stand against the excitement and did everything they could
to suppress it.

In August, 1883, at the time that the authorities first became aware of the new development, the agent was no longer
resident at Skokomish. His office was at Puyallup and his
administrative deputy at Skokomish was the school teacher.
When the call came announcing the big meeting at Slocum's
camp, the response was so general and after a few days the
reports of its consequences so alarming that the school

teacher decided to go with a police escort to try to put a stop to it. He succeeded in getting most of the Skokomish to return to their reservation, by what means we do not know. Myron says that he talked to them "plainly." [10]

There followed the turmoil over the illness and death of Ellen, the wife of David Charley, who was one of the principals in the opposition to the missionary. By this time the agent had been notified, and in September he made a trip to Skokomish where he interviewed the reservation leaders of the disturbance and "made some threats of what he might do if the foolishness was not stopped." It is important to note in this connection that the agent had only a nebulous and uncertain authority over Slocum and the real leader, Mud Bay Louis, the reason being that they lived off the reservation. The Office of Indian Affairs had not settled upon a policy with regard to such Indians at this date, nor for some time after, and Eells was repeatedly disconcerted and thwarted in the exercise of his authority by those who defied him and then moved out of his reach. He appealed to the Commissioner upon several occasions for a clarification of his jurisdiction and the powers vested in him but without any immediate results. In the meantime he conformed to the letter of his commission and applied his authority only within the boundaries of reservations. John and Louis nominally belonged to the Squaxin Reservation; but this was confined to the island by that name. Mud Bay and vicinity were not a part of it, and John and Louis were in effect squatters or homesteaders. Eells was therefore unable to attack the Shaker agitation at its source.

In the middle of October he again returned to Skokomish and finding no improvement in the situation he determined to take up the fight in earnest. He seems to have been aware that coercion might produce effects the opposite of those which he hoped to accomplish, but he nevertheless decided upon this course. He forced the resignation of David and Dick, hoping thereby to make them contrite and ridiculous.

Although Myron would have his readers believe that this accomplished its purpose, we may be permitted some skepticism, especially since the abstract manipulation of rights and duties and the concept of an office as we understand it was beyond the experience of these Indians. Furthermore, Myron himself admits the chiefs did not care if they were "deposed" when the threat was made. Nevertheless agent Eells reconstituted the council, which was composed of his appointed "chiefs," and, of course, secured its pledge of co-operation in eradicating the evil. Before this new council and all the rest of the Indians assembled for the purpose he then declared that the shaking must stop and that if Billy Clams did not concur he was to return to Port Madison to join his Catholic friends, for his sympathies lay more on that side than with the majority wishes at Skokomish.

We have seen that this action did not put an end to the ferment on the Skokomish Reservation but it did slow it down and drive it under cover. And no sooner was this accomplished than more serious manifestations confronted Eells. Even while the Skokomish matter was being dealt with Big John was agitating and proclaiming his visions among the Indians congregated around his wife's parents' home on Mud Bay against the orders of the agent. Then followed his ride through the streets of Olympia, and since his home and that of some of his adherents were within the jurisdiction of Eells the latter "was obliged to imprison the alleged 'Christ,' punish some of his followers, and discharge a number of Indian judges and policemen in order to regain control." [11] After that Big John was ordered to remain on the reservation and stop shaking. He did neither and was again arrested and confined in jail for another four weeks.

Not long after, and before the turmoil had subsided at Mud Bay, an opportunity presented itself for the agent to strike at the heart of the trouble. A woman on the Nisqually Reservation became sick and her friends called upon the

Shakers for help. John Slocum, Mud Bay Louis, Mud Bay Sam, Charlie Walker (Chehalis), two other men, and one unidentified woman answered the call. Agent Eells heard of this violation of his order and sent Indian policemen from Puyallup to arrest them. At Puyallup they were imprisoned for seven weeks; and the men, bearing balls and chains, were required to cut wood along the road where the other Indians were encouraged to ridicule them. On Sundays the prisoners were brought into the Presbyterian mission church and placed in the front row, likewise to humiliate them before the congregation. Eells hoped by these means to induce them to renounce their unorthodox practices. In this he failed. Mud Bay Sam, who later made the most of his martyrdom, appears to have weakened under the pressure and urged Louis to submit, but without avail. Charlie Walker was a practicing shaman, and he let it be known that he was going to use his power to stop the mockery of the Indians who supported the agent's tactics. Soon after, one of his tormentors died and it was asserted and believed by most that this was due to Charlie's supernatural influences. It was, at any rate, an effective block on the agent's efforts, and the prisoners were later released without having recanted.

On the Chehalis Reservation it was not possible to maintain such a close watch on the cult, but when it obtruded itself Eells again acted with firmness and dispatch. In the early part of 1884, Peter Heck, a "nephew" of Charlie Walker, returned home from a visit to Mud Bay. He had not yet been converted, but he had learned one or two of the Shaker songs. Shortly thereafter a program of entertainment was given for parents and their children at the boarding school, and the school master, understanding that Heck knew some entertaining songs, invited him to sing. Everyone seemed pleased, including the schoolteacher. It was not until later that he learned of the source of the songs through the protests of the opposition who spread the story that the Shakers had recently undressed a sick woman as they worked over her to cure her. He was indignant and, with the aid of the agent, applied himself to the suppression of the cult.

It was during the first years of their existence and under agent Eells, that the Shakers experienced the most vigorous opposition. But they also remember that the agents at Tulalip and Neah Bay actively resisted them upon first acquaintance. By this time the cult was protected in its status as a religion, and Eells had so far relinquished his former stand against it that he was able to commend it for its moral principles, whether out of conviction or resignation we do not know. Nevertheless, at Tulalip the first Shakers were treated rather harshly.

Johnny Steve and his wife had been visiting friends to the south when they returned to Tulalip as converts. They attracted the attention of the Indians there and alarmed the priest, the physician, and the agent. They were jailed, along with others, and the men were put in chains to work on the road under demands to stop their excesses. Upon their release they resumed their meetings and were again promptly imprisoned. They sent out a call for help, and Louis with thirty others went to Tulalip to plead for them. The agent gave the delegation twenty-four hours to leave the reservation. When he was finally released, Steve made a trip to appeal to the Yakimas, but without success.

Among the Makahs at Neah Bay the situation was more complex. Samuel G. Morse was the agent there from 1897 until the fall of 1902, during which time the Makahs first became acquainted with Shakerism. Morse was, in fact, instrumental in introducing it there, and it may be that his attitude toward it was a critical factor in his removal. In 1901 he wrote to the Commissioner in his annual report: "The Shakers have done good work among other tribes of Indians on the Sound, and arrangements are being made to have them come in here this coming winter and see if they cannot do something along the Christian line for our poor people." In his next report he expresses the same hopes, saying that Shakers were then among the Quileute "and doing much good there." In these same reports, and also in a previous one, Morse lamented the failure of missionaries to attend to the Makah Indians, stating that little or nothing had been done over the years to make Christians of them and that the field was crying for someone who could understand their needs.[12] By implication there was no missionary at Neah Bay at the time of his writing this plea. The truth was, however, that Miss Helen Clark, supported by Presbyterian missionary groups, had arrived at her new station on this reservation in November, 1899.[13] Morse had indeed heralded her arrival, saying, "We expect that this year a good Christian worker will be among these people." [14] In his next report he ignored the subject of religion entirely, and in the two that followed he praised the Shakers in the words that have been quoted. Apparently he did not approve of Miss Clark; and it may be presumed that his attitude toward the Shakers was in part, at least, the expression of a reaction toward her. Whether this difference of opinion over Shakerism was the cause of his resignation is unknown; but he was relieved of his post in the latter part of 1902 and Edwn L. Chalcraft, a former superintendent of the Puyallup school, temporarily replaced him.

Whether out of sympathy or practical necessity, Chalcraft and his successor the next year, Claude C. Covey, compromised with the Shakers and permitted them to hold meetings, but only on Thursday evenings and on Sundays after the Presbyterian services were over. Miss Clark had instituted a Wednesday evening class in adult religious instruction at her home, hence the Thursday evening stipulation.[15] This did not represent a sacrifice on the part of the Shakers, for they followed the Thursday evening pattern initiated by the original group around Mud Bay and Skokomish. This was not the only restriction, however.

While granting the Shakers the privilege of holding meetings at assigned times the Neah Bay authorities laid other restraints upon them that practically negated this concession. A time limit of three hours for each meeting was set, and a policeman was usually present to see that this and other regulations were observed. Most of the local whites who disapproved of shaking partially justified their stand upon hygienic grounds. In addition to pointing out the deleterious effects of the shaking itself, they decried the unhealthy conditions in the poorly ventilated rooms. Somehow, this became a critical issue in this region. Of the Quileutes Reagan wrote that "they shake in a room so ill ventilated that no reader of this article would care to stay in it for five minutes, though the Indians are shaking till the perspiration drops off of them and forms in rings around them on the floor. Moreover the exhaustive shaking, quivering, trembling will in time surely effect both the nerves and the brain." Miss Clark believed that they deliberately closed all windows and doors as a means of inducing shaking, and reasoned that nobody could stand the physical strain of shaking and living a normally industrious life, so that only the lazy ones were shakers.[16] The assistance of the field matron was enlisted in the health crusade, and she believed, after six years of labor, that "among Shakers [she had] promoted cleanliness as a cardinal virtue in their religion, next to temperance and anti-gambling." [17]

More critical was the attack upon Shaker ideology and ritual. In particular it was demanded that the Makah adherents abandon the use of bells, stamping, and trembling and that they renounce their pretensions of marvelous cures and other miracles that called up repugnant associations with shamanism. The efforts of the authorities were directed toward destroying the influence of the local leader of the cult, Lans Kalapa. It was said by his friends that he was required either to go to jail or "sign a paper" renouncing this part of the religion. As has been noted, he chose an evasive course that simulated conformance but was designed at the same time to maintain his leadership if not to perpetuate the shaking as such. His compromise was not acceptable to the majority of the local Shakers, and the oppressive demands of the authorities simply caused them to hold their meetings in secret or go to other villages beyond the jurisdiction of the Neah Bay office.

Edwin Minor became the superintendent of the Makah-Quileute jurisdiction in 1904. He co-operated with Miss Clark and her assistant Miss Hanna and continued the policy of suppression. Reagan's manuscript contains a copy of an order relative to this subject dated February 21, 1906. It reads:

REGULATIONS

FOR

SHAKER . . . . . . MEETINGS

QUILEUTE

1st. Meetings may be held any time Sunday afternoon, and shall not continue after dark.

2nd. Meetings may be held on Wednesday evening of each week; but must not continue longer than three hours.

3rd. No school children shall be allowed to attend night meetings.

4th. No bells or other instruments for making noise shall be used, except one bell may be used to give signals.

5th. The room where meetings are held must be well ventilated by opening a door or at least two windows.

This order superceeds [*sic*] all other orders.

(*Signed*)

Edwin Minor

SUPERINTENDENT.

That this and previous orders did not have the desired effect is attested by an instance commented upon by Reagan in the same manuscript: "At a shaker meeting recently it took the leader more than ten minutes of terrible effort to reduce his power. At times he would contort his body in hideous shapes and would utter a hoarse, coarse sound like a bark. A similar phenomenon was noticed at a shaker medicine performance in the early part of 1906. The U.S. Officials came upon a group of shakers performing over a little girl at 2:30 A.M. After looking at them for an hour or more through a rent in the window curtain, the officers burst open the door and arrested them for violating the regulations of the Indian Office. An amusing, 'grotesque' scene followed. Some of the performers instantly ceased their shaking and tried to pretend that they had not been violating the regulations, but others, in spite of themselves, shook and writhed their bodies for more than twenty minutes." And again: "At a meeting on May 5th (1907) it took the combined efforts of all the shakers for more than twenty minutes to free a twelve year old girl from the power which they had put on her in their efforts to make her shake." Several other instances are given by Reagan, most of which indicate that the Makah and Quileute managed to continue their meetings, usually for doctoring the sick, by making excuses to leave the reservation where they could not be interfered with by the agency policemen.

The effect of the official attitude was therefore rather the opposite of what was hoped for. As had happened at Skokomish and Tulalip the Shakers of the Olympic Peninsula resorted to secrecy and subterfuge to carry on their meetings. Either because they lacked the courage, or because they had no sponsor comparable to lawyer Wickersham in Olympia, they chose the course of passive resistance rather than to boldly assert their rights to religious freedom as the Mud Bay Shakers had eventually done. They were advised on this course by Louis. During their trials with the Neah Bay authorities he sent them a letter—doubtless written, if not dictated, by someone else, for Louis could not read—enjoining patience and hope. With characteristic admixture of ethics, doctrine, and expedient declarations and protestations, it read:

"I, as head of the Shakers, understand the government at Washington allows Indians to worship God according to their own conscience, so long as we are law abiding and live good lives.

"I wish as a leader you would try very hard to have peace with the agent. Follow our rules as Shakers:

"Believe in God, and Jesus as our head.

"Keep the laws of Government of United States.

"Drink no whisky, nor use tobacco.

"Steal not, lie not, gamble not; love one another as Christians, and lead pure, clean lives.

"I have the license and sanction to lead and will do my best.

"Leave all troubles to me for the present, until I see you again.

"Yours, in Christ Jesus,

Louis Yowaluch." [18]

Gradually the Makah and Quileute Shakers won the right to hold their meetings out of the sheer inability of the officials to control them. It was a slow, piecemeal process, however. They won one missionary, Miss Ober, over to their side before 1910; but her superior, Miss Clark, was relentless, and as late as 1914 while she was still at Neah Bay the restrictions on Shaker meetings were theoretically in effect. Two representatives of the Woman's Board of Home Missions (Presbyterian) visited her in that year and reported upon her difficulties with the sect. They noted, however, that there was some consolation in the fact that the agent limited each meeting to a two hour period.[19] The time limit was probably three hours, as it had been during previous years. But by this date other restrictions were being ignored, and possibly the time limit was not enforced. Reagan states that the Quileute Shakers met for nine hours on Sundays—from

9:00 to 12:00 A.M., from 2:00 to 5:00 P.M., and from 6:00 to 9:00 P.M.—and also on Wednesday evenings for three hours. Eventually the Makah, and still later the Snohomish and others under the Tulalip jurisdiction, were permitted to hold meetings as they pleased.

Elsewhere there were few instances of persecution or restraint after 1892. Bolstered by Wickersham's assurances, most Shakers were quick to assert their rights to a native faith; and after the incorporation of their church in 1910 they were not to be intimidated. Their claims might have been contested with more legitimacy than at Neah Bay and Tulalip upon those reservations where they were still treated as wards of the federal government, but little seems to have been done to thwart them. There have been investigations upon complaints of indiscretions at Warm Springs, Klamath, and elsewhere; but no concerted efforts have been made in recent years in the United States to destroy the cult.

The faith emerged with vigor on the Skokomish Reservation a short time after protection was assured its adherents. Soon they were meeting openly in their homes. Submitting to the necessity of recognizing it as an influence to be reckoned with the authorities there philosophically made the best of it. Almost immediately the agent forced himself to take a more benign view of the Shakers, commending them for their sincerity, temperance, and their Christian virtues.[20] In a letter appended to the schoolteacher's report to the Commissioner of Indian Affairs in June, 1893, Myron Eells wrote a qualified approval of the situation: "Lately the Shaker sect has revived considerably. This singular freak is a new religion which originated within twenty miles of this reservation about eleven years ago; it is somewhat akin to the Messiah craze of the Dakotas, but much more civilized and moral, and when it first originated was kept under control quite firmly by the agent. Lately, however, they have learned that the freedom of citizenship allowed them this religion as much as they wished, and consequently it has revived quite strongly.

Some things about it have been rather discouraging to me." [21] Thereafter, it was not uncommon for Indian service employees within the jurisdiction of Edwin Eells to comment upon the Shakers, and to credit them with good. Thus, the superintendent of the Chehalis schools believed that they represented the most moral element on the reservation and that their influence upon others was beneficial.[22] Field Matron Quimby in 1897 accorded the Shakers the status of a church along with the Presbyterian and the Catholic converts among the Puyallups; and in the following four years she endeavored to work with rather than against them in order to eradicate some of their more objectionable practices and beliefs.[23]

The attitudes of missionaries toward the cult were reflected in the repressive measures of the agents, if indeed they were not the motivations for them. It should be pointed out, however, that in addition to deprecating the emergence of the cult and being scornful of it, they characteristically adopted an air of ignoring it and advised their native followers to do the same. The theory seems to have been that to take notice of it would have been tantamount to signifying an interest, and that in turn might be construed to imply a recognition of its importance. The alternative was to discourage it by disregarding it. This attitude is implicit in every account by Myron Eells; and in one place, describing his part in the funeral of Big Bill, he asserts that this was the first time that he was unwittingly drawn into partnership with their "Catholic" ceremonies and that it was also to be the last.

The importance of this position for an historical analysis is that most of what Eells knew about the Shakers came to him by report and rumor. Nowhere does he tell us that he ever witnessed a meeting, and the internal evidence of his descriptions bears out the conclusion that he did not. Some of the reports of his informers that were publicized were admittedly secondhand.[24] It is on record that Mrs. Edwin Eells, and therefore presumably her husband, the agent, was present at a performance at Skokomish, but the date and other circumstances are not given.[25] As with Myron Eells, so with Miss Clark at Neah Bay. Although she attempted a brief characterization of the Shaker cult, she admitted that she had never attended a meeting, and for the same reasons that motivated Myron Eells.[26]

The reactions of these two missionaries may be regarded as typical, and, considering the circumstances, they are understandable. On that account it is interesting to note that Mann took a somewhat different attitude toward the cult. He deplored it, but he also took a more optimistic view of it, as it is evident from the following excerpt of a report to his home congregation: "The religious condition of the Indian members at Chehalis gives me much joy and confidence at the present time. They had been for a while back much under the influence of the false prophet, an Indian from Skookum Bay, who pretended to have heard a special revelation from God, and used mesmerism and other semi-heathenish rites as a means of conversion, and whenever an Indian 'trembled' or 'shook' it was supposed to be a sign of his acceptance and favor with God. By patient and constant preaching of the Gospel of our Lord, and by the love that never tires, but always wins, they were brought back to the true doctrine of justification by faith, and the all-sufficient work of redemption by Jesus Christ." [27]

Clearly, Mann hoped to gain ground by assimilating this new movement, and the local representatives of the Presbyterian Church seem to have agreed with this tactic. In consequence, we are left to wonder over the way in which he reconciled the course he chose with his own conscience and with the expectations, if not demands, of his fellow missionaries. His relations with the Eells brothers, agent and minister, are not clear. Myron Eells made no mention of his fellow missionary, except in his impersonal history of northwest missions, nor did Mann refer to him. The agent, on the other hand, seems to have been on good terms with Mann,

at least to the extent of officially commending his work; and
Mann in turn was much disturbed at the prospect of Eells's
replacement as agent by one with Roman Catholic sympathies in 1887. A year later he draws a warm-hearted picture of the agent, then stationed at Puyallup, playing the
violin and singing for his church services. And these were
the years when he was consorting freely with the Shaker
leaders once denounced by Eells. In short, there are reasons
for one to believe either that Mann was sympathetic and co-
operative with the Eells brothers or that he insisted on carrying out his work independently—or that both relationships
existed but at different times and places.

In any event, it seems that Mann felt justified in making
certain concessions in his efforts to convert the Indian. He
was less meticulous than his fellow missionaries about reject-
ing anything that might be construed as an encouragement of
the native religion. Even before Shakerism became an acknowledged religious movement Mann exhibited a sympathy with emotional fervors under certain conditions that
were anathema to the Eells brothers. He regarded Indian
enthusiasms as acceptable religious expressions. Praising the
temper of a meeting that was conducted by a native elder,
James Shipman, at the Nisqually church in January, 1882,
he wrote: "Such a prayer and praise meeting as we had that
Sunday evening I have never attended before. After a short
sermon by myself I gave an opportunity for those to speak
who would seek Jesus. There was no halting or waiting; sometimes two or three would rise to their feet at once. Though
it grew cold and late, those ardent Christian Indians evinced
no desire to go home. It is so much like living in the early
apostolic times, to see the fervency and simple faith of
these newly-converted people." [28] Very likely he did not know
that John Slocum had a few months previously made these
words more real than they appeared. Somewhat later, when
the Shakers were in the fullness of their conviction, Mann
describes his struggles with the encroachments of the Catho-

lic element at Puyallup and continues, "When a Presbyterian Indian got sick, to thwart the Catholics, Presbyterians
sat with the patient night and day until he either died or
got better. It was a hard contested battle. Our elders worked
hard and nobly. . . . How they sing and pray and edify and
console in the sick room and in the prayer meeting!" [29]

In order to convert the Indians, Mann knew that it was
important to stimulate their active participation in church
affairs and in his eagerness to achieve this he was prepared
to establish important local leaders in positions as elders at
newly founded missions. He was not as demanding in his
choices as were some of the other missionaries. Perhaps he
thought that he would be able to adapt them to his ends.
Latterly, he certainly knew that he was committing himself
to an issue, for five years after the Shakers had created such
a widespread stir we note that he had adopted a policy of
patronizing its leaders by making them elders in Presbyterian
congregations. In one of the missionary journals to which
he was a regular contributor he recounts his experiences on
a proselytizing tour to the coast and remarks that he took
with him "three Indians, my elder John Smith, his son, and
uncle, who were related to these Quinault tribes"; and that
later, before their meals, "My Indian elder returned thanks
to God." [30]

John Smith was a Chehalis Indian, one of the first to be
converted to Shakerism and the first locally to hold meetings
in his house. Later, when the church was organized with the
aid of Wickersham, he was made an elder. His son was Ed
Smith, who during the church's formative years was the English interpreter for its spokesmen. His uncle was Charlie
Walker, who, it will be recalled, had served a sentence in the
Puyallup jail for his convictions.

Although Mann had relinquished the Squaxin Reservation
to the ministrations of Myron Eells in 1885, he did not forego
his interest in the Shakers there or cease to visit them. Mud
Bay Louis, the leader there, was drawn into the Presbyterian

Church, like John Smith, with the title of elder. Wickersham states, apparently on good evidence, that this was done with the knowledge and support of a conference of Presbyterian ministers after a full discussion of the position of the Shakers and in the hope of absorbing the entire Shaker membership. He adds that by 1893 Louis had for some time occupied his dual position and apparently did not know how to extricate himself.[31] Wickersham, like the ministers, very probably took these formal dispensations more seriously than did Louis or John Smith.

According to the account of Peter Heck, John Smith and Mud Bay Louis declined overtures for more active roles within the framework of the Presbyterian ministry. He related that soon after Wickersham had championed their cause they were asked to appear before a group of ministers at Vancouver, Washington. Louis was asked to state his views upon religion, whereupon he opened with a prayer, thanked his listeners for inviting him to speak, then told them what he knew of Jesus and his understanding of religion. When he had finished "the preacher looked in the Bible and found it said the same things there. And when John Smith was called upon the same thing happened. So the preacher said, 'Good. You are all right. Louis, I want you to be a missionary of this church. We will call your church The Presbyterian Shaker Church, and we will try to get fifteen hundred dollars a year for you. And John Smith you can do the same, and we will offer you one thousand dollars a year for this work.'" Both men refused this offer, declaring that it was against their principles, as expounded by John Slocum, to accept pay for spreading the message and attending to the sick. Doubtless this account has been colored in the course of time to make it impressive, but its elements are probably founded on real facts.

Mann continued in his indulgent attitude toward the new religion apparently with the hope of sublimating its excesses and adopting its converts. In the summer of 1893 he visited the Chehalis, as he was accustomed to doing once a month, then traveled on to Mud Bay where he found "our mission prosperous and very encouraging." Elaborating upon his visit he continues: "The last time I was there I learned that an Indian named 'Big John,' living about five miles from Mud Bay on an inlet called 'Oyster Bay,' had built a meeting house or church for the use of the Indians of that region. So he invited me and the Mud Bay people to come over and have a union meeting of all the tribes and bands in the vicinity. . . . One of the Indians led in singing and prayer and I preached to them the Gospel of Jesus. . . . I could make myself intelligible in that plastic language, the Chinook jargon. . . . After the morning service was over, Big John invited the congregation to dine in a room intended to be an annex to the church, and there being room for about fifty he treated them to boiled beef, clam chowder, bread and coffee, and I found everything very palatable. . . . We had another preaching service from 5 to 7 o'clock, after which I rode home with one of the elders and instructed him more with regard to the doctrines and usages of the Presbyterian Church in order that he might teach his people 'the more excellent way.' " [32]

With Big John we are already familiar, and the assembly to which Mann refers as "our mission" must have been the Shaker congregation meeting at the church built for its use. In 1893 there was no other meeting house or religious focus in this isolated section. That Mann witnessed and, over a linguistic barrier, participated in a Shaker meeting at Big John's is evident. That, further, he was somewhat disturbed by it is indicated by his last sentence; but this veiled expression of apprehension is one of the very few that appears in the records he has left. Evidently he took a less serious and a more opportunistic, if not a more tolerant, attitude toward the cult than most of the other missionaries. It is regrettable that he did not record his observations and leave a more extended account of his relations with the early Shaker leaders.

PREVIOUS TO 1892 the Shakers paid scant attention to the matter of organization. They were without formal leadership and their group was amorphous. On account of Slocum's revelation he was given all credit for showing his people the way to a new and better life, but it would not be accurate to say that he was the recognized leader of the cult or that he had any prior claim to this distinction. Any one might assume the initiative in calling a meeting, conducting it, or altering its character without disturbing precedent. The idea of membership was absent since there was no accepted notion of a religious congregation; and there was no framework establishing the relationships of one individual adherent to another nor of all of them to outsiders. The only unifying force was the opposition of the authorities, and this did not have any positive structural effects.

Actually most of these ambiguous features still characterize the cult; but in 1892 James Wickersham attempted to impose upon it a pattern of organization which would be effective in meeting its administrative and survival needs. This called for formal leadership and the dignity of an established church. Accordingly, when the first meeting took place under Wickersham's tutelage the concept of a generic Protestant hierarchy was adopted. The Indians were already familiar with the design to some extent, but it is clear that the plan

was not their idea. Four offices were instituted, and the ideas
of election and appointment formulated. Louis was elected
"headman," and seven others, including Louis and John
Slocum, were elected "elders." The elders then appointed
and licensed five men, again including Louis and John, as
"ministers." The office of "missionary" was also instituted,
but no appointments were made in the beginning. There
was also to be a clerk to keep records. No provisions were
made for tenure in office.

This charter meeting lasted two days. There were about
forty Indians present at Louis' home on Mud Bay. A brief
record of the meeting exists in the form of a mimeographed
copy of the minutes kept by the clerk, Ed Smith. It is bare
of details and it may be an ex post facto document. It does,
however, bear witness to the fact that the church at this
time officially adopted a name. Up until that time the believers had no common term by which to identify themselves. Wickersham urged the propriety of adopting a name
at the first opportunity; hence the minutes of the charter
meeting record that those assembled were members of the
"Shaker or Tschaddam Church." The meaning of the latter
term is in doubt. It is never used today, and few Shakers know
the word. The inference is that it represents a translation
made and suggested by Wickersham. Beyond its mention
in the record of this meeting it appears only in his writings.[1]

The establishment of formal administrative machinery had
little effect upon the actual operation of church affairs. It
is doubtful whether the functions of the officers were ever
clearly defined in the minds of the Indians. They were at any
rate never made manifest. The old pattern of spontaneous
individual leadership, with lack of direction by, and absence
of responsibility to, officially constituted officers continued.
Slocum was said to be "first," while Louis dominated the local scene and Sam assumed the unofficial position of paramount healer. The formal conditions for holding office were
of small moment, and the concept of elder and minister

faded into the background. Under the circumstances the need for determining rules of tenure and succession was not felt. Therefore, when Louis died in 1905 the church was left without a head for two years while older mechanisms were brought into play to bridge the gap.

It was the custom in this region to hold memorial pot-latches in honor of the dead. To do this it was necessary for near relatives of the deceased to accumulate as much property as they could after a death in the family for the purpose of distributing it among invited guests upon an appointed day. The sooner this could be done, the better; but sometimes a bereaved family was unable to undertake the expense immediately, and often years intervened. In essence, the ceremony was a formal and necessary announcement of the social fact of the death of the individual, and until it was accomplished he was, in social theory, still alive. At the same time the principal donor and host at the potlatch tacitly or formally announced himself or a near relative as the heir and successor to the status of the deceased. This custom and the ideas associated with it began to be abandoned after 1900, but it seems that when Sam gave the potlatch in honor of Louis in 1907 he had the matter of his succession to his brother's place in mind. He invited many Shakers to Mud Bay for the distribution of gifts and at the same time brought up the question of filling the vacancy left in the church by Louis' death. Members from almost all the distant churches came; about thirty of the Yakima Shakers were present. After the potlatch Sam was "elected" headman and Enoch Abraham was made clerk.

By this time the elders were functionless if not forgotten; not one was elected to fill the vacancies which had occurred since 1892, and those who still lived did not figure in the proceedings in an official capacity. When the meeting was over Sam, Abraham, and several others made a trip to Victoria for a visit and then went on to Duncan to help open the new church there. At this time eleven new ministers were licensed for a fee of one dollar paid to the clerk. Abraham kept the money and spent it. "It went into my pocket," he said, "because nobody knew what to do with it."

Within a few years the affairs of the church were so muddled that it was apparent that something had to be done about it. In addition to their organizational difficulties the church members were suffering from the unsettling effects of discrimination and ridicule on the part of outsiders. Consequently, in 1910 Sam called a meeting at Oakville for the purpose of determining ways and means of obtaining relief. In the course of the discussion it was agreed by most of those present that their difficulties would be solved if they could adhere more closely to the model of Christian churches and thereby get the respect and protection that was due them as a religious congregation. In line with this Peter Heck proposed that they organize themselves "under the laws of the State." The proposition received unanimous approval, and Sam stated that he would get the advice of his friend Milton Giles, a white man who lived in Olympia.

This was done, and two unusual documents were drawn up as a result. One is known among the Shakers as their "Articles of Incorporation," and the other as their "Rules and By-Laws." These quasi-legal instruments renewed the self-confidence of the church members and gave them what they today regard as a legal warrant for their existence. By no means all Shakers have read or even seen copies of these declarations, but most members know about them. The original record of the incorporation proceedings was deposited with the Secretary of State in Olympia and is now on file in that office. A true copy of it follows:

ARTICLES OF INCORPORATION

of the

"INDIAN SHAKER CHURCH OF WASHINGTON."

Place of business—Olympia.

Filed 2:10 P.M. December 17, 1910,
at request of Milton Giles.

INDIAN SHAKER CHURCH:

This is to certify that on the 20th day of June 1910, Mun Bay Sam, Alex Teio, Peter Heck, Ike Kineo, Peter John, Tenas Pete, Charley Walker, Capt. Carson, John Smith and Milton Giles; charter members, met and formed a church of the Shaker Faith at the City of Olympia, Thurston County, Washington, and entered into the following agreement in writing, duly subscribed by them and each of them of which the following is a true copy:

That the corporate name shall be the Indian Shaker Church of Washington; Its chief place of business the City of Olympia in said State;

> No terms of admission to members allowed, only good behavior;
>
> The object for which this corporation is formed—
>
> The elevation of the Indian race of this state and the North West,
>
> The encouragement and enforcement of temperance;

The elevation of the female Indian, they to be equal in government of the church, which shall teach honesty, virtue, economy and cleanliness, doing to others as others should do to you; the worship of God in our own way subject to the laws of the state and of God; the owning of all church property, charging no dues or salaries to Preachers; accepting all donations the same being used for charity and improvement of church property.

The officers shall be as follows:

One Bishop, term of office four years,

Five Elders, term of office four years,

Secretary and organizer term of office four years,

Bishop to fill all vacancies.

The following officers were elected for the term of four years: Mud Bay Sam, Bishop, Alex Teio, 1st Elder, Tenas Pete, 2nd Elder, Peter John, 3rd Elder, John Smith, 4th Elder, Ike Kineo, 5th Elder, Milton Giles, Secretary and Organizer.

All people of the Indian Shaker Faith, both male and female shall be licensed as Preachers on payment of One ($1.00) dollar to the Secretary, he to receive all moneys and pay out the same. Preachers license to remain in force during good behavior.

Subscribed and sworn to before me   his **X** mark
this 15 day of December, 1910   *Mud Bay Sam*

                                                     BISHOP
John M. Wilson
                                                     Milton Giles

NOTARY PUBLIC IN AND FOR THE STATE   SECRETARY
OF WASHINGTON, RESIDING IN OLYMPIA, WASH.

O

The second document is not on file with the first, and it is not available for direct quotation. In the preamble it states, however, that it was drawn up by "Judge Milton Giles, who has labored with the Indians and tried to uplift their morals, and is the only white man admitted to their ceremonies." Following this there is a rambling exposition of Shaker principles which is remarkable mainly on account of its fragmentation and confusion of a wide variety of ritualistic, dogmatic, and ethical elements. In part, a paraphrasing of these by-laws is as follows: Members of the church must rid themselves of all thoughts of evil and superstition, think right and do right, cross themselves when they pray, pray often, use only candle light for lighting their churches, enter their church before the service begins and go around the inside in a counterclockwise direction shaking hands with all those assembled before their arrival, refrain from murder and adultery, go to church regularly every Sunday from ten until twelve o'clock, keep the day holy, ring bells, dance, and sing according to their rites, use garments of pure white which must be kept clean, and "not give false witness against neighbors because it will cling to the garment as a sin, for it is sacred." It is stated further that there shall be five head elders for the entire church, one of whom is to be recognized as the principal elder, and for each local congregation three elders, one minister, an assistant minister, and a field missionary; that ministers and bishop must be ordained in their appointments; that they may perform the offices of marriage and baptism; and that their power is the power of God, which can heal the sick and be transmitted to others.

Thus reconstituted and legally fortified it might seem that the foundations had once again been laid for a full and independent growth of the Shaker Church. This might have been the case had these written formulations been spontaneous creations of the Indians themselves and had they expressed their convictions. As it happened, the need for expounding their views was more apparent to Giles than to the Indians; and the concept of crystallizing dogma and ritual in letters of sanction which would serve as a source of authority was entirely alien to them at that time and remains so to the majority today. While most Shakers value these documents as supposed instruments of legal protection, they do not respect them and appeal to them as we do our national constitution or the Bible. Even though this were not the case, the formulations themselves have inherent inadequacies which inevitably impaired their usefulness. The heterogeneous character of the items chosen for inclusion in the bylaws and their commingling and equation on a common level of importance has not contributed to their clarification in the popular mind or to their unqualified acceptance as a unit.

In addition, many matters of practical concern and many contingencies were not provided for in either of the two documents. Although the articles of incorporation stipulate that the bishop has the authority to appoint new officers when vacancies occur, no provision is made for procedure in the event of his own death. And as it happened, this question was one of the first to arise after the reorganization of the church and the institution of the office of bishop in place of the position of "headman."

Mud Bay Sam died in 1911, only a few months after his elevation to the position of bishop. A convention was held at Oakville the same year to settle upon a successor. Peter Heck had just finished building a new church on his property there, and he took advantage of the occasion to dedicate it. About six hundred Shakers responded to his invitation. Most of them stayed several days, interspersing their services with discussions of the problem of electing a bishop. Finally Alex Teio, the head elder, proposed the name of Peter Heck. Heck modestly replied that someone else should be nominated as he was "not smart enough." With that he left the church and retired to his house a few yards distant while the discussion continued. Late in the afternoon his uncle came to inform him that he had been made the new bishop, chiefly upon the insistence of the Skokomish contingent.

Just what happened at this meeting has in later years become a matter of critical importance, since the manner of Heck's appointment became the focus of a bitter controversy which eventually split the church. For years Heck maintained that he had been elected for a full four year term without reservation or reference to his predecessor. His opponents insisted that he was simply appointed by Alex Teio, as he should have been, to fill out the unexpired term of Mud Bay Sam but that Teio, being ignorant of his appointive powers, called for the show of hands which Heck took to be his *de novo* election. The issue did not arise until 1914 when it became apparent that Heck did not intend to call for an election that year. Nothing was done about it then, however, or in the following year, which marked the completion of a full term of office for the new bishop. By that time the status of the church's officers was once more uncertain, for the tenures of bishop and elders were not running concurrently.

During the next ten years a few halfhearted efforts were made from time to time to clear the slate and start over but nothing came of them. Heck continued as bishop without serious opposition and with an easy disregard of the formal requirements stipulated by the reorganization charter. Little attention was given to the tenure of the board of elders; and no one was sure how many there were or just what they were expected to do. They were elected or appointed by the bishop as the situation seemed to demand. No one seemed to care enough to adopt a course of action, and, as a result, the church again fell in danger of disintegrating through indifference, disaffection, and lack of effective leadership.

This period of drifting came to a close in 1927. For a long time there had been a scattering of individual and ineffectual complaints about the bishop, but as these became more numerous and more articulate there eventually developed a strong sentiment in several quarters in favor of his removal. Some of the complaints lodged against him were trivial and personal—those of the sort that could be expected from a long term of leadership—but others gave evidence of a realistic frustration and disquiet with the whole system and with the viewpoint that the bishop represented. Some of the dissidents objected on principle to his tenacious and alleged unconstitutional hold upon his position; others declared that he refused to attend to the calls made upon him by the various churches; others asserted that he was too autocratic; and, finally, vigorous protests began to be heard on the grounds that he rejected the authority of the Bible in his teachings.

There was some justification for all these charges, but the real issue turned out to be over the question of the use of the

Bible in church. Many Shakers could read, and most of those who were able read the Bible. To this there was scarcely any objection; but one faction, led by Heck, maintained that the Bible should not be used in church services. His opponents declared that they were Christians above all and that the Bible was an inspired book which should be used by the Shakers just as it was by other Christians. The controversy was not new. It had taken shape during the first days of Shaker persecution, but at that time it forced a consolidation of cult members to fend against attacks from outsiders. By 1927 it had become an internal problem.

The advocates of the Bible were in the minority, but they were more articulate and determined in their attacks on the bishop than were the other complainants. Naturally, most of them were younger people with varying degrees of education and some insight into the strategy and techniques of control employed by the white man. The leader of this group was William Kitsap of Tulalip. He accepted Shakerism in 1924 and soon became a forceful speaker and a dynamic leader of the local congregation. When the sentiment for a change in leadership began to crystallize, his supporters encouraged it and pressed for a convention in the hope of electing him bishop.

The meeting took place in October, 1927. Four men were nominated for the office of bishop: William Kitsap of Tulalip, Peter Heck of Oakville, Lee Cush of Skokomish, and Charlie Howiatl of La Push. At this point, however, the forward movement ceased. The machinery of election was so unfamiliar and the distractions, delays, and arguments incidental to it so exhausting that it never had an opportunity to function. Bishop Heck's term expired in the midst of the discussion and the advantage that had been gained in placing other names in opposition to his was lost when apathy again settled upon the crowd of electors. When at length no decision could be reached about the qualifications to be required of nominees, the manner of voting, and other points of difference among the delegates, Harry Teio rose to declare that Heck had been elected to his office for life in the beginning and that there was no point in going on with the argument. Enoch Abraham was principal elder at the time and presumably acting bishop at that moment; but neither he nor anyone else raised objection to this dogmatic pronouncement. Instead, Dick Lewis, the old Skokomish antagonist of Eells, made a speech which indicated his agreement; and the weight that his word carried was sufficient to swing the opinion of the confused or indifferent crowd. No vote was taken and Heck retained his position.

Kitsap's supporters did not have the strength to force the issue at this session. But they did not give up. Instead they held a conference at the Tulalip church in December to review their position, sustain their enthusiasm, and attract additional support. The response gave them hope for the future.

Four years later the bishop called for the regular convention to be held at Siletz. Presumably the meeting was for the purpose of a general election, and Heck did indicate upon that occasion that his term was up. Very few people attended this session, however, and those who were present were not interested in voting. The Siletz church was in an out-of-the-way location and its members had not become embroiled in the issues that had brought on the internal disturbances farther north.

The opposition felt that it had been tricked by this maneuver. It countered by holding another meeting at Tulalip at which it was decided that the question must be settled at the next annual meeting, which would be in October, 1932. The Yakima church was the host group on this occasion. The bishop was present, but he fell ill soon after the controversy opened and left for home before anything was accomplished. His followers, seconded by those who felt that, by whatever reckoning, the year was inappropriate, succeeded in forestalling an election. Encouraged somewhat, the dissenters made another attempt the next year, this time by circulating ballots by mail instead of holding a meeting. The score that was announced on this balloting was Kitsap 297 votes, Heck 97, and Howiatl 31. The bishop and his supporters considered this apparent show of sentiment serious enough to call for some direct action. They therefore secured a court order restraining Kitsap from assuming the functions and title of bishop on the grounds that his alleged election had taken place on an unscheduled year. They pressed their case and judgment was eventually rendered in their favor. The court set 1935 as the time for deciding the question, thus sanctioning the schedule of tenure initiated by Heck in 1911.

The 1935 convention was held in Tahola on the Quinault Reservation. This was also in a remote location and few persons attended the meeting. At the election which took place there Kitsap received 38 votes and Heck 34. But this did not put an end to the controversy either. The bishop refused to acknowledge the vote, claiming that it was not representative of majority opinion. To bolster this contention he maintained that the election was void since it had taken place in 1935 instead of 1934. He thus reversed his previous position and put his sanction upon the former claim of his opponents who had maintained that the quadrennia should be based upon the 1914 base as the date of termination of Heck's first term. According to this reckoning the next election should be held in 1938. Standing upon this claim, Heck continued to act as bishop and ignored the protestations of Kitsap and his followers. The latter attempted to get satisfaction by legal action upon two occasions, but the actual situation remained unchanged in spite of their nominal success.

During the summer of 1938 both candidates undertook campaigns to organize support. They went as far afield as northern California, Kitsap holding a series of meetings at Hoopa in August, to be followed by Heck who visited Siletz and Smith River the next month. The Californians were much agitated by the contest, about which they had heard only rumors before. The result was that the conflict was extended over new areas, and the breach was widened. Kitsap announced that he would lead a convention at Neah Bay in 1939, while Heck declared that the orthodox meeting would be held within a month (October, 1938) at his Oakville church. Both of these meetings took place, with expectable results: by the fall of 1939 there were two contending Shaker bishops and two panels of elders and clerks.

In addition to this major cleavage, other fissures appeared in the leadership structure of the church. In order to rally support to his cause, Heck in 1938 promised the California Shakers a "sub-bishop" of their own choosing. Stimulated by the controversy and eager to take advantage of the opportunity, the Californians prepared to hold an election immediately. At a meeting held on September 18 at Johnson's Landing those assembled chose Archie Roberts as their sub-bishop. At about the same time the Canadian Shakers were given permission to set up a special division on their side of the international border. They chose Peter Joe of Koksilah as their bishop. In 1942 Burt Underwood of Duncan succeeded him. It is said that the same charter and bylaws apply to this division as in the United States.

In January, 1940, the Kitsap faction drew up a written statement of its position on the question of leadership. It is integrated with the declaration of faith that has already been quoted on pages 40–44 and reveals the motivation in composing this document. It reads as follows:

"Mud Bay Louie was able to carry the message of the simple faith to the Yakima tribe of Indians. In the year 1910, a white man by the name of Milton Giles, seeing the suffering of the Indians in their desire to serve God, according to the dictates of conscience, assisted them to Incorporate under the state laws of the State of Washington, (June 20, 1910).

"At the death of Mud Bay Louie, his brother, Mud Bay Sam, succeeded as leader. In the year 1911, at Mud Bay Sam's death, Peter Heck became the leader or Bishop. He was from the Chehalis tribe. Although he was not legally elected by the members of the said Shaker Church, or ordained according to the Incorporation, among the Indians he went on to proclaim the title as Bishop. However, by the faithfullness of some of the members of the Shaker Church, who sacrificed their time and money, little groups were gathered into the faith from various tribes in the states of Washington, Oregon, California, and the Province of British Columbia, in Canada.

"With a holy fear, and reliance on the directions of God through the instrumentality of the Holy Ghost, a number of ministers of the Indian Shaker Church were made to feel, from time to time, the great responsibility weighing upon them, as the saints of the most high God and Saviour, Jesus Christ. Finally, at a special convention called by these faithful ministers, at the Tulalip Indian Shaker Church, Dec. 23, 1927, and 1931, messages were given which seriously impressed all those present with a conviction that greater and more earnest efforts should be put forth to promote the work of God and to his glory; to build up his church on earth and carry out in a practical way his word to us, 'Go ye into all the world and preach the good news, or Gospel to every creature.' In order to accomplish this more fully, they were inclined to believe that it was necessary to have a new Bishop for their Indian Shaker Church.

"So that all members of the church might be used to determine the will of God in this matter of proper selection of leadership, it was decided to cast the ballots in all the churches, with prayers. Three names were on the ballot: Peter Heck, then acting Bishop of the said Indian Shaker Church; Charles Howeattle, outstanding Indian of the Quilleute tribe, and William Kitsap, outstanding Indian of the Tulalip tribe, (Snohomish).

"At the annual fall convention, the ballots were counted. William Kitsap, receiving the most votes, was declared elected to the office of Bishop of the INDIAN SHAKER CHURCH OF THE STATE OF WASHINGTON. This automatically makes him Bishop of all the Indian Shaker Churches in all of these other states, as well as the State of Washington, and Canada.

"Pursuant to the plan adopted at the special convention of December 23, 1927 and 1931, and ratified at the fall convention, October 15, 1932, in the Indian Shaker Church of the Yakima tribe at White Swan, Washington, Bishop William Kitsap called a special conference to compile and put into written form, the Doctrines of the Church, and rules to govern the activities. Also, to designate the duties of its officers, and order of its service. It was generally agreed upon that the Bible, which is the word of God, be used as the guide book; for all that was given John Slocum was based upon the written word of God, as they later found it in the Bible."

With these developments the breach between the two factions was complete and without any foreseeable device for reconciliation. Mutual suspicions and avoidances were rife. The customary summer "camp meeting" was called off in 1941 for fear of unpleasant consequences. This created dissatisfaction in a new quarter. Aroused members on the Quinault and Queets reservations joined forces and called a meeting at Tahola. They proposed to solve the dilemma by setting aside both contending bishops and raising the head elder, Enoch Abraham, to the position of acting bishop until a new election could be held. Abraham rejected this scheme; but its backers were not discouraged. Early the next year they circulated a petition calling for support of a plan to get a court order restraining Kitsap from preaching and issuing licenses, in effect revoking his commission as bishop. They were not successful and their activities only served to add to the existing tensions as the time for the 1942 camp meeting approached. Arrangements were made for it to be held at Tulalip without the sponsorship of either bishop. Kitsap appeared at the meeting but he was dubious of the motivations of its backers and held aloof. Heck was not present. The political issue was not raised, however, and nothing happened to change the situation.

The expected development did not take place until October. Heck announced that the annual convention and the election of his successor would take place at that time in Oakville. A large number of delegates attended. Among them were several advocates of Kitsap. When Heck's name was proposed they reacted by maintaining an aloof silence, thus tacitly asserting that this was neither the time nor the place to vote for a bishop of the church since the office was already being legitimately filled by a properly elected incumbent. The Queets-Quinault combination was not disposed to solve the problem in this way. They offered the name of their candidate, Frank Bennett, a Queets man, in opposition to Heck. They had, moreover, planned their revolt against the Heck regime, and when the voting was over Bennett was declared elected.

Peter Heck was chagrined. He felt that he had been betrayed, and he did not take his defeat without a counter-stroke. He refused the use of his church to those who had voted against him and continued to think and speak of himself as the rightful head of the Shaker Church. He has not yet abandoned this attitude, and perhaps never will, but since the defection of a large segment of his supporters under the leadership of Bennett his position is weaker than at any time in the last thirty years.

The new party is both technically and numerically in the strongest position. Bennett's principles do not differ from those of Heck; hence he can hope for the support of the large anti-Bible faction. He is also in possession of the seal of the church and has already made use of it for affixation to another quasi-legal paper which purports to establish the legitimacy of his position and the continuity of his principles with those expressed at the foundation of the church. This document, a single typewritten sheet of paper, was deposited with the Secretary of State of Washington in the fall of 1942 to accompany the original charter filed by Milton Giles. A true copy of it follows (the word Chehalis has been crossed out):

CHEHALIS INDIAN SHAKER CHURCH
COUNTY OF GRAYS HARBOR
OAKVILLE, WASHINGTON

We, the present members of the Board of Head Elders, meet this 25th day of October, 1942, to discuss the foundation of the Indian Shaker Church.

We therefor agree to acknowledge the rules and regulations of the original corporation based upon our belief in the death and resurrection of one John Slocum some sixty years ago at Mud Bay, near Olympia, Washington.

We truthfully pledge to support the Indian Shaker Church, its principles, using only bells and candles for instruments, worship God in our own way, subject only to the laws of the State and God. Charging no dues, or salaries, to preachers; accepting all donations the same being used for charity and improvement of Church property.

We further agree not to permit other denominations to disturb our meetings. We do likewise not to disturb other churches.

(Seal of	APPROVE BY BISHOP	
Shaker Church)	*Frank F. Bennett*	*Gilbert Sotomish*
O	SECRETARY	*Joseph Mitchell*
	Ruth Pete	*George J. Sanders*

This is a rather typical gesture of appeal to the foundation documents. A similar reference to its authority will be noted in the previously quoted declaration of principles at the point where Heck's title to his office is called into question. One frequently encounters verbal references to it in similar situations; namely, those in which some private advantage is to be gained by appealing to its venerability. Actually, the charter means little one way or the other to the ordinary Shaker. This attitude toward it, combined with its artificiality and the ambiguities and lapses contained in it, has fostered the confusion that now afflicts the church. No attempt has been made to remedy these basic defects.

Most congregations start out according to the accepted pattern with a full complement of officers: a minister, an assistant minister, three elders, and sometimes a clerk and a missionary. This impressive structure rarely survives the succeeding decade intact, the reason being that it is superfluous to the actual functioning of church affairs. It has been superimposed upon a native religious movement by a white man whose model was a generic Protestant church. It did not evolve in response to an internal need, and it has failed to meet the demands for leadership definition that have developed. Consequently, the promotion and regulation of the secular and religious interests of the congregation are left to other unformalized standards of leadership while the duly selected officers either take themselves seriously or not depending upon individual attitudes and circumstances. In general, newly chosen officers value their positions more than older incumbents, and among newly established congregations their prestige is greater than otherwise. In any case, their functions are not restrictive or exclusive, and in most instances they are only nominal. The individual makes of his honorary title whatever he chooses. This is as true of the board of principal elders as of the local units.

Presumably it is the duty of the elders to deliberate and decide or to make recommendations on questions of church policy, both secular and religious. This plan is adhered to only in exceptional instances. There are no regular meetings of either the local or principal elders. Many Shakers do not know who their elders are—if they have them. In the past Enoch Abraham has tried to adhere to the plan of consulting with other members of the board of principal elders before annual conventions with the idea of formulating recommendations to be voted upon by all the assembled members. In his view "the board of head elders is like the Congress of the United States and the members are like the President, who has the power of veto." This is not a generally accepted opinion. Very few people have any idea about what elders are supposed to do. Consequently elders are ignored and their functions usurped by spontaneous expression of opinion from the floor during an interval in church services which has come to be set aside for this purpose. This is today the manner of introducing and deciding issues both in local meetings and during the annual assemblies. Strong personalities initiate issues, dominate particular situations, and influence the course of events regardless of whether they hold offices.

The office of minister affords the same scope for the operation of the variables of personality and circumstance. The presence of the minister is not necessary for a church service. Anyone may lead a meeting, and anyone who is willing is likely to be called upon to do so. An assistant minister to act in lieu of the minister is therefore superfluous. Since the services of neither is indispensable they have no binding obligation to their congregations to be present. Normally they are, either out of vanity or because they are among the most zealous of the group; but if they fail to appear within a reasonable time on Sunday morning someone else volunteers to lead the meeting. This is acceptable because the concepts of divine appointment and the consecrated vehicle do not apply to the Shaker minister and because he possesses no private and exclusive ritual knowledge.

The duties of the field missionary are only vaguely defined and they do not entail any particular responsibilities. A missionary is not expected to undertake missions. Anyone can proselytize, and when a call comes asking for assistance in establishing a new congregation or in strengthening the faith of one that is failing the missionary is not more immediately concerned than other members. For church dedications and the ordaining of ministers and elders the bishop is expected to officiate. Upon other occasions the responsibility for responding to an appeal for assistance devolves upon no particular individual or office. Those who feel prompted to do so join together and make the required trip as their finances will allow, with or without the missionary.

Upon occasions the secretary or clerk has been called upon to act in an official capacity. His educational qualifications have been serviceable when letters and manifestoes have been required. These demands are at a minimum, however. Surprisingly little communication takes place by letter, and when it does usually it is routed through informal channels and does not pass through the hands of either the bishop or the elders. When information cannot be passed on in the preferred manner by visits, individuals on their own account write to friends or relatives at another place and leave it to them to convey the message as they see fit. No regular records or minutes are kept by any of the local churches, thus reducing still further the proper sphere of a secretary's activities. There are no official lists of church members, nor any written records of official actions taken with the few exceptions that have been mentioned.

It is very seldom that the church as a corporate body has any business relations with outsiders. The churches themselves are built upon private property or upon tribal lands protected or held in trust by the United States government. Materials and labor for their construction are contributed by members. They do not make use of public utilities. There is, therefore, no necessity for entering into leasing, building, or maintenance contracts. The Yakima church has been exceptional in possessing valuable property and in attempting to capitalize upon it by leasing its farm lands to a white man. The head elder was behind this move, and he undertook the business negotiations. Rental proceeds were in the form of farm produce part of which were converted into cash. This was in the care of a secretary-treasurer. It was expended on the order of the entire congregation acting on the advice and argument of a few prominent members moving without regard to official capacity.

Internal financial matters are disposed of with the same informality. Ordinarily a church as such has no income and no expenses. There are no dues, fees, or periodic collections. No officer receives any compensation, and those individuals who work over the sick will accept nothing beyond meals and traveling expenses when these are offered by the family of the sick person. Often they spend their own money for travel and expect nothing except food during the time they are the guests of the person who has invited their help. Those who wish to go on such a mission or to attend a meeting find someone who will take his automobile provided they pay for the gasoline and oil to make the trip. Similarly, funds are raised at times for special projects, such as the purchase of bells or the making of repairs; but few if any churches have a treasury, and therefore even less need for a business officer.

Individual churches conduct their business by means of informal discussions during an interval in any Sunday morning service. The same provision is made when members of several congregations meet to decide upon matters of more general interest. The custom of holding annual assemblies dates from the time of the first big conversion meeting in 1883. This took place in August, but a call to assemble on the next Fourth of July set the pattern for meetings upon that date. These midsummer meetings, called conventions, continued to be held until the second decade of this century. Essentially they were revival meetings, but in the course of time they became forums for the expression of opinion as well. All manner of subjects pertaining to the policy of the church were discussed, and decisions were made either privately or collectively. The procedure was always informal and the decisions often not definitive or final. The practice of conducting business as a part of the religious meeting nevertheless came to be an established custom.

The last regular Fourth of July convention was held in Oakville in 1915. By then it was becoming increasingly apparent that many people who had jobs could not afford to spend three or four days at this time to attend a distant meeting. Had it been a question of taking a vacation from steady year-round employment, in all probability no complaint would have been heard. But the wage labor of Indians has always been in the greatest demand mainly during harvest seasons through the summer and they saw no reason why an adjustment could not be made to meet these conditions. It was therefore decided to set the convention date in the middle of October when the hop picking was over and most people had more money than at any other time during the year. This scheduling exists at the present time. Although there are contending factions each holds to the October date for its business meetings. One in every four is supposed to mark the election date for the bishop and principal elders.

One of the local churches volunteers to play host upon these occasions. Ordinarily this is not an expensive undertaking for any single individual. Most churches have a kitchen and dining room associated with them, and most of the guests and their hosts prepare and take their meals in these buildings during the meetings. Otherwise the guests are taken into the homes of their Shaker friends or visit with non-Shaker relatives. The ideal is to free the visitors of all expense except for their transportation. Usually this is done by asking local members, and others if they wish, to contribute whatever they can to the table fare. Sometimes money is collected. Some of the churches are proud of their reputations as generous hosts. The Yakima Shakers have been especially fortunate in the past in having had a treasury to draw upon for this purpose. Although they have not been so securely financed, the Skokomish congregation also boasts that it has never asked for subscriptions in advance from prospective visitors. Other churches are forced to do this at times.

In 1926 an attempt was made to revive the custom of midsummer meetings, and at the same time to establish a new tradition. During the convention held at the Muckleshoot church it was suggested that "camp meetings" be added to the annual calendar, and that they should be held at the "mother church" on Mud Bay. The suggestion was approved, and for two years it was followed. In 1929, however, the Bishop and his followers declared themselves against the designation of the Mud Bay church as a mecca. Presumably this was too near the center of influence of the pro-Bible faction. The meeting took place that year nonetheless, but the opposition bolted and held one of their own at Tahola. Since that time camp meetings have been held, extending over the third, fourth, and fifth of July, but not in the same place, and not every year. As might be expected, confusion has been injected into the annual schedule by the conflicting demands of the different factions.

It is apparent from this discussion that the definitions of leadership embodied in the Shaker constitution have proved to be irrelevant to needs of the organization. It does not follow that a more careful formulation would have functioned to forestall the disruptive influences that have been operative. In fact, the probability is that no formal design in itself would have done this, even if it had been complete. The Shakers have evolved their own patterns, as other groups have done, by trial and error; and these are more significant than any arbitrary norms that might have been suggested to them. Quite without plan they have developed an informal design for leadership which has had nothing to do with secular government. It is a pattern of religious specialization which has no counterpart in Christian churches.

With the institution of shaking by Mary Slocum a tripartite division of function was possible and it very soon materialized. Mary became the source of inspiration, the arbiter of dogma and ritual form; her brother Isaac became the exhorter and converter; and Sylvester Yucton assumed the role of divine healer. This triumvirate was almost immediately deposed by their more aggressive functional counterparts: Louis, Big John, and Sam. With them the pattern was crystallized. As the cult diffused, expertness in the three fields was perpetuated, not by any formal provisions, but by the tacit acknowledgment that they represented distinct areas for exploitation and because they appealed in varying degrees to different types of personality. Beyond this the concept was not systematized; the idea that a trio of leaders was indispensable to the completeness of the cult was never formulated. Louis was pre-eminently a visionary, but neither he nor his followers regarded his specialty as complementary to, or as a necessary foundation for, the evangelistic temper of Big John or the shamanistic predilections of Sam. The phenomena were distinct. Therefore, when these men died there was no compulsion to perpetuate the linkage of their activities in the form of an official triad. As other leaders rose to prominence they naturally revealed a temperamental preference for one or the other of the possible emphases, but without consciously conforming to a trimodal pattern. As a consequence, there have always been individuals of recognized proficiency in the three fields, but their number has been variable and they have had a random geographic distribution.

The tripartite division of leadership is manifest today. It is, in fact, a fundamental factor in the disorder that we have noted. William Kitsap is an evangelist; he speaks well and forcefully, and he obviously enjoys it. He believes in the necessity of salvation and in his personal responsibility to save sinners by his preaching. He relies upon his oratorical abilities to persuade his listeners and differs from his predecessors in this field only in the expanded view that he takes of his area of discourse and in the almost exclusive emphasis that he places upon the acceptance of the word of the Bible as the means of salvation.

Peter Heck, and the majority of the Shakers, are impatient with sermons and wordy admonitions. For them the mark of spiritual regeneration is the reception of divine power, and this does not require preaching. Divine power is manifested in shaking, and the principal reason for appealing to it is to obtain relief from distress and bodily pain. Practitioners of this theory of salvation occur everywhere. Almost every church has one or two members who take the lead in healing the sick. The most outstanding example is C. J. Johns. He has carried the idea through to its logical extreme by becoming a professional healer. He has placed himself on call and allows nothing to interfere with what he considers to be his obligations to the sick at any hour of the day or night and for any length of time. His ethics do not permit him to accept compensation for his services, but this has not prevented his earning a fair living at his calling. The pattern tolerates board and lodging and even gifts of food in the name of hospitality. Johns has capitalized upon this so that he is a frequent dinner guest at the home of his patients. He is only secondarily interested in church affairs and has very little to do with them.

Once parallel and congruent, these separate emphases have now become so pronounced and self-contained that they have opened up divergent and antipathetic areas of elaboration and expansion. The tendency might have been restrained had there been an equally emphatic leadership in the third modality, namely the visionary. A dynamic successor to Mud Bay Louis, claiming divine sanction for his revelations, could have dictated the character and controlled the limits of orthodox faith. There have been, and there are at present, many individuals whose visions have been taken as guides for action; but all have lacked the stature that is necessary to direct the fortunes of the church. Their revelations have been trivial and unintegrated. They have not conceived a purpose or been sufficiently moved to forestall the dangers that threaten the disintegration of the church.

In the manifesto drawn up under the guidance of Milton Giles it is stated that no terms of admission to the Shaker Church are to be tolerated beyond the requirement of good behavior. This is undoubtedly a true reflection of Shaker sentiment. It is founded primarily upon their basic rejection of any form of financial levy for the privilege of enjoying the benefits of the religion. They want no dues or payments for services of any kind. This religion is free of charge.

Not quite so clearly a part of the original Shakers' thinking was the refusal to erect any dogmatic barrier to participation in the blessings of the new faith. Their experience with persecution and sectarianism may have prompted them to take a stand for the principle of religious freedom; but it is more likely that this emphasis came from Giles rather than from them. A more positive explanation of their refusal to institute membership controls relates to their individualistic bias, a point of view which has found favor with all subsequent adherents. They have never shown a desire to define the boundaries of membership in objective terms of any kind. They prefer to let the individual decide whether he is a member, why he is, and what he should do about it. He is allowed to establish his own criteria of membership to his own satisfaction. This permits a gratifying personal fluidity and avoids the psychological deterrent that is inherent in any symbol of irrevocable commitment. The ease with which one can "join" the church—and drift out of it—has undoubtedly been a factor in the appeal of the religion. Participation in a meeting does not signify conversion or even conviction, and this fact accounts for the large number of individuals who have at some time been affiliated with the Shaker Church. The result is that the concept of membership is vague and shifting with a minimum of organization, controls, and concerted action.

The most decisive step that a Shaker can take is to give verbal testimony to his conversion. He does not take a public vow, not even a pledge to lead a reformed life. He does not attest to his support of the principles proclaimed in the manifestos. He merely testifies to the regenerative and healing powers of the religion as they have been disclosed to him. There is an appropriate time in the Sunday service when anyone may thus declare his conviction and exhort the rest of the congregation; but the act is entirely voluntary and many individuals never give public expression to their sentiments even though they may regard themselves, and be generally regarded, as good Shakers. In individual instances the neophyte is urged to kneel before the altar and make an avowal of his acceptance of God or of the Shaker beliefs, but this is not necessary. No pattern of acceptance has been established. It is implied in the act of shaking, and this alone is generally taken to mean conversion without any verbal expression to that effect.

There are no ritual acts which signalize spiritual redemption. Baptism comes to mind at this juncture, for it will be remembered that the bylaws provide that ministers may perform this sacrament. It is, however, most unusual for them to do so. Like the ministers themselves the act is superfluous. It is not understood by most people, many of whom are not even aware that it is an acceptable function of their regular officers. The latter are frequently no more enlightened on the subject. Very few of them would know what to do if called upon. The church regulations do not provide a ritual for a model, and when ministers have undertaken to baptize they have drawn upon their individual Christian backgrounds or prejudices.

The ordination of officers is also provided for in Shaker regulations, but again without a sanctioned procedure. In consequence, the status of this rite is the same as that of baptism. It is more consistently performed because it affords occasion for public recognition of a distinction which is more generally prized. It is not imperative, however. Some acting ministers and elders today have never been formally consecrated to their tasks. Individual variation in the ritual is great. Kitsap performs the ceremony differently from Heck, the one using biblical quotations, the other not. Head elder Abraham followed a third pattern.

In the statement written by the Kitsap adherents it is affirmed that Peter Heck was never ordained as bishop. This is not strictly true. There was a formal induction rite, but the person who administered it was George Waters, an Indian Methodist minister on the Yakima Reservation. The reason given for this aberration is that Alex Teio, head elder at the time, protested that he did not know what to do when the obligation presumably devolved upon him. Some of Heck's opponents argue, therefore, that technically he never has been the Shaker bishop. The problem of a bishop's ordination arose again in 1935 when Kitsap was elected. Without precedent, Enoch Abraham, as head elder, was obliged to contrive an appropriate ritual.

With so little that is positive and imperative to mark the threshold of induction into the Shaker faith, and so little that is definite to differentiate functions within its membership, it is expectable that no patterns would have been developed for expulsion or excommunication. Except for the bishop and his general board, who are elected for a stipulated term, all members and officers retain their standing for an indefinite period. An officer may resign, and anyone might neglect the church without overstepping his rights as a freewill member. He removes himself from this classification only when he makes it plain that he wants to be dissociated from it. Theoretically, membership and office holding are dependent on good behavior. In practice, however, this condition has little meaning. One member does not expect another, even if an officer, to be more perfect than himself; and in the present deteriorated state of Indian society moral and ethical standards are not remarkable for their purity or idealism. Some of those who do take the moral precepts of their religion more seriously do often complain about the lapses of others; but they are in the minority, are often in disagreement among themselves, and seldom persist to force the issue. No stereotypes for adjusting fact with theory have been developed.

There is a report of one attempt to oust a church officer. Billy Clams was chosen minister of the Skokomish church when it was formally organized, but by 1899 he had fallen into disfavor with an important element in the congregation. When Louis and Abraham visited the church that year the complaint was made that Clams had abandoned his wife for a younger woman and had run away with her to Port Gamble. As headman, Louis was asked to prosecute him. Louis could not write so he asked Abraham to send a letter to James Wickersham inquiring whether Clams could be expelled for his unbecoming conduct. The reply was, of course, that there were no existing provisions for such action. At the same time Wickersham prepared a form that could be used within the limits of church government for the purpose of formally divesting an unqualified officer. Abraham, in the name of Louis, signed one of these expulsion papers for Billy Clams. In spite of this auspicious beginning the idea was short lived. None of these papers appear to be in existence today. The noninstitutionalized alternative is to resort to demagoguery and intrigue to frustrate incumbents and bring about their voluntary resignations. This is an old affliction of the Shaker community.

Personal rivalries and factional disputes appeared almost at the inception of the cult, and they continue undiminished at the present time. Mary Slocum and Mud Bay Louis were in conflict from the time the latter usurped the dominant role in the cult until he died. Their differences became an issue as early as the fall of 1883 when the first big meeting was held at Slocum's church. Louis took a more extravagant view of the implications of the religion than Mary did and it seems that much of the disturbance and the excess that characterized the first general session were due to his influence. The emphasis that he apparently placed upon an impending destruction of the world developed into a terroristic situation which almost engulfed him. A number of the participants had visions of hell with its flames consuming their enemies. The missionary Eells was an obvious scapegoat, but the tensions and rivalries between the supporters of Mary and Louis also found expression in this guise. Someone saw Louis down below sitting alongside the devil. The controversy that followed almost divided the movement from the start. Eells alludes to the incipient schism when he relates that the Shakers saw him and "Mowitch Man" in hell.[2] Louis did, in fact split up the meeting by inviting his supporters to continue it at his home on Mud Bay. Unlike many others who have been accused, he decided to stay with the religion and fight back.

Speaking in the presence of Wickersham in 1892, Mud Bay Sam said, "Among the Shakers, John Slocum is first. Louis is next. I take power and cure people when they are sick."[3] This is an interesting statement from several points of view. While giving appropriate credit to Slocum it nonetheless obscures his true relationship to Louis with respect to leadership and influence in the movement. Even more importantly, it ignores the part that Mary Slocum played in inaugurating the really distinctive aspects of the religion. Indeed, Mary is not even mentioned in the Wickersham and Eells reports, a fact that has had important consequences for historians of the cult. The reason is clear: Louis was determined to discredit Mary among those who knew her and to suppress knowledge of her among those who did not. Slocum's relation to Louis is therefore even more difficult to explain because Mary did not docilely submit to this treatment. She in fact encouraged an active opposition to Louis which, extending to their respective sympathizers, created a serious division in theory and practice. Until quite recently the Skokomish and other churches to the north obstinately followed a form of service that was instituted by Mary while the southern groups adhered to the ritual forms sanctioned by Louis.

There have been other major divisionist threats, such as the one instigated by Lans Kalapa at Neah Bay, in addition to the more recent and serious ones that have just been described. Individual departures in ritual have been a source of embarrassment and confusion at conventions for many years. Often such differences have to be ironed out and compromises reached before general meetings can proceed. From time to time influential members have made pleas for consistency in the interests of harmony at the annual meetings. Without attempting to level congregational differences it has been urged that no matter what forms are followed at the home churches one standard should be adopted for the general assemblies. At the 1926 convention Enoch Abraham suggested that the ideal model would be John Slocum's service and that an effort should be made to determine what the nature of this was. It was just as well that no interest was shown in this particular proposal, however, for if it had been taken seriously even greater confusion might have resulted.

In addition to these major stresses, a closer inspection reveals a considerable amount of friction and bickering among the members of most congregations. Despite their dedication to the spirit of brotherly love most churches have had an unfortunate history, marred by personal animosities and factional disputes. Sometimes members are justly offended by the rumors that are spread about them and subsequently not only withdraw from the church but seriously damage its opportunities for further growth. In other instances the group as a whole has made scurrilous charges against sinners who have refused to join them and thereby have done irremediable injury to local prospects of success. This was the case among the Yurok.

Soon after the introduction of the cult at Requa anxiety

and resentment were aroused over the witch hunts that the local converts inaugurated. They revived the slumbering fear of "Indian devils," an aboriginal concept that envisioned the transformation of seemingly innocent individuals into nocturnal agents of death. There was an orgy of accusations, with impassioned congregations streaming out of their meeting halls behind one of their number who was impelled by the delusion that one of his personal enemies was prowling about the church attempting to "poison" him and his Shaker friends. Four or five prominent Yurok who did not join the church were vilified in this manner, the visionary leading his entranced followers either to the door of some innocent man or upon an erratic chase that drove the alleged devil into the night. Others were accused of secret sins that were revealed to ardent Shakers in a clairvoyant trance.

Jackson, the leading Siletz elder at the time, attempted to squelch this disruptive development by publicly admonishing the Yurok at one of their meetings. He rebuked their leader for fostering the idea and declared that the impulse to seek out one's enemies was contrary to the Shaker ideals. His vigorous opposition to irresponsible visionaries had a sobering effect on the Yurok, but the damage had been done. Some of the most influential men in the community were offended and thereafter opposed the religion in every way they could. When the faith spread to Hoopa and to Johnson's Landing there were identical expressions of hate and jealousy, but they abated more quickly. Gradually a reaction set in against devil baiting, so that at present church leaders either disclaim the ability to see devils or admit that they can but refuse to say anything about their visions because it would only stir up trouble.

The Skokomish Shakers went through a comparable phase of accusation and alienation. Their fears did not permit them to dispose of shamans simply by denouncing them. They went on to charge them and those who continued to believe in them with all manner of evil designs. For a time almost every case of sickness was attributed to malicious individuals who were believed to have the power to "shoot" their spirit familiars into the body of a victim. Meetings were turned over to the business of extracting these deadly agents from those who presented themselves for help, with the Shaker leaders laying the blame for them upon their enemies. Doctor Jim was a favorite Shaker target, and Isaac was his special persecutor. Upon at least two occasions Isaac claimed that he had captured the spirit of Doctor Jim, but he was unable to "kill" it and cause the shaman to die.

In other places contests with shamanistic powers have been and continue to be sources of discord. Among the Yakima one of the leading Shaker healers is an assiduous exposer of the secret deviltry of ostensibly innocent people. His preoccupation with the idea amounts to an obsession. He finds malignant designs in the most unlikely events, and no one is above suspicion and forthright condemnation for instigating them. He lays his charges indiscriminately within and outside the church membership. If taken more seriously his libelous statements could bring enough censure and discredit upon the religion to make its local survival doubtful.

Many capable people have refused to accept offices or other responsibilities in the church because all too often it involves them in a tangle of petty intrigue and criticism. One of the most intelligent of the Chehalis Shakers has consistently refused an office on these grounds. Others are disillusioned after the trial. A principal elder under Heck tried for years to resign his position, publicly protesting his incompetence while privately complaining of the dissension and criticism as the reason for his dissatisfaction. This is also one of the principal reasons why members drop out entirely and sometimes disavow their former affiliations. Doctrinally this is a dangerous decision, for true Shakers cannot repudiate or deny expression to the power once they have it. Many do it with impunity; others, like their spiritual leader, Mary Slocum, are not so fortunate. Her decision, it is said, cost her

her life. As she grew older she became so disillusioned and embittered with the strife and turmoil in the church that she finally declared that she would have nothing more to do with it. A few nights later she died in her sleep.

Most Shakers deplore the disunity of their church, but they are not distressed about it. They agree that it is unfortunate; but what can be done about it? Few feel it to be their individual concern, and no one is sufficiently motivated by altruism to place the good of the church above his private indulgences and ambitions. The attitude throughout is one of individualism and self-satisfaction. Most people do not want to be leaders; they take what the religion offers them and do not worry about the rest. Those who have not been disillusioned by the fruits of leadership and continue to strive for it do so only by disregarding the seriousness of disunity. Attacks and controversies take place on the personal level, thereby leaving little room for sacrifices and compromises to maintain principles. Typically, the reaction of present day leaders and their supporters is blandly to ignore the pretensions and allegations of their opponents in so far as this is possible. Rather than face controversial issues with a demand for unity at all costs the alternative of avoiding friction by dividing the group is preferred. It is not too late to reverse this process, but a stronger leadership than is now in view will be called for.

FIVE ✠ Doctrine
✠

THERE IS a pronounced feeling among most Shakers that their religion belongs to the Indians. It is regarded as a special dispensation of God for the benefit of all members of this race, irrespective of tribal affiliation. As such it is not for the white man. This attitude does not spring from a background of resentment. Therefore it is lacking in aggressiveness except when the white man obtrudes and makes a nuisance of himself. Basically there is no animosity toward whites; they may attend church services, participate in them, and even become recognized members. Many have, and there are today a number of whites who go to church regularly. The Indians think them strange and do not fraternize with them but make no objection unless they reveal a disposition to project themselves into the limelight or exercise control.

Shakerism in the beginning was and still is an expression of conscience. Slocum and those who followed him were oppressed by a sense of guilt greatly abetted by the Christian concept of sin. This mental state of necessity has a personal reference. No one save the individual himself is responsible for his misfortunes; he can blame no one else and must do something himself if he wishes relief. Although the Puget Sound Indians had suffered at the hands of the whites before and during the days of Slocum, this factor did not play a part in the inspirations of John and Mary Slocum. The religion they founded therefore lacked two common features of messianic cults elsewhere: the urge to preserve or revive aboriginal distinctness and the militant denunciation of the whites as the cause of native distress. Given the fact that Slocum was intent upon defining a means of personal salvation neither of these developments was possible without a distortion of the original doctrine.

The Shakers do not encourage the following of native customs as a bulwark against the incursions of Western civilization. In most places the issue has never even been raised. But where it has the opposite position has always been taken; that is, Shakers deplore Indian traits and beliefs and they advocate abandoning them. This is especially true, and expectable, in the field of religion. Shamanism is totally and unequivocally rejected—which does not mean that Shakers do not credit its powers, or imitate it, but that they fight against identification with it. They will not have anything to do with native dances of a religious character. In California, members who persist in attending the native Deerskin, Jump, and Brush Dances are upbraided and called hypocrites.[1] On the Yakima Reservation the members of the so-called Pom Pom religion present a strongly reactionary front to white acculturation, one of their principal tenets being a declaration for strict adherence to aboriginal customs. The Shakers avoid and condemn them, even while admitting a striking similarity between the two cults. Both Enoch Abraham and C. J. Johns explain the Pom Pom religion as "another kind of Shaker" but shun association with its followers because they gamble, drink, and sing pagan songs.

But it is not only the ethical and religious aspects of native life that Shakers find repugnant. Upon one occasion a Yurok woman was ill and her friends were called upon to cure her. There were a number of articles of aboriginal manufacture in her house, and when the Shakers "got the power" they began to collect all these articles and place them around her body. One woman went outside and returned with a carrying basket; another brought a basketry hat. One of the men started to climb the stairs to the attic but the brother of the sick woman made him turn back. Later he said that he had seen a light like a coal of fire directing him to a mortar and pestle upstairs and that he was going to add it to the pile of Indian goods which the patient must renounce and destroy in order to recover. This is not typical doctrine, but it indicates that if there is any opinion at all on the question of the retention of aboriginal patterns it is negative.

The truth is that the Shakers have struggled to weave a new fabric out of the strands drawn from two religious systems, and in attempting to maintain its distinctiveness they have renounced quite as much as they have embraced. To their way of thinking, they are within the Christian fold but as a distinct sect. Their religion was given to them by the same God and for the same purposes as was Presbyterianism and Catholicism. It naturally had to be presented to them in a special way in order to meet their special requirements; but this does not commit them to the Indian way of life. Contrariwise, any suggestion of adulterating their religion with the precepts and practices that are more definitely Catholic or Protestant arouses resentment and suspicion. On the defensive, its advocates resist encroachment and assimilation with the assertion, "This is an Indian religion. We do not want any white men in it." It is the only effective means that they know of asserting their independence.

As a rule Shakers do not spend much time in thinking about the meaning of their religion. It is primarily an instrument for action and not something on which to meditate. Its theoretical elements are not well integrated, and they rarely if ever are neatly conceptualized. They are implicit in Shaker practice and can be elicited in some fashion by questioning. Otherwise they are given only fragmentary verbalization. There have been few if any attempts to rationalize the various aspects of belief into a systematic whole, and for any individual there are always a number of unexplained components. In this respect the ordinary Shaker is perhaps no different from the lay adherent of any other religion, but among Shakers the tradition of a true priesthood dedicated to the intellectual pursuit of exploring the meaning of their faith has not taken root. Very few individuals have been interested in this abstract exercise and those who have engaged in it have done so for the personal satisfaction that it brings. They have, moreover, been handicapped by a lack of depth or breadth in understanding. Therefore, any attempt to give a systematic exposition of Shaker belief is certain to err on the side of sophistication and to some extent on the side of fact.

On the whole, Shaker belief and practice is an individual matter. There are personal and group emphases which obscure or deny any over-all pattern. Theoretically, everyone accepts the uniqueness of John Slocum's supernatural experience and the truth of his message. This contained the fundamentals of Christian dogma which, in brief, can be stated as follows. The divine ruler of the world is God, who is good and has unlimited power to help men if appealed to in a humble spirit. The expression of His power can be direct and immediate. He can also reveal His wishes directly to the individual by vision or intuition. In order to receive His blessings it is necessary to avoid sin, worship Him regularly, pray to Him for support and assistance, confess one's failures to Him, and praise Him for His help. Almost as important in this respect is Jesus Christ, the Son of God, who once lived on earth and will return at some future time to inaugurate a new existence for the faithful.

In addition there is the whole matter of shaking, which was introduced later and has had a confusing and dulling effect upon the simplicity of this doctrine. In fact, as a consequence of its infusion three factions have developed within the church, each with a different emphasis upon the elements of the pagan and the Christian components of the religion.

Ostensibly their differences are over the use of the Bible in church, but they are divided over more fundamental issues than that. For convenience of reference we may call the three groups the conservatives, the moderates, and the progressives.

The conservatives are in the majority. A rough estimate would give them perhaps three-fourths of the entire membership and until quite recently, as was indicated in the last chapter, their control was not seriously disputed. Their position was stated by Mud Bay Sam in his speech in Wickersham's presence. "No, we do not believe the Bible," he said. "We believe in God, and in Jesus Christ as the Son of God, and we believe in hell. In these matters we believe the same as the Presbyterians. We think fully of God today. A good Christian man is a good medicine-man. A good Christian man in the dark sees a light toward God. God makes a fog —good Christian man goes straight through it to the end, like good medicine. I believe this religion. It helps poor people. Bad man can't see good—bad man can't get to heaven—can't find his way. We were sent to jail for this religion, but we will never give up. We all believe that John Slocum died and went to heaven, and was sent back to preach to the people. We all talk about that and believe it." [2]

In other words, to the majority the most important aspect of the religion is its most distinctive one; namely, the gift of "power" and all that goes with it. They are the Shakers pure and simple. Their attachment to the faith is emotional rather than intellectual. Their position logically presupposes John Slocum's mystic experience and its fulfilment in Mary. When they know about this they freely espouse its verity. Many, however, are unaware of the facts concerning the origin of their religion and are undisturbed by this lack of knowledge. It is not a necessary condition for the acceptance of that part of the faith which appeals to them. Implicit in this view is an unquestioned admission of the reality of direct inspiration and the repeated occurrence of miracles in the form of cures and other demonstrations of divine power.

This in turn entails the recognition of an omnipotent source of the power, which is, in practice, taken to be Jesus Christ rather than God.

Beyond this the conservatives are doctrinally weak. They have no clear conception of the metaphysical implications of their beliefs. They have no articulate explanation of the nature of the soul or its destiny; they have no theology or definition of God's relation to man. Most surprisingly they do not have any consistent theory of disease and its cure. Few have any explanation at all of why they do what they do in doctoring a patient. Finally, ethics is a minor consideration. Much is said about moral behavior by some Shakers, but failure to conform to the standards weighs lightly in any particular consideration. Today the code has been narrowed and stereotyped into the dual prohibition against smoking and drinking. Among those who join the church for the sake of shaking only the most self-righteous stress even these evils. Conformance to an ethical tenet is a personal matter; divine sanction and retribution for its neglect is not a compelling motive for upholding it.

Understandably, those who hold to this view are intolerant of exegesis and exhortation. The question of sanctions is unimportant to them. Some have not read the Bible. They may admit that it is true, or "true for white people," but in any case the issue is irrelevant. Others know the Bible well but still insist that Shakers can do without it. As C. J. Johns says, "We do not have to study what to preach. I just open my mouth and the Lord fills it with words, just like the apostles. They had no Bible, and we need none. The Shaker faith was a spiritual thing in the beginning, is, and ever shall be."

Whatever their competencies in explaining their position all conservatives therefore agree that they do not need the Bible, and the attempt to force it upon them has caused a vigorous reaction. The result has been that their leaders have abandoned any pretense of compromise or tolerence and have taken the extreme position of condemning the Bible and all who advocate its use. They accuse Kitsap of preaching in Pentecostal churches and accepting money for it. They say that he attempts to discredit John Slocum and advises the younger Indians to forget about the episode of his death and resurrection. Some of them have allowed their rancor to lead them into perverse and unwarranted assaults upon the opposition. At the 1933 convention one of their leaders declared that "all of those people who carry Bibles under their arms are preaching lies. The Bible is the devil's book," he continued, "because it approves of horse racing and gambling. I am a preacher, but I never had anybody tell me that I converted him by preaching. You have to convert a person by shaking."

Members of the progressive faction led by Kitsap engage in shaking and they in fact acknowledge the significance of John Slocum's mission for the Indians. Members of this faction place their accents differently, however. While not denying the validity of John Slocum's experience they view it as a singular phenomenon that is unfortunately subject to vulgar distortion and misrepresentation. Like other miracles it is something to be accepted but not expected or needed as a token of God's omnipotence. Divine intervention in human affairs, and the revelations proclaiming them, are rare today; they belong mainly to a bygone period when God was establishing his law on earth. Shaking is recognized as a real demonstration of divine power acting through mortals for their physical and spiritual well-being. But this is not enough; it is not even of primary importance. The essential thing is to be a Christian, and this means to accept Christ and all his teachings.

At the height of the contest for leadership in 1938 Kitsap spoke to the congregation at Hoopa, quoting from the Bible to substantiate his contention that "if you don't believe in God and His good works you cannot be saved no matter how much you stomp and shake." He dwelt upon this theme at some length, placing the emphasis upon moral regeneration and depreciating the value of shaking as the essential means of salvation. The separation in his mind appeared to be fairly complete, but neither the divorcement of the two elements nor his long sermon on the subject found favor with the majority of his listeners. They wanted to "go to work." The progressives, in short, play down the unique features of the religion and stress the common ground that it holds with other evangelical churches.

The moderates have a difficult time maintaining their equilibrium between the two extreme elements. They are few in number, unorganized, and have no spokesman. They probably represent the attitude of John Slocum more faithfully than the rest but they make no pretensions on this score. They are simply individuals who have worked out their own private solutions to the problem of a religious faith. They quote freely from the Bible but do not press it upon others. They take what consolation they can from the Bible and from shaking and harmonize the two to the best of their ability.

Enoch Abraham has always used his biblical knowledge to defend Shakerism and rationalize some of its practices. He quotes, for example, from Psalm 150 to justify the Shakers' "dancing before the Lord" and their use of bells to keep time, drawing an analogy between these instruments and David's harp and tambourine. The Bible has had an important influence upon the life of Silas Heck, too, but it failed to give him the spiritual satisfaction that he looked for in it. Only after he became a Shaker did he gain a clear understanding of the nature of things and of God's will. Since his conversion the things of the Bible have taken on a new meaning; now they "are as clear as water" to him. Without this insight provided by Shakerism the stories of the Old Testament were distorted and misleading, a fact which he attributes to the faulty understanding of scholars who have attempted translations from the Semitic language. "The Bible is true," he says, "but so is Shaker. Both are the word of God."

In the following discussion of the details of Shaker belief it will be assumed that the remarks apply primarily to the ideas of the conservatives, that is, to those who accept the act of shaking as the fundamental and essential part of the religion. The attitudes taken toward them by the others who place their emphasis upon the spiritual lessons of the New Testament can readily be judged by the ordinary reader. Furthermore, it is with theory rather than practice that we are at this point primarily concerned; or, in some instances, it is with the implied belief rather than the one expressed.

The fundamental tenet in the whole theoretical structure is that the Shaker religion was ordained by, and is sustained by, direct revelation. The original sanction for this belief was, of course, Slocum's alleged visit to heaven and his divine commission to deliver a message direct from God. But Slocum was not the last to be granted this privilege. Many others have received special charges, so many in fact that it has become a commonplace in Shaker theory. Mary set the pattern with her disclosure that the shaking trance was an indication of supernatural rapport. While in that state she is supposed to have saved her husband from death. It was soon discovered that others were susceptible to the same uncontrollable force and while under its influence they exhibited extraordinary insight and ability. From that there evolved the concept of "power."

Psychologically, power is a projection of the experience of conviction. Intuitive understanding is so vivid and compelling that the Shakers have objectified it and identified it with supernatural force. Not only have they attributed a revelation to God; they go beyond this to externalize and often to personify their impression of its truth and certainty. Sometimes the force thus conceived is referred to as "the shake." In either case it is regarded as an undifferentiated and generic supernatural agency. It is not uncommon, however, to find that it has become individualized with the result that each person is believed to have his own distinct and personalized guiding force. Very often individuals speak of *their* shakes. A common justification for a private belief is that "My shake told me so." And with reference to the orthodoxy of some individual it is said that his shake is good, or bad, as the case may be.

The principal effect that power has upon the individual who receives it is to give him enlightenment, discernment, and clarity of understanding. It suffuses him with the sensation of being right and true. The locus of this intuitive under-standing is not in the head, but in the heart. Those who have not abstracted and personalized it to the extent of calling it "my shake" nonetheless refer it to their heart in the same way. Enoch Abraham, for instance, says that his heart tells him that a certain person is not long for this world, that an-other will get out of jail, that he will achieve something that he hopes for, and so on. Most Shakers involuntarily point toward their left breasts when asserting that they "know" something.

Shaker power is supposed to emanate from God and act through the human body after the latter has been prepared by an attitude of submission and humility. It is not always present in the body. The act of shaking is an overt manifesta-tion of its presence. The force or power is controlled by God. The individual through whom it acts is, in himself, unim-portant and he takes no credit for the passive role that he plays in its operation. It can be transmitted from one person to another, or it can come directly from God. Some people are more susceptible to its influences than are others. In some phases of its diffusion power is conceived of like a contagion: it "spreads," or it is "catching," and a number of people succumb to it in quick succession. When someone comes under its influence and begins to shake it is said that it "falls on him" or "hits him." When necessary one person "draws" or directs the power toward another and "throws it into him." Almost always power comes to a person or is directed into his body during a meeting while others are shaking. There are a few instances, however, of an individual being moved almost to the point of shaking under other circumstances. A Chehalis man who suffered acutely from rheumatism one night cried himself to sleep, and in that state he had a dream in which he saw himself as a Shaker. He woke up shaking, and when he attended the next regular meeting the power came over him so strongly that he was convinced that he must join the church.

The principal virtue of power is its curative and restorative properties. Its acquisition brings mental and physical relief. Also, even though a person has not experienced its healing effects by possessing power himself he can be relieved or cured of an illness by the manipulations of one who has. Acting through the hands of one who is possessed, power cures by "drawing" and "brushing" sin or some evil force from the patient's body; or it finds and helps to restore the soul of a sick person. Since it guides the search for such disembodied souls and leads the hands to sickness, power, therefore, has preternatural insight and volition.

These superhuman attributes of power find expression on other occasions. Many people "under power" are clairvoyant. In the trance state they have visions of future events or are given insight into the causes and results of developments that are obscured from ordinary view. They are able to foretell deaths and to discover the location of lost or hidden objects. In the latter instance the outstretched hands of the seer "lead" him to the objective, just as they do in curing. In theory the power directs this action. Some Shakers are better vehicles for this form of power manifestation than they are for healing, and some are more characteristically visionary than motor minded. No formal or conceptual distinctions are made between these capacities, and any person without training or certification may exhibit them.

To every Shaker who gives thought to his religion the most important ingredient is faith. This is the explanation of all the good and wonderful things that have happened in the

name of the religion. One must believe in order to cure or
be cured. He must believe to experience the emotional uplift
that comes with conversion. Nothing can be accomplished
without faith in God's power, and nothing is impossible when
it is brought to bear. Once Enoch Abraham was summoned
before the Yakima Indian agent to justify the Shaker's pretensions to curing. Appealing to the Bible, Abraham explained that what they did was neither more nor less than
faith healing, a practice sanctioned by Christ and admitted
by many white people. C. J. Johns attributes most of his
failure to cure sick people to their skepticism. "They are
given the test," he says, "and if they have no faith, they can't
be cured by anyone."

As this tenet implies, submission and appeal to God for
his blessings is essential. Since all power comes from Him
He is to be given credit in prayer and in song. The songs are
sung during church services. Usually they are composed of
one or two lines that are repeated several times. They are
expressive of love and gratitude, containing such refrains as,
"Oh, what a friend is Jesus," "How can you believe Jesus
when you are not true to Him," and "I am so glad since Jesus
came into my heart." These songs are "received," that is, bestowed upon an individual either in a dream, or in the wak-
ing state, or while under power. He sings his song until others
become familiar with it and then it becomes public property. Johns often sings at his everyday work, and very often
a song "has just come" to him. Once as Abraham slept a
song revolved in his mind and he woke up singing, "I praise
Thee, my God on high." At another time he was ill and too
feeble to feed himself at a time when his friends had for-
saken him. In despair he wept, and as he cried the words to
a song came to him: "Lord have mercy on me, a poor sinner."

Some songs come from the "wrong side." Good ones are
believed to come from above, the bad ones from other directions. In almost every congregation unsanctioned songs have

had to be repressed. Often they can be identified because they have been lifted from pagan contexts. When Lincoln White, one of the Cowlitz men who introduced the religion to the Yakimas, fell under the shaking power he could not restrain himself from singing the tune of his old curing spirit song. The Yakimas adopted it before they knew what it was. It continues in use, although under protest by some who know about it, and has spread to Warm Springs and other places. Abraham's mother was a shaman. Another Yakima woman who became a Shaker adapted one of her curing songs in spite of his strenuous objections. Two other women appropriated it later, again over his objections, each one claiming its tune as original. At the height of their agitation over the new religion some Yurok Shakers alarmed both their Siletz brothers and the conservative Yurok element by appropriating songs from native ceremonies, especially the "doctor making" dance. One woman adopted her father's "good luck" song to the consternation of old Yurok men.

Prayer is important, but in the main its use is a matter of individual conscience. Every devout Shaker should pray in the evening before retiring, in the morning upon arising, and before and after each meal. Beyond this, private praying is left to the individual, and he resorts to it very much as does the Christian. In addition there are occasions for public prayer: during church services, at specially designated prayer meetings, at conventions, and before beginning and ending curing ceremonies. At these times one person is called upon or assumes the function of praying for the rest, although at one point in the Sunday service everybody prays aloud individually. Appeals to and praises of God and Jesus Christ are individualized and extemporaneous, though they are replete with stereotyped phrases and sentiments.

The quality of spontaneity is stressed in praying. The interpretation given this ideal is that unpremeditated expression is a mark of divine inspiration. A person in the proper frame of mind need not reflect upon what he is going to say; God will speak through his mouth just as He acts through the vehicle of a man's hands in curing the sick. John Slocum phrased this belief thus: "for it is said, it don't make any difference if he [a person] prays good and does good [i.e., perfectly]. God gives him help and words to speak." C. J. Johns says of both songs and prayers that no one has to give thought to them; God puts the words in a person's mouth and all that he has to do is open it and they begin to flow out. "We must let the Lord have His way. We cannot quench the spirit."

Theoretically it is essential that Shakers not only pray to God in private but that they attend group worship. Of this Slocum said: "While one man can try to start a religion here on earth, it don't do much good; we don't believe him much. That's why we join to worship." There has never been much emphasis upon this point, however. It is expected that most members will want to go to church, but the decision is left to each individual entirely. There are no sermons or reproaches by ministers upon the obligation to attend public services. The reason for this is that the concept has never been crystallized as a divine injunction.

The same can be said of several other tenets that received an even more precise formulation in the early days of the church. The speech made by Mud Bay Louis in 1892 contains a dogmatic portion that is relevant at this point: "Long ago we knew nothing at all. When Slocum came back from God, we found out there was a God. From that time we have prayed for anything we want. We follow God's way. God teaches us if we do bad we will go to hell. That's why we pray and avoid bad habits. If we don't ask grace, bad things come when we eating. When we drink water, we think about God before drinking. If we don't think of Him, maybe we get sick from water. If traveling, maybe we die if we don't think of God. We are afraid to do wrong against God. Long time ago we worked on Sundays, but no more now. Our brother Christ has given us six days to work. On Sunday pray to God. God put people here to grow—puts our souls in our body. That's why we pray so much. If we quit, like a man quit his job, he gets no pay. We would go to fire in hell. We have no power to put out hell fire." [3]

John Slocum set Saturday as the day of worship, but under later influences this was changed. Sunday became, and remains, the proper day for regular church services. Two meetings are held, one in the morning and one in the evening after dinner. Lip service is still paid to the injunction that this is a day of abstention from all labor by those who have heard of the Fourth Commandment. Many have not, and for them relaxation from work does not signify abstention from worldly activities. The two are concomitant, but the one is not the dogmatic basis of the other. Those who object to manual labor on Sunday do so by way of claiming a right for themselves rather than out of a sense of sacred obligation to their creator. And the idea of complete abstention is foreign to almost everyone. In short, for modern Shakers religious principles are not the compelling or even the primary factors in their attitude toward Sunday as a day of rest. Their rest is literal, not symbolic or commemorative. At an early period, and in some places, this might not have been the case. To judge from the statement quoted above, Louis took the commandment seriously. Perhaps the proscription was more generally observed around 1900 than it was later. After affirming that "the Shakers are very strict in keeping the Sabbath, doing no unnecessary work on that day," Miss Ober goes on to describe a meeting that she attended at Neah Bay for which food had been prepared in advance, only the hot drinks having been made on Sunday.[4] It is difficult to say whether this was the result of practical expediency or of religious scruple. In either event, it does not appear that Shakers today make a point of avoiding work on Sunday. One does not hear it advocated in sermons, and observation does not disclose the operation of the idea in practice.

The Christian concepts of atonement and redemption have not been grasped by the Shakers. The notion of original sin has escaped them, therefore the interpretation of Christ's suffering as a mechanism of vicarious atonement is meaningless. The meaning of sin as a spiritual stigma odious to God is only faintly sensed. Sin is egocentrically conceived. Primarily an evil act is an offense against oneself rather than God. It is the cause of personal distress, and for that reason it is to be avoided. The exhilaration that is experienced as a result of the admission and fervent denunciation of sinful ways is an end in itself. To interpret it as a spiritual rebirth into a new life acceptable to God is to place it beyond the metaphysical reach of most Shakers. At most they regard it as a relief so phenomenal and gratifying that it is awe-inspiring. That it is an act of grace which entails the obligation to continue in the ways of righteousness likewise does not hold. Backsliders are not reproached because they have offended God or broken a sacred covenant. They have hurt themselves, but their souls are not at stake.

In fact, concern for the fate of the soul is not projected upon this abstract level. All Shakers are anxious about their souls, but their interest is in keeping them in their bodies rather than in providing for them after death. Their thinking does not run to speculation about an afterlife. Heaven, when it is thought of, is vaguely imagined as a good place somewhere up above without positive attributes or inducements. Ideas about it are too nebulous and wavering to qualify it as a goal to be striven for. The glimpse that Slocum had of heaven was apparently not vivid enough to bring the imagination of his followers to a focus upon it. At the present time there is seldom any reference to it and one hears nothing of angels or other possible elaborations upon the idea. It enters figuratively into Shaker thinking, but not as a guiding reality.

In view of these facts, it is not surprising that the concepts of purgatory and eternal damnation are not a part of Shaker doctrine. Not only is the idea of punishment absent; it has been consciously rejected. Slocum never mentioned hell or the devil, and he advised others not to. Today most people do not like even to talk about such subjects. Mud Bay Louis and his brother Sam, however, insisted upon the threat of hell fire as a deterrent to sinners. In the excerpts that have been quoted from their speeches made in the presence of Wickersham it will be noted that both men stress this idea. Sporadically it crops up in other contexts.

Charles D. Rakestraw has published an elaborate version of John Slocum's experience in death which is almost certainly apocryphal, but it illustrates this point. According to his informant or informants:

"Additional accounts say that soon after John Slocum's soul had left his body he came to a fine-looking house but could not see anybody in the yard. As he approached, the front door opened, apparently of its own accord. He entered the front room but found it empty. As he looked around he heard a voice say, 'Go into the next room.' The door swinging open, he stepped into the room and found a fine-looking, well-dressed man who greeted him pleasantly. The man asked him, 'Did you believe in God while you were on earth?' 'Yes,' said John. (This of course was not true.) 'No, you didn't,' said the man. Slocum was then shown into a side room, where he saw something that looked like a large photograph. This picture revealed to John all of the bad deeds of his life and he saw that he had been a very wicked man. The man said to John, 'Now, what about that?' pointing to the picture; and, without waiting for a reply, continued, 'I will now take you where you can see the fire.' They went into another room, which was really the entrance to a very large furnace. Slocum looked into the horrible place and saw a large number of men whom he had known and who had died before him, and, among them, hideous serpents fighting, writhing, and biting each other, making a most awful place.

"The man said to him, 'This will have to be your place, John.' At this, John began to plead but the man said that God alone could change the decision, at which John begged for an interview with God himself, and this was finally granted.

"God said, 'John Slocum, you have always been a drunken, gambling, worthless Indian while on earth and now that your life there is ended you will have to go into the furnace.'

"Slocum said, 'Oh God, I can't go into that terrible place and I will do anything if you will only not send me there.'

"God said, 'John, you had your chance when on earth but you were bad and now the furnace is the place for you.' Slocum said, 'Oh God, for mercy sake don't send me there. I will do anything you ask of me if only you will keep me out of that furnace. Just tell me what it is, God, and give me just *one* more trial, and you will see how good I will be. Oh, please do, God.'

"God said, 'John, I will think about it,' and told the man to show John around and to bring him back afterwards into his presence.

"The man took Slocum out on top of the house and into an upper room where everything was beautiful. There was a great, bright light and everything to make one happy. After showing him the spaciousness and the beauty and the comforts of this place, the man said to Slocum that God had prepared this place for all Indians who believed in Him and lived good lives while on earth, but that all bad Indians would have to go to the furnace when they died. They then went again into the presence of God, who said, 'John, I have decided to give you one more trial on certain conditions. I will let you go back to earth and come to life again and you are not only to be a good man yourself and live a sober, honest, upright, Christian life, but you are to teach your people (Indians) to be sober, honest, upright, Christian people. Now if you will do this, when you die again and come up here I will not have to put you in the furnace.'

"John said, 'Oh, God, I will gladly do that and please let me go at once,' which was done. And John had just returned from this interview when he rose in his burial cerements before his awe-stricken friends as they were about to deposit his body in its final resting place." [5]

While Shakers are cautioned not to sin, each upon his own responsibility, no charge is laid upon the individual to rescue his fellows from their wickedness. A man is not his brother's keeper. Neither is he counseled to avoid those who sin, out of regard for his own safety. Very few persons give any thought to the danger of temptation. When they do they render an individual judgment that applies to their own case. C. J. Johns represents one extreme. He deplores athletic sports, shows, Indian games and dances—in fact, "all of the pleasures of this world, for they are temptations." Even an innocent contact with these evils is dangerous, as one instance which he adduces will show: Not many years ago a man who was a reformed gambler jumped upon his horse, struck him with a quirt, and raced by some of his friends shouting, "This is just like the old days." The next day he was sick and nearly died because he had relaxed his guard against temptation.

A more general point of view is embodied in the interpretation of Silas Heck. If others were more thoughtful and articulate they would probably express their attitude as he did: "You do what your shake tells you to do. Some Shakers say that you shouldn't go near gambling, movies, horse races, and so on. This means that *they* can't do these things. When they say that Shakers can't do these things they are really talking about themselves, because they are weak and can't resist temptation. They should stay away, but I feel no temp-

tation. I avoid sins myself, but it is because I don't like them.
I can associate with anyone. I can go around with a murderer
and it won't hurt me. That is between him and God, not
me and him." In part this is a rationalization, but it could be
taken as a dogmatic basis for common, unpremeditated practice.

The confession of sins has never been strictly enjoined upon
Shakers. The doctrine of its necessity was preached by John
Slocum, but by no means all of his followers adopted the
practice. Those who did came to him in private, and he,
according to his sister-in-law, went every Friday to Olympia
to confess to a Catholic priest for himself and his communi-
cants. He did not long maintain his prerogative in this respect, for soon Louis assumed the role of confessor, and
shortly after that another Mud Bay man, Dick Jackson, did
likewise. Still later, around 1903, Joe Riddle, who lived on
the Yakima Reservation, proclaimed his right to act in this
capacity. Ministers and bishops are not ex officio confessors.
The function is in the nature of a special blessing. At present
no one claims the "gift," and the necessity of confession is
not an article of faith. Many congregations, among them
those in California, have never known about it other than
by hearsay. Lee Cush, at Skokomish, recently "received" the
idea that people should make an open confession on the
floor of the church, and he has been advocating this mode. It
has not been accepted.

The belief that miracles can take place is consistent Shaker
doctrine. Instances in which prodigies have been expected,
and in some cases realized, bear testimony to the prevalence
of this hope. Ober affirms that "At first the Shakers 'shook'
for everything they desired, for fair weather, favorable winds,
for success in hunting or fishing, for escape from danger
or deliverance from trouble; to exorcise evil spirits, and cast
out diseases, as well as for salvation from sin." [6] There are
no specific data available to substantiate parts of this gen-

eralization; but there are instances which indicate the scope of Shaker faith in spectacular demonstrations of power.

There have been attempts, probably inspired by the story of John Slocum, to return the dead to life. It will be recalled that Eells heard the rumor that four persons had been raised from the dead during the big meeting around Mud Bay in 1883. Later, Lans Kalapa of Neah Bay acquired a wide reputation because he was alleged to have brought two children back to life by restoring their souls to their lifeless bodies. The idea has cropped up in other places, too. When a Siletz man was proselytizing among his Yurok friends in the late 1920's a skeptic remarked to him that he seemed to be claiming the powers of an Indian doctor. The Shaker replied that his power was greater than any shaman, that he could "raise a person from the dead even if he has been dead one-half day." A few years later when a young boy died at Johnson's Landing the local Shakers held services over his body for three days in the hope of reviving him. They were finally stopped by the store keeper who threatened to call the sheriff if the corpse was not buried immediately. Doubtless there have been other instances of attempted resurrections.

Reagan states that some of the early Shakers believed that they could walk on water in imitation of Christ. When another imitator, Big John, was imprisoned for his impersonation of the crucified Christ his followers crowded around the jail and prayed for its walls to be cast down to vindicate him. Once a Puget Sound Shaker demonstrated his command of power before a large number of Indians gathered for hop picking in the Yakima Valley. He raised his hand and closed it on the "soul" of a passing bird. The bird fell to the ground, but when its captor opened his hand it revived and flew away unharmed. Lans Kalapa was believed to have healed the eyes of a nearly blind boy. The youth's eyes were so sensitive to light that he had to wear a blindfold, but Kalapa is said to have restored his normal vision with the use of candle light. Kalapa removed the black cloth from the boy's eyes three times while directing him to stare at the flame. Twice the boy flinched with pain, but on the third trial he was able to see and the light did not trouble him.

The ability to do such things the Shakers term a "gift" or a "help"; that is, a blessing bestowed by God. Any remarkable ability is called a gift; but the term is more inclusive, and its implications relate it closely to what is intended by the word "teaching." A teaching is a precept, and because it is "received" from spiritual sources, it is also a gift; but not all gifts are teachings. Some are not intended to establish precedents for others to follow. They represent personal convictions and compulsions. One of the more articulate Shakers summed up the nature of gifts in these words: "Some people have special power to give the shake to others just by touching them, some to cure, some to sing a song, and so forth. These helps come at any time, while you are working, or shaking, or sleeping. You know it when they do; and you have to do what your shake tells you to do, and other people have to let you do it. You help them in doing it and you help yourself. You know it when you get a song. It is not like other songs that are just made up and have no life in them and do not touch your heart. A real Shaker song makes your heart glad, and you have to sing it."

Gifts include a great variety of ministrations and ritual devices. Some are trivial, with only a personal reference; others are of such a character that they call for the co-operation or the concurrence of other persons and are therefore in the nature of privileges or prerogatives. The gifts of prophecy and confessorship belong to the latter category. Still others, such as ritual forms, demand not only the admission of truth from others but their active participation as well. They may more properly be called "teachings."

Any person is eligible to receive these blessings. Almost every prominent Shaker has been favored with one or more and some members, such as Mary Slocum and Mud Bay Louis, have acquired a reputation for the number and significance of their inspirations. Since a gift or "teaching" is supposed to be sanctioned by God, the extent to which the claim to true reception can be established determines the degree to which the inspired persons gain popular approval. If the circumstances surrounding their realization and demonstration carry conviction, they are incorporated into the morphous body of Shaker lore and ritual. Some fail to meet this pragmatic test, and they are simply ignored. Others may gain some support but are rejected by an opposition group. The opposition may admit that the teaching or gift has been "received" with all the earmarks of truth but maintain that the receiver has been the victim of deception. He has obtained his gift from "the wrong side." In the minds of some people this expression is a euphemism for the devil; for the majority it means only that unanalyzed forces of evil are constantly at work to undermine and destroy the true faith. These evil influences are subtle and deceptive; they show themselves under the guise of their opposites to beguile the unsuspecting person. All true power and revelation comes from above; evil lurks in every other direction. Shakers must be on their guard and when they find that one of their number has been deceived the evil power must be taken out of him. Some people so possessed disclose their misfortune by displays of violence while under power; they want to fight, kick, hit, or bite others.

George Pike was a good Chehalis Shaker; but not long before he died he began to advocate a change in ritual which most of the local congregation considered unacceptable. The conservative members, led by Peter Heck, decided that the devil's power had taken possession of him and that to cure him this must be taken out. They "worked over" him, drew the power out with their hands, and threw it away. He was "saved," but did not live long afterwards. In another instance, Peter Heck was called upon to settle a controversy about ritual procedure between two Skagit women. Each claimed that her revelation was the true one, and their differences were disturbing to the rest of the congregation. During the course of a shaking session to determine which of the women was right, Peter's shake told him the answer. Secure in this knowledge he set to work on the erring contender and took out her bad power.

Success in healing the sick is a gift. There are gradations of ability, but every Shaker shares to some extent in this blessing. Any person under power may work upon the sick, and it is expected that all will. The healing power in everyone is the same; it simply manifests itself more strongly in some individuals than in others. Not only may one individual help another; he can also help himself. By manipulating his hands he can "work on" himself just as he does on others.

Shakers credit a materialistic explanation of ordinary ailments. Cuts, bruises, broken bones, and some of the common complaints such as colds, intestinal disorders, and contagious diseases are most often regarded and treated as we regard and treat them. At the same time, the possibility is always entertained that the ostensible causes of these misfortunes are merely secondary and that the fundamental cause is the operation of forces set in motion by some malignant agent. Usually the offender is considered to be an enemy with evil power; that is, a shaman or a magician. His evil power must be overcome by God's power. Also, whatever the cause of an ailment, divine power can cure it even more certainly than can drugs and mechanical operations, and frequently this recourse can bring relief when all hope has been abandoned for help from surgery or other therapeutic aids.

In general, the more inexplicable a physical or mental disorder the more probable is it that it will be attributed to the operation of some occult force. The mechanics of the connection is by no means clear to the great majority of Shakers. Most of them have never given the subject any thought and do not care; they do not trouble to find a rationale for their curing practices and do not consider it necessary to explain them to others. No one is able to formulate a consistent theory of disease and cure that will comprehend all aspects of the subject or even to provide a self-satisfying explanation for those parts of it that are known and practiced by himself.

For some of the more incomprehensible ailments the Washington Shakers have one explanation which is fairly generally recognized and rationalized. They believe that many people become ill through the loss of a vital life essence or force. Practically no one will use or accept our word "soul" as an appropriate term for this force. Actually, however, that is a rather accurate translation of the Salish word *sale*, which is what the Puget Sound Shakers use to designate it. In English, they use such words as "mind," "breath," or "life" or employ personal pronouns like "his," or "he" to convey the significance of its vital quality. It is the loss of this life principle that causes illness. C. J. Johns and a few others make a differentiation. Johns says that it is not the soul which abandons the body but the "soul's companion." This is a refinement to which we will return at a later time.

Usually the younger people can offer no reasons for the loss of the soul. Some of the older people say that a person "loses his mind" when he is despondent, or when he thinks too much about his dead relatives, or when he wishes he were somewhere else and cannot go there. In these cases, which are perhaps the most common, a wandering soul is vaguely related to a preoccupied or nostalgic state of mind wherein a person longs for other times and places. Given this state of mind it is conceived that the afflicted person's mind *is* elsewhere, and unless it is recovered in time he will die. Sometimes it is said that his soul "gets stuck" in some place where he has been, or it travels on to some destination when its owner stops, or it is attracted to, or stolen by, the ghosts of the beloved dead. For some individuals—those in whose minds the evils of shamanism loom large—more sinister forces are at work. In their view an equally imminent danger is the kidnapping of the soul by shamans. According to some, a shaman might abduct the soul of a person and tie it to the top of a tree, thereby causing the tree to fall upon him, or place it on the ball of a bullet and cause him to shoot himself. Others believe that the shaman simply captures and hides the soul until his victim dies.

The loss of the soul does not mean immediate death. "You see," said one informant, "we have two parts to our bodies, the corruptible and the incorruptible. The incorruptible part cannot be destroyed. It can leave the body for a while and the body runs on like an automobile after the engine is cut off, but before long both of them will stop." The loss of the soul, then, marks the initial stage of death, and the bodily symptoms that appear are suggestive of this state. Shaker power enables a person to diagnose this condition, locate the errant soul, and replace it in the patient's body.

Some Shakers under power are said to be able to see a soul. One night Enoch Abraham's first wife saw another woman sleeping at the foot of a tree. As she watched she saw the woman's soul climb the tree to the highest branch and then vanish. A soul is said to look "like a fog." When it cannot be seen some Shakers are led to it by following a "thin line like a cobweb." Many never see anything, but they can feel a soul when it nestles into their grasp. Upon one occasion Abraham accompanied C. J. Johns to help a sick woman near Toppenish. As he was shaking, Abraham "got something" in his extended hand. He soothed it, took it to an altar candle "to clean it," then placed it in the sick woman's head. He did not know how to explain his actions, but when the meeting was over Johns told the woman and her family that she must have been sorrowing for her dead relatives who had lived over in the direction in which Abraham had extended his hand and that her soul had lodged there. It was drawn back from the ghosts by Shaker power.

In the early years of Shakerism another concept of illness was prominent. This was the belief that a shaman could send his spirit familiar into the body of an enemy and cause him to die if it were not removed in time by another person with stronger spirit power. This is one explanation of John Slocum's "death," and possibly of the later attempts upon his life. A shaman was believed to be able either to "shoot" his power secretly from a safe distance or to place it in food or drink so that it would be ingested by his victim. This thought was uppermost in the mind of Mud Bay Louis when he said, "If we don't ask grace, bad things come when we eating. When we drink water we think about God before drinking. If we don't think of Him maybe we get sick from water." [7]

The first Shakers were obsessed by shamanistic threats, and it was due to an epidemic of such fears that so much dissension was created around Mud Bay and Skokomish at one time. Aboriginally it was thought that only another shaman was powerful enough to extract the intruded spirit. Pitting his helping spirit against that of the killer shaman, he encompassed it and withdrew it with his hands. As he grasped it he was flung violently around by its superhuman strength, sometimes to such an extent that two assistants were required to hold him down. At length, as he mastered it, he rose, dipped it in a container of water "to weaken it," and finally either threw it away, kept it as his own, or shot it back to its owner. If he withheld it from its master, the latter died.

The Shakers with their new-found power took over this curing function. Isaac Thompson once extracted a spirit belonging to Doctor Jim from a patient, dipped it in water, then sealed it tightly in a glass jar which he buried on the beach at a location known only to a few. The next day Doctor Jim was seen paddling around the bay, allegedly in search of his imprisoned helper. Alice James stood on shore watching him. He came up to her and said, "Have you seen anything?" Alice did not answer him; but he called aloud, and his spirit must have heard and answered him, for he looked pleased and went off in the direction of the spot where it was buried. At another time Doctor Jim is reputed to have sent some of his spirits into the Mud Bay church during a meeting "just to see what was going on." The Shakers discovered and picked them out of the air. After wetting them "to cool them off" they were capped in a strong jar; but they were so powerful that the jar was broken in Isaac's hands and they escaped.

At a meeting of the Skokomish congregation in 1922 Spier presumably witnessed a cure by spirit extraction: "Suddenly a sharp exclamation announced that one of their number had caught the 'disease' above the patient's head in his cupped hands. The 'disease' dragged the captor about despite the efforts of the others, who held him about the waist, into a corner near the altar. There his hands, still held together, could be heard knocking rapidly on the wall. One of the group was dispatched outside for a crock of water into which they put the captured 'disease,' hastily screwed on the lid and carried it out to be buried." [8]

At the present time the Washington Shakers follow the practice of removing an evasive "something" from sick people. The hands are used as Spier describes, but only infrequently is the captured thing dipped in water or imprisoned. It is just "thrown away." Both the patient and the manipulator claim they experience a sensation of change at the moment of removal. The patient is relieved at once. The captor feels the thing wriggling vigorously to escape his grasp, and sometimes he is even swung around by the strength of its exertions. He knows that it is not a soul, which is soft and fluffy, because the thing writhes and contorts itself in spasms that seek release. Its captor must get rid of it by throwing it up into the air, not straight out, and never toward another person.

This is as far as most Washington Shakers go now in rationalizing this kind of illness and its cure. They are not sure what the thing is that gets into a person's body or how it comes to be there. Or perhaps it would be more accurate to say that they have heard an explanation of the phenomenon but are a little dubious that it will be believed by others because they are somewhat skeptical about it themselves. Among the Shakers around Puget Sound the belief still lingers among some older people that the intruded thing is an evil spirit and a few of them do not hesitate to describe it as a shaman's familiar. Others are more cautious; they are content to call it "something bad." Johns says that many Indians today have an "animal power which they shoot into you just like with a gun." Most other informants are not so forthright.

Peter Heck once visited Shaker friends at Muckleshoot. He did not feel well, so after dinner his host, Bob James, began to shake over him. Bob discovered that "somebody was trying to do away with him." After announcing this, Bob and his wife began to shake again. They extracted "what was going to kill" Peter and threw it back where it came from. The patient felt better after this, and when he returned home he discovered that a shaman, Charlie Walker, had fallen out of a buggy and killed himself. This was regarded as proof that it was he who was responsible for Peter's illness. Asked whether it was his spirit power that Walker had sent for this purpose, Peter replied, "I don't know. I think it was his bad thoughts."

Silas Heck explained his views thus: "If you catch a person [soul] in your hands, your shake knows it. It is different from an evil spirit. People around here believe that there are evil spirits. If you catch one of these in your hands it swings you around like you are drunk. They get into a person's body and have to be taken out. I don't think that this will go on very long though. The young people don't believe this anymore. They have been to school—but these professors don't know it all either."

Two other causes of illness are more commonly recognized and treated by the Washington Shakers. Their statements with respect to them, however, are even more tentative and inarticulate. No one is able to give a satisfactory account of their nature or operation. One set of causes gives rise to all the physiological afflictions recognized by medical science: diseases, wounds, disfunctions, and even mental disorders. In explanation of cures in this category the Shakers simply say that they "draw the sickness out." Joe Young of Oakville is said to have been cured of rupture in this manner. Some years ago he took his wife and a white man and his wife from Tenino to a meeting at the Skokomish church. The white man's wife had a swelling in her throat which a Shaker told her would be gone in seven days after the treatment. It was. Joe was so relieved by the help he received at the meeting that he was able to discard his truss. Johns has helped at least two women in childbirth by bringing their infants into position for an easy delivery. He has also "worked with" the victims of contagious diseases. While the influenza raged in 1918 and 1919 he and his wife visited many of the homes of the stricken to hold shaking exercises. He has likewise gone into more than a score of Yakima homes to help smallpox patients. "The shaking helps what there is there besides the smallpox and the flu," he says. "It helps the sick person to breathe better, clears his head, and then nature takes its course."

Less common, but still important, is the concept that sin makes a person ill. It makes him sick by "covering his body." No one is certain whether sin penetrates beneath the surface, but most of those who have been asked think not. It clings to the outside and has to be "brushed off." Eells wrote of this idea when he learned of it soon after the religion started: "They would also brush each other with their hands, as they said, to brush off their sins, for they said they were much worse than white people, the latter being bad only in their hearts, while the Indians were so bad that the badness came to the surface of their bodies and the ends of their finger nails, so that it could be picked off."

Several years ago an Indian who lived near Victoria, B.C.,

was distressed because he smoked so much. He wanted to break the habit, so he appealed to the Shakers for assistance. They "worked over him and took the smoke out of his mouth," thereby curing him. According to Peter Heck, no one who drinks, smokes, or gambles should be permitted to shake over a patient because "all of those bad things cover the sick man and make him worse."

None of these conceptions of illness prevail among the California Shakers. For them any incomprehensible sickness is caused by the presence of "pains" in the body—the aboriginal theory. The presence of the pain entity explains any disorder of mind or body. As with "sickness" in Washington, it must be removed, and by the same means. But it differs in being conceived of as a thing and not as a state or condition, although it may produce exactly comparable symptoms. Pains can be felt in the hand, and a patient feels them being drawn out. They are visible, but not to everyone. Some Shakers can see them; others cannot, but their hands are led to them and they can extract them. A person under power can take pains out of his own body.

Informants are divided on the question as to whether the pains they remove are the same kind with which shamans deal. Most of them say they do not know or hesitate to reply in a way which indicates that the question has not previously occurred to them. Jimmy Jack maintains that they are the same. He has had occasion to consider the question because his claims as a healer have been contested by a Yurok shaman. This shaman, a woman, appears to have been genuinely interested in Jack's pretension to power, and she once suggested to him that the two of them treat a certain sick man in order to see what kind of pains each of them took out of him. Jack refused, saying that her presence would "spoil his power." Later, when another sick person came to this shaman for help, she "saw hands playing over his body and felt slime on it." She did not know what this meant, but she was able to take several pains out of his body. Afterwards she learned that the Shakers had previously treated him, so she concluded that whatever kind of pains they claim to get out of a sick person they are not the same as those she extracts; otherwise they would not have left the ones she found in this man's body.

Pains get into human bodies either as a result of natural but unknown causes or because they are "shot" in by malevolent persons who have control over them. Shamans have the power to shoot people; so have "Indian devils," a special class of wizards who take on monstrous shapes at night and are capable of prodigious movements. Indian devils operate secretly; hence anyone might be suspected of engaging in the nefarious business of covertly destroying his enemies while assuming the pretense of friendship or innocence. Shakers can detect these devils and remove the pains that they magically implant in their victims.

The beliefs that sin, spirit intrusion, or soul loss cause illness play no part in the ideology of the California Shakers. Jimmy Jack knows that sometimes a person's soul leaves his body and that Shakers can recover it. This he learned while he lived at Siletz. He says that he has tried to explain the idea to his people but they do not understand it. Like the Washington Shakers, those in California also treat ailments due to natural causes, but neither so extensively nor with as much rationalization. They claim to have cured hopeless cases of pneumonia and Bright's disease, but do not have an explanation of how; they do not extract the sickness.

The emphasis upon curing which is apparent in all Shaker communities has made them the natural foes of shamans and magicians. It is this which has framed the definition of good and evil to the comparative neglect of other possible polarizations, such as those which can develop around ethical behavior or the man-god relations. Sickness has come to be the primary evil; hence its agents, and especially its human perpetrators, have been the embodiments of wickedness in the past. Shamans and Shakers have everywhere been in conflict, either fictitious or real. Shakers consistently in the past have supposed themselves to be plagued and tried by their underhanded adversaries.

There are many stories of shamans sending their powers to disturb a meeting or to put a Shaker's power to the test. Once before a shaking service among the Skagit people Peter Heck, according to the custom, shook hands with everyone around the room. When he came to a certain man, he knew intuitively that he was a shaman. Later, while under power, his diagnosis proved correct, for it was apparent that the man had come there to pit his power against Peter's. Subsequently the shaman was forced to admit that his was the weaker. At another time a certain Chehalis shaman sent his power to a meeting hoping that someone would step on it and get sick. It moved about near the floor, like all bad spirits, but one Shaker discovered it, picked it up, and threw it away toward the west, "the place of darkness."

Closely associated with the antipathy toward shamans is the abhorrence that has developed toward the payment of fees for medical aid. So marked has this feeling been that it is a principle of faith to righteously reject the suggestion of compensation for relief of the sick. Shakers ridicule and condemn both white physicians and shamans for this practice. Mud Bay Sam, the foremost healer of his day, expressed his views upon the matter in these words: "I can cure people now. I have cured some white men and women, but they are ashamed to tell it. I cure without money. One big, rich man, Henry Walker, was sick—had great pains in his ear and leg. Doctor at Olympia failed to cure him, and he came to John Slocum and me. We worked for him, prayed, and he lay down and slept and was cured. He offered us twenty dollars—but no, we refused it. God will pay us when we die. This is our religion. When we die, we get our pay from God." [9] This is an idealistic statement of the compensatory aspect of the rejection of payment for cures. It is in the John Slocum tradition if not directly suggested by him. There is no evidence that it was ever a commonly accepted interpretation of the refusal to take pay for curing. Certainly Shakers at the present time do not regard the spiritual reward as a substitute for the material. The question is irrelevant, for they help others because they get an emotional satisfaction out of the experience of shaking which is sufficient compensation in itself. At their altruistic most they rejoice in being able to help another; at the least they enjoy what they do for its own sake or because they can be helped in return.

As Sam's statement indicates, white people as well as Indians can be benefited by Shaker power. They may even possess it themselves. Almost always the ailments that are treated in them are regarded as being due to natural causes, for there is a very general belief in and outside of Shakerism that white men are not subject to the mystical afflictions from which the Indian suffers. It is said that shamans and magicians cannot harm them, hence it is unusual for a Shaker to claim that he has recovered a white patient's soul or removed a foreign object from his body. Sins he may have, and they sicken him as well as others.

Theoretically, before a person anywhere can be treated he must make a voluntary appeal for help. This establishes the necessary premise of faith. But in practice there are numerous instances where Shakers have undertaken a cure upon their own initiative or have responded to the appeal of the relatives of a sick person without consulting his wishes. It is further stipulated that before beginning their performance those who are to undertake the cure of a patient must kneel and pray for God's help and direction. This is almost always followed, for it is the means of preparing the minds of the participants and of calling down the healing power to take possession of them.

The Shakers' watch for the millennium was long ago relaxed. Even by 1900 very little thought was being given to the subject of the time and nature of the world's end. At present the belief in Christ's second coming can hardly be said to be a living part of Shaker doctrine. For those who neither read the Bible nor listen to Christian sermons the idea poses something remote and purposeless—purposeless because its philosophical context is lacking or only vaguely present. It is not a necessary or an integral part of their faith. For those to whom Christian dogma is truth but not incompatible with the pre-eminent truth of inspiration through shaking, the way is open for individual interpretations of the dispensation yet to come. An example of such an interpretation is Silas Heck's view of what must happen when the appointed time arrives.

"My shake told me," he said, "that a new day is coming just before Christ returns to this earth. At that time there will be a new voice and a new vision, because as it is now all of the people in the world would not be able to see and hear Him no matter where He appears. Millions of people could not crowd around Him in Seattle if He came there—all could not hear His voice or understand what He said. So before this happens there must be a new understanding, some way that everybody will know at a distance. It will be something like radio, which needs instruments to pick up voices in the air; but when that time comes our bodies will be so cleansed of sin that we will be able to see and understand everything without instruments. That must be the way it will be. My shake told me that, not all at once but gradually as I thought about it, and I believe it must be true."

✠
SIX ✠ Faith
✠

THERE ARE numerous expressions of faith in the virtues of the Shaker religion. Every adherent knows of a variety of instances which testify to its truth and to the wonders that it makes possible. In general, the recognition of its value stems from four things that it does to or for the individual that are believed to be otherwise impossible. First of all, submission to a benign, omnipotent will brings with it assurance and consolation, at the least, and beyond that the opportunity for a regenerated life. In addition, it brings a compulsion to accept certain individual charges and obligations; it offers relief from physical distress; and it bestows supernatural insight into hidden forces and events. Although a single individual may not experience all these demonstrations of divine power, he knows of others who have.

Testimonials to the redeeming power of the faith are common. They may be heard at almost any evening meeting in a Shaker church. They follow a pattern that is varied mainly by artistic elaborations on the theme of a debauched life that has suddenly been purified and strengthened by an act of divine grace. Typically, in giving testimony a person reviles himself and the iniquitous state in which he lived before he became a Shaker, then goes on to rejoice in his new-found happiness. Men magnify their wickedness in terms of the cardinal sins of drinking, smoking, and gambling, stressing less frequently their weaknesses for lying and stealing. Ordinarily women do not confess to such a lurid past. Generally they testify to the vanities, ignorance, and mental depressions from which they suffered before the new hope came. Occasionally someone with more sophistication admits that he "was tired of the world" or "was lost and had to do something."

The statements of Mud Bay Louis and Lans Kalapa are in the characteristic vein. Louis said to Wickersham: "Well, my friend, we was about the poorest tribe on earth. . . . I was worst of lot. I was drunkard—was half starving—spent every cent for whisky. I gambled, raced horses, bet shirt, money, blankets—did not know any better. . . . John Slocum came alive, and I remember God and felt frightened. We never heard such a thing as a man dying and bring word that there was a God. I became sick for three weeks, four weeks. I hear a voice saying to soul, 'Tomorrow they will be coming to fix you up.' Had just heard about John Slocum, and knew it was punishment for my bad habits. My heart was black—it was a bad thing. Now I have quit swearing—my heart is upside down—it is changed. After I heard the voice I heard another say: 'There it is now—someone to fix you up. Have you prepared your heart? If you don't believe in Christ, you will go into a big fire and burn forever.' I saw a man's hand coming to my heart. That day I got up—was well —talked to my friends, advising them. I will remain a follower of Christ as long as I live." [1]

Kalapa's testimony has been recorded by Miss Ober. He said, "One time I bad—drunk—steal—lie—no like work— dirty bad (meaning immoral). I go white man's church—hear about white man's God—I say He no good for Indian—He not keep white man good. I go to Shaker church—I say—that fool religion—no good. But God speak to me—I no like hear God speak. I go way—git drunk—no like hear God speak— I sleep—all drunk. Then Jesus Christ come down to me— down from sky—look at me—I no can look—all bright—

like sun. But Jesus Christ look down in my bad heart—and love my bad heart clean." [2]

Mabel Teio, the wife of Alex, who later became a minister, was one of the first Shakers among the Yakima. She and her two sisters, Alice and Elsie, received the power on the same evening. The account of her conversion reveals the common feature of an unanalyzed emotional relief which comes with submission. Upon this occasion the Shakers had been summoned to the home of Elsie to cure her of a lingering illness caused by some shaman; but as they worked her sister began to succumb to the power: "Alice began to shake her hands. They [the Shakers] saw her and told her to stand. The spirit was coming to her. They told her to pray: she said she did not know how. They said, 'Never mind; God will bless you and show you how to pray: we will not help you.' Soon her hand began to pat her breast: she was helping herself. Elsie, my sister, was shaking too: her body was cold. The man said, 'That girl is getting the spirit.' So he made her stand up too. . . . The sick girl looked at Alice and said, 'Oh, Alice is going to join.' Then I cried. Then my cousin, the first woman convert, came and brushed me. I cried and cried: I did not know what was the matter. I felt funny; all my body felt different. That same man said, 'You cannot separate from your sister. You are all of one mind.' I thought how I was always sickly: we spent lots of money for doctors: my husband was a hard worker. And at last the spirit came to my mind. There were four of us: no one told us: the spirit came to us." [3]

From the Quinault comes a similar story of pent-up emotion given release by grateful surrender. "A young Indian from Oregon visited the reservation and asked the local members to shake over him. He had had tuberculosis and white physicians had given him up. But now, a year later, through the Shaker faith, he had nearly recovered. He told his story at a meeting. He stood with his right hand raised and said, 'Jesus wants us. Jesus wants us. But some of us he can't get.' Then he cried." [4]

Before his conversion Enoch Abraham was not dissolute or unprincipled, but he paid no attention to the Christian preaching that he had heard. He liked to have a good time, but he was not a gambler or a drinker. He liked to dance, and he, Alex Teio, Joe Riddle, and others of their age were accustomed to assemble on Friday nights during the winter for quadrille dances. It was because of his love for this pastime that Abraham caught pneumonia on New Year's Eve in 1899. Then before he had fully recovered he went to another dance and had a relapse. A shaman was called upon to treat him but failed to do any good. Another Indian doctor with a better reputation for this type of sickness was summoned, but Abraham showed no improvement. He became so ill that he believed that he was going to die. With that he became frightened and began to pray that his life might be spared for a time so that he could "clean" himself.

He was sick for seven weeks, and during that time he thought a great deal about the meaning of religion. In the end he was convinced that there was a God, that only his praying had saved him, and that he must become a Christian. As he lay sick he was visited by a Catholic priest who was calling upon a neighbor. His cousin, George Waters, also dropped in to see him. Waters was a Methodist preacher; but neither he nor the priest mentioned religion during their calls and Abraham was disappointed. He concluded that their kind of religion was not for him.

A few days after these visits Sophie Cree, who was a cousin of Abraham's wife, came to urge him to attend a Shaker meeting that she was planning at her home. He resisted because he had already found a previous experience when Shakers worked over him an unpleasant one. His wife insisted that he give them a trial, and at last he assented, saying, "All right— if you want them to kill me." He was still weak and had to be assisted in making the trip to Sophie's house. Aiyel was in charge of the ceremony there. He told Abraham that he must pray for help, and since Abraham did not know what to say

Aiyel gave him a prayer. He was told to stand in the center of the floor with his hands uplifted. This he did for several hours that night in spite of his feeble condition, but the power did not come to him. Another long trial took place the following night with no more success.

When the time came for the third meeting on Sunday night Abraham decided to offer his own prayer for help. Again he raised his arms and stood for four hours. His hands and arms became numb, and his back and legs were stiff; but before midnight he began to tremble slightly. His little fingers began to quiver and his hands descended to his right side—"pointing to" a rib that he had broken several years before. Aiyel thereupon motioned to his wife and told her to "get it." She placed her two hands close to Abraham's side. She did not touch his body for he had warned· the Shakers "not to fight" him. The woman appeared to scoop something out of his side and throw it up in the air. He raised his arms again, and soon his hands came back down to indicate the place where he had previously broken his collar bone. Aiyel again motioned to his wife and she withdrew something and tossed it away. Meanwhile Abraham's wife had begun to shake.

By that time it was midnight and Aiyel called a halt for supper. He announced that although Abraham had received the power, it was not yet strong enough in him and that they should resume the meeting. Abraham's wife was eager to continue, and he agreed to go on. After the meal he took his position in the center of the floor and stood there until dawn. He did not lose control of himself; but he did feel stronger and "cleaner" than he had before the meeting. This change he attributed to his own earnest prayer and the faith that he had in the religion. "You have to have faith," he said. "If you are just testing shaking you can't get help; and if I don't believe that you are sincere, I can't help you."

Sometimes an individual at the time of his conversion feels

compelled to perform some public act as an expression of contrition or thanksgiving. This was so with Joe Riddle when he was converted in 1901. Previously he could claim few virtues. He was disliked by many people, especially because of his promiscuous love affairs. "He had more women than Solomon," to quote his cousin and confidant. But when his son died he was overcome with grief and decided to reform. He found his vehicle in Shakerism. When he was converted he stood before the congregation and repudiated his evil life. In doing so he proceeded to strip himself of his clothing, one garment at a time, and with each one that he cast off he described and confessed some sin. The majority of those that he mentioned were cases of adultery. Ultimately he was naked, because "this is the way we come into the world, clean and innocent." The members of the congregation were embarrassed. They hung their heads in shame for him, and a few left the church.

This was not the last time that such a dramatization of rebirth took place. A few years ago a Nisqually woman imitated Riddle, though not to the point of exposing herself indecently. She had previously enjoyed a frivolous life and was very fond of dancing. At her conversion she cast off her dancing shoes, her party dress, and the tawdry ornaments that she wore. This manner of symbolically expressing a renewal of life may have been exhibited in other cases besides these two.

There are numerous special instances in which an individual has felt that he must perform some private ritual or satisfy some personal obligation as a result of conversion. Willie Yucton, Sylvester's brother, was a young man when the shaking part of the religion began. He was a frequent visitor at Slocum's home and had attended several meetings before he received the power. This experience was preceded by an illness of an undetermined character. He was helping his father slash timber for a white man when he fell unconscious.

He was taken to his house and put to bed where he remained for several days. As he lay there in a feverish state he began to shake and at the same time had a vision. "It looked like a Catholic picture," and a voice come out of it telling him that he must get out of bed and go tell John Slocum that "he was making a mistake." Just what the mistake was he did not know. He hoped for further enlightenment but it did not come. Nonetheless he was worried and was torn between the compulsion to obey the voice and his shyness about "going to the headman who knew more" than he did. As a consequence he did nothing about the charge, but he did join the Shakers.

Olson obtained the following account of the conversion of a Quinault girl: "My daughter C. (an adopted white girl) used to love to dance at parties. Some other girls were jealous because the boys liked her so much and they placed poison in her food. She was sent to the hospital in Aberdeen. She vomited blood continually and the doctors finally gave her up. One night she felt something shake the bed. Three nights this happened. The fourth night she saw a man standing by her bed. He had long hair, a face like a woman's, and was dressed in a long white robe with a yellow band across his chest. He looked at her and said, 'I am Jesus from heaven. Your time to leave this world has not yet come. You will live to see the girl who poisoned you suffer more than you have. You must send a man to Quinault Lake to get water from a creek which never runs dry. There he is to get water from a quiet pool. Do not get the water in the riffles, for there it is full of worms. That water is my blood. When you drink, it will become good blood in you. Now I am leaving this gown and its band for you to wear. It is to be your helper, and you will get a song.' J. C. and a white man got the water as directed. C. drank a half glass. What remained in the glass soon turned red. The doctors (white) marvelled at it. A Catholic priest pronounced it the blood of Jesus. In a year

C. was well. She never went to (social) dances afterward, for in her vision she saw that dance floors were three inches deep with blood. On Sundays she wears the gown and ribbon band to church and sings the song which came to her." [5]

In 1913 Boston Bill, a prominent Tulalip Shaker, received several special injunctions regarding his personal behavior. A circumstantial account of his vision is not available. However, Reverend Paul Gard, the Catholic missionary for that reservation, gave a brief notice of the event in these words: "This very year in Tulalip the Lord appeared to Boston Bill and ordered him to let his hair grow, to wear only white garments, forbade him to till the ground, to travel on a steamer or by rail—to which ordinances Boston Bill added on his own hook, to abandon his family and to 'hear confessions'; and that spider got some flies, too!" [6] The stipulations with regard to the length of Boston Bill's hair, the tilling of the soil, and travel by modern conveyances are clearly parts of a whole. They are reflections of the anti-white reaction that was aroused at the time among the Tulalip Shakers as a result of the attempts to suppress them. The gift or privilege of hearing confessions, on the other hand, was in the familiar Shaker tradition inaugurated by Slocum and continued by Louis, Riddle, and others.

John Slocum himself received the charge to travel among Indians outside his own group and spread the message of salvation that he had obtained. His reticence caused him to make only halfhearted attempts to accomplish this mission. Not so for Louis, who appears to have accepted a similar responsibility. In 1903 Joe Riddle also received the call to go abroad and proselytize. Enoch Abraham agreed to accompany him, and this was the reason for their visits to Neah Bay, Jamestown, and other villages in northern Washington during that year. Riddle's mission was to preach and convert and, as it happened, to attempt to rectify the errors in faith and ritual that he encountered. The details of his vision and his accomplishments are not at hand. Other men about whom more is known have experienced the same missionizing compulsion in later years. Silas Heck was one.

Heck's religious experience has been more complex and mystical than most. He first became a Shaker in 1895 but only outwardly as measured by his later outlook. He attended meetings and shook like the rest but without any inward conviction of its worth or understanding of its meaning. He gave no thought to it and had not aligned it with his attitude toward life. Then, in 1918, his uncle died, and he attended the funeral. He "did not feel especially sorry," but the mourning of others upset him. It was a cold day, and when he returned to his home he went directly to the heating stove in the living room and began to pat the pipe to warm his hands. Suddenly he could not control himself. His hands began to shake in characteristic fashion and his body started to jerk. This was about four o'clock in the afternoon, and he continued to shake until midnight, stimulated by the encouragement of others who were called in immediately. Phases of high physical excitation alternated with intervals of prayer and other verbal eruptions during which he sorrowfully reproached himself with all his faults and shortcomings. The mood which predominated was one of gloomy foreboding and despondency: "Every time the clock ticks I come nearer to death; every day my life gets shorter; every step I take I come nearer to Jesus. Soon I will have to face God. All these years my heart has been small; it is getting smaller, shrinking all the time, closing out my life. . . ."

From that time on Silas Heck was a "true Shaker." His emotional crisis brought with it a more reflective cast of mind and a deeper understanding of the nature of things. It marked his real conversion. He had his shake, with its locus somewhere near his heart, which brought to him a new enlightenment and told him what he must do. In addition to being a good Christian his shake required that he do several specific things. First of all, he was to be baptized in running water,

an obligation which he fulfilled by going to the Chehalis
River near his home every day for a year to duck his head
three times. Then he was to confess his sins every day between
two and three o'clock in the morning "when the day was
young and clean." For the next three years, as his conviction
grew, other acts were demanded of him. Foremost among
them was the call to undertake a missionizing tour.

He set out upon his journey in the winter of 1921. His
shake had told him that it must be a sacrifice and a hardship,
and consequently that he was not to ask for any favors en
route. He must travel on foot. Carrying a pack on his back
he went first to Tahola, where he preached for a few days.
On his way north to the Queets Reservation he became discouraged. There was no road and scarcely any path. The
forest was a thick tangle of vegetation and difficult to pene-
trate. Downcast, he stopped at a creek and seriously contem-
plated turning back. At that moment he had what appears
to have been a mystic experience. Of it he said, "I can't explain it to you. Words can't tell about it. It came like a
lightning flash, and for a second it was wonderful. What I
saw was a beautiful thing. It was like a scene in a beautiful
land." He did not lose consciousness and the sensation passed
in an instant. The occurrence strengthened him immeasur-
ably, for his shake reproached him for his feckless heart:
"Now, see what you would have missed if you had turned
back!"

From the Queets Reservation Heck went on to Mud Bay
and then to Potlatch. He did not ask for rides, but on the
way to Potlach a white man picked him up in a car. This appeared as an act of divine intervention, since by the man's
conversation it was made clear that he did not make a practice of picking up strangers on the highway. From Puget
Sound Heck went on to the Yakima Reservation. He visited
Toppenish and Pasco, then went south to the Warm Springs
Reservation in Oregon. There his friends urged him not to try
to walk the distance to the Klamath Reservation in the winter

because it was too far and food was hard to get. He insisted on going, so the Shakers took up a collection of thirty dollars to send him to Klamath Falls by train. Although he could not ask for such help the Chiloquin congregation likewise took up a collection, amounting to seventy-eight dollars, to send him home.

This trip, however, did not fully discharge his obligations. It gradually came to him that he must make another journey sometime in the future when the call comes, this time to the Colville Reservation in northern Washington and to the Nez Perce in Lapwai, Idaho. Speaking of this in 1943, he said, "When the time comes I will leave everything—cows, wife, property—everything. I will take two or three of the faithful with me—just the ones that think only of Jesus. I have been ready to go any time, but maybe it is too late. Maybe I have done something wrong and the call will be given to somebody else."

His shake has also revealed to him the meaning of faith and other mysteries, including the necessary condition of things at the second coming of Christ and the meaning of death. Through it he has learned that there is no hell, that death is a total destruction of the body but not of the soul, and that the world is composed of "two elements—like night and day, life and death—that are always working against each other." Finally, he has been charged with a last obligation with respect to this knowledge: when the spirit moves him he is to sit down and write out what his shake has told him for the enlightenment of others.

By far the greatest number of people who have become Shakers attest to their faith in the religion because of cures that they have either witnessed or experienced. There is apparently no limit to credulity on this score. The claims of healers have expanded with their knowledge of physiology, medicine, and the malfunctions of the human body. By premise the cure is a miracle, and the most spectacular and well remembered cases are those which clearly demonstrate

this quality. Nowadays this is measured by a comparison between the limits of modern medical practice and Shaker healing: typically the faithful heal and are relieved of complaints
that have been given up as hopeless by white physicians. Frequently this results from the fact that physicians are unable
to determine the real cause of the ailment due to its supernatural character, hence they are powerless to effect a cure.

Any disorder may be treated by shaking. Instances have
already been described in passing of alleged successes with
blindness, rupture, goiter, the smoking habit, influenza, pneumonia, Bright's disease, dropsy, and smallpox. There are
many others. One of Peter Heck's sons has been afflicted with
partial paralysis for eight years. He is unable to take care of
himself, but he receives temporary relief from the treatments
that the Shakers give him periodically in his home. Once
there was a Hupa man who had had an unhealing sore on his
leg for twenty years. The government doctors at the hospital
could do nothing about it. Some of his friends prevailed upon
him to let a visiting group of Shakers from Washington work
over him. He agreed, although he could no longer walk and
had to be carried to the church. After three nights of treatment his leg was well enough that he wanted to stand alone.
He was not permitted to, but the next morning he was found
chopping wood.

As previously mentioned, C. J. Johns has assisted at two
difficult child births. The first time he was called upon by
the Shaker relatives of a woman in labor. After several of
those attending her had begun to shake, Johns placed his
hands at her sides and drew them over her belly with a twisting motion so that the child was soon delivered with ease.
Another time he and his helpers were called to treat a woman
who was ill with rheumatism. After shaking over her all night
the party sat down to breakfast. Johns was asked to say the
blessing. As he prayed "it came to" him that some one else
needed his help. When he had finished breakfast he therefore
told his companions, "My brothers, we have some more work

to do. I don't know what it is, but I want you to help me."
They began to ring their bells and shake around the table.
After a while Johns's hands led him out of the kitchen and
into another room where he had not been before. The daughter of the sick woman lay on a bed there. Unknown to him
she was expecting a child, but it was overdue and the family
had been contemplating sending for a physician. Johns's
hands were drawn to her sides, which they proceeded to pat
and rub. It was not long after this treatment that the baby
was born.

Again, in 1942, Johns was called to help a woman and her
new born baby. Both were ill, the woman suffering from the
effects of a difficult delivery. Johns and his party of Shakers
worked over her for two nights and she improved. However,
on the afternoon of the second day a neighbor came to see
how she was, and from that time on she suffered a relapse.
The visitor, Johns explained, was a shaman, and she was envious of the Shakers' success. She therefore "covered the sick
woman over with her devil power," and laid the blame on
the Shakers.

Jimmy Jack's first experience with Shakerism was at Siletz
in 1926. At one of the meetings that he attended as a spectator a young man under power approached him and allowed
his shaking hands to play over Jack's chest. Afterward the
young man announced that he had seen blood clots there,
and that Jack "was in danger." The latter was amazed at
this diagnosis, for he had been suffering from a disorder of
the lungs that caused him to spit blood occasionally for seventeen years. The young man did not say specifically that he had
done anything about the blood clots that he saw, but Jack
never afterwards had any trouble with his chest.

Willis Norton, a former Hupa minister, had a similarly
critical experience that immediately altered his life. Previous
to his conversion he had been an inveterate smoker, always
carrying a pipe and a package of tobacco in his pocket. Like
many others, he attended some of the first Shaker meetings

at Hoopa out of curiosity. At one of the meetings a Yurok woman shook in front of him for a long time with her arms extended as if she were struggling to reach him. She did not touch him, but finally a second woman approached and her shaking hand led directly to the pocket where he kept his tobacco. She extracted the package, turned toward the prayer table, and held it out as she prayed. Finally she returned it; but that night Norton felt for the first time in many years that he did not want to smoke before going to bed. The next day he found that he still lacked the urge. He questioned one of the visiting Shakers and was told that whenever he felt the desire for tobacco he should cross himself instead and the craving would vanish. He did this, and within three days he had no use for tobacco. He decided that the power possessed by the Shakers must be a true and wonderful thing and that he must join them.

There are many instances of Shakers healing an individual through the restoration of his soul. Ghosts might be the cause of the misfortune; or a fall; or a fright; or the enmity of a shaman. The idea is not well understood by the Yakima or by some of the Siletz people, and it is completely alien to the Californians. The Quinault were fully conversant with it as the following example shows. "Three years ago Mrs. T. S. had an operation. She grew steadily weaker and finally was taken home, nearly dead. She could not even speak. That night the Shakers shook over her until morning. The next night they did likewise, and she began to improve. The third night Mrs. C. S. found her soul in the road in front of H. S.'s house. It had fallen out on the way to the hospital when the truck went over a bump. The Shakers put the soul back and every night kept up the shaking. She mended rapidly and in a year was entirely well." [7]

Pat Kane, a Klamath Indian, once cured his friend Hassenblower of the same complaint. Hassenblower was not a Shaker at the time but he appealed to some of the Klamath members for relief from an illness of undetermined cause.

Of this Kane says: "He asked Billy Moore, Coley Ball, Jim Jackson and me, and Susan why he was sick. They didn't answer. They shook three nights, pretty hard. They stopped during the day, and shook only at night. They finished after three nights. They didn't tell anything.

"H[assenblower] asked, 'Did you find out what made me sick?' I took him outside. 'Those fellows up there couldn't answer because they couldn't see anything. I want to tell you what I saw, what you got.' I told him. 'That's right, brother, Mr. Kane. Tell me; I don't care if I die. I am not afraid. Tell me,' he said. 'Now I am going to tell close,' I said. 'All right, tell me.' 'I shook three nights in there in the house,' I told him; 'I finished last night. You remember what I shake. You don't belong in this house; it is Jim Jackson's house (near Chiloquin). Your house is way down at Yainax. When you were asleep at night in your house, you saw ghosts. While you slept they came; lots of people came. I tell you exactly what it is. That way the ghost caught your life; they hold your life. That's why you are sick. Your own brothers, sisters, and children like you. That's why they want to catch your life (hokis). I couldn't make you well in here; this is J[im] J[ackson]'s house. Even though there are lots of Shakers here they can't make you well. I show you the best way to find it (your sickness). Maybe we make it so that for several days or a week you will feel good, but then the sickness will come again. If I take all the Shakers to your home and we shake there, then in a little while we will drive out the ghosts. You can't get well in J[im] J[ackson]'s house. Your sickness is in your house; because there are lots of ghosts there. I will try my best to save you up there.'

"Hassenblower listened to everything I said. 'Do you understand?' 'Yes,' he said; 'All right, brother, then you know my sickness?' 'My belief, God, Jesus, up there tell me why you are sick. They showed me; told me. It wasn't me.' He said, 'You tell me the truth. Already you found it for me. That's what I want to know. You tell me all good: I believe it.'

"Hassenblower said, 'I was sick. At Klamath Falls, the (white) doctor said I would die. Lots of ghosts came in my gate; they came in and filled up the room. I looked at them; "Where do you come from, people? What's the matter?" They didn't say anything. I looked at them: I didn't sleep. They were all Indians. So many times they came up in there; in the day, not at night. Pretty soon I got up. "What do you want, so many coming?" I said. They didn't answer. I talked to them. They went back, all of them. They went through the gate without opening it, just as they had come. What you told me was true. God is a good help; you find out my sickness. Other Shakers could not help me, but you (Pat) were the only one who could tell me.' Then we all come home: we needed no more cure for him." [8]

Silas Heck's wife, Alice, lived at the Cowlitz mission as a girl and was raised a Catholic. When the early interest in Shakerism was at its height, she joined the cult. Later on she returned to her Catholic faith but with full sympathy for the Shakers. They have helped her several times. Once she was quite sick, feverish and delirious. She had a nightmare in which she found herself being pursued by her dead aunt. She tried to escape by crawling under a fence, but she got stuck and her aunt caught up with her and held her fast. When she awoke she told this to her family. Her mother was a confirmed Shaker and she at once made preparations for a healing ceremony. As it progressed she discerned that the nightmare was indeed a fact: her daughter's soul was being held captive by the ghost of her aunt who wanted her to join the dead. To prevent this she alternately pleaded with the dead aunt to release Alice and shook, making brushing motions with her hands to push the aunt away. The next morning Alice was well and happy.

Later, after she was married to Silas, Alice had other encounters with death and was saved by the shaking power. Upon one of these occasions she had just returned from a visit with some Yakima relatives. It was during the winter and on her way home she caught cold. As she lay fitfully sleeping it seemed to her that she was not at home in bed but in the Chehalis Shaker church. Its floor was covered with a foot or more of water upon which scraps of food and paper plates were floating. On the benches around the walls sat a number of dead women, eating and talking unconcernedly. Alice was clinging to the prayer table, afraid that she would be washed away in the swirling water. She awoke crying out to Silas to help her. He and another man immediately arranged to shake over her. When the power descended upon this companion he discovered that "Alice" (i.e., her soul) was in the church: "she" had gone past her house on her return from her visit and had stopped in the church, drawn there by the ghosts of the dead. He therefore proceeded to "draw her back" with his hands. In this way he was able to restore her soul to her body.

Silas was able to do the same thing upon another occasion. His wife had been out picking berries when she returned to her home feeling unwell. He decided to cure her himself. As he proceeded to sing, pray, and shake, it was revealed to him that Alice was ill because she had fallen down while picking berries and at that moment "she" had left her body. His cupped hands were pulled in the direction of the spot where she had fallen. Soon he felt "her" nestling in his hands, warm, soft, and gently moving. He carefully replaced "her" in her body and immediately afterward she felt better.

In cases of this kind, according to Enoch Abraham, "You never know what you have in your hands, or what to do with it, until you pray." While this may be true, most Shakers are not concerned about the question. The interpretation of what has happened is left to the few who have a flair for it. Abraham himself had no clear ideas about curing except that it is accomplished by faith. One evening while he was shaking along with others in the Yakima church he felt something in his hands. He knew that it was good because it was soft and light. He therefore took it to a candle on the prayer table and warmed it. Then he just let it go. When the midnight intermission came a certain woman who disliked him charged him with soul theft, saying, "Where is my grandchild that you took away?" With that his wife, who was sitting next to the woman, began to shake. Reaching over the woman's head she cupped her hands together and started to move around the hall. She stopped in front of the woman's grandchild, hesitated, and then moved on. Coming to another child she made the motions of restoring a soul to its body. Later she explained that she had caught the "breath" of someone over the woman's head, but it turned out to belong not to the woman's grandchild but to some other child that the woman had hoped to kill.

Another time Abraham and his wife were working over a sick man when she got something in her hands. He took it from her because it made her jerk violently. As his hands clamped tightly over it he was pulled around so vigorously that he was almost thrown to the floor. Eventually he mastered it and "threw it out into the grave." When the shaking was over his wife told the patient that she had pulled from his body the tamanawus of a shaman who had shot his spirit into him in the hope of killing him. She named the shaman and described the circumstances under which the patient had taken ill. When asked for verification the patient admitted that what she said was true.

Some individuals are not only prone to give a spiritualistic interpretation to most illnesses, but, like Abraham's wife, are quick to attribute them to the hatred of an enemy. C. J. Johns's diagnoses are frequently of this character. During an influenza epidemic he and his wife were treating her grandson who was very low with the disease. While shaking over him Johns had a vision of a large rattlesnake coiled up in the corner of the sick room "calling for the boy to be its master." Johns knew by this token that some shaman with rattlesnake power had been employed to kill the boy and that it was too late to save him—as indeed it proved to be. Johns was also convinced that his wife's death was due to the spite of her enemies although the immediate cause was clearly an accident. She was badly burned when her clothes caught fire from an improvised stove that she was using for cooking in the hop fields. Although suffering from third degree burns on her back she refused to go to the hospital and her husband attempted to treat her with applications of Unguentine and the tannic acid solution that he obtained from the government physician. Eventually it was clear to both of them that she could not live. And then "it came to" Johns that the reason for her misfortune was that one of the women who had worked with her in the hop field, pretending to be her friend, was in reality an enemy with evil power who had "covered her back" and caused her skirt to catch fire. Questioned about her fellow workers, Mrs. John finally agreed that one of her companions did seem strange occasionally, although she had thought nothing of it at the time. Her husband then recalled that he had not been entirely in sympathy with her going to pick hops. He did not know why, but he "was afraid that something might go wrong."

The gift of preternatural insight was from the inception of shaking an important aspect of the new power and one of the principal reasons for accrediting it. Whereas John Slocum proposed to heal without a diagnosis by a laying on of hands accompanied by prayer, the Shakers were able to see the cause of the sickness which they treated. Their powers of discernment in matters pertaining to illness almost immediately began to manifest themselves in other contexts as well. It is not certain what part John Slocum played in this development. He foretold coming events, but it is not known whether he claimed the power before or after the introduction of shaking. At any rate, soon after Mary discovered the healing power all manner of hidden knowledge began to be revealed to those with the gift to know intuitively. And this gift has been less restricted than some of the others. Almost every Shaker has at some time claimed at least a modicum of clairvoyant power, not as a special gift but almost as a matter of course.

Many of the forecasts are mere forebodings or vague warnings; others have a particular reference. Some are exhibitionistic stunts intended to impress spectators; others are called forth in response to a demand, either private or group. Many are aimed at disclosing the insidious evils against which Shakerism contends: sins, shamans, animal spirits, and the devil. An equal number are intended as warnings against impending death or danger. Frequently they are trivial and inconsequential, contrived for purposes of display and not intended as guides to action. Some people are said to be able to divine one kind of thing and not another; a few stand out preeminently from the mass in all respects. Most Shakers give their dreams the same validity as the visions they have in the shaking trance without sensing the need to explain the identification of the two states of mind.

Among the earliest evidences of clairvoyant power that are remembered are certain descriptions by the Slocums of events transpiring at a distance. It is said by some that Mary was the first to be able to tell what was going on far away and that she revealed her ability at a meeting soon after news of shaking began to spread. She declared upon that occasion that Billy Clams would arrive at the meeting within a stipulated time and that he would be riding upon a certain horse, dressed in a particular manner, and carrying a hand bell.[9] He arrived as predicted, although no one knew that he planned to come or that he was aware that a meeting was being held.

John Slocum made similar predictions, but it is not definitely known whether they were subsequent to Mary's or preceded them. To convince skeptics he once told them that a certain individual was going to pay a call on him that day, that he was at that very moment saddling his horse, would arrive at three o'clock, and would say certain things. Events transpired as he had said. Again, at another time, one of his logging oxen strayed and was not to be found. John announced to his congregation that the ox had broken into the pasture of a certain white man who in anger had declared that he was going to sell the animal to pay for his broken fence. A doubting listener forthwith called upon the white man and found that Slocum had spoken the truth.

Aiyel was likewise credited with knowledge of impending events. While he was still minister of the small Yakima church his son failed to arrive from over the mountains for a scheduled visit with him. Aiyel announced to his congregation that he was going to discover the reason for this during the shaking to follow in the course of the meeting. At the end he disclosed that his son had been delayed because of a storm, that he was stopping with a certain friend en route, and that he would arrive two days hence. Needless to say, this proved to be the case.

The Shakers also very early demonstrated a flair for locating missing objects. Maggie Slocum, the oldest daughter of John and Mary, sought to impress Willie Yucton with the new faith by this means upon his first acquaintance with it. Yucton was visiting the Slocums at the time, and Maggie displayed her power by finding coins that she requested him to hide from her. With closed eyes and trembling hands she either induced shaking in herself or simulated it. In this state she twice found the coin that Yucton secreted in the room. Then he threw it out the open door into the yard. Her hands led her to his feet, "and kind of stopped there," but she finally followed them outside and picked up the coin. Later on Mary gave a comparable demonstration. Yucton was preparing to leave the house in search of a horse that had wandered off when she told him to wait. She began to shake, or pretended to, and as she did so one of her extended arms moved slowly around to point in a certain direction. The other arm soon followed and pointed the same way. Yucton set off in the indicated direction and found his horse.

Aiyel, the Kelso Shaker, gained a notable reputation for his abilities in locating lost objects. His talent for this kind of divination first brought him to the Yakima Reservation and stimulated a wide interest in the new religion there. His success in discovering the body of a man that had disappeared in the Yakima River led to subsequent appeals for similar assistance. He is said to have apprehended several thieves, among them a man who had stolen money from a woman in the Moxee hop fields and another on the Umatilla Reservation who had looted a house. Spier obtained an account of the latter episode from Mabel Teio in 1924. It is still well remembered by the Yakima Shakers. Spier's record is the fullest and is as follows:

"A [Umatilla] man came from the Pendleton reservation about sixteen or eighteen years ago [1906–1909] to get a Shaker to help him catch a thief. There were no Shakers there. He asked Aiyal, who was afraid to go alone. They might harm him if he picked out a thief. He came to Alec Teio because he was the head elder of the Shaker church. So Teio and Mrs. Teio, Aiyal's wife, and two local men went.

"There was a French half-breed who had been stealing extensively and cleverly. When he got there Aiyal prayed: he saw this man as though in a picture: a tall slender man and a short woman with light hair. He also saw a long house with a rough shed behind it. First he saw another man. They went to this house, a white man's. He was angry and would not let them in, so they went away. Then Aiyal woke in the night and heard the sound of a wagon driving. It was a vision of this man escaping. So he told the Indian policeman in a nearby house. Early next morning they started. The others rode or drove but Aiyal walked. The (holy) spirit made it possible for him to keep up with them.

"They came to a gate. Aiyal held out his hand and it seemed as though someone was leading him in. They opened the gate for him. They reached the long house and shed and peered in. Everything was disarranged. They heard wheels; then the man and his wife, who fitted the vision, drove up.

The man was angry. He said to the Umatilla man whose things had been stolen, 'I can shake like that (like Aiyal), too.' But his wife said, 'Yes, you stole it. You had better open the house.' He did, but he was angry. So Teio said, 'You had better sit down.' They found the stolen dishes but no blankets and beads. They told the woman it would be all right if he [her husband] restored the stolen goods; he would not be punished. Aiyal had a vision that the sacks of beads had been taken by another man. A year later the Umatilla [man] found the beads on his doorstep." [10]

Shaking is still resorted to for the purpose of discovering the whereabouts of people and things. About ten years ago the son of Ida James, a Yurok Shaker, disappeared. After a week had elapsed and nothing was heard of him she decided to apply to a shaman who had a reputation for locating missing people. Using some of the boy's clothing he divined that the owner was still alive and visiting with a family near Orick. His charge for this service and the assurance that he gave was fifteen dollars. Mrs. James, however, was not satisfied, and as her anxiety grew she decided to test the assertion that anyone with shaking power could see things for himself. When the power fell upon her she did indeed have a vision, but it was disturbing: she saw a dead body, presumably her son's, with the sheriff standing guard over it so that she could not approach it. She became hysterical and could not stop shaking. She was seized with intermittent fits of trembling for several days. Six weeks later her son's body was washed ashore near Cresent City.

In sequel, the Shakers were summoned to hold the funeral service. While they shook over the body, Mrs. James went outside the room to prepare the scented water that the Yurok aboriginally believed to be requisite for the purification of bereaved relatives. When the rest of the Shakers discovered this they were indignant. They stopped their ritual and left immediately, declaring that only Christ, not water, could cleanse and protect them.

Much of the preternatural insight of the Shakers has been directed toward the exposure of the hidden forces of evil as they are understood in Shaker ideology. Almost exclusively the evils that are envisioned are those which threaten life and limb or lead to sinful ways, particularly those which encourage drinking, smoking, and gambling. It is unnecessary to elaborate upon the statement that the preponderance of revelations have for their purpose the discernment of disease, the exposure of shamans, and the persecution of witches. These are the inveterate enemies of the Shakers who avow intuitive knowledge of their presence and the danger that they forebode for the unwary or the unseeing. But Shakers also claim an unfailing sense for the sinner and and the shackles that bear him down. It is said that no one who smokes can conceal the fact from Shakers under power, and although many times a skeptic has thought to test them by secreting tobacco on his person before coming to church, such a person is always found out. An addiction to liquor is likewise transparent. At one of the first meetings among the Yurok a woman under power claimed later that she had a vision of Robert Spott with empty whisky jugs and wine bottles hanging from his lips. Gamblers are sometimes similarly embarrassed or openly accused. Upon the occasion of a revival meeting among the Hupa one of the men under power led the others out of the church to a neighboring spot where he dug up the gambling sticks of a local wastrel. Occasionally the violation of other dictates has been drawn into the orbit of Shaker omniscience, as when it was alleged that Louis intuitively knew when a penitent omitted a sin at his confession, and when Mary knew whether the water had been polluted in the creek where she received her inspiration.

The forecasting of things to come is usually in an ominous vein. The predictions are generic and freely applicable. Willis Norton often had visions of death under power or in a dream. Sometimes he saw an automobile skid and capsize over an embankment; or some unidentified person pull a pistol and

shoot another equally unknown adversary; or someone drowning in the river. Then he knew that "soon, but not right
away," someone would be killed. Annie James has had comparable premonitions. Not many years ago she attended a
meeting at the Skokomish church on Sunday evening. The
power came to her with such force that she could not stop
shaking. The rest of the participants continued with her until she was finally exhausted. But during her seizure she saw
that the door of the church was closed and could not be
opened. That signified to her that before long someone
would die—a prediction that was fully justified within the
year. Stella Brown, an ardent Hupa Shaker, had several
dreams or shaking visions of a coffin, sometimes with reference to a particular family. Thus she knew that a death was
not far off, but rarely did she tell anyone in advance save
her own family for fear of causing anxiety or trouble.

Mrs. Case was one of the Siletz Shakers who helped to introduce the religion to the Yurok in 1927. During one of the
meetings upon that occasion she had a vision of death. After
she had recovered from shaking she announced that someone would die before three o'clock in the morning two days
hence. It did happen that a white man was drowned sometime during the night that she had designated. The excitement among the Shakers was in consequence so alarming
that Jackson, the Siletz elder, felt obliged to dampen their
enthusiasm. At the next meeting he warned the Yurok novices
against the excesses into which their ardor was likely to lead
them. He cautioned that Mrs. Case's revelation was an unusual manifestation of power. Not everyone should expect
it to act that way nor even try to bring it to bear upon such
things. One person in twenty, he said, might do what she
had done; but "the real work is different." More important
was its saving grace and the things that it promised here and
in the hereafter.

Most predictions have a nonsubjective reference. Occasionally a Shaker has premonitions about his own fate or that

of his family, as in the case of a Quinault woman in 1925. "All last year I felt sad," she said. "Every time I prayed I cried, and often I cried between times. My helper [shaking power] seemed to tell me that something was going to happen, but I didn't know what. Then two weeks before O. S. was drowned my crying stopped. My heart no longer cried. When he died I knew why I had been sorrowful, because his mother and I are cousins." [11]

The dream character of some Shaker forebodings is shown by Mabel Teio's diagnosis of her own illness. "Once I was very sick for months," she said. "I had a pain in my left chest. I prayed. In the morning I was all right but in the afternoon I had to lie down. My husband was ditch foreman. Elsie [her younger sister] was a young girl. In the evening I slept. I dreamed a woman gave me wild huckleberries. A person whom I could not see told me, 'The food she gives you is not good. She is angry because you are making a ditch here. You would get sick, perhaps with consumption. Place the berries on a white cloth in front of you. Pray and the berries will be all right.' That was a woman shaman who had given us the berries. I was not acquainted with the Yakima; she was one.

"Soon I dreamed of our oldest sister who had died long before. She was standing. She said, 'Look at yourself.' I looked down at my breast and saw a person's face with closed eyes. It was a snake biting me, someone's tamanawis [spirit]. So I held up my arms; 'Oh, sister, I want you to get it out.' She said, 'Sister, you have to make up your mind. People give you that sickness: all the shamans who are against your husband for building that ditch here.' I did not see how she did it but she pulled it out. It pained. The snake hung over my shoulder. I told her to throw it into the water so it could not come back. It could not swim, being a snake. So she swung it around and threw it in. I was crazy: I sweated and sweated. I called my relatives. We looked under my dress— nothing; in the bed—nothing. It was the sickness.

"Pretty soon I crawled to our tent. I told my sister Elsie to bring the berries. So I put them on a white cloth and prayed. Then they were all right and we did not get sick from them. I told my sister, 'You be quiet for a while: I want to pray.' After I prayed I told her I thought I would be all right again. I changed my clothes entirely. It always hurt. I told my husband when he returned that I was saved now: someone had put the tamanawis there. I got better from that time without any (white) doctor or medicine. The sister I dreamed of had a white cloth about her, not a dress, and long hair. I think she helped me like the angels: that accounts for the white cloth. It is my religion that saved me." [12]

Perhaps it is only human nature that many of the older Shakers regard the modern manifestations of the spirit as decadent. They look upon the past as the golden age of shaking and speak regretfully of the trivial character of contemporary cures and predictions. They say that "the power is getting weaker," thinking of it somewhat as a reservoir of energy that is gradually failing. Or they attribute the decline to aberrations and weaknesses in the faith of contemporary members. Annie James used to be able to foresee the future clearly, but now nothing important "comes through." This she said was because she worried too much about her soldier son, and because "everything is getting mixed up"; that is, there is contention, uncertainty, and alteration in Shaker practice and theory. In the same way, Willis Norton said that "there are only a few John Slocum Shakers left. Nowadays people don't get power, or they don't get it good. Too many people are turning into white men."

With this gilding of the past the best remembered figures in Shaker history assume greater stature. During the summer of 1943 the partially decomposed corpse of a man was discovered in the hills near White Swan. Officials were unable to identify the man or explain the circumstances of his death. A Yakima Shaker volunteered that if Aiyel were living he would have no trouble answering these questions. The capabilities of Louis and others in the early days of the movement are similarly magnified. The younger people accept these elaborations without question. But they are primarily concerned with the power of the faith as they know it, and this is sufficiently impressive. The age of heroes may have gone, but the workings of the faith are still evident enough for all ordinary needs.

✙

SEVEN ✙ **Ritual Elements**

✙

THE CHRISTIAN CROSS is a prominent feature of Shaker ritual. A large figure of the cross surmounts the belfry of most churches and occurs again as the central part of the setting for the altars. Crosses rise above Shaker cemeteries and appear on headstones. Smaller forms are to be found on every altar and on prayer tables in the homes of the devout. Ordinarily they do not hang upon the walls of either the church or the home; and Shakers do not wear them as necklace ornaments or as parts of rosaries. Customarily, those that are to be found in homes have been made of unfinished wood by their owners. They are, at the same time, candle holders. Nails or other crude clasps are affixed to hold the candles, one at the top of the upright and one at each end of the cross piece; or each cross makes an individual candlestick. These forms are quite plain and are considered to be sufficient for the need. In recent times some people have preferred to buy their crosses, and for this reason it is not uncommon to see crucifixes of glass, plastic materials, or polished wood in homes and churches. They also are made as candlesticks.

A few individuals have received special revelations regarding the cross. One person's shake told him to construct a form without the upper extension of the vertical arm and to place four candles upon the cross-piece in recognition of the

Father, the Son, the Holy Ghost, and some mystical entity about which he could not be very explicit. This was a gift or a help; and it had reference only, or primarily, to the cross that he uses in his home. Lans Kalapa, on the other hand, received a teaching that every Shaker should have a cross of cedar wood made in the conventional design with three candles along the top and that he, Kalapa, should either distribute such crosses to all the faithful or induce them to make their own. Later on, after his trouble with the Presbyterian missionary at Neah Bay, he received a countermanding teaching to the effect that all crosses should be destroyed, and he proceeded to advocate burning those that he had made.

Candles have acquired even more significance than have crosses. John Slocum used them in his original services, and they have ever since been a necessary appurtenance, both in the home and in the church. Almost from the beginning it became an article of faith to reject any other form of light during evening ceremonies. John Slocum called candlelight "the light of heaven"; others now refer to it as "the holy light," or "the purity light." Eells, describing Shaker practices near the end of the last century, wrote upon this subject: "They use candles both when they attempt to cure the sick and in their general service, eschewing lamps for fear of being easily tempted, as they believe coal-oil lights to be from Satan." The same attitude has been extended to gasoline lamps and electric lights; they are called "the devil's lights." Although most people employ one or the other of these more modern means of illuminating their homes, for religious services they must be dispensed with and replaced by candles.

The question of installing lamps in churches has inevitably come up. Several years ago some of the younger members of the Yakima church began to bring gasoline lamps to the meetings and hang them up for additional light during the services. There were protests; but Enoch Abraham worked out what he regarded as an acceptable compromise. He brought a storage battery and an automobile headlamp and set the lamp up for use only while people were entering the church and during the preaching. When the shaking began it was turned off. At a subsequent convention at Mud Bay the whole issue was discussed. Abraham stated that in his church the electric light didn't seem to bother the shaking, but the consensus of opinion was strongly opposed to the innovation. Perhaps not more than three or four churches now use electricity; those known to be so equipped are at White Swan (Yakima) and Concrete (Skagit).

Originally candles were used only as sources of illumination during religious services. For this purpose they rested in brackets on the walls of churches or homes or were set in holders on prayer tables. If there did not happen to be any provision for supporting them, the candles were held by individuals. Thus, when Enoch Abraham attended a meeting in a home at Oyster Bay in 1899 there was no prayer table available and no candle holders; instead, four men stood near the corners of the room, each holding two lighted candles. Not long after churches began to be built without interference, it became the custom to install chandeliers in them in addition to the simple bracket supports on their walls. Inside the building that was erected under the leadership of Mud Bay Sam just after he became "headman" an octagonal wooden framework was suspended from the ceiling to accommodate candles. They were fixed at intervals along this frame and along eight spokes radiating from a central point within it. It would seem that their total number was intended to be some multiple of four.[1] The Yakima, the Tulalip, and perhaps other churches now have similar lighting fixtures. At Tulalip a slightly arched strip of wood hangs from each quarter of the ceiling as a support for twelve candles. Then from the center there depends a circular frame circumscribing a cross; this is likewise set with twelve candles. In the Yakima church a wooden framework outlining a large cross is suspended a few feet from the ceiling over the central part of the floor. Nails set along the sides of the long arm provide holders for twelve candles, those on the short arm hold seven.

Soon after shaking was introduced by Mary Slocum candles began to be carried in the hands of the performers as an aid in the curing rites. It will be recalled that she placed them in the uplifted hands of her relatives as they stood around John's body upon that first occasion when he was supposed to have been cured by her. This became an established pattern. Equally early was the custom of placing lighted candles at the head and feet of the dead. Subsequent visions instituted other ritual manipulations involving candles. One person received the teaching directing healers to circle a patient three times holding lighted candles in their hands before putting them out and setting to work. Another received the gift to carry a candle in his hand as he searched for the illness because candlelight enabled him to see it. Others by the same sanction introduced the ideas of "putting the holy flame on the sore spot," either by "scooping" it on or by holding the hands over it, then laying them on the patient's body; of taking the sickness out with the hands and holding it over the flame; and of "warming" a recovered soul over a candle flame. The rationalizations for these actions are that the holy flame dissipates sin and sickness or forms a protection against them and that a lost soul gets cold and may also have been subjected to evil influences. All these practices are current, but the explanations can usually be elicited only from someone who remembers the original teaching by its sponsor.

Enoch Abraham advocated the teaching that before the prayer movement in a Sunday service both the leading man and the leading woman should carry a lighted candle during their circuit of the room. His enigmatic explanation was that "men and women are different." This precept has been followed; but with another of his teachings he was not so successful. He attempted to introduce the idea that a person under power could take a candle from the altar or prayer table and carry it around to "draw people to it," that is, convert them; for the flame is, like Christ, the "light of the world," and He draws people to Him. Joseph Sam, a Columbia River Shaker, objected to the removal of the altar candle, and Abraham acquiesced. He brought his own candle from home on later occasions, "but it didn't work." He said that he did not know why: "I guess if I prayed over it before I started it would be all right; but I never think what I am going to do beforehand."

Both Eells and Mooney have stated that Shakers placed lighted candles upon their heads during their ceremonies. No living Shaker could be found who knew anything about this; none had ever heard of it. The presumption is that it was a gift or a teaching of someone which was abandoned long ago. Mooney, however, has left a description of an elaboration upon this practice which does not seem in keeping with Shaker ideology or ritual. The Yakima members, he says, were called "blowers" by others of their tribe. "In doctoring a patient the 'blowers' usually gather around him in a circle to the number of about twelve, dressed in a very attractive ceremonial costume, and each wearing on his head a sort of crown of woven cedar bark, in which are fixed two lighted candles, while in his right hand he carries a small cloth, and in the left another lighted candle. By fastening screens of colored cloth over the candles the light is made to appear yellow, white, or blue. The candle upon the forehead is yellow, symbolic of celestial glory; that at the back of the head is white, typical of the terrestrial light, while the third is blue, the color of the sky." [2]

In addition to the mechanical difficulties involved in effecting this display, there are several considerations which render its attribution to the Shakers suspect. For one thing, color symbolism is entirely foreign to their thinking. So is elaborate preparation. Shaking is a rugged exercise. It does not rely upon ornamental fixtures and even derogates them.

Mooney's informants, moreover, were not Shakers. They were followers of the local offshoot of the Smohalla Cult, in which precisely this color association occurred. It therefore seems most likely that either they or Mooney confused the subject of their discussion. In any event, whether the wearing of lighted candles was ever a part of Shaker ritual or not, it has left no mark either in memory or ritual at the present time.

The candles that are used for all the purposes that have been described are of the plain tallow variety that can be bought in any general store. There is no ritual for their consecration, and they are given no special attention. Anyone may assume the responsibility of supplying them, and there are usually a few partially used ones to be found on church altars. The candles themselves are without sacred connotations, but their light has mystical properties.

The bells used by Shakers are the most striking—and to some observers the most incongruous—feature of their ceremonies. They are ordinarily made of brass, four to six inches in diameter, and have a wooden handle that will fit the full male hand. They are of the type once used in rural districts for calling children into the schoolhouse. During curing ceremonies, and throughout certain phases of other rites, they are rung continuously and as loudly as possible in unison by volunteers. Women do not swing them. Any number of men may assist in this accompaniment to the singing and shaking. Bell ringers need not be Shakers, and often young boys offer their services just because they like it. They hold a bell in each hand, grasping it like a club. Keeping their elbows bent, they proceed to bring the bells up and down in front of them and at the same time stamp the rhythm with their heels as heavily as their enthusiasm dictates. As the fervor spreads, the noise rises in a deafening crescendo. The floor resounds and vibrates with the added tread of the Shakers, and after an hour or more of this mass movement the walls themselves seem to pulsate to the rhythm.

Most churches have one or more pairs of bells that have

been donated to it by some member. They are kept on or near the altar. In addition, practically every Shaker who takes his religion seriously has two bells of his own that he keeps at home and takes with him to the meetings. No formality is involved in acquiring or keeping them. Normally they are placed upon prayer tables along with their owner's crosses and candles when not in use. Devout Shakers often grow attached to their bells because of the associations which they have, but a mystical attitude toward them is either lacking or is so faint and unformalized that it is not apparent. It is not uncommon for an owner's bells to be placed upon his grave at death; and a few people have had the bell figure incised upon the headstones of their dead Shaker relatives.

Besides their function as an accompaniment to the stamping of feet, bells are also employed to mark the divisions of a ceremony. For this purpose only one bell is used, and it is swung over the arc of the upper quarter of a man's forward reach; only rarely does the leader of the service drop it into the lower quarter. The minister summons the congregation into the church in this way, and he indicates the beginning or the end of each subsequent ritual movement with the same signal. John Slocum used a hand bell for these purposes in conducting his original services. There was therefore one in his home upon the occasion of his cure by Mary. She gave it to her brother Isaac with instructions to ring it while she prayed and wailed. As a result the hand bell came to be used as a continuous accompaniment to the shaking exercises in addition to its function as a signal to mark the phases of a ritual. It also acquired another meaning. Of the Shakers of 1890 Eells wrote: "Especially do they use bells, which are rung over the person where the sickness is supposed to be. The others present use their influence to help in curing the sick one, and so imitate the attendants on an Indian doctor, getting down upon their knees on the floor and holding up their hands, with a candle in each hand, sometimes for an hour. They believe that by so holding up their hands the man

who is ringing the bell will get the sickness out more easily
than he otherwise would." [3]

As this quotation implies, someone had the inspiration or
teaching that the hand bell when rung close to a patient
would draw the sickness out. This is not a prevalent concept
today, but it does appear sporadically. Jimmy Jack, for example, claimed that when a pain was difficult to extract,
ringing a bell close to the spot where it was localized would
facilitate its removal by the hands of other workers.

Shaker churches now have small belfries. The Slocum
church did not have this feature; but the one built by Louis
on Mud Bay in 1892 had a small steeple surmounted by a
cross to accommodate a large bell that was paid for mainly
by a contribution of Jack Slocum's wife. It was principally
because of this investment that the church came to be regarded as the property of the Slocum family at the death of
Louis. Bells of this kind are used, as in Christian churches,
to summon the faithful to worship. They are rung three times
at approximately fifteen minute intervals just before the meeting begins. They are sounded again at the conclusion of the
service. Normally the belfry is directly above the altar, so the
bell cord hangs just to one side of it.

The term altar is not used by the Shakers; they employ the
word "prayer table" to designate the fixture that has a comparable function. It is a plain four-legged wooden table that
stands before the large cross at the end of the church opposite the entrance. It is covered with a white cloth upon which
rest the hand bells and the candle holders. When not in use
these articles are ordinarily covered with another white cloth.
They should be kept on the prayer table and not elsewhere;
and, according to majority opinion, no other objects should
be placed upon it.

In recent times, flowers, both real and imitation, have
made their appearance on prayer tables. By 1942 they were
to be seen in the Tulalip, Yakima, and other large churches.
In the past this innovation has encountered some vigorous

opposition. One Sunday evening in 1934 a Siletz elder severely berated a woman member of the congregation who persisted in putting "brush" on the prayer table before their meetings. God, he said, intended that the table should be kept "clean." Again, at a convention held at Tahola a few years ago, a man from British Columbia protested against imitation flowers, saying that if flowers are going to be used at all "they should be real, God's own, not made by man; because if we use false flowers we will be like that, with false hearts and bad minds."

The antipathy toward the use of flowers for altar decoration, together with the fact that they do not appear in other ritual contexts, throws doubt upon the authenticity of another of Mooney's statements. Speaking of the Shakers, his Yakima informant apparently told him that "Frequently also they carry in their hands or wear on their heads garlands of roses and other flowers of various colors, yellow, white and blue being the favorite, which they say represent the colors of objects in the celestial world." [4] If this usage ever existed, contemporary Shakers have forgotten completely about it. Any question about it mystifies them.

Protests have also been made about other extraneous items on prayer tables. Once while under power Enoch Abraham was inspired to correct their abuse. His power made him look at his left hand, as though reading what to do. He was led to follow his right hand toward the table where it came upon a woman's belt, "which should not have been there"; then to a picture of Jesus hanging on the wall, from which his hands "brushed the dust"; then to a bell which rested on the bench to the left of the table, "where it should not be." He made no teaching of these revelations because he was "too bashful," but the implication is clear. Alex Teio was minister of the Yakima church at the time, and he was accustomed to place his watch on the table so that he could bring the meeting to a close promptly at twelve o'clock. Abraham likewise perceived that this was wrong, and, while still not making a teaching of it, he unobtrusively removed the watch

on several occasions. His explanation was that the prayer table "should be clean, like our hearts." He knew that his inspirations were authentic because "we do not study what we
are going to do in advance; the power just shows us."

Every practicing Shaker is expected to have a prayer table
in his home. Slocum made use of one, and he was followed
by Louis and other prominent men. At present most Shakers have them. If it is at all possible the table should be placed
against the east wall of the living room. Sometimes the shape
of the room or other requirements make some other disposition advisable. In its construction and furnishing this table
does not differ from the one found in church. Ordinarily
two, or preferably three, L-shaped wooden brackets are fastened to the wall above it to receive candles. Rarely, a large
cross is to be found against the wall behind it. Frequently
it is provided with three hand bells and a three-candle arrangement.

Serious Shakers feel it their duty to pray at the table at
least twice a day: immediately before retiring and immediately on arising. Properly, the candles are lighted, one of
the bells is sounded gently, the suppliant kneels, prays to his
satisfaction, arises, rings the bell, and extinguishes the light.
It is not possible to determine the extent of adherence to
this practice, but the impression obtained from talking with
Shakers is that it is much neglected, and even when it is
followed the ritual is often abbreviated and perfunctory. In
addition, the prayer table at home is used during healing
ceremonies and other special meetings that are held there on
week day evenings by invitation of the householder.

At the same time that Lans Kalapa received the teaching
directing him to burn his triple candlesticks he also advocated revolutionary details respecting the prayer table. There
was no church at Neah Bay at the time, in 1903, and Shakers were holding their meetings in the homes of those who
had been converted. The agent by then had given them permission to meet at any time except on Thursday evenings

and Sunday mornings. Kalapa held his unorthodox services in the home of his convert, Skyler Colfax. There the prayer table was placed near the door of the living room, and it was turned so that the corners, rather than the sides, were oriented to the four cardinal directions. His vision rejected the large hand bell but substituted a much smaller one which was placed on the table between two parallel rows of five candles each. Kalapa sounded the small bell three times as each member left the room after the service. These innovations were never widely accepted. Even members of Kalapa's family rejected them.

When John Slocum held church services he wore a plain white vestment which, from the descriptions of it, appears to have been an ordinary shirt with an open collar or, more probably, a dress shirt with no collar at all. It is described as coming down to his hips, from which statement it would seem that the tails fell outside his trousers. Up until the time that shaking was introduced no one else wore a ceremonial costume, and there was thus a symbolic as well as a conceptual difference between religious leader and congregation. The conceptual distinction was modified, however, with the inauguration of shaking, and very soon its symbolic expression took a similar turn. For it was not long after her first inspiration that Mary had another revelation which impelled her to "teach" that during their curing rites Shakers should wear special clothing. Specifically, she advocated that the women wear white dresses with blue ribbon belts and collars covering the throat and that the men wear collarless shirts with wide sleeves.

The precise specifications recommended by Mary were never strictly adhered to, but until a few years ago it was considered important for women to wear some kind of a white dress and for men to don an ordinary white shirt when they went to heal the sick. Women were more observant of this formal requirement than were men. In recent times both sexes have become lax. By 1942 so few Shakers around Puget

Sound were observing the custom that it could hardly be recognized. Only one woman wore a white dress at the Tulalip camp meeting in the summer of that year. The usage is still current among the southern Shakers, although with less conviction than formerly. Twenty years ago almost every woman who participated in the Sunday evening meetings at Siltez wore a plain white dress on the pattern of a nurse's uniform, and a few men were to be seen in their best shirts. In 1938 the Hupa held this up as the ideal but were not consistent in their conformance to it.

More attention is now paid to another type of vestment. The inspiration for this came to Mud Bay Louis a few years before 1900. He fell sick and believed that he was about to die, but during his illness he had a vision of a "long white dress." Upon regaining his health he instructed his wife to make a copy of the dress so that he could wear it during church services. This was his "help," and he made a teaching of it, saying that all those who believed, as he did, that he had been deathly ill but had been saved by the grace of God should follow his example. The explanation which he gave for the general adoption of the vestment was that in heaven everybody dresses alike, so here on earth on those occasions when Christians are preparing their hearts and minds to enter heaven they should also clothe themselves in the same way.

Louis had just begun to preach this doctrine when Enoch Abraham visited him in 1899. Few Shakers knew about the teaching at that time. When Abraham left Mud Bay the following spring Louis asked him to tell the Yakimas about it. Abraham therefore called a meeting at his home upon his return to make the announcement. The local Shakers were his guests, and to feed them he killed a beef and used a quantity of pilot bread which he had received at a potlatch given by Tyhee Jack of Port Gamble. Louis had, up to this point, called the vestment simply a "white dress." Abraham gave it the name "garment," and it has been called that ever since. As described by Louis, it was to be a loose ankle-length gown with long sleeves that could be worn over ordinary clothing. A strip of blue ribbon should be sewed around the neck and on the breast with a cross at the end. The woman's garment was to have a collar, but the man's was not.

Garments were not immediately adopted. Johns asserts that when he became a Shaker in 1909 "nobody" on Squaxin Island wore one. There was considerable talk about them and some hesitancy and opposition toward them. One prominent Squaxin man declared that he was "afraid of them because they were of such shining brilliance." Mary Slocum was resolutely opposed to their use, maintaining that dressing in such fashion was an imitation of angels that was not appropriate for sinners here on earth. She countered with another teaching; namely, that worshippers during the Sunday services should wear a black garment with a white stripe down the front that was symbolic of the way to heaven. Her suggestion was not adopted; but she did succeed in prejudicing the Skokomish and some of the northern Shakers against Louis' teaching.

Although the Yakima heard about white dresses in 1900 they did not see any until three years later. In 1903 Louis and his wife visited the small church on Tom Simpson's homestead and displayed their garments. A short time later Johnny Johnson claimed to have had a revelation and presented himself in a white gown decorated with a yellow band running from one shoulder diagonally across his breast. He maintained that this was the true garment, but only one man followed him in this teaching.

Light cotton garments, buttoned up the back, with a narrow band of blue ribbon forming a V and a cross on the breast, are now quite common everywhere. The California Shakers wear them more often than members in Washington. Those for men and women disclose no differences; neither has a collar. They are worn only at the Sunday morning service, which is conceptually not a curing ceremony.

There is therefore no connection between them and the healing rite, although this is the implication of some of the reports about them.[5] Upon occasions a Sunday service becomes an impromptu curing ceremony and garments are then in evidence, but this is not their ritualistic context.

Anyone may own and wear a garment. Years ago Alex Teio, the Yakima minister, received the teaching that garments should be prayed over in church "just like a new church is dedicated." Lately another Yakima Shaker has attempted to initiate the custom of requiring garments to be made by a leading woman member. Neither of these teachings has become well established. They have not acted as controls on the wearing of garments, nor have any similar devices been instituted elsewhere for this purpose as far as could be learned. The use of the gowns is optional and there is no moral or other compulsion acting on members to garb themselves in this fashion. One need not receive the gift or be tested in his faith to wear a garment. Consequently, it does not figure as a reward and does not confer prestige or stimulate emulation. Johns has "been shown," that is, had a vision of, a garment four times, yet he has not regarded this as a divine commission. A friend gave him one in 1940, the first that he had owned. Most true Shakers say that they should have a garment, but many either do not own one or neglect to wear the one they have. In explanation they say, generally, that "it is too much trouble."

Some Shaker women carry a large white handkerchief while they are under power.[6] This is an uncommon sight at the present time but it was formerly a more widespread usage; and, if Mooney's information on this point is reliable, men also carried them. He reports that while two Shakers "from the north" were visiting at Woodland, near Longview, Washington, in 1900 they cured a woman of sickness caused by a local medicine man and that when the sickness was withdrawn from her body one of the men seized it in the cloth that he held. The cloth was also used to wave in front of the patient's face on this occasion.[7] Cloths are still used in this fashion and also with a fanning motion before the Shaker's own breast when she wishes to help herself. The origin and the rationale of this practice has not been investigated. It appears likely, however, that it is restricted to women.

Shaker churches are not impressive structures. All are frame buildings. The walls of the simpler ones are made of one-by-twelve boards with weather strips over the cracks. The better ones are of clapboard. In most cases their exteriors are unpainted. They are rectangular in ground plan, usually with a projecting anteroom at the entrance and a slight extension at the other end to provide a low, shallow interior recess for the prayer table. Three or four windows open along the sides. In modern churches whose congregations can afford them, windows are narrow with a pointed arch. Earlier buildings, and the cheaper ones today, were provided with ordinary household window casings.

The long axis of the church should be oriented in an east-west direction. The entrance should be at the west end, opposite the altar. The belfry, topped by a cross, should be above the altar. This is the plan established by Louis' original church at Mud Bay. Nothing is known at present about Slocum's church at Skookum Chuck. Louis advocated his orientation of the church but he did not make a teaching of it. Apparently he took it for granted, and most churches have conformed to the pattern without question. There have been some departures, however. At Jamestown the houses of the village line the beach and face it. The front doors of the houses therefore open to the north in this village, and when the Shakers erected their first church there it was oriented in the same fashion. The belfry was also placed at the north and over the entrance. During their visit to Jamestown in 1903 Enoch Abraham and Joe Riddle attempted to persuade the Shakers to correct these errors but they were opposed by the conservative sentiment which was expressed

The Shaker church near White Swan, Washington, looking northeast

The dining hall next to the church, looking southeast

The interior of the church

by the headman of the village with the words "the front of a house is anchored to the sea, the back to the land." Other churches in northern Washington reveal departures from the rule, among them those at Tulalip and Elwha.

To the unprepared observer the interiors of Shaker churches seem somewhat primitive and secular. Rows of rough benches extend from the entrance to one third of the distance to the prayer table on either side of an aisle. These seats are for the spectators or other nonparticipants. The forward area of the floor is vacant except for a string of similar benches that line the three walls. At the far end a gap is left to accommodate the prayer table. The seats along the forward walls are for the participants. The benches are not painted, but the walls are usually colored white, as is the table and the alcove which forms its background. Sometimes the latter is a recess in the wall; in other churches it consists of a projecting archway only deep enough to suggest a shelter for the table. Against its back wall a large cross is fixed. Around the arch smaller crosses, often twelve in number, are fastened. There is no altar rail.

A few odd chairs and a wood stove completes the list of furnishings for most churches. The chairs are used as seats for patients who present themselves as subjects for the "workers." They are placed in the middle of the open part of the floor. The stove is for heating purposes, and is mainly for the spectators. It is set up near the entrance of the building. Some churches have sacred pictures on their walls. These are prints of the Sacred Heart, The Virgin, Jesus, and other religious subjects with an unconscious emphasis upon Roman Catholic ideology.

From the foregoing descriptions it will be apparent that Shaker ritual is relatively barren of material detail and diversity. Few objects are needed for a religious service, and the few that are required are simple and easy to get. More emphasis has been placed on the multiplication and elabora-

tion of behavioral complexes. There are a number of stereotyped action patterns that figure in various combinations to
make up a ceremony.

The act of shaking, although seemingly uncontrolled, is itself stereotyped. It comprises a variety of bodily movements,
some of which are spontaneous, but the majority recur repeatedly with different individuals in the same situation.
Though various, they are limited in number and their multiple combinations and permutations give a greater similitude
of individuality than actually exists. In addition, consistent
shaking patterns according to sex and age differences are apparent to the close observer.

The facial expression of a Shaker under power assumes
one of two characteristic configurations. In all cases the
eyes are closed, but under some circumstances the lids and
the lips are lightly drawn together, the muscles of the face
and neck are relaxed, and the whole expression is one of peaceful repose. At other times the eyelids are compressed, the
brow wrinkled, the teeth clenched, and there are grimaces
that suggest emotional strain. It may be that the two facial
patterns represent characteristic individual reactions to the
trance experience; but it is certain that they can also be
phases in the experience of a single individual. Shaking usually begins with relaxed muscles, but as the ardor mounts
many individuals become more tense, their expression more
concentrated, their movements more spasmodic. At such
times their whole behavior is expressive of an intense and
even a painful preoccupation. The body posture conforms
to these two phases of intensity: in relaxation a person stands
with normal erectness, his face set straight to the front; as
the tension grows his neck is bowed and he leans slightly forward.

These muscular postures reveal themselves indifferently
among individuals, but in the stamping which accompanies
them there are some group differences. Stamping is always
done with the heels, alternately with the right and the left,

but there are three ways in which this is accomplished. In part they also conform to the intensity of the emotional involvement. In the initial phase everybody begins with a stiff-kneed, treading motion that rocks the upper body. Some individuals may continue this action throughout their seizure, modifying it only by sharpening and quickening it as their absorption deepens. This is especially true of women; and older women seldom display any other foot movement. This is also the typical step of all Shakers when they perform ritual circuits and when they apply themselves to the cure of a sick person. As their preoccupation develops, men usually alter their leg action in one of two ways: either the knees remain relatively stiff and the feet are kicked out in front or the knees are sharply flexed, raised high, and the heels alternately brought down with a vigorous thrust. Young men, especially, do the latter. Women never flex their knees and thrust their heels down in this fashion. Young women do sometimes kick their feet out like the men, but not typically. This step, incidentally, is not easy; it requires some practice. Since the object is to strike the heels as sharply as is possible a vigorous performer appears to be falling over backwards—and may be.

The hand movements of a Shaker are most complex. There are, nevertheless, a limited number of them, and they vary according to purpose and context. In making a prayer the right hand is held in one of two positions. In both the elbow is bent and the hand is raised to approximately shoulder height; but in one case the palm is turned outward, as if in blessing, and in the other the hand is lowered slightly and the thumb is turned upward. Both gestures may be seen today as Shakers sit or stand and address themselves to God either in prayer or in song. They are also used as symbols of affiliation and faith in the cult.

Equally typical of the initial stages of shaking, and even more directly connected with it, is another gesture. This is an upward extension of the arms to a position not quite vertical above the head. The act is consciously interpreted as an invitation to the power to descend, and a person who is seeking to join the church is always placed in the middle of the floor with his arms in this position.

One or another of these preliminary postures might be steadily maintained by a Shaker until the power comes to him. Sometimes, though, he interrupts them with two or three claps of his hands, by swinging his arms at his sides once or twice, or by making one or more gestures of rubbing the power into his body. A familiar act of the latter sort consists of alternately rolling the fist of one hand in the palm of the other. Others consist of the patting and brushing motions noted below. When the bells sound and the stamping begins most participants begin to clap their hands in rhythm.

As this preparatory stage passes and the power begins to take possession a Shaker raises his arms so that they are extended in front of him at shoulder height. His hands are relaxed with the palms downward. This is the typical position for a person who is simply shaking for his own good or for one who is "searching" for something such as a lost object, a lost soul, sin, or disease. In healing the sick one hand may remain in this position while the other is applied to oneself or another patient or both hands may be engaged in these movements.

Healing gestures are the most varied, but it seems that all fall into one or another of the following categories. The laying on of hands: either one hand or both rest upon some part of the patient's body for variable lengths of time. Brushing: one hand or both follow along the contours of a patient's limb or body, either lightly, with noticeable pressure, or with sharp sweeps. Some healers do not touch the patient, and when they make the gesture of brushing from a few feet away their rapid arm movements degenerate into a series of counterclockwise revolutions. A handkerchief may be twirled in this way, too. Scooping: the two outside edges of the palms are placed a short distance apart on some part of the patient's body and are then pressed together to form a cup. Patting: one or both hands flutter rapidly against the patient's body or against the breast of the Shaker himself. Fanning: the hands wave rapidly in a horizontal plane before some part of the patient's body. Rarely, a handkerchief is held in one hand when this is done. Scraping: the edge of one palm is drawn along the patient's body to a point where the cupped palm of the other hand waits to close with it. Smoothing: the hands are rubbed slowly down over the head, face, or limb of the patient. Flame application: a lighted candle is held in the left hand while the other passes rapidly through it and toward the patient's body.

As has been said, most Shakers do not know why they do these things. None of them have received any instruction in them. There have been no teachings about them that any-one remembers. Some persons are rougher than others. Some touch the body of a patient and others do not. All maintain that their movements under power are spontaneous, unpre-meditated, and even unique. The motions are not cate-gorized or even differentiated as they have been above. A Shaker insists that the power does everything and that no one has any control over it. As one of them said, "I don't know what John Slocum or Mud Bay Louis did with their hands. Nobody taught me anything. If I am right with the heavenly power it will come into my hands. I don't think what I am going to do. The power does it. Look, now, I'm a Shaker; so is my friend George. But our hands don't go alike."

Nevertheless, from those who could be induced to give explanations, the following rationalizations of the different movements were obtained. The laying on of hands is for the purpose of locating illness or transmitting power from healer to patient. Brushing is to sweep sin from the body. Scooping draws out internal sickness and, in addition, for those who credit the theory, it pulls out evil spirits. Patting brings power to focus and taps it into the body. Fanning blows away sin-

ful things. Scraping takes sin off the surface of the body.
Smoothing is for the purpose of restoring a lost soul and fix-
ing it in the body again. The application of candle flame de-
stroys sin and sickness and forms a protective coating that
is relatively impervious to their further inroads upon the
health of the patient.

Correlated with the extractive manipulations are others
which relate to the treatment of the captured substance.
Brushing sweeps sin downward and casts it away. Scooping
and scraping yield something in the hand that must be disposed of. Commonly, therefore, these movements end with
an upward and parting thrust of the hands. In between each
reapplication the healer usually claps his hands three times.
Sometimes instead of throwing the evil away a Shaker takes
it to the prayer table in his clenched hands and releases it
over a candle flame. The movement to the table takes some
time, for all the while the person is under power and his
stamping retards his progress. Some nevertheless make repeated trips between patient and table carrying sin to the
powerful light. They rapidly pass their hands back and forth
through the flame so that it will purify and adhere'to their
palms. Returning to the patient they transmit its curative
and protecting properties to him by contact with their
hands. Those who have caught a soul hold it tenderly in the
cup of one palm and cover it with the other; normally the
palms are crossed but sometimes they are matched together.

Many individuals "work" on a patient at one time. Consequently, all the above activities are likely to be going on at
once. There is no concert or agreement as to the cause or
method of curing a sickness and each individual pursues his
own diagnosis (if he has one) and the remedy that the power
directs. The diversity of attack is not a source of disagreement. Indeed, the incongruity of it is not even realized. If the
question is brought up it is simply suggested that the patient
had a variety of things wrong with him. Otherwise there is
no reflection, and it is certain that a majority of the partici-

pants in a curing ceremony are indulging themselves in the shaking experience with the patient serving only as the necessary justification for it.

The tremors that have given rise to the name of the sect begin in the hands of a person as they are held out at shoulder level in front of him. The fingers are relaxed and slightly apart. In the beginning the hands are usually in the prone position, but as the seizure comes on they are often turned so that the palms face each other with the thumbs up. The quivering is due either to a rapid flexing of the wrists or to an equally rapid torsion of the lower arm. The onset of the involuntary stage of shaking is commonly induced by a preliminary controlled fluttering of the hands. Once it has been initiated the autonomic quivering continues throughout the ritual manipulations that have been described but with due regard to their requirements. That is, a Shaker with something to do, such as holding a candle, maintains a relatively steady hand for the purpose. His localized muscular agitations are contained within more inclusive and directed operations. Also, the tremor itself, when applied to a patient, becomes a ritual manipulation; much of the "patting" and "fanning" mentioned above is of this character.

At times, as a Shaker's seizure becomes more pronounced, his hand tremors pass into or become combined with clonic spasms of the arms or neck. Like the trembling of the hands it is often induced by preliminary voluntary movements, such as a patting of the breast or a jerking of the extended arms. This larger involvement of the arm and shoulder muscles is interpreted as fanning or patting when directed toward a sick person. In some instances the fluttering action of the hands disappears and the arms of the performer beat inward with vigorous jerks that pull at his entire upper body. In this state he rarely if ever maintains the placid facial expression that has been described for one phase of shaking. The jerking of the neck muscles, however, may be independently activated. It may or may not accompany the trembling or jerking of the hands and arms. When it occurs the head bobs up and down rapidly or is shaken from side to side, the face meanwhile maintaining an aspect of repose or its muscles contracting tightly in a painful expression. It is uncertain whether other parts of the body become involved in these exertions. The stamping action assumes a convulsive quality, and it may well serve as the foundation for subsequent developments.

From this description it can be seen that there are all degrees of intensity in the emotional experience of shaking. Yet it is important to realize that no matter how spontaneous and oblivious to control a Shaker may appear and believe himself to be, he nonetheless follows definite patterns in his ecstasy. The generic picture of a Shaker engrossed in his own experience presents the figure of an individual with his eyes closed, his hands trembling in forward extension, and his feet treading the floor in one place. As his prepossession intensifies his muscles grow more tense, their contractions and relaxations more automatic and rapid, and their involvement of the larger elements of the body more pronounced and vigorous—all according to standardized patterns. When he directs his attention toward a patient these stereotypes continue in part, and in part they are replaced by others that are appropriate to the situation. In spite of the fact that every individual in the milling crowd on a Shaker church floor seems intent upon his own private fancies, the departures from the forms that have been described by any one of them are so slight as to rule out spontaneity in any sense except that of variation by combination.

The intricacy which results from a host of people weaving their individual designs out of a stock of common elements makes it more difficult to perceive the ritual norms appropriate to the shaking phase of a service than most others that pertain to the rest of the ritual. Many of the latter are obvious. It is apparent, for instance, that men and women are spatially separated during all parts of a church service except during the shaking when they mingle indiscriminately. When seated the active women participants occupy the benches along the wall to the right of the prayer table as one faces it. The men are on the opposite side. Children of all ages accompany their parents to these places, which are unassigned, the girls going with their mothers, the boys with their fathers. During the prayer service the women take their positions on the right half of the open floor space, the men the left, facing the table. Spectators occupy the benches near the entrance on both sides of the aisle, and among them the sexes are mixed indiscriminately.

At several points in their rituals the Shakers revolve in position or form circular processions. In all cases the movement is in a counterclockwise direction. This is the general practice at the present time, but it has not always been so uniformly accepted. Mary Slocum and Mud Bay Louis disagreed on this issue as well as others. In the beginning, Mary advocated a clockwise movement and it seems that the earliest Shakers followed her without question. The Skokomish and others who derived their knowledge of the cult from them conformed to this standard for many years. However, not long after he assumed leadership Louis had a revelation to the effect that moving in clockwise fashion was the "way of the world" and that in heaven "everything went the other way." It is uncertain whether Louis was referring to the movements of the celestial bodies, but that is the suggestion. In any event, by 1903 all the southern churches, those which had come under the direct influence of Louis, were following his teaching, while the Skokomish, the Clallams of Port Gamble and Jamestown, and the Makah of Neah Bay were making a clockwise circuit at those points in the service where a decision upon the issue must be made.

Enoch Abraham and Joe Riddle visited the Jamestown church in that year and were distressed by the perversion. Riddle made an issue of it and tried to induce a change. William Hall, the local minister, was adamant. He made a speech, giving three reasons why the Jamestown Shakers made the circuit as they did: first, Mary Slocum was the original Shaker, and she did it that way; second, John Collier had received knowledge that he could cure a certain insane white man if he, Collier, were to lead him by the little finger around the room three times in a clockwise direction, and this had proved true; third, a girl with an incurable sickness had received instructions that if she prayed in each corner of the church successively and in clockwise order she would be healed, and this also had proved true.

The issue was settled at the same meeting, not by argument but again by certain evidences of divine intervention. During the shaking that followed the discussion a new convert was made. He fell to the floor unconscious when the power "hit" him, and when he revived he began to move around the room in a counterclockwise direction. This was proof enough for some people, but Hall was unconvinced. When the final movement, the "handshake," was begun, Riddle led the group and went around in a counterclockwise direction. Hall and his wife dropped out and refused to shake hands as the procession filed by them. But a month later Abraham received a letter from Mrs. Hall in which she told him that her son had died from no apparent cause and that she was convinced that it was because she "had gone against God's way at the meeting."

The ritual handshake that has been mentioned is not the one with which we are familiar as a symbol of greeting. At the time of his resurrection John Slocum is said to have called for a handclasp from those present who believed what he told them and wished him well. Later he received the same expression of confidence from his followers as they filed by him upon arrival at his church. He also shook hands with them at the close of the service as a token of brotherly love, his preachment being that, according to one informant, "maybe somebody will die between now and the next time you see him, and you would be sorry not to be able to tell him good-bye."

The Slocum handclasp, imbued with these solemn meanings, was the one that we employ in our everyday social intercourse. It no longer has the same implications for Shakers. It does not have a place in their ideology and its connotations are purely secular. The ritual act that is now called "the handshake" is a distinct formality. In it a person bends his elbow and presents his right hand, palm outward, at about shoulder height. His vis-à-vis does likewise and their two palms meet and cross each other. Usually there is a slight grip and a barely perceptible shake; sometimes the hands merely touch for a brief moment.

It may be that Sylvester Yucton was responsible for introducing the Shaker handshake. There is no direct evidence on this point but the statement in the document already quoted implies that in asking the sick who wanted help to come forward and take his hand he was establishing a precedent; and it may well have been the handshake, for the other elements in the situation were not new. In making the plea he was apparently exploiting the same reasoning that Slocum had, which was to the effect that "If you believe that what I say is true, come forward and take my hand." This, at any rate, is a meaning that the gesture did acquire.

For a number of years the symbol retained its special meaning as an attestation of confidence in the teaching of another. It did not have a wider area of usage until after 1900. When Enoch Abraham visited Louis just prior to this date, the handshake was not a part of the religious meetings that they attended. There was much handshaking in those days but it was the secular kind, and it was not integrated with the devotional exercises. The step of substituting the elevated handclasp for the other as a token of greeting, and welding it to the ceremonial complex came in 1903 as another teaching of Louis. He taught that everyone should "shake hands" with fellow members when they met inside the church and before they left it, for the church, like heaven, was a different place from the outside world.

The ritual handshake therefore theoretically opens and closes every Shaker meeting. Each member, as he or she enters the church or a house where there is to be a meeting, is supposed to go directly to the first person seated on his right, "shake" her hand, proceed to the next one, and so on around the room from right to left. Women are approached first because, in church at least, they are on the right side of the room and the movement must be counterclockwise. Women should make the circuit too. This feature is only semiritualized. It takes place as members begin to come in individually or in groups, before the minister "takes the floor." It precedes the service proper; therefore some people frequently neglect it.

Joe Riddle of the Yakima church introduced an innovation about 1910 which, if it had been accepted, might have made the ritual handshake preceding the services a more definite part of them. His teaching was that a person upon entering the church must go directly to the prayer table and kneel down for a short prayer before shaking hands with his fellow members because "when you die you go straight to God's feet to be judged; then if you pass you can go around and get acquainted with the other people in heaven." A few influential Yakima Shakers followed him in his practice of this teaching, among them the minister, Alex Teio, his brother Harry Teio, and George Barr. For a time it appeared that the idea would become accepted, at least among this congregation, but it did not achieve a wider recognition and was eventually abandoned by the few among the Yakima who adhered to it.

The handshake that concludes a Sunday service is an integral part of it. It is performed in concert, and the fervor of the meeting is carried over to it. It begins with the women lined up in single file along the right wall and the men in a line on the opposite side of the room. The bells sound the rhythm and everyone begins to stamp. The woman at the end away from the altar steps out and begins to shake hands with each of her sisters as she tramps down the line. Each of them in turn steps out from the end position to follow the procession as it moves slowly across the room to file by the men. As the last woman touches his hand the man nearest the prayer table falls in line behind her, and the rest follow suit, each shaking hands with the rest as the women have done. As the leading woman comes back to her original position she stops; the others do likewise, and the entire procession unfolds in reverse order, each person who had previously given his hand to the others now receiving theirs as he stands in place. The movement ends with the two lines and their component individuals in the same position as in the beginning.

This activity takes fifteen minutes or more, depending upon the number participating and the pace set by the leading woman. The rhythm is usually quite fast but the forward progress is slow. Before touching hands each person makes the sign of the cross. All look straight ahead and not into the face of the one they greet; many keep their eyes closed. In the moving line a person follows close upon the heels of the one in front of him, so the crossing and the handshake are often much abbreviated. At one convention William Hall of Jamestown made an attempt to accelerate the movement. He introduced the teaching that those in the moving line should squeeze together as close as possible because "leaving spaces in between gave a chance for the devil to get through." He also rang the hand bells faster, so a person had to exert himself to keep up and barely had time to cross himself and touch the hands of those he passed. When it was over Enoch Abraham "took the floor" and argued that this was the wrong way to do the handshake, that people needed more time, and that the omission of the crossing was what permitted the devil to enter people's hearts and not the space in between them. Some months later his wife received a teaching that Shakers must always make the full sign of the cross and not distort and abbreviate it. Theoretically this view is the accepted one today; but the preoccupation of an individual with his own emotional state, which is intensified by the rapidity of his foot movements, often makes the crossing perfunctory and the handshake a mere touching of hands.

In crossing himself a Shaker touches the fingers of his right hand to his foreheard, lowers them to the center of his breast, then crosses them first to the left and then to the right. John Slocum instituted this practice. He recommended it as an introduction and a conclusion to prayer. The Shakers extended the occasions for its use. Eells remarks that "They became very peculiar about making the sign of the cross many times a day, when they began to eat as they asked a blessing, and when they finished their meal and returned thanks; when they shook hands with anyone—and they shook hands very often—when they went to church and prayer meeting on Thursday evening, and at many other times, far more often than the Catholics do." [8] The other occasions that he refers to included the private prayers at night and morning and any situation that might be fraught with evil. Silas Heck recalled that the earliest adherents among the Chehalis crossed themselves before passing through a doorway, either to enter a house or leave it, because "you never know what danger you are going to meet, and with the cross you have the protection of the Lord." They crossed themselves before eating or drinking for similar reasons: to protect themselves from the effects of swallowing food contaminated by malignant spirits and perhaps sin.

The Shakers still cross themselves before and after each prayer, including those at meal time, at night and morning, and on every ceremonial occasion in church and at home. They do not do so before greeting a stranger or on many of the other occasions that were formerly considered to be dangerous. It is uncertain to what extent this fear still prevails. It may be compelling in individual instances, but it does not make the Shaker conspicuous; and one gets the impression that the practice of crossing has dropped out of secular situations. Lans Kalapa attempted to eliminate it altogether but without success. He taught that making the sign of the cross over the chest "cut the life short" and advocated what he regarded as a fundamental innovation; namely, that the hand should first be placed on the top of the head, then on the right breast, then in the center, then on the left breast.

The custom of crossing oneself before shaking hands has survived only in the ritual handshake, the only occasion when the act is performed without a verbal accompaniment. Shakers everywhere know and recite the Puyallup or Nisqually words for this devotion. It is an expression that is universally used, always at conventions and camp meetings and usually at local services from California to British Columbia. It is translated as "In the name of the Father, the Son, and the Holy Ghost. Forever." It is not known whether the Californians have put this meaning into their own languages; but most, if not all, of the Washington groups have done so, even though they do not normally use it in their services. When asked why they do not, they usually reply that it "sounds better" in Puyallup. The English translation is not used.

The Puyallup words for the sign of the cross are naturally very often distorted by those to whom the tongue is alien. Were it not for the fact that there are periodic reunions, the modifications and their divergences would no doubt be much greater than they are. As it is, there are several dialectic variants resulting from the fact that some of the Nisqually phonemes are intermediate between two or more known to other peoples who therefore now hear them as one, now as the other of their familiar sounds. To our ears, for example, the Nisqually, Puyallup, and Snohomish seem to use *b* and *m* interchangeably; likewise for *d* and *n*. The Yakima make the sign of the cross in the Nisqually dialect, to which John

Slocum's language belonged, as follows: "Thwasnaksmans, titumunas, titusantosple, qu:musistu." The Chehalis made this "Twaksnaksmans, tetumunus, tetusantospli, qo:busistu." The Snohomish say "Dwulksnakuman, etamenas, etasentospli, tlomasista." These are but variants of the same original translation of the sign of the cross made by the early Catholic priests.[9]

When the Cowlitz, under the leadership of Aiyel, became acquainted with this form they made a translation into their own language, and in doing so arrived at a different meaning. The Cowlitz form is not available, but both the Yakima and the Wishram (Chinook) followed the interpretation established around Longview and they reveal the following modification. Instead of saying, "in the name of" the Yakima say, literally, "here is." Consequently their sign of the cross, as they touch the forehead, center, left, and right breast regions, signifies "Here is the father, here is the son, here is the good heart. All the time this way good." Not quite parallel is the Wishram meaning, which runs: "This is the father, this his son, this his good heart. Thus always good."[10]

Shakers everywhere occasionally use the ejaculation "masi," or some variant thereof, in very much the same contexts that the expressions "Hallelujah" and "Praise the Lord" are used in Christian revival meetings. Very few of them, however, know what it means. Enoch Abraham has puzzled over it, and years ago asked his cousin Joe Riddle about it. Riddle replied that he did not know but "guessed" that it meant "thank you." Abraham was not satisfied. He suggested that it sounded much like the proverbial negro corruption of "master." The word does indeed mean "thank you." It is taken from the Chinook jargon in which it was incorporated as a corruption of the French "merci." Some of the older Indians speak this jargon today, but the majority of them fail to link the word with the old trade language. The young people know nothing of this background, have not inquired into, and therefore have not been taught, the literal meaning of the word. It is quite comparable to "Hallelujah."

Other verbalizations reveal close analogies with Christian revivalistic patterns. An interval is provided in every Sunday service for the conveyance of all manner of public information pertaining to the church. At this time any person may speak his mind upon doctrine or ritual and criticize the interpretations of others. He may testify to his faith, ask for prayer and help in sickness or trouble, and describe the benefits that he has obtained from his affiliation with the church. Announcements relative to meetings, finances, and other aspects of church business are made then, too. Whatever the subject matter might be, the speaker characteristically quavers his voice and intones his phrases with the billowy, histrionic inflections of the camp meeting preacher. He likewise interlards his speech with frequent addresses to "My dear brothers and my dear sisters." The effect of embodying mundane ideas in this theatrical form is sometimes incongruous. All the speaking on these occasions is in English.

Shaker songs have revealed a tendency to vary within limits. It is not certain what kinds of songs John Slocum used in his services. Probably they were in the Chinook jargon, patterned after Protestant hymns and carrying simple burdens reiterative of the bounties of heaven, the wonder of God, and the blessedness of being a Christian. In 1878 Eells composed several songs of this character, had them printed, and taught them to his congregations. In 1892 Wickersham recorded two such songs and it is likely that they were inspired by Eells's example if not composed by him.[11] They are strange to contemporary Shakers; and other songs with Chinook words are rarely if ever used today. The presumption is that they became less popular after the introduction of shaking.

It is said that Mary received a song at the time of her supernatural experience. All that can be learned about it is that it was a mixture of wailing, gasping, and sobbing fused with repetitions of such phrases as "Jesus is good. Jesus saves." It is likely that her performance introduced the elements out of which subsequent Shaker songs were composed; but it is also probable that Mary was herself unconsciously drawing upon already existing patterns.

There are two kinds of songs today. In one there are no words but only nonsense syllables. Typically the syllables are compounded of *h* or *y* and the vowels *ai, i, e, u, o,* and *oi.* The syllables are variously combined. Reagan recorded the following three sequences, constituting as many songs, sung at La Push around 1907: "ai hai ha ai hai hai hai hoi hai hai hi hu hai hi"; "ai hai ai hai ai hu ai hai ai hai"; and "oo o he ye hi i." Another, which he calls Lans Kalapa's song, runs thus: "ai yi u haw ai ha."

Characteristically the melodic range within such songs is great, the first few measures being in very high notes, and the final ones, by an abrupt transition, in very low notes. When the song is first started the syllables are drawn out and the tempo is slow; as it is repeated and the stamping which accompanies it becomes more animated the time is quickened. Frequently in its first repetitions the singers quaver the notes, insufflate between the syllables, and otherwise give the impression of wailing and sobbing.

There seems to be a limited number of melodic patterns but a great number of syllabic variations based upon them. Everyone agrees that there are very few new songs composed. Most that are called new have only a new syllabic structure. A Siletz leader admonished the first Yurok Shakers that not more than one person out of ten ever "came out with" a new song. A Yakima man said that he often thinks of new songs while he is humming at his daily chores, but these never "come to" him under power; when the spirit is upon him he almost always begins to sing one that he has heard before.

The other song type uses English words only. It may have been modeled in part upon the Christian hymn, which its words recall, but its melodic structure is different. Refrains such as "I am so glad since Jesus came into my heart" or "Jesus is here to show us the way" are typical of the sentiments expressed; and the repetition of each expression an indefinite number of times make up a song. The tempo is always slow, and the notes are held for long intervals. Without knowing the entire range of songs, and without a more competent musical analysis, it is difficult to say whether the English words are set to the same tunes as the nonsense syllables.

The two types of songs are not used interchangeably. Those with nonsense syllables are the real shaking songs; they are accompanied by the ringing of hand bells and the stamping of feet. The leader of a meeting, or one upon whom he calls, begins a song of this character and at the same time holds up his or her hands and starts to tread the floor. Others join in. At each repetition the tempo and the volume of the singing increases until the stamping can go no faster. The singing continues as long as anyone wants to carry on; gradually as the shaking and stamping become more vigorous the voices subside and only the bells accompany the resounding tramp of feet.

The songs with English words figure as introductory or concluding elements, sometimes both. From observation it would appear that whether or not such songs are sung depends very much on whether the leader knows one and prefers it as an opener. Whenever they are used they either precede or follow the shaking part of a service. They are therefore not accompanied by bells or by hand or foot movements. Occasionally they do induce ecstasy in the more susceptible members who thereupon begin to tremble and move their hands over their bodies. During the singing of a song of this kind a person usually stands facing the prayer table with his hands lifted in one of the positions that have been described as appropriate for the invocation of the spirit.

Shakers almost always pray in their native tongues. Therefore, at conventions relatively few individuals understand the prayers of the rest. It is uncertain whether there are any fixed prayers. Ober states that "Slocum had a beautiful prayer, which is translated as follows: 'Our God is in heaven. If we die He will take our life to heaven. Help us, O God, so that we shall not die. Wherever we are, help us not to die. Our Father, who is there, always have a good mind to us.' " [12] In the manuscript already referred to, Reagan also quotes this, and calls it the "watchword and prayer" of the early Shakers.[13] It may be current today but if so it is not an obvious feature. Most praying is quite individualized, and none of it is in unison as is the sign of the cross.

When John Slocum prayed he got on his knees facing the prayer table. The devotional exercises that he advocated consisted of silent prayer or of voiced supplications alternating with singing. While the rest of the congregation remained on their knees any person who felt prompted to do so could rise to his feet and sing or pray aloud. This continued until everyone who wished had expressed himself. Then followed a very long interval of meditation and silent communion while all remained kneeling. The experience was extremely tiresome, especially since Slocum would brook no noise or movement during the period of silence. It is reported, as an instance of his ruling on this point, that at one of the meetings William Choke, a Chehalis man, had to kneel close to the heating stove, that it became too hot for him, and that he tried to quietly shift his position. Slocum could not see or hear him, but he called out for him to be still.

Sometimes such devotions lasted from eleven o'clock in the morning until three o'clock in the afternoon, under Slocum's insistence that a true Christian could not feel tired or cramped. Jack Slocum said that during those early meetings as the worshippers knelt in concentrated silent prayer they could hear a concourse of voices swelling in the heavens; that the voices grew more audible until by twelve o'clock distinct words could be made out; but by three o'clock they had faded away again. Presumably the reference was to the anticipated return of Christ with the multitudes of the faithful.

The Shakers did not continue with Slocum's custom of silent prayer as a part of church services. At first they did follow his practice of kneeling for a long time while individuals rose to their feet and sang or prayed aloud in turn. The Skokomish in 1900 did this in regular order, the first man on the left starting it, to be followed by the man on his right, and so on, until the last person in the rear had finished. Louis, however, opposed kneeling. He protested that the position was too uncomfortable to be maintained through the long series of prayers. Accordingly he instituted the practice of standing while each person took his turn offering a song or a prayer. Later on this was modified so that today Shakers pray while standing during one part of their Sunday service, and during another they kneel. They all pray aloud, individually and simultaneously.

When kneeling some Shakers rest on one knee, others on two, according to preference. Old people who have difficulty getting on their knees either stand up or turn on the bench where they sit so that they partially face the prayer table. Some of the others who are lazy or indisposed also make this perfunctory gesture. While praying the right hands of most supplicants are raised with palm outward or are held in the handshaking position. As their appeals become more fervent some individuals extend both arms upward and go through the motions that have been described for the gathering in and absorbing of power. When the babel of prayer has subsided someone usually begins one of the wordless songs, and others may follow when he has finished. The number sung is indefinite and appears to depend upon the mood of the moment. Singing at this time is not accompanied by the ringing of bells and, of course, not by stamping. Instead, the participants clap their hands.

Shakers do not genuflect on entering the church or on crossing in front of the prayer table. They do cross them-

selves and turn once around, counterclockwise, when they
pass the table in the course of their ritual circuits of the room.
This should be done at both positions on the diameter of
the circuit in line with the table. Recently, lapses in this
requirement have become noticeable. Not more than half
of the participants observe the rule, and none do when they
are shaking or are absorbed with their inward experience.
Among the rest there is a tendency to make only the turn
directly before the table and ignore the one farthest from it.
In the beginning, at least, and up until 1910, it was customary
to make three turns instead of one.[14] Gradually this has
been reduced to one or none.

As this example indicates, the outstanding ritual number
of the Shakers is three. It is not clear what part John Slocum's
religion had in the establishment of this feature. From his
testimony as recorded by Wickersham it would appear that
he regarded the number four as having mystic significance.
If this is so, his predisposition for it did not survive the introduction of shaking except possibly in one instance; namely,
in the number of candles on the prayer table. Perhaps this
was the extent of his objective recognition of the number
four. From the beginning the Shakers have characteristically
thought of and done things by threes; and this pattern has
inhered in their ritual wherever it has spread. As a minister
of the Hupa church said, "We do everything three times—
go around the room three times; cross ourselves three times;
ring the bell [signal] three times: once to open the meeting,
once to begin the preaching, and once to start the work
[shaking]." Even when theory does not meet the fact the
ideal of the trinity is not lost. In discussing the healing of
the sick, for example, it is said that Shakers "work" on a
patient for three nights. Not so pronounced are the embodiments of the number twelve. Still less important are a few
sevenfold duplications.

Sometime before the year 1890 an unknown person in one
of the congregations in the southern Puget Sound area an-

nounced a teaching to the effect that women should un-
braid their hair and let it fall loosely down their backs while
shaking or when they asked for shaking help. At about the
same time someone else declared that women should wear
no jewelry upon these occasions. The reasons given for these
pronouncements have not survived, but the teachings themselves were accepted and for many years they were rather
carefully followed. Rakestraw's illustrations, while inaccurate
in other respects (e.g., women ringing bells and the use
of long, trailing garments), correctly incorporates this treatment of the hair and gives an idea of its prominence around
1900.[15] Mabel Teio, one of the first of the Yakima Shakers,
also mentions it in recounting the story of the introduction
of the religion in the White Swan district.[16] Among the
Siletz and California Shakers the custom is still almost universally followed; but in Washington this is not the case.
At the Tulalip convention in 1942 there were few women
who still had long straight hair; most of them bobbed or
curled it. Not more than a dozen wore their hair in braids
that were done up at the back of the head and they did not
take it down for the services.

A number of other teachings have appeared from time to
time to leave only a passing impression upon Shaker behavior. Mary Slocum attempted to enshrine the creek where
she first experienced the afflatus of the shaking power but
without any lasting effect either for herself or others. She
also taught that the tableware used at meals by Shakers
should be arranged in a definite way that is no longer remembered. Enoch Abraham's first wife, who died in 1924,
announced a teaching shortly before her death admonishing
Shakers not to spit on the floor of the church. She reasoned
that "the church was the body of Christ, and spitting on
it was like spitting on Him as the Jews had done on the way
to Calvary." Spitting on church floors is not at present a
flagrant evil; but it is safe to say that most Shakers have
never heard of this doctrine.

Mooney relates that the Yakima Shakers got their nickname of "blowers" because upon meeting a stranger "instead of at once shaking hands with him in the usual manner, they first wave the hand gently in front of his face like a fan, and blow on him, in order to 'blow away the badness' " from him.[17] In 1942 and 1943 no one could be found who had ever heard of this custom or anything like it with one exception. The brother of Sylvester Yucton recalled that Mary Slocum sometimes blew on a patient when it was a difficult case. It is probable that this behavior was her special gift. A few others may have claimed it later and thereby made themselves conspicuous to some of the Yakimas. It almost certainly was never a common practice.

There are some suggestions that there have been attempts to introduce food taboos into Shaker ideology. Of his second wife Enoch Abraham recalled: "She was a strong believer in not touching eels." In explanation he said that Shakers were not supposed to eat eels, sturgeon, trout, white swan, suckers, duck, or pig; that this was being preached at the time when he joined the church in 1899; and that he did not know whose teaching it was—"maybe Louis or Slocum made the rule, I don't know." No one else could be found who knew about such prohibitions. In 1937 a Yurok Shaker fell ill and invited her friends to her house to work over her. Her daughter prepared a beef roast that was offered to the guests during the intermission at midnight, but they refused to eat the meat because it was Friday. This was the only explanation offered, and no other has come to light from other sources. Nor have other Shakers that have been asked found anything familiar in the idea that there should be a day of meat fast.

THE SHAKERS recognize, or have at times recognized, some ten ritual occasions. In large part they coincide with the Christian sacraments or other acts of consecration. Some are divergent; and among those which parallel the Christian forms the pattern of emphasis is so different that quite another system results. The most important rites are those of healing, worship, thanksgiving, divination, and burial, in approximately that order of significance. Less consistently observed are the rituals of conversion, ordination, dedication, confession, and baptism. The Shakers do not have any ceremony which resembles or purports to be an act of holy communion. Nor have they, except in theory, adopted or evolved a rite of holy matrimony.

Shaker ceremonies are likely to strike the Christian observer as a curious mixture of solemnity and informality. The ecstatic absorption of an individual in his own shaking experience at one moment contrasts with his detached and inattentive air at other times when his friends are going through the same passionate exercise. A matter-of-fact attitude predominates with only occasional evidences of awe or reverence. The shaking and the praying are impressive demonstrations of fervent hopes and real needs, but they are set in a background of mundane behaviors.

Bell ringers, who at other times are themselves shakers, characteristically exhibit an indifferent and indulgent attitude toward those whom they are helping with the necessary accompaniment. And when they tire they set their bells on the prayer table and unceremoniously walk outside the church for a rest. Others, at their leisure, may take their places. Those who have tried for a long time to induce shaking in themselves or others without success frequently leave the floor for short recesses. Spectators constantly come and go while a ceremony is in progress. These secular distractions are incongruous with Christian religious expectations; but with respect to sermonizing and testimonials the detachment of the Shaker is perhaps more understandable. Preachments and testimonials from the church floor are as keenly felt by the deliverer, and often are as touching, as any to be heard at a Christian evangelical meeting; but one finds the same wandering gazes and unresponsive faces among the listeners in both places.

The ceremony of worship takes place on Sunday mornings. It is by far the most elaborate of the Shaker rituals. Its enrichment and systematization has been due to a series of reorganizations that have taken place as a result of the introduction of the innovations in ritual behavior that have been noted in the preceding chapter. As reported by living informants, John Slocum's Sunday service was a relatively simple ceremony. It opened with a ringing of the hand bell, which was immediately followed by making the sign of the cross, perhaps three times, by everyone in unison. After ringing the bell again, Slocum then began his sermon, in which he reiterated his experiences and his faith in the message that he brought from God. This portion of the service was concluded and the interval of individual singing or praying was introduced by another sounding of the bell. Finally there was the long period given over to silent meditation.

In 1903 Louis decreed that the service should start at nine o'clock, that each person as he entered the church was

to go to the right, cross himself and shake hands with everyone, then remain standing until all had taken their places
along the two walls, the men on the left side, the women
opposite them. When the minister rang the bell they were
to make the sign of the cross together, and as he rang it
again they were to sit down. Then anyone, after making
the sign of the cross, could preach, testify, or otherwise
give evidence of his faith. When all had finished the minister again sounded the bell and all who wished to participate lined up in ranks facing the prayer table, the men on
one side, the women on the other. After another stroke
of the bell and another sign of the cross, the man on the
extreme left and front began his prayer or song, to be
followed by the one next to him, and so on until all had
been given the opportunity to appeal or in some way give
thanks to God. This portion of the service differed from
Slocum's in that everybody stood up throughout and each
one was called upon in order for some expression of devotion. Also, the period of silent prayer was eliminated. Instead, as the stamping and bell ringing began, a procession
was formed to march around the room three times. The
circling ended with the women in a line on the right (south)
side of the room and the men facing them on the left side.
The last woman in the line then began the handshake.

This was the mode of Sunday worship for several years
after the death of Louis. In some churches it appears to have
persisted until relatively modern days. Of it, Miss Ober
wrote: "They [the Shakers] have their prayer services where
there is only prayer and singing, where men and women
stand for sometimes five or six hours in devotional exercises. They wear long, full white robes, bound about the
neck with blue ribbon that forms a cross on the breast. At
Jamestown both men and women were clothed in spotless
white when not wearing the robes. In their prayer services
any one prays upon whom the spirit comes. . . . Some of
the prayer services are very beautiful. There is none of the

dancing, or but little of the bell ringing. There is a kind of intoning in which all join between the prayers. Different ones pray, as they have 'God's gift.' It is at these services that the most spirituality and Christianity are shown." [1]

The description given by Waterman also seems to conform to this type of service. The group to which it applies, and the date of his observations are not stated; but it is known that he visited the Puget Sound region in the early 1920's. "The church service," he wrote, "consists first of a sermon, which serves to quiet everybody down and induce a feeling of solemnity. The leader then turns to one of the worshipers who stand facing him, and says, 'Pray!' The member called on delivers an extemporaneous prayer which, like the sermon, is in the native Indian language. At the close of his devotions he repeats, the others following his words, in a deep chorus: 'In the name of the Father, the Son, and the Holy Ghost, it is well.' . . . Every member of the Shaker congregation in turn (every convert, that is) leads in prayer or singing, or both. At the close of each petition, the well-remembered chant rolls forth, 'In the name of the Father,' deep toned, thrilling with fervor, and a thing moving even to a neutral observer. At the end of the terminal prayer, a deacon or assistant grasps two of the bells and begins to shake them, as Indians do a rattle, one in each hand in a pounding rhythm. . . . The progress of this deacon around the premises, in a sort of crow hop, followed in Indian file by the devotees, is accompanied therefore by a considerable din. Meanwhile, a song mounts up in time to the clang of the bells, and as each dancer passes the altar he (or she) revolves once. This exercise or parade is repeated as often as necessary or convenient. The worshipers often in going by the altar pass their hands through the flame of one of the candles, trying to purify themselves by driving away sin. At the close of the dance or parade, every worshiper shakes hands, or touches hands, with every other worshiper and with every spectator, sometimes blessing his vis-à-vis with the sign of the cross." [2]

This ritual may yet survive in some localities, but the one presently used at conventions and camp meetings, was given shape by Alex Teio, the Yakima minister, and probably by others as well. After the death of Louis, and perhaps subsequent to 1910, Teio began to teach that the Sunday service was too long and that it should end at twelve o'clock instead of running on until midafternoon. He advocated that while standing only two men and one woman should individually sing or pray. Then, after thrice circling the room as Louis had taught, the ranks should be re-formed facing the altar and every one should kneel and pray together aloud. Finally, there was to be another circuit of the room, followed by the handshake. Teio kept his watch on the prayer table to be certain that the service did not run beyond twelve o'clock. This precaution was not considered to be necessary and was even regarded as objectionable by some; but the inspiration to bring the Sunday meeting to a close approximately at noon was generally welcomed.

In 1913, during a convention at the Muckleshoot church, Enoch Abraham introduced another teaching which seems to have had an important effect upon the evolution of the Sunday service. Formerly, the ceremony opened rather abruptly with a sermon or exhortation. Abraham proposed that the minister begin the meeting with an invocation. He intended that this call to worship should be only a prayer, and for a time it was no more. Its nature is still somewhat variable, depending upon the disposition of the minister. It may be simple and perfunctory, or it may be complex and consciously extended. It has, in other words, become a focus for free elaboration. At times, and in places, especially at large meetings, it becomes a replica in miniature of the central part of the service which follows it.

The Sunday morning service now, therefore, consists of

four main divisions: the invocation, the exhortation, the concerted prayer, and the handshake. The first part is performed by the minister, who, with the proper introductions and conclusions by means of the bell and the sign of the cross, utters the first prayer and, if he chooses, sings one or more songs. As he sings he claps his hands and stamps one heel, then both. He is joined, except for the singing, by the seated congregation. For the second part, the minister delivers a sermon himself; or he "turns the floor over" to a specified person; or he "throws the meeting open" to anyone who feels that he has something to say.

Part three begins with all participants lined up informally in ranks facing the prayer table, the men on the left, the women on the right. There they begin to put on their garments. As many men as wish provide themselves with two hand bells. The minister or leader, who is in the front row of men closest to the prayer table, holds a single hand bell at first. He rings it with a long sweep and, if there are strangers present, he turns to face the ranks and briefly intones the outline of the procedure to be followed. This is necessary because there is still some individual and local variation at this juncture. In general, however, the pattern includes these features: All stand while somebody, usually a woman who has been called upon, sings a song. At its conclusion the minister begins to sing a wordless song while accompanying himself with a rhythmic ringing of two hand bells, and everyone begins to stamp his feet in time. At a signal from one bell (a more rapid ringing), all turn half around, counterclockwise, so that the company faces the door of the church. At a second signal another half turn is made so that all face the prayer table. Three complete turns are made in this way. Signalling again, the minister treads around to make a complete turn where he stands; then he begins the steady tramp that will take him slowly around the room. As he passes in front of the man on his left the latter makes the same movement and follows him. Simultaneously the woman on the inside of the rear rank turns around and begins the slow circuit behind and around her sisters to be followed in similar fashion by the woman on her right. As she reaches the opposite side of the hall the last man has joined the procession and she falls in behind him. At the same time the leading man steps in behind the last woman on the other side of the floor. Thus the circle of tramping, singing individuals is complete; and progressing slowly they make three circuits of the room. When this is finished, the procession unfolds in the reverse order of its formation and each person is once more back in his original position in the ranks facing the prayer table. The singing and stamping is stopped at a bell signal by the leader and all kneel in postion. Then begins the babel of individual praying which lasts until the leader signals for all to rise.

To begin the fourth movement another circuit of the room is made just as before; but upon its completion, instead of returning to ranks, the men unfold in a single line facing the center of the floor on the left of the hall and the women line up on the right side. Without intermission in the stamping, the woman farthest from the prayer table turns around once and starts down the line of her sisters for the handshake. She is followed by the woman to her right and that woman by the next so that a moving line is formed with each passer-by touching the upraised palm of each woman who is still in place. The line of women crosses over to pass before the men who in turn fall in behind the last person to pass by. At the conclusion of this handshake, if order prevails, the ceremony ends with the two lines of men and women facing each other across the hall as in the beginning.

This is the scheme of a full-dress Shaker service of worship, and normally, in all its details, it is reserved only for Sundays. However, there has been a growing tendency to duplicate it on other occasions. It is usual, for instance, to hold a full service on each morning of the customary three during which a camp meeting or a convention is held. During the camp meeting held at Tulalip over the third, fourth, and fifth of July, 1942, a service was witnessed on Saturday, the fourth, which conformed to the preceding plan in most respects. Upon that occasion the leader was a young man of the Tulalip congregation who called himself the "floor manager." He informed the visitors, of which there were some two hundred all together, that he had been asked to act in that capacity by a local committee who had sponsored the meeting. He called the assembly a "Fellowship Meeting." Others, in conversation, referred to it as a "Revival Meeting."

The floor manager on this day rang the large belfry bell twice, at approximately 9:30 and 9:45. Then about ten o'clock he stood in the doorway of the church and rang a hand bell, at which signal the people still outside got out of their cars and began to straggle inside. Upon entering, the majority of those who intended to join in the services went around the hall to shake hands with others already seated there on the forward benches. The latter did not rise for the greeting. The performance was leisurely and perfunctory. No one spoke and the church was quiet for some time afterward until it appeared that no others were going to join the company of thirty or forty worshipers seated along the walls in the front part of the church. There was a large crowd of perhaps seventy-five persons seated on the spectators' benches near the door. They entered and left the church as they pleased while the ceremony was in progress. So did the participants themselves. A doorkeeper sat on a stool at one side of the door and opened it to permit exits and entrances. He made no inquiries of anyone and appeared to exercise no restraints upon admissions.

Finally the floor manager rose, took the bell from the prayer table, sounded it twice or three times by a long sweep from over his head and along his side as he faced the congregation. He then replaced the bell, faced the table, and began

The altar of the Shaker church near White Swan, Washington

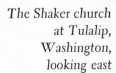

The Shaker church at Tulalip, Washington, looking east

to make the sign of the cross. The others joined him, and together they crossed themselves and repeated the words twice in the Nisqually dialect. This routine marked the beginning and the end of each subsequent phase of the service.

The floor manager spoke briefly, welcoming the guests, explaining his position as leader of the fellowship meeting, and urging participation to make it a success. He then called upon a visiting minister "to lead in prayer." The minister went to the prayer table, took the bell, and swung it five times. Facing the table he made the sign of the cross as the rest turned on their seats and joined him. Raising his right hand he began to pray in his own language. Many of the others sat silently with their right hands raised and their eyes closed. After five minutes the sign of the cross was made again and the minister faced the congregation. He started to sing a wordless song, and after it had been repeated two or three times he began to stamp one heel. With another repetition he began to stamp both heels, and the rest of the participants, still seated, did the same. The singing, which was by the minister alone, did not last long and at its conclusion he again faced the prayer table and made the sign of the cross, accompanied by the others. With that he returned to his seat.

The floor manager rose to ask whether there were "any announcements." A sermon or testimonial was in order, but as no one responded the leader "turned the meeting" over to another man "to open the service." The latter approached the prayer table and made the customary introduction to this third phase of the ceremony. About thirty of the participants along the walls stirred themselves at this point and rose to their feet to assume positions in ranks before the prayer table without prearrangement or guidance. There was an approximately equal number of men and women, separated by a four-foot aisle to the table. Five or six of the men held a bell in each hand. The women carried nothing. No one wore a garment. The leader was in the front rank of the men on the inside end nearest the table. When all was ready he turned to face the others and, in the characteristic intonation used by the Shakers, outlined the main figures of the service to follow. First, one of the women, whom he named, was to sing a song; second, they were to go around the room three times; and finally, there was to be the handshake. The rest of what followed was apparently taken for granted.

After the bell signal the appointed woman started her "Hai, Hai" song, at the same time raising both arms. Many of the others raised their right hands. As the song was repeated more fervently others joined in the singing. Some of the older women began to fan or rub their arms, heads, and chests; made motions of casting off something; stretched their arms upward; and periodically clapped their hands or swung their arms at their sides. About ten minutes were taken up with these exercises. Finally the voice of the woman subsided and she led the rest in the sign of the cross. The sound of the bell concluded this opening part of the movement.

The leader rang the bell again, made the sign of the cross, and, taking another bell from the table, began a song with the syllables "Yoi, yoi." The bell accompanied him and everybody started to tread in place. At the end of one refrain the leader raised his right-hand bell high up and shook it without interrupting the ringing of the other or breaking the rhythm. Thereupon everybody stamped slowly around in a half turn and remained facing the door of the church for another refrain. By this time most of them had joined the singing. The steady tramp of their feet combined with the sound of the bells and the swelling chorus of voices to produce a stirring roll that grew in volume with each repetition of the song. All participants kept their eyes closed. Some allowed their arms to hang limply at their sides as they jogged; others bent their elbows and held their hands out in front at approximately waist level with their thumbs up. As the bell sounded rapidly again they tramped around to face the prayer table. This movement was repeated twice.

As another signal was given, the other men who held bells added their clang to those of the leader and the stamping became sharper. Simultaneously the leader turned around once and began to pass slowly along the front rank of men while the woman on the aisle in the rear rank turned and proceeded in the same counterclockwise direction behind the other women. In order, the other men and women followed close behind the two leaders.

The single file of participants moved slowly around the hall three times. Each leader twice passed the point where he had initiated the movement before returning to it. The time required was twenty to twenty-five minutes. Roughly one in three people crossed himself and made a complete turn in passing before the prayer table. As the noise of the stamping and the bells increased, the words of the song were drowned out and most people ceased to sing. Each one was wholly absorbed in his emotions and with closed eyes was apparently unable to see where he was going. But the leaders at least were aware of their surroundings and the rest did not lose control of themselves. They returned to ranks, assuming their original positions by an unfolding of the procession in the same order as its formation.

The bells ceased to ring a few minutes later and the tramping subsided. Then upon a signal all knelt. The sign of the cross was made, to be followed immediately by a few voices lifted in prayer. Some supplicants spoke English, but the majority used their own language interspersed with English words. Gradually others added their supplications to the unintelligible chorus in a crescendo of fervent ejaculations, wailing appeals, and monotonous repetitions of the same words or phrases. Some individuals raised their arms heavenward; others applied their hands to their bodies or held their right hands with palm outward or thumb up. At times the confusion subsided until only one voice was to be heard, loud and ardent. Then again the rest would start. This continued for ten minutes or more and finally ended with one voice trailing off in a whimpering, exhausted appeal to Jesus. The sign of the cross was made, the bell sounded, and the company rose to its feet.

At this point there was an awkward break in the ceremony, due no doubt to mismanagement. The leader indicated that the ranks were to be broken and the men and women unceremoniously took their positions as they saw fit in single lines along opposite sides of the floor. The two lines faced each other. When everyone was ready, the bells began to sound and the tramping started again. Heretofore the spectators had taken no active part in the ceremony, but with this movement the doorkeeper motioned for all of them to stand up.

The handshake was started by the woman nearest the door of the church. While still standing in place she made a complete turn, then began to shuffle down the line of women to touch the raised hand of each. Before crossing palms for an instant each person crossed herself. The leading woman was immediately followed by the one next to her until all were moving across the floor in single file before the prayer table. The same few as before crossed themselves and made a complete turn as they passed in front of it. The line crept forward along the line of waiting men as each received the handshake from every woman. As the leading woman approached the end of the line of men the doorkeeper motioned for the spectators to stand up and receive the advancing procession.[3] They obligingly held up their hands but did not cross themselves. Some, however, joined the moving line by wedging in as it passed by.

The leading woman made another circuit from the point of her departure and then returned to the position that she had occupied while the congregation was lined up in ranks. Following her, the rest of the marchers regrouped themselves on this pattern and, hence, once again stood in rows facing the prayer table.[4] After a few minutes had passed the bell signal was given and the stamping ceased. The sign of the cross was made, and the same woman who had opened with a wordless song began another in English. It consisted of the words, "Oh, what a change Jesus has brought," repeated several times. At its end she made the sign of the cross, the leader gave the bell signal, and the formation dissolved as the worshipers went to their seats.

This concluded the service. It was then almost twelve o'clock, but since the food was not ready for the meal that was being prepared for the visitors and their hosts, the floor manager rose and asked whether anyone had something to say "to kill time." A white man, who evidently was a Pentacostal minister, consumed the greater part of the waiting period with a sympathetic and impassioned speech commending the Shakers as witnesses of the direct expression of divine will. There was no reply to his remarks and little interest was shown in them. Before lunch was announced two Shakers volunteered with testimonials of their personal regeneration through the workings of the faith.

These lengthy exercises took place on Saturday, and they were almost exactly duplicated by those which followed the next day. An even more interesting instance of the way in which this ritual is being extended into other contexts is noted briefly by Upchurch, formerly the superintendent of the Tulalip agency. The occasion for the ceremony which he describes was a business meeting called to discuss the tribal reorganization of the Skagit people remaining near Concrete, Washington. He writes: "A strong unit of this [the Shaker] cult is maintained in the Upper Skagit country. Recently a reorganization council meeting held in this vicinity was opened by prayer at the Shaker altar of the home where we gathered. It is significant that a woman was asked to lead the prayer. The home altar was arranged on a table with images, a cross, two burning candles and two large hand bells. First the right hand bell was rung raucously for some time, all arising; then followed a brief litany in Indian in which all joined at the same time crossing themselves; next, in English, a prayer of invocation evidently extemporaneous, followed by a second litany in the Indian tongue accompanied by the sign of the cross, then a few taps of the left hand bell seating the audience and completing the invocation. . . . After the business meeting was concluded in the home they adjourned to the nearby church where they enjoyed a further exercise of their religious spirit in a formal 'Shake.' " [5]

As a rule Shakers do not actually become ecstatic during the Sunday service. The power is invited and most of the outward manifestations of possession are displayed during the concerted praying, the ritual circuit, and the handshake. But normally the time is too short to properly prepare most people for the seizure, and they do not get beyond the stage of welcoming it by consciously simulating its presence. Genuine transport is far more typical of the curing ceremony.

The healing rites take place either in the church or at the home of a patient. There is accordingly some variation in the ritual due to circumstances. Usually there are specified evenings for the performances in the church. In the beginning they were called "prayer meetings," like the meetings held by Eells, Mann, and others on certain weekday and Sunday evenings; and in imitation of them they were held at the same times. Eells, for instance, had prayer meetings on Sunday and Thursday evenings. So did Slocum, and later the Shakers. The Makah and Quileute wanted to hold their weekday services on Wednesdays like Miss Clark. Other exigencies of time and place have made the regular dates variable; but in most places either Friday or Saturday nights have been preferred, the former being the more general perhaps.

Evening meetings begin at any hour after dinner. Commonly people begin to assemble around eight or eight-thirty depending upon the wishes of the congregation and the location of their church. Normally the latter is at some distance from any home, especially if there are whites nearby, for it might otherwise readily be adjudged a public nuisance. The shaking is usually in full swing by nine-thirty, and it continues indefinitely. Its duration is governed by the enthusiasm of the participants. If they are uninspired the meeting may end within an hour. If, on the other hand, the presence of the spirit is evidenced by a rather general seizure, or if there are candidates for conversion, the shaking may go on until one or two o'clock, or even later. Ordinarily at camp meetings, and when the Shakers have been called to a sick person's home, a break comes around midnight during which food is served. After that the shaking is resumed if the enthusiasm continues or if the patient feels no better. Usually as long as any Shaker feels the compulsion of the power the rest will co-operate and continue their exertions for his benefit.

The healing of the sick in homes naturally takes place when and where the circumstances demand. On the other hand, the rites held in the church often assume an artificial character. Since they take place at stipulated times, frequently there are no really ailing individuals to be helped by them. This, however, is not a deterrent. It offers a welcome opportunity for hypochrondriacs and chronic invalids to call for attention; and when they are not forthcoming with their complaints any one may oblige by offering himelf as a necessary subject. It is questionable how frequently the people who make an appeal for help on the church floor really believe themselves to be afflicted and in need of aid. Certainly the difficulties they complain of many times strike the observer as trivial if not wholly imaginary.

The curing ceremony, as performed in church, has also undergone a transformation since its inception. It is not known what formal procedure Mary Slocum instituted for administering to the sick. It is highly probable that her behavior, and that which she demanded of her brother, mother, daughter, and sister-in-law over the prostrate body of John at the time of her inspiration, was the core of the ceremony. For those postures and movements have persisted in the curing rite and have been extended beyond it into others. But nothing is known of any conventionalized forms or procedures sanctioned by her inspirations. Perhaps there was a minimum of indispensable routine and an allowance of flexibility according to circumstance. Doubtless the ceremony was simple. The evidence indicates that it had only two major components: a phase of prayer and one of shaking.

Rakestraw witnessed a healing ceremony sometime before the year 1900 which, according to his description, embodied only these two features. "It was my good fortune," he wrote, "to witness the treatment and attempted cure of a sick child by the shakers. This child, a little girl of twelve years old, was brought into the room by her father and held in his lap. There was every evidence from the appearance of the child that it was indeed very sick. The ceremony began with the lighting of the tallow candles on the numerous crosses. The father and child were placed in the center of the room and the shakers arranged themselves in circles around them and began ringing their bells in unison. Soon they began to jump in unison with the ringing of the bells. After this had continued for some time, one after another proceeded to the child and, by feeling over its body, took out some of the *masache*, which was burned over the candles.[6] Then, in a most reverential and devout manner, they knelt around the sick child and most earnestly prayed for its recovery. Their prayers were intermingled with responsive exercises in which they all fervently took part." [7]

At about the same time, Enoch Abraham assisted Louis at the healing of a Skokomish boy and girl. By his description the plan that was followed then was as simple as the foregoing; and according to him, their performance "was altogether different from what Louis taught in 1903." Upon this occasion, in 1899, the shaking party consisted of four people, Louis and his wife and Abraham and his wife. The little group was led into the house of the sick children by Louis. The three others followed without any attention to the separation of the sexes. They all made one circuit around the room without shaking hands with the people sitting along the walls waiting for them. Louis stopped at the east end of the room and knelt down. His three companions got to their knees where they stood. Louis then prayed for help in the task they were undertaking. When this was over the four Shakers stood around the bodies of the children as they lay on the floor and began to sing. Two or three around the room began to ring bells, and eventually the healers began to shake. At the end the Shakers informally shook hands with the others in the room.

Four years later Louis taught a more formalized procedure for healing the sick. He stipulated that upon entering a house or a church the "workers" must go around the room to touch hands with everybody and then divide themselves so that the women took seats on the south side of the building and the men opposite them. The sick person was to be placed in the center of the room and he or his relatives must ask for help. Thereupon the Shakers were to take their positions in ranks facing the east (prayer table), with the men on one side and the women on the other. Standing thus, anyone could pray or sing as the spirit moved him until all had finished. At the bell signal three tramping circuits of the room were to be made, at the end of which the men and women disengaged themselves from the procession so that they formed two parallel lines or arcs of a circle across the hall from each other. While the stamping and bell ringing continued without cessation this formation was to dissolve gradually as the power took possession of individuals and they began to mill indiscriminately around the patient. Finally, after all the shaking was over, the two lines were to re-form and the ceremony concluded with the ritual march of the handshake.

This soon came to be the regular pattern for a curing

ceremony. Its main outlines are apparent in Miss Ober's generalized description of those she witnessed in north-western Washington just after the turn of the century. Of them she wrote: "The usual evening service is the Shaker dance. This resembles the dance of that nearly extinct sect, the Shakers of New England, but this Indian Shaker religion has no connection with that sect. The worshipers form in ranks, the men on one side, the women on the other, facing the cross. All join first in a chant, and large silver hand bells are rung rhythmically. The leader starts off in a peculiar jog-trot of a dance, singing, 'hi, hi, hi, hoi, hi, hi, hi!' All join in, and in turn follow him, each one turning about three times, first. This motion is repeated when passing the cross. Soon the dancers form a large circle, and if there are any who seek salvation from sin or disease they are standing or sitting in the center. The rhythmic clang of the bells, the wild singing, the regular thud of heavy feet grows faster and faster, wilder and wilder, as the ardor of the worshipers in-creases.

"With upturned introspective faces, closed eyes, clasped hands, all seem oblivious to any outward thing, but somehow keep perfect step and time, avoiding all obstacles. They begin to gesticulate, and to me, every motion is full of meaning, and seldom devoid of grace. Some extend their arms, with waving motions, as if swimming through seas of ecstasy; others reach upwards, their hands outspread as if to grasp some occult power; some stroke and brush their bodies, ending each movement with an outward, downward fling, as if removing accumulations of sins; some with intent, ab-sorbed countenances, in attitudes of petition, are lost in devotion. These all seem to me the outward expressions of groping souls—the instinctive yearnings of poor, benighted humanity for divine revelations.

"The scene baffles description. More and more violent grows the dance, the noise, the whirling figures. Twirling like dervishes, weaving in and out of the circle, they dance.

Old Klootchmen [women] foot and jig as lightly as the young girls at their side, though fat, unwieldly and shapeless. Rough, sin-scarred men are transfigured, their faces shining with some mysterious inward power, their gnarled hands outstretched as if to take hold of the very God Himself. Young men and women lithely spring and dance, totally oblivious to sense or sex, completely dominated by that strange ecstasy. Suddenly the 'shaking' comes upon some one, every nerve, muscle and limb shaken in a manner impossible to describe. Sometimes it comes upon several, or it might be that it is withheld from all. The Indians assert that it cannot be produced by their own volition, neither can it be stopped at will. They claim it is an answer to prayer, and is the power of God, coming into their lives. They say that only when that comes upon one is sin and disease taken away." [8]

The ritual framework of this curing ceremony has, since the time of Louis, interacted with that of the Sunday service and each has been effected by the other. All the phenomena of shaking and the gestures of power invitation and absorption have been incorporated into the Sunday ritual from the curing rite. Contrariwise, the curing rite has absorbed many of the formal elements of the other ceremony. A noticeable recent transposition of this character—and one which is objected to by many people—relates to the expansion of the introductory phase of the curing ceremony. It is becoming the mode for the minister or the leader to "open the meeting" and then to preach before the shaking can begin. In other words, there has been a transfer of the invocation and the exhortation from the Sunday service. This is more typical of the healing ceremonies held in the church than of those that take place in the home of a sick person.

Theoretically the full church ritual should be performed in the home of the sick, but practical considerations often bring about its modification. In many homes there is no prayer table, or the sick room is too small for freedom of ritual movements, or the patient cannot be placed in its center. Then, too, the demands of the moment sometimes invoke greater spontaneity and this results in ritual short cuts and abbreviations. Upon occasions the power is too strong to resist and formal requirements are perforce ignored.

Once Moses Sampson, who lived near White Swan, was quite ill and the Shakers were called to help him. They came from the hop fields several miles away in buggies, and C. J. Johns was among them. They had been having regular meetings in the hop yards and Johns was "in good trim." On the way Shaker songs began to "come up" in his throat in an uncontrollable fashion and he had to sing. By the time the party arrived at the Sampson home he was "singing good." When he entered the house he started to go around to shake hands with all those present, as he should have done; but Sampson was lying in the middle of the floor, and Johns "couldn't go by him." He dropped his hat, peeled off his coat, and "started to work." Some of his companions joined him, others began to ring the bells, and the ceremony proceeded without any preliminaries. By midnight Sampson was able to sit up and the Shakers stopped to eat the food that had been prepared for them. After the meal they set to work again and continued until four o'clock.

Another instance of the way in which the home situation can alter formal requirements was afforded by an occurrence which the author was privileged to witness as a guest of Mary Black. Also present upon this occasion were Mary's husband, her father, her uncle, and her good friend and cousin, Maggie Jones. Maggie was not a Shaker; she was a Catholic. She was visiting Mary this day after a call at the hospital where her three children were being treated for advanced tuberculosis. Anxiety over the serious condition of one of the children weighed upon the minds of all those present and was the explanation for what followed.

When the afternoon meal was finished, while every one sat at the table, Mary bowed her head, crossed herself, made the sign of the cross and began to pray. At first for a minute or more, she spoke in her native language, meanwhile rubbing her hands and forearms. For another minute she prayed in English, praising God and asking His blessing. Then without moving from her chair she started to sing in low tones, "Hai, Hai, Hai, ho, ho, hai, hai." There was no accompaniment; only her uncle joined her as he held his right palm on edge by the side of his plate. The others remained silent with bowed heads. Mary sang the song three times, each rendition requiring three or four minutes. She uttered the syllables with forced catches in her breathing, and gave to the notes the quality of a moan or a sob. With each measure she seemed to become more distraught. On the second repetition of the song she rose from her chair and, with eyes still closed, began to cause her right hand to tremble in a voluntary manner. Her voice subsided each time in a whimper, to be caught up again in a high-toned wail as the song started again.

Maggie apparently knew what to expect, for as Mary rose she turned her chair away from the table so that she faced her and continued to sit in a passive manner with bowed head and hands relaxed, palms up, on her lap. Mary began to flutter her trembling hands over the head, shoulders, and hands of her cousin. For a moment she pressed Maggie's head and then began an extraordinary variety of manipulations over her body, all the while singing with growing intensity. She rapidly and gently patted Maggie with one or both hands; strongly patted or slapped her; brushed her and clapped hands after each sweep; fanned her while holding one hand on her head or breast; made scooping motions at various points on Maggie's body and then tossed her hands upward; touched Maggie while fanning her own breast; gently patted Maggie while holding a cupped hand before her; or held both hands loosely cupped in front of Maggie.

Mary was not without control of herself during this performance. She co-ordinated her actions and was aware of her surroundings. At one juncture she was taken with a coughing fit and had momentarily to cease her ministrations. At another she needed to wipe her nose and did so by taking up a piece of tissue from a nearby table. At length she indicated by a touch on Maggie's arm that she wanted her to get to her feet. Maggie responded and remained standing for the rest of the time. She seemed to be praying in a fervent, sibilant whisper throughout the treatment.

At the end of fifteen minutes Mary began to brush Maggie's limbs and breasts with sharp, passionate, downward sweeps of her two hands. As she did so she exclaimed, "Hai! Hai! Oh hai! Lord Jesus! Oh Lord, hai!" The movements had a sadistic quality about them, and they were obviously attended by strong emotional discharges. At the end Mary raised both arms upward and began to turn slowly around a step at a time as she whimpered "Ho, ho, hai, hai," in an exhausted voice. After she had revolved once or twice she ceased to cry, lowered her arms, took up a cloth and wiped her face. Both women then seated themselves and Mary began a long prayer in English. It embodied a thanksgiving, an appeal for mercy for Maggie and her children, and an admonition for her to accept God's will and not to grieve. It ended with "Amen. Glory to God. Amen. Glory to God." Maggie joined her in this then said, simply and humbly, "Thank you, Mary."

Just what purpose this ceremony was expected to accomplish was not plain, nor would it have been appropriate to ask. As has been mentioned, the curing gestures have become conventionalized and the question of their propriety in a given instance is ignored. In so far as was known, Maggie was in no way ailing physically herself. She did, of course, have a troubled mind.

The ritual of thanksgiving is quite simple as it is ordinarily practiced. But it, too, can become involved with other rites, as the instance just cited indicates. Shakers are supposed to have candles and a hand bell on their dining tables. When all are seated for a meal the candles are lighted, all bow their heads, and one of those present "asks the blessing." He does this by first ringing the bell softly before leading the others in making the sign of the cross. He then prays in his native tongue (usually) while all rest their right hands with thumbs up beside their plates. When he finishes the sign of the cross is made. During the meal the candle is kept burning. It is extinguished at the end after a repetition of precisely the same ritual as in the beginning, the prayer of which is interpreted as "giving thanks."

This is the full ceremony of a family thanksgiving, but there are many individual departures from the ideal. Some Shakers ignore it entirely at times, and among others it is abbreviated. At present there is a general tendency in Washington to neglect to use candles and bells. Candles are usually to be found on tables but they remain unlighted during meals. Bells are less common. In 1942 some of the leading Shakers of Oakville, Nisqually, White Swan, and Skokomish paid no attention to these accessories although all prayed before and after meals in typical fashion.

The blessing is also asked at meal time during public gatherings, as at camp meetings and conventions. Very early there developed a tendency to elaborate this ritual by including in it features belonging to other occasions. Instead of sitting down immediately, as at home, those who are gathered for the meal remain standing in their places around a long table for the preliminary rite. Someone is called upon to ask the blessing; but instead of concluding it after a brief prayer it is customary for him to supplement his petition with one or more of the wordless songs, as in the invocation for the Sunday service.

The ritual after the meal at conventions has been still further elaborated. At an early date, in the first decade of this century, it conformed rather closely to the service of worship instituted by Louis. Miss Ober has left a description of such a ceremony as she witnessed it during a convention at Neah Bay: "After the feast, all the company stood around the table for an hour and a half, and different ones prayed alternately. I could not then understand Chinook, but the earnest fervor of the petitions, the reverent faces and complete devoutness of all the worshipers attested to their sincerity and devotion. In all that time not one except the smallest children relaxed from their attitude of devotion, or opened their eyes. At the conclusion of the prayer service, they sang several chants, and then danced about the table seven times, ringing their large hand bells. When the leader passed my chair, he gave me the Shaker salutation, both our hands meeting in form of a cross, and most of the Indians did the same." [9]

In this description the long period of standing for successive individual prayers, the ritual circuits, and the handshake of Louis' Sunday service are apparent. Later the thanksgiving rite was modified but only to conform to the altered Sunday service. It became the rule, and remains so, for some one, after thanks has been offered, to deliver a sermon to the crowd still seated at the table. After this, all stand up, a song is started, the bells begin to sound, and a procession is formed to tramp three times around the table. In some places, when and where it is convenient, only one circuit of the table is made now, then the procession files out of the dining hall and into the church where the two last circuits are made.

The interposition of an exhortation in the thanksgiving rite has been subjected to serious criticism. Enoch Abraham and others have objected to it for years; and, according to him, they have "put a stop to it twice, at Mudbay and Oakville." The reasons given for the objections are not religious but practical. Seldom are the dining halls that are adjacent to the churches large enough to accommodate the entire company in attendance at a camp meeting at once. Therefore the guests must eat in groups. If the time at table is unduly prolonged those unfortunate enough to come last get hungry, have nothing to do in the meantime, and must eat cold food when their turn finally comes. These are the candid objections raised to the after-dinner sermons; but a few people have rationalized their displeasure by arguing that preaching should be done before all the people, not just a part. Nonetheless, the impulse to carry on with the custom is strong, and it is still practiced. At the Tulalip camp meeting in 1943 there were preachments after dinner, but they were short.

In some respects it is artificial to segregate the performances which result in the discovery of some hidden knowledge. In a sense, every shaking ceremony has this character. Almost always during a shaking session someone has a revelation of some kind: an insight into the cause of the sickness that is being treated, a threat of impending evil, and so on. Also, as with conversion, an ordinary meeting can develop into a concerted effort to seek out and destroy some evil influence.

There are, however, occasions when this is the purpose for which the meeting is called. There is nothing elaborate or distinctive about their ritual framework or about the behavior of the seekers. In curing, the trembling, extended hands of the healer are believed to be automatically guided to the source of illness; the individual "just follows his hands." Likewise in divination, when it is a question of locating something. As a clairvoyant Shaker moves about in various directions in the course of his stamping, his arms, reaching out in front of him, are said to be "searching for something." When they come in line with the object of their search they are drawn toward it and the Shaker follows. Others troop after him if he is led from the room. The devil chasing of the Yurok and Hupa will be recalled in this connection as will the occasion when Aiyel set his prayer table up on the bank of the Yakima River and led his companions in the direction of the missing body that he was called upon to locate.

A typical instance of a search occurred among the Quinault in the early 1920's: "Three years ago H. M. and H. C. got the shake power the same night. They took bells in their hands and went outside, ringing them as they went. The people followed them. The two went to the river, got into a boat, and rowed across the river (with closed eyes) to the cemetery. They walked into the cemetery and the bells soon 'pointed' to a particular place. The onlookers dug there and produced a woman's shoes, dress, and a lock of hair. Someone was trying to bewitch her. The people threw the things in the river and saved her life." [10]

Shakers feel that they should perform their own service over their dead, and when this is possible they do hold a ceremony. Despite this, no distinctive ritual seems to have been developed for the occasion. The procedure is left to the individual leader, and usually it resolves itself into a shaking exercise that differs little from the curing rite. The corpse is present, lying in state in the center of the church floor if it has been brought there, or in the living room of a home if not. Lighted candles are placed around it. After an interval of prayer and song, during which the Shakers stand facing the prayer table if there is one, three circuits of the room are made, and the participants end up in the two arcs of a circle around the corpse, still singing, tramping, and ringing bells. This activity may be concluded after a short time if all maintain control of themselves; but frequently it develops into the likeness of a curing performance with the corpse instead of a patient as the focus of the activity.

Alex Teio attempted to inject a new element into the funeral service. He once led his congregation past a corpse in a ritual handshake at the end of the funeral ceremony, "shaking" the hand of the dead individual along with all the rest. A few people followed his example, but most were revolted or terrified. They objected, and the innovation never became established.

It is probable that similar attitudes have caused the entire funeral service to remain unformalized and indistinct. Even though fellow members might not object to a Shaker performance over a dead relative, nonmembers, also related to the deceased, usually find the demonstration barbarous and will not permit it. About ten years ago a certain Yurok Shaker died. His family did not belong to the church, but a group led by Jimmy Jack decided to go to the funeral and hold their own services. The body of the dead man was at his home and, according to Indian custom, all his friends and relatives were expected to appear and mourn before the body was taken to the grave. As the rest were sitting solemnly around the room, Jack rose and began to pray and sing. His followers joined him, and soon about sixteen of them were stamping about the room to the rhythm of their hand bells. The rest of the mourners, including the relatives of the deceased, found this very disturbing. Even some of the other Shakers who did not participate thought that it was disgraceful. Nevertheless, since no one assumed the initiative to bring it to an end, the shaking continued for over an hour. When the corpse was taken to the cemetery a short distance from the house the Shakers followed and lined themselves up on one side of the grave. Jack again assumed command of the situation and began a long prayer followed by a song. He then called upon others to do the same; but before this could develop into another shaking session, the bereaved relatives ordered the gravediggers to close the grave and others to leave the family alone in its grief.

The conversion of a neophyte—that is, his introduction to shaking—always happens in the course of a manifestation of power among the participants in one of the ceremonies already described. It does not matter what the ceremony is primarily. Any of them may develop into an attempt to bring the power to some one who shows signs of being ready to receive it. Conversions may therefore be made upon any occasion when the excitement becomes so infectious that persons other than members are affected by it. When this happens a susceptible person is steered toward the center of the floor, his arms are raised above his head, the noise is intensified, and all the Shakers converge on him with their multiple and varied efforts to convey the power to him. Sometimes this occurs quite unexpectedly; in other instances it is generally known that a certain individual is trying to "get the shake," and at every meeting he is watched for evidences of his surrender to it.

Some individuals present themselves for conversion. This often happens at an evening meeting, and the candidate is treated almost exactly as a patient. He stands, often for hours on end, with his arms raised, whereas a patient sits on a chair; but the ritual and even the hand manipulations of those who work on him are ordinarily the same. Indeed, a patient often rises from his chair to become a shaking convert, and there is no break in the ceremony.

The hand gestures over a convert, when they are rationalized at all, are interpreted to have two functions: to remove the evil (of whatever kind) from his body, and to place the holy power in it—just as with a patient. Hands are applied, as in curing, during the confused intermingling of Shakers that follows the formal preliminaries of praying and circling the room. The various manipulations continue until the convert begins to shake or until everyone is exhausted. When the "worker's" efforts fail upon the first attempt the performance is resumed on successive nights until they succeed or until all are agreed that nothing is to be gained for the time being by further effort.

Some persons, like Louis, Big John, and others after them, have claimed the special gift to bring power to a candidate. Under such circumstances a division of function and a more distinctive ritualization has resulted. The pattern in this case is for the women to go around the candidate first to brush him. A selected number carry candles, the flame of which is smoothed into his body or is used to purify the evil collected on it. The men then follow, also to brush the candidate. After these purificatory rites the brushers withdraw slightly, although without ceasing their gestures or stamping, and the person with the gift approaches. He raises his hands above his head, gently grasps the power and smooths it into the convert's body. Theoretically this act takes place three times but in actual fact it goes on indefinitely. All of this, of course, happens slowly and without disturbing the rhythm of the bells, the stamp of the feet, or the oblivion of the participants who circulate about indiscriminately, each lost in his own ecstasy.

Candidates for conversion are sometimes spun around in a counterclockwise direction until they get quite dizzy. Often they fall to the floor where they lay without attention until they revive. This was at one time a more prevalent custom than at present. The recollections of a Quinault convert illustrate a moderate treatment of this kind: "Quite a few years ago I went to the church and stood up to 'join.' For two or three nights nothing happened. On the next night, after several hours, J. C. and another man started to 'shake me.' They are strong for giving the shake. They shook around me and finally began to work on my arms. Soon I began to feel my arms, then my hands, get warm. Then my hands began to shake. Soon I felt that warmth in my breast. Then my arms began to tremble all over, and my shoulders, too. But I didn't feel the shake in my feet. They took me by one arm and turned me around. Then one of my heels began to tap the floor. Soon I began to stamp with both feet. The shake came strong in me. Soon I was shaking all over and jumping high with every step. Some say they see things (a vision) when the shake comes to them, but I saw nothing. Only the shake came to me so that I couldn't help shaking." [11]

The pattern comes out more clearly in an account of the reconversion of a Quinault woman. She initiated the revolutions herself in this instance, presumably because she considered them appropriate to the conversion situation. "Mrs.

T. S. was a backslider but decided to rejoin. One night during the dance the power came to her. She bent over until her fingers nearly reached the floor and in this posture started turning round and round counter-clockwise. She spun more and more rapidly and finally fell heavily to the floor and lay motionless. Some of the dancers were alarmed and wanted to carry her to the bench but were restrained by others. After some time she arose and walked over to the bench and sat down." [12]

At one of the Quileute meetings around 1907, Reagan observed a similar performance. Of it he wrote: "At one of the meetings here recently, an old woman on receiving the inspiration put herself in a stooping, almost a sitting position; and then, after twisting her body around in a sort of corkscrew shape and bending forward at the same time so that no one under ordinary conditions could have maintained his equilibrium, she danced to the time of the chant as she screamed, cried, and moaned. At the same time she tried to pick up some imaginary thing from the floor with one hand as she waved the other trembling, shaking, quivering hand above her head." [13]

When the turmoil has quieted, if a neophyte has succeeded in getting the power and is convinced of it, he is supposed to kneel before the prayer table, raise his right hand, and unburden himself. Others pray with him. He is not expected to say anything in particular. This is his own private act of submission. The minister or some friend may kneel with him and by fervent prayer encourage him to give some sign of contrition. Many converts weep. Some are frozen in silence. Others release the tension in an outpouring of praises, pleas, and self-castigations. As has been said, this act is the nearest approach to a formal rite of induction into the church. Although desirable, it is not essential, and many Shakers regularly participate in meetings without having declared themselves publicly.

Robert Spott never conceded that he was converted to

Shakerism, although he did shake and members claimed him as one of the fold until he disclaimed them and refused to have anything further to do with the religion. He succumbed to shaking involuntarily and even against his conscious will. The occasion was the last night of a two-week revival meeting in the town of Klamath in northern California. Spott had attended several of the previous sessions out of curiosity mixed with a real interest in evaluating the new religion. As the shaking mounted to a climax on the final evening, one of the Shakers stood before him with hands trembling near his face. Spott felt himself "going to sleep" and became frightened. He made a move to leave the room but was restrained by his cousin, who later told him that he did so because he did not want the Shakers to have reason to charge him with being a devil. Spott cried to him, "Hang on to me! Don't let me go!" At that point several Shakers converged on him with jerking hands, some of them "throwing" candle flame on him. Suddenly he lost consciousness of what he was doing.

Later he was told that he pulled away from his cousin's grasp and got to his feet, shaking like the rest. He made his way slowly to the prayer table, on which there were six lighted candles. He ran his hands over the flames until his friends thought that he must be searing his palms. Then he began to stamp with the Shakers and move around the room, intermingling with them. He approached several of the spectators and brushed their heads, arms, and legs in the conventional manner. He continued in this way for an hour, his eyes closed, oblivious of what he was doing.

When he regained his senses he was in the middle of the floor with the Shakers around him. The noise had ceased. Jackson, the leader of the meeting, took his arm and led him to the prayer table where he was asked to kneel. He "felt foolish but didn't know what else to do," so he complied. The others knelt behind him. Jackson told him that he "had a contract with Jesus" and that he must pray. All the others began at once, but Spott remained silent. At the conclusion of the praying, Jackson told him to cross himself "in the name of the Father, Son, and Holy Ghost," which he reluctantly did. But when told to raise his right hand and swear to be a good Shaker he refused.

The following night, upon the insistence of Jackson, Spott attended the meeting; and while he was ringing the bells for the others, he again began to shake. He did not want to become a member of the church, to which he was opposed on several counts, and realizing his weakness for shaking he refused to attend any meetings after this second experience with it.

Candidates, like patients, are often roughly treated by their overzealous helpers. Later many of them either complain of or rejoice in their bruises. The "workers" also often injure themselves or bring on a state of exhaustion by overexertion—without any recognizable fatigue the following day. Shaking is strenuous exercise, and the participants perspire freely on warm nights. The more ardent male members meet the situation in a practical manner. As a curing or conversion ceremony begins they soberly remove their coats and shirts and hang them on nails provided along the walls. Usually only a few of the older men do this, and there is no warrant for the charge which has been made that Shakers expose themselves indecently.

Although somewhat overdrawn, Ober's description of a scene she observed during a convention at Jamestown over fifty years ago conveys a fair impression of the vigor and elation which frequently attends a conversion today. After watching the efforts of a crowd of Shakers to convert a young man on that occasion, Miss Ober wrote: "I never before witnessed such intensity of emotion as was expressed by those Shakers that night, or such strange ceremonies. Every one of that large gathering did all in their power to bring the 'shake' upon the boy. Here is where the hypnotism comes in. They clustered about him, dancing frantically, ringing many bells close to his head, making hypnotic passes over him, stroking, rubbing, whirling him round and round, but he never moved an eye-lash, or flinched. I saw women whirling round and round him for over an hour, until I could scarcely distinguish their separate figures, so rapid were their dizzy evolutions. Then they whirled him about with them, till severally they fell out, exhausted, and only one was left, a small woman whose head did not reach the boy's shoulder. How she did it I cannot tell, but she whirled that stiff, motionless body round and round, and all over the room, and he never moved even his feet. They passed so close to me I could see them clearly, and the boy was like a wooden statue, without sign of life or motion. Finally both fell to the floor, the boy's head striking with an awful crash.

"The woman was soon resuscitated, but the boy lay without life or motion, in the very same attitude that he had taken at the beginning. For an hour the Shakers continued their performances, until at 4 A.M. I left. But the next morning, when I went to the first meeting, there was Daniel [the boy], as lively as a cricket, dancing away, and full of happiness, for he had 'got the shake.' " [14]

On July 5, 1942, the author witnessed a lengthy ceremony which culminated in an attempt to convert a young man at the Tulalip church. A camp meeting or convention was in progress, and the ceremony was properly a Sunday morning service for the large number of Shakers assembled from other congregations. But, as sometimes happens, the finale after the handshake developed into a vigorous session of shaking, and this provided a propitious atmosphere for the induction of new members. The ceremony was also noteworthy because of the elaboration of the invocation. The particulars of the service are noted for future reference.

The steeple bell was rung three times, at approximately fifteen minute intervals. Most of the people were already congregated around the church yard, sitting in their automobiles and talking. As the last bell sounded, around ten o'clock, some of them began to straggle to the church door. In a listless manner both spectators and participants seated themselves, those among the latter who entered late usually proceeding to make the rounds of handshaking with others seated in the forward part of the church.

The prayer table was in a recessed alcove at the back of which was a large wooden cross with a smaller one nailed at its center. Twelve other small crosses were spaced along the arch of the recess. The white cloth on the prayer table reached half way to the floor, and three blue crosses were sewed to the front apron. On the table were six hand bells and four lighted candles; and toward the back there were some artificial flowers. Overhead, near the corners of the room, were four candelabras with twelve unlighted candles in each. From the center of the ceiling was suspended another candle holder in the shape of a circle circumscribing a cross.

When it appeared that all were present, the "floor manager" approached the prayer table, grasped the hand bell, swung it twice, faced the prayer table, and made the sign of the cross accompanied by the others. Turning to the congregation again he intoned a few preliminary remarks to "my dear brothers and my dear sisters"; then called on a man by the name of Richards to "open the service."

Richards came forward and sounded the hand bell for the invocation. The participants along the benches in the front part of the church got to their feet. About twenty of them proceeded to line up in ranks facing the prayer table, the men to the left, the women to the right. An equal number simply remained standing in their places along the benches. This was not by prearrangement; it was optional with the individual. Richards then led the congregation in making the sign of the cross, following which he raised his voice in a song beginning with "Hai, hai." He sang alone, and after repeating the song he started to clap his hands and stamp his feet.

The others joined in the clapping and stamping for two or three further repetitions of the song. Richards concluded it with a prayer in English. Then he again raised his voice with the song, "I praise my Lord and Savior, Jesus." This was sung six times. At its end Richards led the others with the sign of the cross, rang the hand bell, and all returned to their seats and sat down.

The floor manager rose to introduce the next phase of the service, namely the exhortation. Several prominent people were present, he said, and he was sure that they had a message to bring to the others. Therefore, he was going to call upon the bishop, William Kitsap, "for a few words." Kitsap rose, read a text from the Bible that he carried, and launched into an exegesis of it. His presentation and his mannerisms closely resembled those of an evangelistic minister. He took about twenty minutes for his message, after which the floor manager announced that he would "turn the floor over" to Mary Krise. Mary, also carrying a Bible, approached the prayer table where she made a complete turn before making the sign of the cross. Facing the congregation she sang a verse of the Christian hymn, "This little light, let it shine," accompanied by a few voices scattered over the congregation. Then she began to preach in a forceful, articulate manner, likewise employing the gesticulations and dramatic inflections of a revivalistic preacher. At the end of fifteen minutes she concluded her message with the sign of the cross, joined by the rest of the participants.

The floor manager asked Isidore Tom of Lummi to "lead the service." At the prayer table Tom rang the bell slowly for several seconds while the others rose to their feet and took their places in ranks. Everyone lined up this time. About ten of the forty or fifty had brought their garments in little bundles which they now proceeded to put on. About six of the men carried two hand bells each. When all were ready Tom outlined the order of the service to be followed with the characteristic intonation. As all faced the prayer table the sign of the cross was made, to be followed by a "Hai, hai" song from a girl in the front rank who had been called upon by Tom. As she continued singing the girl began to move between the ranks of her sisters, and as she passed behind each one she gently drew her hands down their sides and crossed herself. At the same time, one of the men from the front row passed along the lines of men, pausing behind each one long enough to hold his right hand over their heads momentarily and cross himself. Many of the women stroked, patted, or brushed their own bodies while this went on. Most of the men simply held their right hands up. When the man and the girl came to the end of the rear ranks they returned to their places and she started a new song: "Jesus is here to show us the way." At its conclusion the sign of the cross was made.

Immediately Tom started to sing, "ai, ai, o, o" and everyone began to tread lightly. After one repetition he raised the bell aloft and rang it rapidly. Everyone stamped around in a half turn which brought them facing the door of the church. Others had by now begun to join the singing. At another signal from the bell they stepped around another half turn to face the prayer table. The completed turn was performed twice more, whereupon Tom sounded the bell again. This was the signal for those carrying bells to commence ringing them to the rhythm of the song. At once the tread of feet became more vigorous and the volume of the singing was increased. Tom turned in place once, then began to move slowly for the counterclockwise circuit of the hall. Simultaneously the woman at the inside end of the rear rank did the same. They were imitated and followed by others in succession. In the course of the circuit a few individuals turned around and crossed themselves as they passed the table.

When the procession had slowly circled the room three times, ranks were resumed, each person in the same position as before. After a minute of stamping in position Tom ceased to ring his bells, the others did likewise, and the noise subsided. All kneeled down. As another sign of the cross ended, first one then another raised his voice in a confusion of prayers. When the last prayer trailed into silence the same girl who had sung before began again with "Hoi, Hoi, Yai," as she clapped her hands in time with it. Others clapped also. At the end of several repetitions she made the sign of the cross with the others. Another woman and then a man sang similar songs, opened, closed, and accompanied in the same fashion. Finally Tom gave the bell signal and all rose to their feet.

Turning to his fellow participants Tom told them that they would now make one circuit of the room as before, then all shake hands. He started to sing, "Ai, Ai," and once again the bells and the stamping began. Raising the bell over his head and ringing it rapidly was the signal for everyone, simultaneously, to make one complete turn in place before the procession began to form and move around the hall. The movement ended with the men in a line on the left side of the hall and the women similarly placed on the right. The woman on the end then began the handshake, which did not differ from the description already given. Several people, however, began to lose control of themselves, jerking their arms and heads violently.

The bell ringers did not participate in the handshake. They stepped out of line into the center of the floor where they proceeded to stamp and ring vigorously for the others. The handshake ended as it had begun, with the two lines of men and women; but because of the number participating the ends of the lines were bent inward and nearly touched, forming two semicircles.

Formally this was the end of the service, but by the time the handshake was completed the feeling ran so high that several people were actually shaking in an unrestrainable fashion. Moreover, it became apparent as the stamping in place continued that a young man, who had come forward for conversion the night before, was approaching a crisis. He had gone through the ritual with the others and now, as he stamped with them with eyes closed and arms outstretched, he seemed to be on the verge of shaking. Sensing this, some of the others intensified their efforts. Someone started the song again, and the bells and the stamping became deafening. Tom moved toward the boy and, touching his arm, led him into the center of the circle. Two of the bell ringers drew nearer to him for greater effect and gradually others who were shaking left their places to focus their hand manipulations on him. Shortly all ritual order had dissolved and each person became engrossed in his own activities, as happens upon any occasion given over to shaking.

The throbbing din continued unabated for approximately half an hour. The boy did not succumb. Although obviously intent upon shaking he did not do more than exhibit a slight tremor of his hands. Gradually the noise quieted although several people continued to shake violently. Among them was a middle aged woman, neatly dressed in white, who throughout the ceremony twirled a white handkerchief in her left hand. By this time most of the spectators were on their feet and had pressed forward to the edge of the floor. The woman in white began to weave among them, gently patting or fanning their faces and breasts with her trembling right hand while she twirled the handkerchief in the other. As the singing died down she started a new song: "Jesus is our savior." This required a change in time, which was promptly adopted by the bell ringers and followed by a change of tempo in the stamping.[15]

The general enthusiasm was renewed, and once again a climax developed. Still the boy showed no signs of losing control of himself. Consequently, after another forty-five minutes the vigor of the participation decreased, the bell ringers stopped one by one, and the demonstration came to a ragged end. Individuals who a few minutes before had been ecstatic distractedly wiped their eyes and faces with their hands or handkerchiefs and went to their seats. There was no formal closing of the service.

It has already been said that, although the bylaws of the Shaker church provide for the appointment of officers, no consistent ritual of ordination has evolved. There is, therefore, not much to be said about it, except that it is felt to be important, though not indispensable, and that each official called upon to perform it does it in his own way. It has not been uncommon in the past for one officer to pass the obligation on to another or to do nothing beyond announcing the accomplished fact of an appointment to an office without any formal act of induction. Enoch Abraham, however, considered this inappropriate. Therefore, when he, as head elder, was asked to ordain William Kitsap in 1935 he had to draw upon his imagination. Asking the bishop-elect to stand before him at the prayer table in the church he questioned him briefly on matters of faith and sincerity. Then as Kitsap knelt with two elders flanking him, Abraham prayed "for the spirit of Christ to descend upon him." This brief rite was followed by one of the women of the assembled congregation singing "Come to Jesus." Finally everybody filed by to shake hands with the new bishop.

The rites of baptism and dedication are scarcely more crystallized or elaborate. Although the dedication of a church is frequently spoken of, as well as the dedication of garments and other paraphernalia, it is difficult to discover what constitutes the ritual of consecration. It seems probable that any ordinary ceremony held in a new church to officially open it is considered the ritual of its dedication. Two new hand bells were given to the Tulalip church by some member to commemorate the occasion of the camp meeting held there during July, 1942. At the first session, on Friday evening, July 3, a visiting minister was asked to "dedicate the bells" before the ceremony of the evening started. This man, without any particular attention or reference to the bells, prayed for a short time and sang a song in a way that differed not at all from what has here been called an invocation and what is referred to by Shakers as "opening the meeting." Indeed, it served just this purpose, for following it came a long speech and exhortation by the floor manager who then "turned the meeting" over to another. In short, the dedication was not a special ceremony or even a distinct one; and that is probably generally the case.

Baptism is not more important than ordination, and it is subject to the same individual variation in ritual. At one time it had a wave of popularity, comparable to confession, but there is no longer much attention paid to it. About 1909 Miss Ober received a letter from an unnamed Yakima Indian which read: "Some [Puget] Sound Shakers come to Yakima Shakers, and they have new God's gift, they got baptism. But near all us Shakers, we get baptised. I glad to get baptism. I read in Holy Bible about Jesus get baptism, and I not know how it mean. Now I know that baptism mean bring me nearer to Jesus—mean my heart all clean like Jesus. I glad I get baptism—God's gift." [16] In other words, some member of one of the Puget Sound congregations had received the help or gift to baptize others.

Enoch Abraham baptized nine children while he was head elder. William Hall, the veteran Jamestown minister, Robert Choke, a former Chehalis Shaker, and a few other men have at times officiated at this sacrament. Bishop Heck has not looked with favor upon these ministrations, believing, it seems, that they pertain to his office rather than to those of ministers and elders. In any event, at the present time the need is not felt for baptism and there is no generally recognized precedent to be followed in administering it. When Abraham baptized he had the mothers hold their children before the prayer table in the church while he quoted the passage beginning: "Suffer little children to come unto me, for theirs is the kingdom of heaven. . . ." Then, sprinkling their heads with water, he placed his hands upon them and consecrated them with the words, "I baptize thee in the

name of the Father, the Son, and the Holy Ghost. Amen."
It was, he said, "the Catholic way," but he knew no other.
Choke and others reject the use of the Bible, so their ritual
must of necessity be different.

The rite of confession has also been individually treated,
and was more popular in the past than now. It, too, came to
the Shakers as a special gift or help vouchsafed a few. It was
Slocum, however, who instituted the requirement before
the days of shaking and established the main outlines of the
rite. It was a part of the message that he brought back from
heaven. He impressed upon his followers the necessity of
confessing sins and asking for their forgiveness in order to
attain salvation. The proper time was on Friday. According
to one informant, Slocum instructed his congregation to
ask silently for forgiveness on Friday mornings within the
privacy of their own home; but Slocum's sister-in-law stated
that he received confessions himself and then conveyed them
to a priest in Olympia on Fridays for absolution. Further, she
said, in receiving confessions Slocum did not hear them, for
he rang a hand bell all the while that the petitioner spoke of
his sins. It is not known whether he imposed penance upon
the sinner, but it is doubtful.

It is probable that the account of Slocum's procedure
during confession accords with the facts. At any rate, it was
the one accepted by the Shakers. Louis was the first to receive
the gift of accepting confessions. Shortly after they joined
the church, Enoch Abraham and his wife confessed to him.
Friday was the day set for this. Louis received them sepa-
rately in the church at Mud Bay, and no one else was present.
They had been instructed to provide themselves with a little
bundle of sticks, each stick representing a sin that was to
be confessed. As Abraham and Louis stood in front of the
prayer table Louis rang a hand bell once and they made the
sign of the cross. Then, as Louis began to ring the bell continuously so that he could not distinguish what Abraham was
saying, Abraham reviewed his sins, and after each admission

he laid a stick on the table and Louis brushed him. Finally both prayed and made the sign of the cross. There was no shaking. Louis burned the little stick counters when it was all over. Nothing more was demanded of Abraham, and Louis did nothing further. It is said that although he could not hear the words of the confession he knew if a sin had been omitted and promptly told a person who tried to conceal it.

Two other people are remembered in their roles as confessors, but not so happily as Louis. Dick Jackson of Mud Bay claimed the right to hear confessions shortly after Louis did. Joe Riddle, a half-blood Yakima, received the same gift soon after he was converted to the faith in 1903. Riddle followed the pattern established by Louis except that he responded to calls from people to take their confessions in their homes. Several Shakers today, however, affirm that "his help was not right," meaning that he offended some of those who confessed to him. Dick Jackson was even more unfortunate. He listened to the words of his penitents and evidently did not feel himself bound to secrecy about what he heard. It is said that he gossiped to his wife, who also lacked the necessary restraint for a confidant, so he "lost his help." Riddle died in 1935, but even before this occurred private confessions had lost their appeal.

NINE ✠ John Slocum's Religion

JOHN SLOCUM's teachings, to the extent that we can determine what they were, derived almost wholly from Christian sources. In ritual and ideology they reveal that he was influenced by both his Catholic and his Protestant contacts, relatively little by his Indian background. In some instances it is possible to assert with some confidence that a particular element in his system is more Catholic than Protestant in its emphasis—or vice versa—and to point to historical facts to give substance to what might otherwise be nothing more than a deduction from general principles. In the meagerness of our knowledge, however, many questions regarding source and emphasis must remain unanswered.

Little more can be said about a large part of Slocum's religion than that it was generically Christian. In historical terms this means simply that the elements in question are common features of the various Christian denominations, certainly those with which Slocum was familiar, and that he undoubtedly had them impressed upon him by all missionaries. The bulk of this common ground lay in the realms of doctrine and belief. Included in it was a recognition of the Trinity, in so far as this concept could be understood: the belief in an omniscient and omnipotent God, together with His Son, Jesus Christ, and His Presence, The Holy

Ghost. The concepts of angels and of the devil and of their localization in heaven above and hell below also influenced Slocum's interpretations of man's relations to his Creator. Equally essential to his belief and to Christian dogma was the notion of a fundamental antagonism between the forces of good and evil in unremitting conflict over the souls of human beings. Closely associated with this was the idea of sin which defined the inherently base character of man, emphasized his vulnerability to evil, and stressed the need for his submission to the will of God for his regeneration. This carried with it the conviction of the immortality of the soul and of its eternal salvation or damnation as reward or punishment for a life of good or evil on earth. The Christian combination of an ethical and devotional code was the accepted measure of the redeemed; there must be a public profession of faith combined with good works dictated by brotherly love. The consolation of the spiritually oppressed and the alleviation of physical pain fell within the definition of divine dispensations granted as a result of faith and prayer. Virtue and spiritual rewards, however, were to be rated above material gain. Finally, Christian eschatology gave dramatic force and urgency to these imperatives. The end of the mundane order of things was imminent; the millennium was to be heralded by the second appearance of Jesus Christ and would be marked by the final judgment of all souls, the destruction of the wicked, the reunion of the saved, and the eternal rule of right, truth, and justice.

Among the overt features that characterized Christianity in general and Slocum's version of it alike was the existence of a church building; that is, a separate structure dedicated as a place of worship and to some extent regarded as holy and inviolate. Along with this went the idea of a congregation with its spiritual leader in the person of a minister or priest and a regular order and periodicity of religious services in the church. In addition, there were a variety of special behavioral sets among which may be mentioned the physical attitudes expressive of solemnity, supplication, prayer, and spiritual fellowship and numerous postures and acts too variable and elusive to be embodied in the religion. There were two gestures that took on consistency under Slocum's influence and became marked features of ritualistic behavior. These were the sign of benediction and the testimonial handshake.

Demers, the Catholic missionary, tells us that upon one occasion he, Demers, combined these gestures. Speaking of his mission to the Indians around Fort Yale on the Fraser River in November, 1841, he wrote: "All drew themselves up in line for the indispensable greeting, and it was necessary for me to present one hand to those 306 persons, while I held the other elevated above my head; a double ceremony for the women who had their infants on their backs; I was completely exhausted." [1] It is supposed here that the missionary offered his right hand to the Indians and held his left above his head. Probably this was not general practice, and Slocum did not institute the combination.

The upraised right hand of the priest and the minister was nevertheless a constant feature of Christian group worship and Slocum adopted it as a mark of his identification with Christians. Whether it was he who advocated its adoption by all members of his congregation is unknown. Someone did, as is evidenced by the fact that very early this gesture became a symbol for the Shakers. As members of the faith, they ordinarily adopt this pose for photographers.

The custom of shaking hands as a salutation and an expression of friendliness was certainly introduced among the Indians by white men, and it is evidently this form that Sloclum used in his testimonial handshake. It is by no means certain, however, that Slocum was responsible for converting what we suppose to be a secular act into a semireligious formality. There is good evidence to indicate that the missionaries themselves were instrumental in consolidating, if not in establishing, a precedent in this respect which Slocum and his associates may or may not have taken more seriously than was intended. In this connection we must not forget that the handclasp is used by ministers of the gospel as well as by other people. Mann, and perhaps Eells and others, greeted their parishioners at the church door in this traditional manner.[2] It is also to the point to note that those who became converted were commonly welcomed into the Christian fold with the same gesture of good will. The Congregational Church formalizes this welcome into a brief ceremony called "the giving of the right hand of fellowship"; and new Presbyterian elders are inducted into office with the same formality.[3] It may be that the Catholic missionaries also regularly took the hand of converts. When Demers traveled among the Indians on the eastern part of Puget Sound in August, 1841, it is said that he "rejoiced to see tribes who had never seen the *blackgown* able to sign themselves, sing and pray around the Ladder when the priest was giving the hand to a newcomer." [4]

Perhaps it is enough to show that these precedents existed in Slocum's experience with Christian behavior. It may have appeared to him that the handclasp was an integral part of a religious system regardless of the sect, and in no instance was it inharmonious with the prescribed forms of Christian faith. The meaning that he gave it might have seemed to him to be the most significant among the many that we impute to it. Considering the context in which he found it, he could have reasonably inferred that the handshake was a humble expression of the dependence, confidence, and faith due a religious teacher. Whether this implication was there by design or whether he read it into the situation, in all probability he was not discouraged in the interpretation once it impressed him.

As has been mentioned, this handshake has not survived with the same solemn overtones. It might be noted however, that a characteristic and unexplained Shaker gesture during prayers is the extended right hand. It is held at waist level, somewhat retracted, with palm open and thumb up. Perhaps this is a survival of the testimonial handshake.

Several aspects of Slocum's religion can rather readily be referred to Catholic sources. Most of them are either objects or acts. The sign of the cross obviously belongs in this category. This was one of the first things taught the Indians by Catholic missionaries, and it became a kind of shibboleth.[5] Slocum advocated its use before retiring at night, before arising in the morning, before and after meals, and perhaps at other times. This gesture and the words that accompany it were employed to excess by the first Shakers who, as Eells says, used it "far more often than the Catholics do." It is also evident from the statement of Silas Heck that with the advent of shaking, if not before, the making of the sign of the cross took on a magical value. He mentioned that the early Shakers crossed themselves at every turn to ward off evil—before entering or leaving a house, before eating, and before greeting a stranger. There is a possibility that this concept was also borrowed directly from Catholic teaching, and was not altogether an Indian invention. Upon this point we cannot be sure, for there is no unequivocal evidence to substantiate the suggestion that the missionaries conveyed the idea that this short prayer and gesture was effective in staying the forces of evil. The idea is not entirely foreign to Catholic precept.[6]

It is likely that Slocum instructed his congregation to join him in making the sign of the cross in unison. This happens repeatedly in Shaker services. Despite the occurrence of some group responses in Congregational and Presbyterian meetings, participation by the congregation is not a marked feature of these forms of worship.[7] It is more characteristic of Catholic ideology. In any case we are probably safe in assigning this particular group response to Catholic influence.

Among other things taken over from Catholic ritual by Slocum were candles, an altar, bells, and a vestment. Perhaps it need not be demonstrated that the first of these items was of Catholic origin. It is true that candles were common means of household illumination.[8] But Slocum specifically associated them with religious services. He called them "the light of Christ." To further establish the point it is perhaps unnecessary to go beyond noting that Eells several times disdainfully mentions the significance of lighted candles in the "Catholic" services conducted by Billy Clams and his associates.

Slocum's altar became the Shaker prayer table. It is not known what he called his altar or what he kept on it; but we may suppose that it did not differ in use from the table that is to be found at present in Shaker churches and in most Shaker homes. The table conforms to its suggested prototype in being covered with a white cloth and in supporting candles, crosses, and bells, all of which are, when not in use, covered with another white cloth. Even though this simple table lacks many of the requirements of a properly appointed Catholic altar it might still be a rather faithful duplicate of the ones that Slocum was familiar with in the rough mission chapels around Puget Sound during his day. Reporting upon the state of the ten churches and chapels under his care in 1881, Boulet stated that there were no regular seats in any of them, only benches, some with backs, some with none; that only two or three of these buildings had altars "that might be considered worthy of the name," while one had none at all and another had a "mere shelf running across the whole end of it"; that some churches had no railings at all to set the altar space off from the common floor and others had only a picket fence; and that only one church had "the vestments and sacred vessels strictly necessary for the Holy sacrifice." [9] Grandidier, visiting the tribes on the Fraser River in 1861, was forced to reduce the requirements for mass to a minimum. For him, "two empty demi-johns served as pillars, my trunk as table, a blanket as altar cloth, and two boxes of matches as candlesticks." [10] Doubtless, a plain wooden table was often an acceptable substitute for an altar even in established missions.

It has been stated that Slocum donned a white shirt, wearing it with the tails out, to conduct his services. This can hardly be otherwise than an imitation of the priest's alb or surplice. These garments were undoubtedly familiar to Slocum from his familiarity with priests, some of whom wore garbs that were not so radically different from his imitation.[11] There were, moreover, other models that might well have influenced him, and they likewise stemmed from Catholic precedents. Chirouse, who was in charge of the Tulalip mission center for the Sound area from 1857 to 1878, encouraged Indian youths to assist in church services and supplied them with vestments as an incentive to participate. For his acolytes he provided red and black cassocks with surplice and belt.[12] To keep the younger children preoccupied with religious matters he also devised a small ritual for them for morning and evening on Sundays and on feast days consisting of a recitation of the Pater Noster, the Ave, the Credo, and the Gloria Patri. To them he gave long white tunics which had to be left in the church and were to be worn only upon these occasions.[13]

Since we know very little of Slocum's early life it would be gratuitous to assume that he was familiar with this attention given to vestments at Tulalip. On the other hand Chirouse was accustomed to taking his young converts to act as choir boys or to offer instructive entertainment on his regular visits to Puyallup, Steilacoom, and Olympia.[14] Moreover, Indians from the southern part of the Sound sometimes made trips to the Tulalip mission after St. Joseph's, the Catholic mission near Olympia, was abandoned. Opportunities were therefore not lacking for Slocum to observe the ceremonial use of a white slipover garment by religious leaders.

Spier has uncovered evidence to show that Slocum could have been stimulated by the Smohalla or Dreamer Cult, a

quasi-native religious movement that reached its climax as
it spread over parts of Washington, Oregon, and Idaho in
the early 1870's. It had its inception around Priest Rapids,
on the middle Columbia River, sometime between 1850 and
1860. Its founder, Smohalla, was supposed to have died and
returned to life with a message for the Indians. We will not
enter into the details of his doctrine and ritual at this point,
but will note, as Spier has shown, that this cult was in all
probability only a special manifestation of an old indigenous
pattern—to which Spier has given the name Prophet Dance
—compounded with Christian elements that spread into the
Washington area on a purely aboriginal level and through
native channels of dissemination beginning in the 1830's. The
source of the Christian elements was the famous group
of converted Iroquois Indians who journeyed westward and
came to make their home among the Flatheads of Montana
and who eventually were responsible for sending a call to
the east for missionaries to fortify their convictions and to
spread the doctrine among other Indians around them whose
interest they had aroused.[15] A number of local derivatives
of the Smohalla Cult appeared toward the end of the last
century and some have continued to flourish. At present the
cult on the Yakima and Warm Springs reservations is known
as the Pom Pom religion in onomatopoetic reference to the
sound of the hand drum that is a prominent feature of its
service.

We shall turn to Spier's thesis from time to time as particular items come up for comparison. At the moment it is
relevant to point out that Smohalla, some years before Slocum's advent, had adopted a ritual garb which simulated
a priest's surplice. We are told that this was simply a white
shirt with a stripe down the back, but "he was pleased to call
[it] a priest's gown." [16] Smohalla's garb may have been an
inspiration to Slocum, but that is improbable. It is very
doubtful that Slocum ever saw Smohalla or had any direct
knowledge of his religion. They had contacts with the Yak-

ima bands which separated them, but on this particular there is no evidence to suggest a transfer of the idea. As far as is known the Yakima followers of Smohalla have always made it a point of doctrine to wear nothing but native dress during their meetings and there is no mention of a white garment to be worn by the leader. The case is stronger for an independent imitation of this Catholic element by the two cult founders.

Slocum used a hand bell to call his congregation to worship. This was a custom very early established by the Catholic, and perhaps other, missionaries. In May, 1840, Demers visited the Chinook Indians near Astoria where, "a little bell in one hand, and a Catholic Ladder in the other, he continued his mission for three weeks." [17] This and several other references to the subject leave no doubt that Slocum used the same kind of bell as did these missionaries and that he employed it as they did to summon the Indians to prayer and religious devotions. Furthermore, Chirouse and his associates were accustomed to training native catechists in outlying districts who could baptize and conduct simple services in their absence.[18] To these persons they gave hand bells, and sometimes a Ladder and a flag, as symbols and appurtenances of their office.[19] Billy Clams used to carry a hand bell with him, "because he was a Catholic," an informant said. Very likely it had been given to him by one of the missionaries, perhaps by Chirouse himself. We do not know whether Slocum was made a catechist or whether he was given a hand bell or procured it on his own initiative. Regardless, he probably followed the long established pattern set by the Catholic missionaries and borrowed the idea directly.

On one interesting point with respect to the use of bells there is no information. The records do not reveal whether the missionaries used the summoning bell also to announce the elevation of the Host or to mark other points in religious services. Neither is there any information as to whether Slocum employed his hand bell for similar purposes. It is quite

probable that he and the missionaries did and that a precedent was thus established which adequately accounts for
Shaker usage. A dinner bell is large and clangorous by comparison with a sanctuary bell; but, again, expediency may
have dictated this adaptation by the missionaries. Chirouse,
while ministering to the Yakimas in 1851, lacked even a hand
bell and so used a blast from an ox horn to announce the
times for prayer.[20]

Catholics and Protestants alike at times demanded a public confession by their converts, especially in cases when a
person had violated a pledge. Slocum, however, like the Catholics, advocated private confession of all sins; and identifying
himself in part at least with a priest he attempted to establish himself as a confessor. At the same time it seems that he
intended to act only in an intermediary capacity. According
to his sister-in-law, he believed it to be his duty to transmit
the confessions in some way to a priest in Olympia. It is not
known whether Slocum ever actually did this or whether it
would have been acceptable practice if he had tried. It is
interesting, however, that he set Friday as the day for confessions, for Chirouse, writing to his Superior General in
1865, reported that Fridays and Saturdays were being especially reserved for the acceptance of confessions.[21] Whether
this continued to be common practice does not appear from
the records available, but it is at least probable that Slocum
was again adopting what seemed to him to be a standard
usage.

In at least two respects Slocum's idea of prayer conformed
more closely to Catholic norms than to Protestant. In point
of posture, he instructed his followers to kneel while praying.
Catholic missionaries did the same. Their earliest reports
make explicit mention of this form, as when Father Blanchet
called upon a local headman's family on Whidbey Island:
"I had them kneel," he writes, "make the sign of the cross,
sing a canticle and I recited, while kneeling, the prayer of
St. Francis Xavier for the conversion of the infidels. . . ."[22]

Members of Protestant churches do, of course, kneel in private devotions and upon special occasions; but in general the practice is to stand, especially when they are assembled in public worship.[23] Silent, individual prayer is also a more marked feature of Catholic public devotions than it is of Protestant. Slocum adopted this manner of supplication for his congregation and gave it an extravagant emphasis. Indeed, the very long periods during which his converts knelt on a hard floor, supposedly in silent meditations and prayer, is one of the features of his services best remembered by informants.

It has been suggested that Slocum believed, or was induced to believe, that he was the prophet heralded by his precursor, Big Bill. If so, the prediction that the chosen individual was to bring word of some great benefit to be bestowed upon the Indians may have planted a seed in Slocum's mind. His announcement that God promised to send some future nostrum was couched in the vaguest of terms. No explanation seems to have been given of the nature of the benefit, the time of its dispensation, or the method of its conveyance. Slocum referred to it only as a "medicine." In this he was doubtless influenced by the Catholic missionaries who from the earliest contacts made use of this term to refer to the Christian sacraments. The practice seems to have been rather general and consistent. We are told that upon the occasion of one of his first visits to Whidbey Island, F. N. Blanchet, using a Chinook jargon interpreter, explained Christian doctrine to the Indians, using images and the Catholic Ladder, and gave to them "an idea of the seven medicines [sacraments] instituted to cure the ills of man, and especially of baptism to wash the spiritual stain . . . and of means to avoid the great fire." [24] Another time, at Fort Nisqually, he reports a difficulty: "Two Indian children only received baptism, because the parents were afraid of that *medicine*." [25] Later on, however, he addressed four hundred Indians at the same place, speaking to them of "the seven medicines to make us good," with better results. He baptized 122 children upon that occasion.[26] Several years later his brother, A. M. A. Blanchet, journeying west to join him, stopped at Fort Walla Walla where he took the opportunity to baptize an old Indian woman who was near death. Using an interpreter the priest made her "understand the existence of God, heaven, hell and also the necessity of Baptism. She then earnestly begged for the powerful medicine (Baptism), saying that she loved God and heaven, and feared the devil and his fiery dwelling." [27]

The use of the word "medicine" with reference to shamanistic practices and magical performances was current in the east, and the Catholic missionaries in Oregon Territory employed it in this sense too. In applying it to the sacraments they doubtless hoped to form a bridge of understanding between native occultism and the Christian mysteries. Slocum's prophecy represents a groping impulse in the in-between zone that took on an unexpected emphasis and a new meaning with the appearance of shaking. That mystery became the fulfilment of Slocum's promise of a new medicine.[28]

It is not so easy to isolate features of Slocum's teachings that are unequivocally Protestant in origin. Apart from those which have been classified as generic Christian, there are only one or two that have a characteristic tone, and even with them the assignment is less a matter of distinction than emphasis. One has to do with the report that Slocum was accustomed to deliver a sermon to his congregation preceding the period of quiet, individual prayer and meditation already discussed. Presumably this took the form of an exhortation, perhaps rather individual and personal in its reference and appeal. If we can distinguish between preaching or sermonizing and religious instruction, certainly the former is more typical of Protestant than of Catholic forms of indoctrination. In the nature of the case Slocum's preaching was more homiletic and expostulatory, more discursive and less formalistic than Catholic exegesis and catechism. At the same time, these orthodox distinctions may not have been so marked in Slocum's experience with the two churches; and even if they were they might have escaped him. It is entirely possible, too, that he was guided by inspiration rather than pattern, and any parallels between his preaching and Protestant sermonizing were merely coincidental.

A more certain Protestant influence is detectable in Slocum's puritanical code of Christian virtues. Like the Shakers who came after him, he placed great stress upon the evils of smoking, drinking, gambling, and swearing. These were the cardinal sins, to which were sometimes added the vices of lying and stealing. The selection of just these temptations was not fortuitous. Together with the practice of shamanism these were the abominations which the Protestant missionaries struggled incessantly to suppress. Much of their energies were directed toward the eradication of these evils, as their writings attest. Eells, under the heading of "Besetting Sins" of the Indians, says that "the more prominent of these are gambling, betting, horse-racing, potlatches, and intemperance." [29] There were other evils, such as wife purchasing, adultery, and Sabbath breaking, against which Eells and Mann contended; but in the main they concentrated their attacks upon the various forms of self-indulgence and the lack of moral discipline which they believed to be so harmful.

In attributing this puritanical strain to Protestant influence it should not be necessary to point out that the Catholic missionaries also deprecated the dissolute and irresponsible lives that many of the Indians led. The assignment derives simply from the fact that traditionally there is a difference in the interpretation of the sinfulness of certain behaviors that is well recognized inside and outside both churches. The difference is mainly one of degree and interpretation. However, at certain times and under certain circumstances, these differences are thrown into relief and take on added significance. Such was the case in the competition for converts around Puget Sound. The Protestant missionaries attributed strength and virtue to themselves and connivance and hypocrisy to their Catholic rivals for the latter's failure to inculcate a stern moral code. Eells, for instance, laments that the Indians were inclined to turn to the easy tolerance of Catholicism which permitted them to continue with their horse racing and gambling while he steadfastly refused to give baptism to a convert unless he renounced these vices.[30] Mann found cause for similar reports. Describing the case of an Indian who was said to have boasted that he was a Catholic when he was reprimanded for his profanity, Mann continues: "The Catholics know that we are strict, and exercise discipline, while they are allowed to swear, drink whiskey, and break the Sabbath, and make quarterly confessions to the priest who comes around once in awhile to forgive their sins." [31] On another occasion, relating the failures of Catholic attempts to lure away converts with impressive rites and usages, Mann recalls that "On that Sunday morning several Indians spoke, among which was also that ex-priest, Spot. He said he had worked long and hard for the Catholic Church, but it was all labor lost; that he felt himself in a rotten canoe, while we were safe in a life-boat; that he called upon us to come to his rescue and take him in. He spoke feelingly and earnestly, and while he did so tears were flowing down his cheeks. While in the slough of despondency the Romish priest, his spiritual advisor, gave him this advice, to use a little spirits once in a while; and not having sufficient discretion as to the quantity of spirits necessary to produce the desired spiritual status in the mind of the Romish priest, the poor Indian took too much, and his temporary 'spiritual' exaltation ended by being put into the jail or guard-house of the Reservation: from that time he wants to know nothing more of Romish 'spiritual' advice." [32]

The question is not whether these charges are true. Some were surely overdrawn. With respect to drinking intoxicants, for instance, it is well documented that Chirouse very early organized a temperance society among the Indians around his mission and administered strict punishment to those who pledged themselves and later succumbed to temptation.[33] The point is that Eells and Mann, in signalizing their differences with the Catholics, stressed their onslaught on drinking, smoking, and gambling. Slocum and his followers accepted the emphasis and carried on with it.

The only features of Slocum's teachings that were at all clearly drawn from his native background were those which had to do with his trance experience. In this connection, the concept of a vision in the sense of a supernatural visitation was a well integrated aspect of aboriginal culture. It was not uncommon for men, and not extraordinary for women, to have remarkable dreams, or to witness monstrous shapes and unnatural events, or to hear strange sounds and voices to which they attributed preternatural significance. The conviction in the reality of these manifestations and in their importance to individual success in life was at the root of the widespread practice of seeking for spirit help to sanction personal ambitions. More to the point, however, was the belief that a person's soul could leave his body and travel anywhere, even to the land of the dead, and that it was capable of sensing and retaining a recollection of its experiences. The soul might remain away indefinitely; but if it could not be restored to its owner within a certain time the person would die. This was the theoretical basis for Slocum's death and resurrection.

In Wickersham's recording of Slocum's speech, as translated by another Indian, Slocum's flickering consciousness is described as a hovering between life and death and his final coma is called death. It is possible that Slocum intended this interpretation, but there are reasons for doubting it. My informants told me that Slocum never said that he died; that he, in fact, avoided the word death out of fear of the consequences of using it. I am inclined to believe that this is true and that the use of the word in Wickersham's account reflects the translator's difficulty in conveying the native view of what soul loss meant in terms of the English at his command. Conceptually a state of unconsciousness was not different from death, but the connotation of finality essential to the meaning of the latter term in our sense was lacking in the native view. This seems clear from Slocum's statements that his soul "would die for two or three hours at a time" and that he died only to "come through the first time" and then die again. His interpretation of his mystic experience was no doubt dictated by the current belief in the possibility of a temporary separation of body and soul which was not necessarily the end of mortal life but only its suspension. Slocum's soul went to the Christian heaven instead of wandering aimlessly or instead of being attracted to the land of the Indian dead, as the souls of so many others had done before him. It was this departure from the norm that provided a logical mechanism for the reception of Christian doctrine.

Spier has called attention to the prevalence of the belief in the resurrection of the dead among Indians all along the North Pacific Coast and has indicated that it provided a ready explanation of Slocum's trance.[34] Accepting what has been said above regarding the native interpretation of death this is certainly true. To the alleged instances of death and revival that Spier gives could be added others gathered from the immediate vicinity of Slocum's acquaintance. Peter Heck's great-grandfather, for instance, is said to have died of smallpox but returned to life after five days. His body had been wrapped in funeral coverings, placed in a canoe, and set in the crotch of a tree. When he revived he had to extricate himself. He told his friends that during the interval he had been to the underworld, the land of the dead, where everyone was gambling, dancing, and having a good time; but his dead uncle had accosted him and told him not to enter the ghostly village "because his clothes were not good enough." Then as he turned to go back he found himself trussed up in his sepulchre. Another man, still living on the Skokomish Reservation, asserts that he died while a young man, that he saw two angels standing on his coffin arguing whether he should be accepted or not, and that finally he was sent back to join the living. These and many other instances of suspended animation attest to the ease with which Slocum's death and resurrection could be fitted into a current pattern without straining belief.

Spier, however, goes a step further. He develops the possibility that Shakerism is historically connected with the Smohalla Cult. The data available to him were not as complete as they are now, and consequently some of the reasons that he adduces in postulating this connection are not applicable at this point in the analysis since we are now concerned with distinguishing Slocum's contributions to the cult from those of Mary and her followers. In spite of this reservation there remains the possibility that Slocum was affected either by reverberations of the Prophet Dance that flourished in the early 1830's or by the Smohalla revival of its principal features in the 1870's.

There can be no doubt that the Indians around Puget Sound had some glimmerings of Christianity prior to their first direct contact with missionaries. Blanchet was aware of this influence and took occasion to assign a cause for it. Writing in 1840 he said: "It is now ten years since they have understood how to speak for the first time of a grand master in the sky, and of the day when they will come to serve him. That idea came to them without doubt from some trader or soldier of the fur trading company; and that knowledge caused them to sanctify Sunday in their fashion, by means of games and dances to the point of exhaustion." [35] In view of the evidence that Spier has assembled we may be permitted to doubt that fur traders were responsible for the Christian elements, especially when the latter are taken in the context of "games and dances." On this point there is some further information on events that took place around Fort Vancouver and Fort Nisqually preserved in the journals of William Fraser Tolmie.

Tolmie, an employee of the Hudson's Bay Company, ar-

rived at Fort Vancouver in the spring of 1833. On Sunday
evening, May 5, the day following his arrival, he rode out of
the fort with Governor McLoughlin to view the farm. Soon
they "heard a low howling and approaching found a party
of from 30 to 40 Indians, men, women, and children, performing their devotions. They formed a circle two deep and went
round and round, moving their hands as is done in [calling?],
exerting themselves violently and simultaneously repeating
a monotonous chant loudly. Two men were within the circle and kept moving rapidly from side to side making the
same motion of arms, and were, I am told, the directors or
managers of the ceremony. Having continued this exercise
for several minutes after we beheld them, becoming more
and more vehemently excited, they suddenly dropped on
their knees and uttered a short prayer, and having rested a
short time resumed the circular motion. During the ceremony so intent were they that not an eye was once turned
toward us although we stood within a few yards in an en-
campment close by. . . . The Governor says that they have
imitated the Europeans in observing the Sabbath as a day of
rest." [36]

As Spier points out, this dance form was the same as that
observed by devotees of the Prophet Dance over most of the
area to the north and east.[37] The only identifiable Christian
element in Tolmie's account is the significance of Sunday as
the day of worship. This was also an important part of Prophet
Dance ideology. Its source, to judge from the last sentence
in the above quotation, is scarcely to be sought in local white
influences around Fort Vancouver. Indeed, the current seems
to have run the other way; for the Company first began
closing its doors to Sunday trade with the Indians on July
21, 1833.[38] In all probability this decision to observe a day
of rest was taken on Tolmie's recommendation as a means
of encouraging the native practice, for it is evident from his
later references to the subject that he immediately became
interested in the religious welfare of the Indians.

In the Fort Nisqually journal which he subsequently kept, Tolmie made regular reference to the Sunday devotional exercises of the Indians. The participants came from different localities, and sometimes as many as two or three hundred individuals congregated at the fort in anticipation of the ceremony. Tolmie also believed that they had been taught their mode of worship by the whites, and in one place he makes it seem as if he were in possession of some direct evidence on this point. His entry for Sunday, February 1, 1835, reads, in part: "The dance was well conducted and all behaved well. This devotional mode was for the present adapted and given to Indians as a mark of their showing they were pleased that they knew who their Creator was." [39] This is a reasonable inference, but I agree with Spier that this religious movement diffused to Puget Sound from the east and that it was in fact the Christianized revival of the aboriginal Prophet Dance. There are several bits of evidence in Tolmie's record itself which point to this conclusion.

For one thing, it is evident that the Nisqually Indians were in regular contact with the Yakimas over the mountains where the Prophet Dance was well entrenched. Tolmie many times notes that Yakima Indians arrived at Fort Nisqually to trade and participate in native affairs. More particularly, however, he mentions a Yakima called Laahlette who was one of the leaders of the religious activities. This individual is referred to as a beggar, and worthless, but it is noted that the Indians assembled at his camp on Sundays for their meetings.[40] Another Yakima, a young chief called Tahkill, who was formerly a slave of the Pend d'Oreille, is also mentioned in this connection.[41] It is probable that these and other Yakimas were instrumental in introducing the cult to their western neighbors.

It is also probable that Laahlette was one of the visionaries who periodically appeared to give renewed assurances of the truth of the cult doctrine. The belief was that the destruction of the world impended and that when this hap-

pened the dead would return and the world would be renewed. From time to time a prophet arose who claimed that
his dreams portended the end or that in death he had been
given an insight into the nature of things to come, whereupon he called his friends together to hear his message and
to engage in a ceremonial dance to hasten the advent of the
new life. This is the basis of the Prophet Dance which Spier
believes was aboriginal. Innumerable individuals appeared
throughout the nineteenth century in this region to make
prophetic revelations of this character. Smohalla was only
one, and one of the last of them, but he came to be the best
known.[42] Perhaps Laahlette was another, less distinguished
seer. It is even possible that Tolmie was himself regarded
in this light. He relates that shortly after his arrival he began to give religious instruction to the Indians on Sundays,
and it is evident that his attempts were well received. For
instance, on Sunday August 6, 1834, he wrote: "The natives assembled and requested me to point out to them what
was proper for them to act in regard to our Divine Being.
I told them that they should endeavor to keep their hand
from killing and stealing to love one another and to pray
only to the Great Master of Life or as they say Great Chief
who resides on high. In fact I did my best to make them
understand Good from evil they on their part promised fair,
and had their devotional dance for without it they would
think very little of what we say to them." [43] While their interest was gratifying to the sympathetic Tolmie it appears
from another passage that he welcomed a relief from their
importunities. On July 6, 1834, he mentioned that the "Indians do not trouble us as formerly with their dance." [44] But
this was not the end of the excitement, for his references to
it continue throughout the next year. In fact, although he
does not make the connection, it is a reasonable interpretation that an episode he describes briefly a few months later
relates to the emergence of a local prophet influenced by the
cult tradition.

Tolmie took notice of this individual in these words: ". . . the forenoon a few Soquamish arrived headed by a young man who is rising up a new religion. He came on purpose to see me, but as yet has not made up his vision of celestial beings. It is reported that in a dream he was presented with a written paper and 18 blankets from above, the latter invisible but the former the Indians say he has about him." [45] The following week Tolmie made another note on this young man: "The Soquamish mentioned on the 21st Ulto. is again doing wonders about his tribe it is said he has a coat covered with dollars and is making present to the natives by giving them blankets of cloth. This is to be a yearly custom with him therefore they [his friends] will be well off." [46] The pretensions of this person created a stir for a time, but his successes were short-lived, for it was soon discovered that he had been robbing graves to provide for his display of mysteriously acquired wealth. This, however, is incidental to the central question of whether he is to be regarded as another instance of a visionary inspired by Prophet Dance ideology; in other known cases reputed prophets succumbed to similar temptations and came to ignominious ends. Unfortunately we know nothing about the dreams of this young ambitious Indian and no more concerning the nature of his "new religion." His appearance at this time is nevertheless significant.

In addition to these contemporary hints, there are traditions, told by Indians in the present century, which bear out the view that pseudo Christian cults flourished at this time west of the Cascade Mountains. In particular, it is related that soon after 1800 a woman from one of the tribes on the north side of the Columbia River near its mouth died, went to heaven, and returned with a message. We are told that she was the one who began counting seven days to a week and instituted a custom of "dancing" on the knees during devotional exercises. Whether this inspiration had any relation to the visit of Lewis and Clark to this vicinity we do not know;

but there are several other accounts of similar visionaries from the Lower Columbia region at about this time or a little later.[47]

So much is to be taken in support of Spier's thesis that the Prophet Dance existed in the southern Puget Sound region by 1833. Still it is questionable whether this movement could have appreciably influenced John Slocum. Spier inclines to the belief that it was a resurgence of the same basic ideas in the 1870's that had a direct effect. He has called attention to the traffic that existed between the coast and inland groups and to the fact that some of the former knew of the word Smohalla. Had information acquired later been available to him he could also have pointed out that there were several dreamers, contemporary with and in the same class as Smohalla, in many of the groups adjoining the coastal tribes, one of special importance being a Klickitat Indian.[48] Furthermore, there was probably an unbroken continuity from the beginning to the end of the appearance of these many prophets, and while each one left his own characteristic imprint the fundamental idea must have persisted well into Slocum's time.

In view of all this it is difficult to resist Spier's suggestion. On the circumstantial evidence there is a strong case for his conclusion. And yet the Slocum manifestation is seemingly so autonomous that I am inclined to doubt that he was himself influenced by the prophet tradition. The principal reason for this doubt lies in the facts already presented; namely, that there was ample precedent and stimulation in Slocum's own local contacts to account for his behavior. The difficulty in coming to a decision, apart from a paucity of data, arises from the similarity of the two possible sources of stimulation. Most of the elements in the Smohalla revival with which Slocum's teachings are in agreement are those that were infused into it from Christian sources. The question of influence therefore seems to turn upon whether unique aspects of the Prophet Dance appear in Slocum's version, and of this there is no evidence that has been forthcoming. That there was some fusion later on when shaking entered the picture is probable; and to this and related matters we may now turn.

TEN

✠ Later Accretions

WITH THE ADVENT of shaking, the re-
ligious revival that had been initiated by Slocum took on
an entirely different complexion. Not only was the ecstatic
element pregnant with distinct interpretations and elaborations; it also took the controls out of Slocum's hands. Nor
was it simply switched to the hands of another individual.
Thenceforth the way was open for any person to contribute
to the development of the cult out of his stock of knowledge,
his prejudices, and his mental associations. And the greater
the number of individuals who in time became attracted to
the cult the greater the number of re-evaluations and accretions that were certain to appear. The range of sources for
contributory ideas was therefore greatly expanded beyond
the limits allowed by Slocum's inspiration. By the same token
the task of assigning provenience to particular elements becomes more difficult and the results sometimes carry less
assurance.

The native background contributed considerably more to
the cult after 1882 than it did in the beginning. Mary Slocum's hysterical performance over the helpless body of her
husband almost certainly laid the foundation for the direct
transfer of the elaborate structure of shamanism. The manner
in which this was effected and the attitudes toward it are
contained in another study.[1] Here we need only point out

that the incorporation, proceeding by variable degrees in different places and at different times, has at one time or another been rather complete, even to details.

In its broadest aspects shamanism is reflected in Shakerism by the fundamental notion that an individual can be imbued with supernatural power—as manifested by trembling seizures—and that while in this state he is capable of mystic insight into the causes of disease and distress which the power directing his movements enables him to cure or alleviate. With this basic concept grafted to Slocum's doctrine—as the fulfilment of his promise of a medicine—the stage was set for an exploration of all the ramifications of the shaman's attributes and abilities and for their transfer to the Shaker context: the means of securing the power, ideas about its nature, mannerisms and actions while under its influence, nativistic notions of disease and its treatment, and so on throughout the implications of faith healing. In short, shaking was shamanism, often unwittingly and even unconsciously transferred.

In his speech before Wickersham, Slocum made no reference to shaking. He stressed the spiritual aspects of the religion and was unspecific about the rest. He said, "It is ten years, now, since we began, and we have good things. We all love these things and will follow them all time. We learn to help ourselves when sick. When our friend is sick, we kneel and ask for help to cure him. We learn something once in a while to cure him. Then we do as we know to help him and cure him. If we don't learn to help him, we generally lose him." [2]

The contrast with Mud Bay Sam's bold interpretation upon the same occasion is marked and significant. "I take power and cure people when they are sick. Long time ago I knew nothing—just like an animal. No doctoring, no medicine—no good. . . . When John Slocum was preaching, I heard that if I prayed I would have power and be a medicine-man, and could cure the sick. From time John Slocum preached I

tried to be a good Christian man. I prayed and was sick—
my soul was sick. I prayed to God and he pays me for that.
There is a lot of difference between this power and old Indian doctoring. This is not old power." [3]

In this Sam clearly envisages himself as a medicine man,
albeit of a new kind. It is safe to say that Slocum did not
make this linkage in the beginning, and that he shrank from
its implications later on. He was much disturbed by the
shaking, being skeptical of its relevance and dismayed by its
resemblance to a shamanistic seizure. He never fully sanctioned it but made a mild peace with it and allowed the
stronger personalities of its protagonists to carry him along.
It is uncertain whether he was ever overcome by power and
succumbed to an ecstatic trembling. There is, in fact, so
much doubt on this score that many of those who were most
closely identified with the cult in the beginning declare today
that John Slocum was not a Shaker.

In the days when Slocum still held his kind of service he
enjoined a solemn demeanor upon his congregation. During
the long periods of strict silence all were supposed to pray.
Meetings were dour and restrained. The church was strictly
the house of God and mundane affairs were excluded. At no
time was there to be any whispering, inattention, or frivolity.
After the introduction of shaking he cautioned against the
assimilation of the cult by shamanism and attempted to establish safeguards against this threat. He tried to discourage the
concern for evil forces and the inflammatory contests that
ardent visionaries were waging against them. The hands
should be held up toward heaven, he preached, for this is
the source of good power; Shakers should not go about the
room seeking bad things in corners, near the floor, and outside the door in the darkness.

Slocum did not want shamans to join the church. Even
though they renounced their old practices he was afraid that
they could not avoid reverting to their evil ways. This is what
he told Doctor Jim when the latter wanted to become a

Shaker. He stipulated that Doctor Jim should not do anything for patients except brush their sins away.

Although it is not known to what extent Slocum was an ecstatic Shaker, it does appear that he gave some who heard him reason to believe that he had the gift of insight and some measure of supernatural power. It is reported that upon one occasion as he rang a small hand bell the clapper fell to the floor. He placed the bell over the clapper for an instant and it was automatically reattached. There are also several accounts attesting to his ability to discern distant events and to forecast their outcome. With all of this, however, John Slocum remains an obscure and minor figure in the background of the shaking phase of the development of the religion, one whose concept of it acted as a restraint rather than as a stimulation.

It is impossible to say precisely what part Mary Slocum played in bridging the gap between faith healing and shamanism. It is clear that she laid the foundations by regarding her shaking as an evidence of power in the shamanistic sense while maintaining that it emanated from God. However, no one today knows just what theory of cure she established by her alleged healing of John; no one can say what God's power, acting through her, did to the sick man. Circumstantial evidence indicates that she took the view that her husband was made well by the dissipation of the aura of sin that clung to his body. This is suggested by the emphasis upon his backsliding as a prelude to his second illness and by her demand that he be cleansed of his association with the shaman who was working over him. Further, Eells, in describing the situation at this time, states that the Shakers "acted much like Indian doctors, only they professed to try to get rid of sins instead of sickness." [4]

Admitting that his information was at all times from hearsay, it is to be noted that in his report to Mooney two years later Eells adds that the extraction of sickness was a prevalent concept. It is certain that this was true; and it is probable that it was during this interval that the ideas of soul and spirit removal were assimilated by the cult, very likely with the concurrence, if not at the instigation of, Mud Bay Louis or his brother.

There is one aspect of Slocum's practice which might have provided an easy point of transition to the Shaker curing complex. That was the outward appearance of his own curing rite. Theoretically he healed the sick by prayer alone. He never claimed the ability to locate or see illness, and he did not extract it. He simply placed his left hand on that part of the patient's body where the distress seemed to be localized, raised his right to heaven, and asked God to make the person well. This posture is not an uncommon sight in Shaker meetings today, although the right hand of the healer sometimes holds a candle or is applied to the ailing part of the patient's body along with the left. By comparison, an obvious characteristic of shamanistic procedure was the manual exploration of the patient's body to locate the illness preparatory to its extraction. In turn, the overt similarity between this act and the Christian custom of laying on hands, with an expanding series of identifications, could have suggested a linkage and at the same time preserved a continuity with the Slocum tradition.

There are other elements drawn from the native religious background. Among them must be listed the ceremonial circuit, which, apart from Mary Slocum's aberration, was counterclockwise. This was the direction for any closed movement in sacred contexts, as during the old winter dances, and the demand to preserve it in Shaker ritual marches and turns was automatic. Mary seems to have founded her sanction for the opposite movement upon an accident alleged to have been divinely inspired; that is, it is said that at the time of her first seizure she found herself turning in clockwise fashion.

Another feature of Shaker practice which seems to relate to native ceremonialism is the pattern of general, unrestrained, infectious participation in the dancing at the height

of the fervor during a meeting. Aboriginally the winter cere-
monials consisted of performances demonstrative of spirit
possession by individuals or organized teams before a crowd
of spectators among whom were others waiting their turn to
exhibit their powers and prerogatives. At times, however, the
tension was too great for restraint to be exercised and any
number of persons might be overcome by ecstatic impulses
and perforce exhibit themselves. An intense Shaker meeting
presents this scene as typical; evidently what amounted to a
necessary conclusion by aboriginal standards was accpted as a
premise by the Shakers. In any event, there must have been
a connection between the two ceremonial patterns.

There is less assurance with respect to two other items in
the Shaker ceremonial repertoire. One of them is the startling
and characteristic manner in which participants strike the
floor of the church with their feet in time to the singing and
the rhythm of hand bells during their praise meetings and
curing ceremonies. There have been numerous individual
variations on this, but typically there are three steps. Least
common, and confined to the initial stages of excitement, is
a tiptoed lift and drop of the body, with the aim of a solid
impact of the heels on the floor. Another is a stiff-kneed forward kick that alternately and rapidly brings the heels into
resounding contact with the floor. Then there is an extremely
vigorous tramping with the heels that is the most common of
the three modes. There are no particulars to draw upon, but
it is likely that all of these forms were to be found in the local
aboriginal dance patterns. Unless they were invented by the
Shakers themselves—and on that it has not been possible to
get information—the other possible source was the Smohalla
Cult. Even this source, however, would account only for the
first step mentioned. It was characteristic of the performances
of this cult as described in the 1880's as it is so with the present day derivative known as the Pom Pom religion. Really
vigorous stamping seems never to have been a part of the
Smohalla ritual.

Shaker churches are supposed to have their prayer tables at the east end of the building while their entrances face the west. It is not easy to say why. There seem to be four possible sources for the idea. The Smohalla (and Pom Pom) ceremonial room is likewise orientated on an east-west axis; but the entrance lies to the east and the leader with his assistants take their places at the west end, the reverse of the Shakers. This circumstance, conjoined with the fact that the two buildings are entirely different in construction, appointment, and function, materially reduces the likelihood that the one served as a prototype for the other.[5] Somewhat the same argument may be offered against the view that Catholic churches were taken as the model. Theoretically they also face the east.[6] We do not know whether, on Puget Sound, they always did. Neither can we say how apparent this pattern was to the Indians even if it was in fact followed consistently by the missionary builders. And then, as mentioned above, it is the reverse of the Shaker orientation, even more obviously than in the case of the Smohalla chamber because an altar is involved. The elimination of this model leaves a choice between the opinion that the native notion of the ceremonial importance of the east somehow came to be embodied in the Shaker church layout, and the view that the latter was founded upon chance circumstances. The vagueness of the first of these alternatives, which could just as well call for an opposite orientation, combined with a bit of positive information attesting to the second seems to weigh in favor of the chance explanation. It will be recalled in this connection that, according to one well-informed Shaker, Mud Bay Louis' church just happened to face the west but that a precedent was established thereby which became a point of doctrine.

There are a few elements drawn from native secular life and attached to Shakerism that are interesting. One of these is the custom of holding feasts in conjunction with large meetings such as conventions and revivals. This was an in-

A Shaker cemetery near White Swan, Washington

The interior of a Shaker home near Tulalip, Washington

herent feature of potlatches; and it was a necessary conclusion to any other occasion when a number of people were
called together. From the beginning it was fitted into the
Shaker setting. It became customary, whenever possible, to
erect a smaller building adjacent to the church to serve
as a cookhouse and dining hall. Many churches have this
adjunct today; and wherever, because of lack of funds or
neglect, none exists, meals are taken outdoors or at some
member's home. Mann noted the custom immediately after
the first Shaker churches were built. While visiting the Indians at Mud Bay he and others there were invited to Oyster
Bay for a Shaker service in Big John's church. After the meeting on Sunday morning "Big John invited the congregation
to dine in a room intended to be an annex to the church,
and there being room for about fifty, he treated them to
boiled beef, clam chowder, bread and coffee. . . ." [7] Today
the different churches pride themselves on their ability to
entertain visitors in this fashion, which in itself may be a
survival of the aboriginal emphasis on wealth display.

Another practice that very likely derives from an aboriginal
prototype appears in the account of a Skokomish Shaker
meeting around the year 1900. Upon this occasion the men
as they entered the church were escorted to their places by
an "usher." The suggestion is that this individual was acting
in a capacity similar to that of the person appointed to give
directions to guests and to keep order in the name of the
host during potlatches, winter dances, and other native assemblies. This function survives at the present time in at-
tenuated form in some places, as at Tulalip, where there
is a doorkeeper and prompter for the spectators at the rear
of the church.

At Skokomish, in 1900, men were lined up across the room
and women took their places behind them. It remains undetermined whether this ordering of individuals had anything
to do with their social prominence or their religious importance. But the transverse alignment, together with the

subordination of the female sex, was contrary to subsequent practice and suggests an appeal to the native custom for a precedent.

It would be an unrewarding task to attempt to indicate all the secular details incorporated in Shakerism from native life; but one in particular is interesting. It will be recalled that Louis instructed those who confessed to him to carry a little bundle of sticks, each one of which represented a sin, so that they might not forget any transgression. This method of prompting recall was a common one among Indians over most of the north Pacific Coast. It was used especially by a man contemplating giving a potlatch; each stick in the bundle he made represented one guest or one wealth item, such as a blanket, to be distributed to a guest. From the Shaker data available it would appear that Louis was responsible for the shift of this mnemonic device to a religious context. Other sources show, however, that the adaption occurred much earlier and indicate a more widespread resort to the practice. Ricard, relating events at St. Joseph's to his Superior General in January, 1857, says of his converts: "To recall their sins, after a general examination, sometimes very long, they use a special method. They cut a bundle of branches in the forest. Each piece represents a sin. They cut it in different fashions according to the nature and gravity of the fault. Having finished the bunch, they kneel at the feet of the priest. At each accusation they hand him one of the pieces of wood until they have exhausted their supply. Then they are sure of not having forgotten anything, and their souls are at peace." [8] In view of the time differential, it is possible that Louis developed the idea independently. It is more probable, though, that he drew upon his knowledge of past or even upon current usage at Catholic missions in introducing this ritual form into Shakerism.

There is little assurance that the information that has been obtained on Slocum's religion is complete, but accepting the facts as we have them it appears that several new Christian elements were incorporated into the cult after 1882. Again, some of them were of a generic character common to most Christian denominations. Among traits of this kind may be listed the following: an accent on the destruction of the wicked, marked by fears of hell and realistic punishment; ritual recognition of the mystic numbers three, seven, and twelve; limited color symbolism; the use of sacred pictures; the reservation of Sunday as a day of abstention and worship; and the asking of the blessing before and after meals.

The records of the missionaries of all denominations leave no doubt that the Indians were given a fearful impression of hell and its tortures. This is especially marked in the Catholic sources. Slocum seems to have avoided this frightful complement of heaven, as Shakers at the present time do. The same cannot be said of Louis, Sam, and others of their time.

In Shaker ritual the number three is by far the most common mark of magic completeness. Most things are done or occur in threes. But there are several references to the ritual use of the number seven. According to one report the Shakers at the Neah Bay convention in 1910 made seven circuits of a dining table.[9] Also in one account of Slocum's visions it is stated that he saw seven candles in heaven representing as many churches. The number twelve is not so important; but it is recognized, as when twelve candles make up the church chandelier.[10] There is not much doubt that this ritual framework was introduced along with shaking. Slocum thought in terms of fours, as is shown by the intervals by which his term of life was recurrently extended after his supposed death. In this he was doubtless drawing upon a native concept that did not survive the impact of the new developments that came with shaking.[11]

It is curious that Slocum, in telling Wickersham of the beginnings of his mission, stated that "every Saturday we worshiped God." If no misunderstanding was involved on the point, the choice of Saturday instead of Sunday calls for an explanation. A likely one is that the day was determined by ritual count; that is, that Slocum must have revived on Tuesday, at which time, as he relates, he was promised four more days of life at the expiration of which he was granted four more weeks when a church for him must be completed and his mission begun. Thus calculated (by multiples of four from Tuesday), the advent of his public teaching would fall on Saturday, a circumstance which might account for its continued observance as the day apart from all others as a day of worship. Substance is given to this speculation by the urgency of the demand for the completion of the church in the stipulated time; the first meeting, by all reports, took place before the building was finished and probably because, even though it was Saturday, the alloted time was up. On the other hand, the reverse interpretation is possible; that is, the ritual count adopted by Slocum does not represent an appeal to the mystic number four, but was an accident of timing. This is suggested by the Shaker document (pp. 40–44). There it is alleged that meetings were from the beginning held on Sunday and Slocum's death and resurrection took place four days before this day of the week, presumably, then, on Wednesday. This reasoning makes Sunday the datum for reckoning and, therefore, makes one suspicious. In other words, this may be another instance, among several to be mentioned later, of a rational interpolation designed to fill in a gap of real knowledge. Without additional data we cannot decide which interpretation to accept.

The sacred pictures that are to be found in Shaker homes today are generally more Catholic than Protestant in treatment and subject matter. All of the missionaries, however, welcomed the aid of visual materials in their teaching and made efforts to get them into the homes of their converts. From the beginning the Catholics distributed crosses, chaplets, and "médailles." Eelles made energetic efforts to obtain appropriate Bible pictures. He says that "they went like hot cakes" even though he had to charge the Indians twenty-five cents for them.[12]

Missionaries of both sects likewise recognized the appeal of singing. The Catholics immediately after their arrival began to render canticles in Chinook jargon and later in the different local languages. They made them an important part of their model, as integral as the sign of the cross, and reported rather remarkable success in getting the Indians to join in singing. Eells experienced difficulty in the translation of Protestant hymns; in fact he found only one that he could transliterate into Chinook jargon and but very few others into the local Salish dialects. He compromised by composing a short line or two of text expressive of an appropriate sentiment, such as "Come to Jesus, now," and set this to a familiar tune to be repeated over and over. There is a marked suggestion of this pattern in Shaker songs. But whether or not the stronger influence came from Catholic or Protestant forms, it is apparent that the Indians were amply impressed by the association of song with religious service in Christian tradition. And apparently it was not Slocum but his successors who exploited the linkage and made the most of the appeal of group expression in song.

As a previous quotation (footnote, p. 296) makes plain, one of the observances stressed by the Catholic missionaries was the offering of a prayer before and after meals. The giving of thanks at this time is equally a part of Protestant tradition, and as such was transmitted by Eells and Mann to the Indians with whom they came in contact. Eells mentions this specifically. "Feeling that a very short prayer would be the best probably for them to begin with alone," he says, "I recommended that they ask a blessing at their meals. This was acceptable to some of them. I taught them a form, and they did so for that fall [1875] and a part of the winter." [13] Although in this, as in other attempts at indoctrination, the response was at times discouraging to the missionaries, the seed was scattered rather widely and it unexpectedly bore fruit in the Shaker revival. Attention to this ritual at meal times is today a fairly definite earmark of the practicing member of this faith.

There is some doubt as to whether Louis was the first to advocate a separation of the sexes in the Shaker church. Some informants state that he was, and this is probable; but the possibility that Slocum also divided his congregation in this way cannot be excluded on the basis of the evidence at hand. In either case the suggestion was very likely due to Catholic precedent. Ethnographic reports on the area lack specific mention of this detail as an aboriginal practice; so do the missionary accounts. Both, however, seem to bear out the view that it was not the native custom to separate the sexes in public assemblies. Any alignment that followed a voluntary pattern apparently took shape on a prestige basis: the headmen ranged themselves in front with the rest of the group at the back and on the sides. Shortly after his arrival in the Northwest Blanchet visited the Indians around Fort Nisqually, and on his last Sunday there he celebrated mass. The ceremony took place outside where "the big chiefs were kneeling on their mats facing the altar, and the men and women were at the sides of it forming the extremities of a half circle." [14] On Whidbey Island soon after, when some four hundred Indians were present for the mass, "each placed himself with great ceremony according to his rank"; [15] and at another meeting in the same place "the chiefs took their places in the first rows and the others placed themselves behind and at the sides just as the women and the children." [16]

The internal evidence of the same documents, as well as other considerations, indicates that early missionaries soon instituted new alignments of their congregations. The separation of men and women in church is an old European custom,[17] and it is known that some of the missionizing orders, the Jesuits in particular, introduced it to their native converts. Father de Smet, who pioneered the mission work among the tribes of northeastern Washington and northwestern Montana, noted that the tradition was being implanted among his charges in 1846. In relating events that occurred at a Christmas celebration at St. Ignatius among the Kalispel he mentions that at baptisms the men were placed on one side of the room and the women on the other "according to the custom of Paraguay," by which he meant the pattern that prevailed in the collectivized communities established by the Jesuits among the Indians of Paraguay.[18] There is no equally precise statement for the Puget Sound area; but there are several allusions to a sexual dichotomy in other contexts. It is mentioned, for example, that when choirs were formed they were in two sections which sang alternately, the one composed of men and the other of women and children.[19]

While it therefore seems probable that Slocum, or the Shakers who came after him, got the idea of separating men and women in church directly from Catholic example, it should not be overlooked that in the Pom Pom (derived Smohalla) services the same division takes place. Moreover, from the standpoint of compass orientation the placement is the same: the women are on the south and the men are on the north side of the building. At the same time, the key points in the two structures (entrance and leader's position) are just reversed. Pom Pom men are on the leader's left as he faces them, and Shaker men are on their minister's right. For the Shakers this local orientation is the important consideration, and there may not therefore be any historical connection between the two patterns.

The Shakers, and Slocum as well, undoubtedly drew upon Catholic sources in their use of the cross. This is a prominent feature of all their churches, inside and out. A large cross forms the back drop for the prayer table and another surmounts the gable at the end of the building above it. Also, where there are special cemeteries for Shakers, as at White Swan, a large wooden cross rises above the graves to mark the site. It is curious that chaplets or crosses on necklaces are not generally worn by Shakers; but the custom may be represented by the blue bands sewed on the front of garments. It is more probable, however, that this appliquéd neckband and cross has as its prototype the bishop's pectoral.

To the historical analyst one of the most puzzling features of Shaker services is the ritual touching of hands. Although this is called a handshake, it bears no objective relation to the token of friendship to which we give that name. It also differs formally from the testimonial handshake introduced by Slocum. Overtly it has the appearance of a reciprocal act of benediction, and that is possibly its origin. Still, the fact that the hands of the two individuals meet requires some explanation; and, since the act is something more than a mere salutation by friends, the most likely source is some precedent in a religious context. There are references in the Catholic missionary accounts which may afford a clue for speculation along this line, but they are not conclusive. In fact, they are as mystifying as they are suggestive.

Blanchet, Demers, and many other missionaries refer repeatedly in their reports to a custom of hand touching that they encountered among the Indians from the beginning of their acquaintance with them. There is every reason to suppose that the missionaries themselves had nothing to do with introducing the practice. In fact, the tenor of their descriptions indicates that they believed it to be a native custom. On this subject Blanchet wrote of the Nisqually, whom he visited in August, 1839: "I had occasion to note their customs, of which some are rather strange. Here is an example. To honor a person of distinction, they form a line, in order to present their hands to him one after the other, from the first to the last. Thus it was that I had to submit to such a ceremony on the part of about fifty persons, all in grand attire. . . . The women also observe the custom. They carry their infants on their backs, and hasten to take the hand of the little ones whenever they have touched that of a chief, in the belief that they transmit to them a certain blessing." [20] Again, upon an occasion when a chief at Steilcoom had one of his tribe lashed for punishment for dishonoring a young girl, the man got up, "and according to the prescribed ceremonial, touched the hand of the chief, in order to thank him, and to prove that he did not hold any rancor." [21]

I know of nothing in aboriginal custom which could account for this behavior. And yet the missionaries met with it all over the northwest. Evidently in every community they visited the inhabitants immediately lined themselves up to file by and take the hand of the priest, the most important men preceding the others. Blanchet, encountering the custom on a mission to Whidbey Island a year after the trip referred to above, spoke of it as "that ceremony of strict etiquette." [22] Demers, who was greeted in this fashion by over three hundred Indians near Fort Yale on the Fraser River in 1841, called it "the necessary greeting." [23] Fouquet noticed it among the Songish around Victoria; and in 1865, Durieu in the Lake Okanagon region and Lejacq among the Kwakiutl described the same performance.[24] Bolduc, who by 1844 had submitted to the tedious requirement many times, referred to it as "that terrible ceremony." [25]

Evidently the compulsion to initiate the formality rested with the Indians rather than with the missionaries. And the accounts of their behavior leave little doubt that they were motivated by considerations that were more mystical than those which demand conformance to ordinary patterns of social intercourse. The quotation from Blanchet's letter indicates this well enough; but there are still others that comment upon the solemn and anxious concern that the Indians manifested in carrying out the ceremony. Everybody, including the smallest child, must touch the hand of the priest. Evidently the act was conceived to confer a blessing or some benefit beyond our power now to define. Chirouse, detailing his day's labors among the Yakima at the Ahtanum mission in 1851, recounts that each evening there was "a class in reading and writing for the children, some hymns and a night

prayer, after which each retires, having touched my hand
as a sign of gratitude." This interpretation would hardly seem
to cover the many instances when the priest was a stranger
to the Indians who nonetheless eagerly lined up to be received by him. There must have been other, more compelling
sentiments involved. In this view, the report of a culprit
touching the hand of his chief as a mark of gratitude seems
out of harmony with the others; it is lacking in Indian flavor
and it may have been instigated and designed *ad hoc* by the
authorities at the fort.

An isolated instance of a new custom is understandable;
but the possibility that traders or trappers were responsible
for originating a pattern as widespread and spontaneous as
the one under discussion is remote. It is unlikely that they
would be able to institute a formality expressive of deference
and awe either toward themselves or toward the priests about
whom they might have told the Indians in advance. The
only other explanation that occurs is that the Indians passed
the ceremony and the word of the "blackgowns" coming
along among themselves so that it outran the appearance of
the missionaries in most places. De Smet did not establish
his mission among the Flathead until 1841, too late to have
been the source of the idea in the west. But, as we have
seen, Catholicized Iroquois preceded him in this region by
some twenty years; and they, it seems, were responsible for
the reinvigorated and Christianized version of the native
Prophet Dance that flourished in 1833. They might likewise
have been responsible for coaching their fellows in appropriate expressions of respect for the priests that all hoped
would come and for inflaming their hopes with accounts of
the benefits that could be expected from the blessings con-
ferred by the holy men. It does not appear that a ceremony
embodying these ideas was ever a part of Prophet Dance
ritual; but it may have been a forerunner and a concomitant
nonetheless. The suggestion is, therefore, that the custom
of touching a priest's hand reached the Puget Sound region

prior to the appearance of the missionaries and that it was fortified by their passive encouragement after their arrival.

Even if this reconstruction represents the facts we still cannot be sure that a knowledge of this early formality persisted until 1883, or if so, that it provided an inspiration for the Shaker "handshake." Much of the uncertainty is occasioned by the lack of specific information upon just what the touching of the hands of the missionaries amounted to. In describing the action they most often use the verb "toucher." The expressions "présenter la main," or "donner la main" are almost as common. Occasionally the phrasing "prendre la main" occurs. Only very rarely are the words "serrer" (to press, squeeze, or shake the hand) or "poigne" (clasp of the hand) employed. From this it seems that in general the intention of the missionaries was not to convey the idea that the Indians took their hands in a friendly handshake; and this is borne out by their reference to the humble and beseeching attitudes of the people. Still, there remains some doubt as to actually what happened: whether mere contact of any kind with the priest's hand was sufficient, or whether in "giving" or "presenting" the hand the prototype of the ordinary handshake was involved. Also, sometimes the text reads as if the priest were offering his hand and again as if it were the other way around; and this, in the light of the problem, can make a difference in the interpretation.

There are very few other aspects of the Shaker Cult, as such, that can be attributed to Catholic influence. After 1883 there was a definite swing toward Protestant forms. For this shift the influence of certain dominant personalities should be held largely responsible. No doubt the close attention that Mann gave the new religion had some positive effects upon the forms and attitudes that were adopted. It will be recalled that he took charge of the missionary work around Mud Bay in 1882, organized an "Indian Church," and tried to maintain a regular preaching schedule, either going himself to attend the Shaker meetings or sending his licentiate, Peter Stanup. In thus attempting to assimilate the Shakers he had an important influence on them. Then it must not be overlooked that Wickersham and Giles, who do not appear to have been Catholics, were instrumental in setting up the formal lines for the organization of the new church and were, in their capacities as protectors and sympathetic advisors, in a position to guide the thinking of the cult's leaders on other matters as well. Finally there was Louis himself. Nothing is known of his religious background, but it is obvious that some of the innovations for which he was responsible are more reminiscent of Protestant than of Catholic forms.

Among Protestant influences after 1883 should be listed the shift from the kneeling to the standing posture for long periods of prayer; the shaping of the church leadership structure, with its emphasis on elders and ministers; the non-hierarchical relations between church leaders themselves and between them and the other members of the congregation; [26] the holding of religious services in the home; the adherence to a Protestant religious calendar; the use of the expressions "My dear brother" and "My dear sister"; the increased emphasis on group singing; the encouragement of individuals in the congregation to speak and testify; and, in general, an over-all adoption of the Protestant prayer meeting as the model for all Shaker services. Other particulars could be mentioned, but these will suffice to indicate the character of the alleged trend. Some of them call for a word of explanation by way of showing that their prototypes were available to the Indians.

Catholic practice demands a consecrated altar, and this prescription puts an obstacle in the way of performing any but the most necessary offices outside the regularly constituted church precincts. Protestants may worship anywhere with a minimum of preparation and paraphernalia, and one of the most likely places outside the church is in the home. In fact, in times past this was advocated as a regular habit by some denominations. The Presbyterians, for instance, encouraged private morning and evening family services as a duty, these to consist of prayers, the reading of the Scriptures, and the singing of praises led by the head of the household.[27] Visiting ministers, of course, also conducted such prayer meetings in the home; and both Eells and Mann made the most of their opportunities in this regard. In the chapter that he devotes to this subject in his book, Eells reviews some of his experiences in endeavoring to make converts by going to the Indians at their camps and in their homes when they could not be induced to come to church. In this way the attributes of the church were readily transferred to the home setting. Upon one occasion Mann held a communion service for Old Jacob, a Chehalis Indian, at which time the missionary was "delighted to see how he [Old Jacob] prepared the table for the sacrament in his house." [28] It is not surprising, therefore, that the Shakers saw nothing unusual in setting up a prayer table in the home and in conducting whatever services need be there.

In the beginning the Shakers designated particular evenings for prayer meetings, and in this they were again imitating the Protestant examples before them. Among the Skokomish they duplicated the Sunday and Thursday services of Eells and at Neah Bay the Wednesday and Sunday meetings of Miss Clark. And on a broader scale, the Shaker religious calendar, in so far as one can be said to exist, conforms to the Protestant rather than to the Catholic. The days of the saints, for instance, have never been celebrated, although this was done at the Tulalip mission under the guidance of Chirouse.[29]

There is not much in any Shaker meeting to remind one of a Sunday morning Protestant church service. The formalities and the attitudes of the two groups of participants are quite different. But there is considerable resemblance between a prayer meeting or a revival meeting and a Shaker Sunday service. In all of these meetings there is an emphasis

on member participation, either in the form of group singing or in individual declamation, prayer, or testimony. The
keynote is informality and spontaneity, and there is not
much doubt that the two Protestant forms were instrumental
in molding the character of the Shaker meeting. They provided the pattern most familiar and congenial to the majority
of the Indians who came under the tutelage of Eells and
Mann. In the atmosphere of the church prospective converts
were uneasy or bored. In their homes or in a glade they relaxed
and were more receptive—and, since it required no effort on
their part, they saw more of the prayer and camp meeting.

For years Eells found it very difficult to get the Indians
to participate in his prayer meetings. Most of them felt that
prayer was nonsense and of no earthly benefit; they ridiculed
the few who were taken in by the claims made for it when
nothing happened in answer to their requests. The act itself,
as Eells relates, and as I have been told, struck many Indians as ludicrous; they could not suppress a giggle when
one of their number had been pressed into an attempt to
pray aloud. It is no wonder therefore that they were "self-
conscious" and remained mute in the face of Eells's pleas.
But he did not abandon his efforts, and he did succeed from
time to time in getting the desired response. The idea of
spontaneous self-expression whenever the spirit moved was implanted and came to sudden fruition when the introduction
of shaking provided a propitious setting and a familiar vehicle.

If we may judge from his reports, Mann was more successful than was Eells in getting co-operation at his prayer meetings. At any rate, he often mentioned the Indians' eagerness
to participate in the speaking and testifying at meetings
he conducted. Upon one occasion he tells us that "there was
no halting or waiting; two or three would rise to their feet
at once." At another time he was moved to exclaim, "How
they sing and pray and edify and console in the sick room
and in the prayer meeting." [30] He also held annual camp

meetings during the hop picking season in a fir grove near the Puyallup fields where, "attracted by the sound of our Indians singing the gospel hymns with their sweet, melodious voices in their own native tongue, not only Indians from other tribes passing along the public highway were drawn thither, but also white people were induced to stop and listen to the singing and to the preaching." It was, he continues, "like an old-fashioned Presbyterian camp meeting. . . ." [31] A large measure of this enthusiasm developed after 1881 and, as has been suggested, probably as a result of the undercurrent of excitement about John Slocum's revelation. But Mann's obvious gratification with the development is sufficient indication of his willingness to regard it as the fruition of his labors. Even more than this, it indicates that he viewed Protestant rule and form as a more flexible sanction for his ministrations than Eells was willing to allow himself.

All Shaker services are lacking in the decorum and the restraint that characterized Catholic devotions. Protestant churches, also, except for their evangelistic fringes, deprecate individual excesses and mass agitations of the sort to which the Shakers regularly subject themselves. Among missionaries, however, revivalist techniques are acceptable approaches to the problem of conversion, and sometimes the mass enthusiasm that they induce gets out of hand. Mann, of course, was not responsible for Shaker excesses, and he definitely rejected their raptures and tremblings as a sign of divine favor. But up to this point he was sympathetic with them and their ardent demonstrations of faith. They were aberrant and misguided, but he evidently believed that shaking was a passing phase of a true religious growth and that with proper instruction it could be eliminated to leave a vigorous and acceptable evangelical movement. The kind of prayer service which he considered a reward for his labors was easily adapted by the Indians and made the groundwork for a climax of complete emotional surrender. He apparently

approached the borderline between Christian fervor and
native spirit possession with less caution than some other
workers among primitive peoples.

There is very little that specifically identifies the Shaker
faith with the Smohalla revival. There appears to be nothing in the contributions of Mary Slocum that would point
to this source of stimulation and to no other. At the same
time it is quite possible, and even likely, that the acceptance
of the new religion by some individuals was conditioned by
their familiarity with earlier Prophet Dance manifestations.
They may have regarded John or Mary Slocum as another
messiah and so promoted a transference of behaviors and attitudes from an old to a new context. The "rumor" reported
on the Chehalis Reservation to the effect that Slocum had
announced that all who did not believe in him would "be
turned to animals" might exemplify such a transference of
ideas from one cult to another through the intermediation
of some individual. So, too, does the anxiety that leaders
were able to inspire in their followers over their welfare.
Smohalla, like Slocum, is said to have threatened to leave his
people if they failed to heed him; and the trances into which
he fell gave them great cause for alarm.[32] Then there is the
reference in one verbal account to the curious spectacle of
women hopping on their knees in momentary expectation of
being taken off to heaven during the first big Shaker meeting in 1883. It is possible that this represents an intrusion
of the custom of knee dancing already alluded to (p. 305).
Several of Du Bois' informants mentioned this mode of worship as the one that was followed by various prophets' dis-
ciples on the lower Columbia up until the last quarter of
the nineteenth century. According to one of them "You
kneel and jog up and down in time. Maybe you hop forward
a step or two." [33]

Other correspondences between the Smohalla cult and
Shakerism have been mentioned previously, but, as in the
case of Slocum's religion, they are not specific for these two

religions. There are a few others which may indicate a closer relationship between the two religions. Spier has identified the Shaker hand fluttering under power with a similar gesture in the Smohalla services. It is doubtful, however, that there is any real connection between them. The hand movement as it is found at the present time among the Yakimas is a fanning motion across the breast, not a to-and-fro action; and this, while it may occur in Shaker manipulations, is not characteristic of them. The latter are closely correlated with the concept of introducing good and extracting evil from the body. Another Smohalla feature which bears at least a superficial resemblance to Shaker form is the plan by which men and women take their places when they enter the long house. The first man to come in takes his place nearest the door, the second stops on his left, the next to the latter's left, and so on to the last man, who stops nearest the leader at the far end of the room. The women follow and file down the length of the room in front of the line of men and take their places by the same "peeling off" process except that the first woman stops nearest the leader. The Shakers do not enter their church in this fashion, but they employ the same technique of unfolding a line of individuals in their several marching movements. Whether they have borrowed this device from the Smohalla cultists or not is difficult to decide. The same holds for another ritualistic figure; namely, the Smohalla requirement that each individual, as he marches out at the end of the service, must pause at the door and make a complete counterclockwise turn in place just before stepping outside. The Shakers do not exit in this fashion either, but in their ritual circuits during a service they are supposed to make such a turn on the near and far points of the circle as they pass in front of the prayer table.

These, and perhaps still other correspondences may be real borrowings from the Columbia River Prophet Dance complex. But, if so, it is likely that they were intrusive; that is,

neither John nor Mary Slocum were influenced by them at
the time of the inspirations which originally gave shape to
the Shaker religion. As the movement grew and converts
with widely different backgrounds were drawn into it, accretions from the outside, including some derived from Smohalla, were to some extent expectable. In this connection,
however, it must be remembered that the Shakers and the
followers of the Pom Pom religion avoid each other. Their
ethical systems are different, and the Shakers regard the
Pom Pom cultists as heathens. No practicing Shaker will
even attend a Pom Pom ceremony, and he, therefore, knows
practically nothing of what goes on there. His objection is
mainly on moral grounds, for gambling and shamanism have
never been proscribed by the nativistic Smohalla and Pom
Pom doctrines. Their sins have been of a different order. This
antipathy, of course, would not prevent conversions from one
group to the other, with the resulting opportunity for ideas
to flow across the barrier. At the same time, the members of
both cults are on guard against such contamination, and
there are reasons for believing that its occurrence has been
rare.

Among the many Shaker practices for which it is difficult
to give an adequate historical explanation one set of ritualistic acts is most puzzling. These are the marching movements during the Sunday services. It has been impossible to
secure any information on where, when, or by whom they
were introduced into the meetings. The suggestion has been
made that they relate to military drills; but there is little
correspondence between the two forms. It is, of course, entirely possible that the figures were instituted as the result
of a dream or vision—"gift"—by one or several members,
the stimulus and prototype for which we cannot know at
this date. I would like, however, to suggest another possibility, remote as it is, to explain this outstanding feature
of Shaker ritual. Wickersham could have been responsible

for it. This suggestion involves an even more speculative proposition, and this is given for what it is worth.

Wickersham was born at Patoka, Marion County, Illinois, in 1857. There is no pertinent information on his early life except that he mentions, in defending the Shakers, that he had seen white people professing Christianity who behaved in the same excited fashion under the influence of religion. Specifically, "In times of excitement many of them [i.e., the Shakers] twitch and shake, but in no instance do they conduct themselves in so nervous a manner as I have seen orthodox Christians do at old Sandy Branch camp-meetings in Illinois." [34] It is probable that he is referring here to some of the peculiar forms of ecstasy—such as barking, jerking, and rolling—that manifested themselves among Baptists, Methodists, and other sects in the periodic religious revivals that welled up in the adjacent sections of Illinois and Indiana during the first half of the nineteenth century. But there is a bare possibility that he had witnessed, or at least had heard about, some of the performances of the United Society of Believers in Christ's Second Appearing, better known as the "Shakers."

This religious society was founded in England by "Mother" Ann Lee around 1747. Her followers received visions, prophesied, talked in strange tongues, healed, and were overcome by convulsive tremors of the body and limbs during their meetings. Their uninhibited shaking, stamping, reeling, and shouting led to persecution; and in 1780 they fled their homes around Manchester and Bolton and moved to America where they founded a settlement at New Lebanon in New York State. From there the sect eventually spread to a few isolated parts of the United States. One offshoot took root in Kentucky. The Society leaders, inspired by reports of the widespread religious ferment that manifested itself there just after 1800, decided that the signs were auspicious for spreading their doctrine. Accordingly, from 1801 to 1811 they took part in the so-called Kentucky Revival and were energetic in establishing churches in Logan, Mercer, and Bourbon Counties. They also expanded to several localities in Ohio. In 1810 they organized a community near Vincennes, Indiana, across the Wabash River from Illinois. They carried on some missionary activity in Illinois, but seem never to have established a permanent community there. No new colonies were founded after 1826, although some unsuccessful attempts were made. In 1827 they abandoned the venture at Vincennes and the participants returned to Kentucky.[35] The movement continued to flourish, however, the period of greatest membership being from 1840 to 1860.[36] This was also the period when their rituals were the most colorful.

These facts do not provide a solid basis for inferring that Wickersham was familiar with the Society. Patoka is not more than one hundred miles from Vincennes, but other circumstances of time, place, and opportunity are more important considerations and about them we know nothing. Still, some of the correspondences between the Society and the Indian Shakers are worth noting. Both sects separate men and women during their meetings and refer to their fellow members as brothers and sisters. Both use hand bells as signals during services. Symbolic colors, to the limited extent that they can be said to exist, are in both cases blue and white.

I do not suppose that these resemblances represent transfers. On the other hand, they might have suggested an identification in Wickersham's mind, and led him to advise the Shakers on still others.

Wickersham, we know, gave the Shakers their name. Without question this could have been spontaneous. It is curious, though, that two other terms are applied in common within the two cults. Members of the Society, like the Shakers, call their revelations, and the ritual requirements sanctioned by them, "gifts." This could have been derived independently from a common source, the Bible (I Corinthians 12), even if we allow that it has for long been, and still is, used by the illiterate as well as the Bible reading Shakers. The other term is applied to the activities under power. Shakers call their trembling, stamping, and marching "the work"; the members of the Society refer to the same kind of exercise as "laboring." [37] Both also appeal to the Bible to justify their "dancing before the Lord" (II Samuel 6:14).

More interesting still are the dance figures incorporated into their services by the Society of Believers.[38] In the beginning their dancing was spontaneous and undirected, but around 1785 this chaotic manner of self-expression began to be discouraged. Their meetings became more restrained, and by 1798 there was no dancing at all. Then came the revival in Kentucky and this led to a renewal of ecstatic expression. This time, however, the movements of individuals were ordered to conform to prearranged designs. Marches were introduced early in 1817; and a few years later the participants were executing dynamic figures based on passing files, squares, circles, and serpentines. The first of these ideas—two lines of participants singing and tramping while moving in opposite directions—was most popular, and was employed in a number of variations. It was incorporated into one of the so-called "union [brotherhood] dances" of the 1830's so that two concentric circles of participants, one of men the other of women, revolved in opposite directions.

Even more reminiscent of the Indian Shakers was another "union" dance which began with a line of men on one side of the room and a line of women on the other. In this figure the last individual in each line passed in front of the others singing a song of brotherly love and shaking hands with each person as he or she moved by. Another figure, developed in 1828, strongly recalls the typical Shaker arrangement at a Sunday morning service. In this the participants first arranged themselves in ranks with the men on one side of the room and the women on the other. Then at a given signal the block formed serpentines as a member moved down the line of his own rank and back along the line of the rank next, the circle being closed by the first rank swinging around the outside to join the tail end of the last. The two units, men and women, moved in opposite directions and they remained closed circuits, whereas the Shakers used the device to unwind their ranks in order to form one large circle. But the static ranked arrangement and the serpentine movement by which it becomes a continuous dynamic figure are strikingly similar.

᛭
ELEVEN ᛭ Turmoil and Prophecy
᛭

IN RETROSPECT it is not difficult to assemble sets of facts which make the advent of John Slocum and the introduction and spread of shaking fairly comprehensible. There are certainly gaps and guesses at many points in the story, but this must be true of any reconstruction of the past.

There were several aspects of Slocum's environment the knowledge of which contribute to an understanding of the attitude of himself and others at the time of his revelation. Among them must be counted the social conditions that prevailed generally among the Indians in the vicinity of Puget Sound toward the end of the last century. As a result of the encroachments of civilization most of the native communities of that region became progressively more disrupted from 1850 onward. Their traditional economies, their beliefs, and their social relations were etched away through the partial and piecemeal acceptance of the white man's standards and demands. In part this was voluntary and in part it was under pressures of one kind or another. In any event, the consequences were not happy from the Indian's standpoint.

The confinement upon reservations was perhaps the least burdensome of the demands made upon the Indians of this area. Although there was necessarily some displacement from homesites, in most instances the reservations comprised at

337

least a part of the native habitats of the local groups assigned to them. It was, moreover, impossible to prevent individuals from passing over reservation boundaries in pursuit of their customary social and economic activities.

More oppressive were the restrictions and the forceful measures employed to interdict native customs and to impose American civilizational patterns upon the agency wards. These coercions varied from prohibitions upon native religious practices to persistent attempts to convert a food gathering, co-operative economy into an individualized commercial or agricultural system regardless of local conditions. Shamanistic practices were outlawed; parents were required to send their children to school; marriage, inheritance rules, and other native institutions were challenged and sometimes forcefully suppressed to install the white man's alternatives.

Quite apart from the opposition and the antagonisms that these repressive measures generated were the numerous indirect and unforeseen consequences that follow upon any rapid cultural change and the state of confusion created thereby. The members of the old communities became scattered with the introduction of new economic patterns; the gap was widened between generations by teaching young people to scoff at native "superstitions"; personal differences were exploited to develop native support for the program of change; and inequalities in status and privilege were seized upon to drive a wedge between the conservatives and those who foresaw an advantage in renouncing the old obligations, disabilities, and constraints.

It need not be supposed that the plan was as brutal as these statements seem to indicate; or that the men who were responsible for modifying the Indian's way of life defined their methods or mode of attack in any such systematic fashion. In all probability neither was the case. But the effect of the policy was a cultural collapse that inevitably brought in its train an atmosphere of disquiet, tension, uncertainty, and the resort to "whisky, gambling, idleness, and general vice" about which the authorities constantly complained without understanding its motivations. With their aboriginal social and emotional controls upset, the Indians, unable to adopt a totally new system all at once, turned in their frustration to sensual and selfish gratifications, fleeting and unsatisfactory as they knew them to be.

This progressive demoralization encouraged a receptive attitude toward palliatives. It paved the way for the ready acceptance of any recourse that gave promise of relief. Slocum's revelation, in part growing out of this background, was one answer to the hopelessness of the situation. No doubt many Indians of the time could say with Mud Bay Louis: "Well, my friend, we was about the poorest tribe on earth. We was the only tribe now full blood and nothing else. We would not believe anything. Minister came here, but we laugh at him. We loved bad habits—stealing—and John Slocum died. He was not a religious man—knew nothing of God—all of us same. We heard there was a God from Slocum—we could see it. Same time we heard God, we believe it. I was worst of lot. I was drunkard—was half starving—spent every cent on whiskey. I gambled, raced horses, bet shirt, money, blankets—did not know any better.

"John Slocum brought good to us his words civilized us. We could see. We all felt blind those times. We lost by drowning—our friends drank whiskey and the canoes turn over—we died out in the bay. Today who stopped us from these things?" [1]

In addition to this rather general deterioration, which developed over the years, there were other more specific and immediate provocations of significance with reference to the timing of Slocum's mystic experience. Among them must be listed the strained relations which by 1881 had developed between the Eells brothers on the one side and the reactionary element on the Skokomish Reservation led by Billy Clams on the other. The enmity began in 1876 when the agent, Edwin Eells, refused to permit Clams to abandon a wife that he no longer cared to live with and take another. Clams was as determined in his purpose as was the agent, and the ensuing struggle between them developed into what Myron Eells called "the most severe contest the agent ever had with the Indians on the reservation." It did indeed become very serious with the agent personally taking a hand in an effort to jail Clams; with the latter's friends assisting him to escape, in consequence of which they were severely penalized; and with the ultimate result that, following a formal complaint filed with the Commissioner of Indian Affairs, Eells' conduct of the case, along with several fictitious charges, was officially investigated.[2] The agent was cleared, but he had made an inveterate and aggressive enemy who never missed an opportunity during the next six or seven years to thwart him and to undermine the efforts of his missionary brother. In this endeavor Clams was able to organize a bothersome opposition through his influence with the appointed Skokomish "chiefs" Dick Lewis and David Charley. The advent of John Slocum provided another occasion well suited to his designs and needs.

Still other developments contributed to the Indian's uneasiness and distrust during the period from 1875–1881. A factor of considerable importance was the agitation over the meaning and the consequences of the policy of land distribution. From the time that the reservations in this region were established the belief had been that the sooner the Indian settled down to make a living from an individually assigned plot of land the better. Consequently, in the treaties of 1855 and 1856 covering the cession of lands about Puget Sound, provision was made for surveys and individual allotments. Progress toward this end was very slow, however. When Edwin Eells arrived at Skokomish in 1871 nothing had been accomplished. He instituted a survey, and in 1874 he began to issue tentative titles to the allotments, supposing that they would soon be validated by the proper federal authorities. In this, he as well as other agents who had the same hopes was disappointed. The authorities in Washington were as yet uncommitted on a course of action in the matter; and since there was little effective pressure upon them to act, they did nothing. There were, nevertheless, protests and demands from many quarters, with interested individuals airing their views through newspapers, missionary journals, and in public forums. Eventually, in 1880, the Board of Indian Commissioners was induced to exert its influence in the Indian's behalf, and by the spring of the next year certificates of allotment were being issued by the Office of Indian Affairs in Washington. Many people, whites and Indians alike, regarded these documents as unsatisfactory. The certificates awarded a title in trusteeship only, and prohibited the sale of allotments except to other members of the tribe. Attempts were initiated almost immediately to replace them with patents recorded in the General Land Office. In the case of the Indians around Puget Sound the transfer was effected and such patents replaced the old certificates for all tribes by 1886. In accordance with them the land was still held in trust by the Government, but it could be leased for periods of two years, and the character of the holding could be conditioned by an act of a state legislature with the consent of Congress.[3]

The delay and the confusion contingent upon this long process of adjustment had an unsettling effect upon the Puget Sound Indians. They were suspicious of the white man's intentions and could not understand his excuses for inaction or his theories of wardship. Furthermore, there were inequalities: the Skokomish received their certificates in 1881, their patents not until 1886, later than the Squaxin, Nisqually, Tulalip, and others who had received no certificates at all. Despite the vigorous efforts of Edwin Eells to see justice done, misunderstandings were rife. Of their troubles over this problem his brother wrote: "This delay [in getting titles] was a source of much uneasiness to the Indians, more, I think, than any other cause, for men were not wanting who told them that they would be moved away; there were plenty of people who coveted their land, and examples were not wanting of Indians who had been moved from place to place by the government. It has been the only thing which has ever caused them to talk about war." [4] And again: "The question came up early in missionary work. The Indians said: 'You profess to be Christians, and you have promised us titles to our land. If these titles come we will believe your religion to be true, but if not, it will be evidence that you are deceiving us.' " [5]

The year 1881 brought with it a further cause for anxiety which may have taken on an uncommon significance in the light of Slocum's death and resurrection in the fall. Beginning in early November there were a series of widespread and frightening epidemics that lasted until March. First there was a severe attack of smallpox; later came an equally disturbing epidemic of scarlet fever followed by one of measles. The diseases affected the white population as well as the Indians. Notices appeared in the local papers reporting the "scourges" in New Tacoma and other towns.[6] Still more informative are the reports of the Indian agent. He speaks of the "smallpox panic" which occurred late in 1881 causing many parents to remove their children from the Puyallup school. And with reference to the Skokomish he reported: "During the winter the scarlet fever attacked the school and was fatal in some cases, and many others were seriously and dangerously sick for some time. . . . This malady also carried off a number of the tribe, so that the rate of mortality has been much greater during the past year than for several years previous." Then in January: "A severe and fatal form of measles prevailed among the scholars and Indians, and a number of them died. This suspended the school for a time and was very discouraging. . . ." [7]

The Indians' distress over these afflictions was concurrent with the unsettling effects produced among at least some of them by John Slocum's doomsday message and by his vague promise of a medicine to save them from their bodily ills. It is therefore not improbable that the two events came to be intimately connected in their minds. Without understanding the full import of the turmoil about which he wrote, Myron Eells gives support to this interpretation. In 1882 in a report to his sponsoring society he says: "There has been considerable religious interest among the Indians [at Skokomish]. The Indians on other reservations have been more interested than usual, and intercourse with these has caused a similar interest here. Then the most severe sickness which has visited the reservation since my residence here came upon us last winter and awakened serious attention in the minds of many. This additional interest has caused increased work, so that I now hold prayer meetings at two logging camps regularly. Some of our young people are taking hold of the work and at times conduct meetings during my necessary absence." [8]

Finally it remains to be noted that the appeal of Slocum had roots as well as branches, and to suggest that his inspiration was something more—or less—than divinely given. As we have learned to expect from other cases of the kind, neither the original idea nor the motivation for its reception was a sudden and isolated phenomenon. To begin with, it is clear from the writings of Eells that the Indians whom he served were by no means unreceptive to his first approaches. It is quite probable that they dimly sensed that the things he told them about an omnipotent and generous God suggested a way out of their impasse. That the first promises frequently failed to materialize in their view raises another question. The important point is that the kind of thing that he represented to them, namely supernatural aid, did have an appeal. Recalling his early experiences with the Skokomish, and their neighbors, Eells relates some of the curious notions that they entertained about certain features of Christianity as they knew it, and which incidentally indicate their appeal. He says that he early met a number of Indians who believed that if they ceased to drink whisky and acquired a picture depicting a biblical scene they were certain of going to heaven. Many also took an equally magical view of baptism: if seriously sick they asked to be baptized, believing that this act would insure their recovery. Or they asked that all of their children be baptized; for, contrasting the mortality rate among their own offspring with the healthy appearance of Eells's four children, they concluded that baptism must be held accountable.[9]

For these and other more elusive reasons Eells was welcomed in many distant villages, logging camps, and homes. During the years from 1874 to 1881 there was a seething interest in religious matters in this section which he was at a loss to explain but which overjoyed him.[10] Writing of the Jamestown church, which the Indians founded on their own initiative, he says: "It is worthy of note that while Clallam County had so many people in it as to be organized into a county in 1854, and had in 1880 nearly six hundred white people, yet these Indians have the only church building in the county, the only church bell, hold the only regular prayer-meeting, and at their church and on the Neah Bay Indian Reservation are the only Sabbath-Schools which are kept up steadily summer and winter. One white person, who lives not far from Jamestown, said to me on one Sabbath, in 1880, as we came away from the church 'It is a shame, *it is a shame!* that the Indians here are going ahead of the whites in religious affairs. It is a wonder how they are advancing, considering the example around them.'"[11]

With reference to the antecedents of Shakerism, this religious interest came to a focus in the visions and prophesies of Big Bill, and in the following he inspired under the aggressive leadership of Billy Clams. Peter Heck's recollection of the circumstances surrounding Big Bill's inspiration has already been given. Enoch Abraham had also heard stories of the wonderful power possessed by this man as a result of his vision. It was related that once while he was preaching out-of-doors he raised his hand as a bird flew overhead and clutched its soul. The bird fell to the ground, but when Big Bill opened his clenched fist it flew away unharmed. Upon another occasion when he was holding a meeting and did not have enough food to provide a meal for his visitors he directed one of them to "go out there behind those trees and get that deer." The implication was that he was clairvoyant, for when the man returned he carried a deer that he had found at the place to which he had been directed.

Eells was rather intimately acquainted with Big Bill; and, having some sympathy for him and his earnest search for spiritual consolation, recorded some interesting details about him. He had received instruction in the Catholic faith and had presumably been baptized many years before Eells's arrival at Skokomish. From their first acquaintance in 1875 he was among those who welcomed Eells to the logging camps, and he was usually the one to take the lead in praying when Eells tried to encourage active participation in the meetings. In time he began to suffer from a lingering illness, and he requested that he be admitted into the Congregational Church and receive baptism. "One reason given was that he had heard of another Indian far away who had been sick somewhat as he was, who was baptized and recovered." Eventually, in May, 1880, Eells admitted him on his moral record, and particularly because in his sickness he struggled to resist the temptation of being ministererd to by shamans. Big Bill was led to repudiate shamanism as one consequence of the visions he had near the end of his life. Eells says that these supernatural visitations combined Protestant and Catholic teachings with an admixture of native beliefs and much reference to heaven. Eells often went to see him as he lay ill, and he was disturbed when Eells refused to admit that his visions were as authentic as the word of the Bible. Eells found nothing particularly objectionable about them except that they involved "a species of spiritualism." That is, he had visions of heaven, and of an old friend who had died years before. This friend told him to do certain things and taught him four songs which Big Bill taught to others. When he became too ill to attend the meetings at the church he held services in his own home at the same times; namely, on Sunday mornings and on Sunday and Thursday evenings.[12]

It is not known whether there was any direct contact between Big Bill and John Slocum, but almost certainly there was a transfer of ideas from the former to the latter. In several particulars their preachments were in agreement: both saw a blinding light at their first inspiration; both had visions of heaven and received messages from there; both instituted services in their homes that had many elements in common; both repudiated shamanism as a result of their regeneration. In addition, there was ample opportunity for indirect contact through the intermediation of Billy Clams, who was himself a precursor and a stimulator of both Big Bill and John Slocum. He had also received Catholic instruction, and prior to the advent of Big Bill had held services in his home. When the latter became ill and began to have visions, Clams cultivated an intimate association with him, which, according to Eells, became quite influential. Then when he died in June of 1881 Clams and his friends continued to hold services in his memory. They, in fact, held a funeral service for him, adopting, as Eells says, a ritual "of his own and Catholic songs and prayers, of lighted candles and ceremonies which they went through with after I was done [with the Protestant service]." Further, "they kept them [the services] up as an opposition, partly professing that they were Catholics, and partly saying that their brother's last words and songs were very precious to them, and they must get together, talk about what he had said and sing his songs." [13]

Big Bill's death occurred only a few months prior to Slocum's death and resurrection. Furthermore, Big Bill had foretold the coming of a religious leader and prophet who should be welcomed as a saviour by the Indians. In all probability Slocum was previously aware of this prediction; and if not, Billy Clams very likely made it known to him after his inspiration. At the very least, we know that there was an intimate association between Slocum and Clams. Eells reports that it was Billy Clams who, after a visit to the Slocums, came back to the Skokomish Reservation with the general invitation to the big Shaker meeting in August 1883. But other references attest to a close friendship long before this date.[14] It is therefore rather certain that the Slocum affair was in one sense the end product of a cumulative series of events; that in the broad view it was simply the most successful manifestation of various promptings to seek relief by religious means.

It is regrettable that we know so little about the personal history of John Slocum. It is also one of the more unexpected conclusions of this study that we can never obtain much of this information. This is because Slocum's friends and followers have not been interested in perpetuating it, and the literate people of the times, the whites in the vicinity, had even less serious interest in him or his pretensions. There are therefore only scanty and scattered references to his career and personality. Much of what follows is frankly by way of inference.

It is uncertain where John Slocum was born or when he died. His followers today do not even know where he is buried. Wickersham gives his approximate age in 1893 as 51. Mooney makes him four years older.[15] His name does not appear on any of the census rolls now available, so that even his tribal affiliation as a Squaxin rests only upon Wickersham's assertion and the supporting inference to be drawn from his residence at Skookum Chuck, in Squaxin territory, at the time he first came to public notice. Eells says that he formerly lived on the Skokomish Reservation, but moved to his relatively isolated location twelve miles away around 1875 or 1876. The missionary therefore did not know him well, although he implies in passing that Slocum had received some religious instruction from him. What his other contacts were before his revelation is virtually unknown.

Ober says, upon what authority we do not know, that John and Mary Slocum had attended Eells's services but later joined the Catholic Church. It is well established that Slocum did adopt the Catholic faith, but some important questions remain regarding the extent of his association with it and the date of his final conversion to it. Eells, in stating that Slocum's teachings at first "agreed partly with what he had learned from me, partly with the Catholic religion, and partly with neither, but that he was soon captured by the Catholics, baptized, and made a priest," [16] implies that his conversion came after his vision. It is more probable, however, that it came before that experience and very likely was almost coincident with it. The evidence for this comes from the Catholic missionary at Tulalip some twenty years after the event. In a brief reference to it he says that "a man by the name of Slocum, who had been baptized by Father Boulet, died. . . ." [17] If this is the case, then Slocum was not baptized until after 1878, for it was at the end of this year that Boulet arrived to take over the direction of the Tulalip mission.[18] It is therefore a reasonable conclusion that Slocum did not formally embrace the Catholic religion until at least three years before his alleged translation, and that very likely this took place immediately prior to it.

Of his other associations and interests we can only guess. In 1942 nothing could be learned about his travels. Presumably he visited friends and relatives on reservations in the area, as most of the other Indians did. What specific connections he had elsewhere, other than those with his wife's relatives among the Chehalis, we do not know. It is practically certain that he had no schooling, or but very little, for he could not read.

There is no direct information on the time of his death; no Indian that I have encountered could give even an approximate date; and no mention of it appears in the local newspapers that I have seen. He was dead by 1900, for Rakestraw, writing in that year, states that he passed away about two years before.[19] Ober, with perhaps more positive evidence, states that, from the time the gift of shaking restored him to health in 1882, he "lived for fourteen years free from sin and disease. . . ."[20] Since there is no need to be more precise, we may conclude that John Slocum finally died sometime within the two year span from 1896 to 1898.

With regard to his personality there are a few facts of significance, and several inferences that are tempting. By all accounts, he was a rather commonplace and timid man. Wickersham took notice of his bright eyes and "unquestioned confidence in himself and his mission," but found nothing striking or commanding in his appearance. He was, instead, modest and retiring with "rather a common expression of countenance." Other reports indicate that he was reticent and taciturn. His entanglements at the time of his conversion suggest that he was more likely to be victimized and used than to take a forceful stand and direct his own affairs. Even though charged to carry his message to Indians everywhere he avoided the mission. People came to him instead; and it was not until Louis assumed control that Slocum was induced to trail along in his wake. He was not called upon by the Presbyterians to give evidence of his faith, as were Louis and John Smith; and he was not jailed and publicly ridiculed for it as these men were. One gets the impression that he was docile and not very alert. In all that is known about him there is nothing to suggest vigor or color, much less of insight or cleverness. It is true that he had undertaken to carry on independent logging operations to support his family, and had acquired a modest amount of capital goods in the form of oxen teams and logging gear. But he was not an outstanding success in this, or conspicuous in any other way among his associates. Wickersham confirms the impression of mediocrity in saying that "up to the time of his translation [he] was looked on as a common Indian, with a slight inclination to fire-water and pony racing, as well as a known fondness for gambling."

If from such meager data a characterization may be ventured, he might be described as phlegmatic and persistent, with perhaps less need for external support and stimulation than was ordinary among his fellows. If more were known of him it might be that he could appropriately be called a mystic.

There is a suggestion that he suffered from some kind of nervous ailment. In the words of the anonymous document already quoted (pp. 40–44), "There were times when the spirit of God brought such heavy conviction upon the heart of John Slocum that he fell prostrate upon the skid-roads while at his work." An attempt was made to follow up this clue with informants, but without success. Questions regarding his various illnesses failed to elicit any significant responses. The only additional bit of information that can be offered to bear out a theory of a chronic nervous disorder appears in the account of Mrs. Heck. She recalled that once while preaching Slocum suddenly stiffened and fell backwards in an unconscious state, much to the dismay of his followers, who were afraid that he was going to leave them again. Taken in conjunction with the central fact of his prolonged state of coma at the time of his visitation, this suggests a common pattern that makes the phenomenon more understandable. It is, perhaps, too late to conjecture whether the attacks, if real, were of an hysterical, epileptic, or some other kind. There is no evidence that they were accompanied by convulsions or muscular spasms, although here, again, nothing positive may be said.

It is intriguing to suppose that Slocum's message emerged from the same psychological need as his seizures. It is possible that his faints provided him with a refuge in times of crisis, and that eventually a conjunction of favorable circumstances made capital of them for him in terms of personal justification and social reward. Despite his reticence, it is probable that he enjoyed the attention he received after his visit to heaven. In this connection it should be recalled he threatened to leave his people if they failed to heed his message.

Even when we discount the suggestions of a chronic nervous disturbance as a factor in Slocum's acceptance of a mission there remain other circumstances which indicate that he had reached in impasse in his personal relations from which any escape would be welcome. From the account of his sister-in-law it appears that he had become enmeshed in an oppressive network of interfamily intrigue and hate. His father and his wife's family were involved in a feud of growing intensity which not only put a strain upon John and Mary's marital relations but made them unwilling parties to it and innocent victims of it. The conflict was the more vicious psychologically in that it played upon suspicion for its harmful effects. Since the weapons were those of magic, there were no overt physical attacks by the enemy, and hence no defense by similar forthright expurgatory means. In as much as deceit and dissimulation are assumed to be the stock in trade of the magician, there was not even any method for distinguishing friend from foe. Under these circumstances families, at least, must stick together to preserve the minimum of emotional security for the individual. We do not know to what extent Slocum himself was beset by the fears that impelled his father to accuse his wife's relatives of poisoning him; but in any case he was confronted with an unhappy choice in loyalties. He must have been phlegmatic indeed not to have been disturbed by this embroilment, especially since it was heavily charged with an element of fear for his life.

Whatever he may have thought of his father's charges against his in-laws, it is evident that by the time of his critical illness Slocum had developed a pronounced dislike for medicine men. The idea of expressing this dislike in the form of a divine injunction against shamanistic practices may have come to him as a result of his familiarity with Big Bill's teachings, but his rejection of them was not due simply to his copying of a ready-made pattern. The statements of informants, and the internal evidence of his message, all indicate that he had strong personal motivations for denouncing the activities of shamans. Most informants in the vicinity of Puget Sound agree in attributing his troubles, including his severe illnesses and ultimate death, to the venal and malicious practices of these dealers in magic. Very likely he shared this view along with most of his contemporaries, from whom the belief undoubtedly stems and from whom it has been transmitted to modern informants. And to judge from the evidence of his teachings, Slocum was not only afraid of magicians for the evil they were capable of perpetrating; he also resented the monopoly they held on the curing art. He made it plain in his message, and it has become a cardinal tenet in Shakerism, that God was to send the Indians a free medicine, something not only different from shamanism but gratis to anyone who led a Christian life.

Shamans, in their dual capacities as killers and healers, were instruments of unrelieved oppression in native society. When they were not a threat to personal security, they were collecting heavily to defend and maintain it for their clients. Slocum found a way out of this circle of compounded evil, and presumably because he was strongly motivated to do so. He was impelled by a personal need for greater security than his society at the time could offer him. It is interesting that he accepted a refuge in fantasy. It was also appropriate to his cultural background, and seemed reasonable to others. The immediate appeal of his solution, the uncompromising stand that Mary and her followers took against shamans, and the surge of witch hunts that marked the emergence of Shakerism, all indicate that Slocum was not alone in his anxiety. Others were grateful for the escape that he offered them. And today, though a Shaker may know nothing in particular about Slocum's teachings, he is clear on the church's stand against Indian doctors.

But even more important at the present time, when shamans are few or nonexistent, is the fact that for many individuals the emotional experience of shaking is a healing instrument. It *is* a medicine, the fulfilment of a prophecy for the afflicted and the oppressed, an unmeasured gift to the faithful.

NOTES

Full bibliographical material for the following references not supplied in the Notes may be found in the Bibliography.

INTRODUCTION

1. Mooney, p. 747.

CHAPTER ONE

1. Mooney, p. 746.
2. He referred, of course, to Mooney's *The Ghost Dance Religion*. Enoch Abraham also knew about this work, although he knew nothing of its particulars. I used it to check specific details with him.
3. At the onset of their first menstruation girls were isolated from the rest of the community to provide for their ritual passage from childhood to adulthood. It was believed that during the interval a girl was particularly impressionable, an easy victim of undesirable influences and evil forces, and also a source of spiritual contamination for men.
4. Mooney, pp. 752–53.
5. Ober, pp. 583–84.
6. Mooney, p. 747.
7. It appears on pages 119–21.

CHAPTER TWO

1. *Presbyterian Home Missions*, May, 1882, p. 105. "Hyas Lee Plet" is Chinook jargon for High or Chief Priest.

2. *American Missionary*, July, 1882, p. 215, and November, 1882, p. 341.
3. Mooney, pp. 753–54.
4. Eells, *Ten Years of Missionary Work*, p. 161.
5. *Ibid.*, p. 165.
6. *Ibid.*, p. 170.
7. *Ibid.*, p. 172.
8. Mooney, p. 747.
9. Eells, *Ten Years of Missionary Work*, p. 173.
10. Mooney, p. 748.
11. *Ibid.*, p. 748.
12. DeKoven Brown published two interesting pictures of the then new 1910 church on Mud Bay in his article called "Indian Workers for Temperance." I am unable to reconcile the information I obtained with his statement that Mud Bay Sam donated an acre of ground for the site of this church.
13. Actually across the bay in a village called Boston.
14. Reagan, *Ethnological Studies*.
15. *The Indian Sentinel*, 1913, p. 37.
16. Olson, pp. 170–71. Spier reports, on information from Olson, that the Quinault became Shakers between 1888 and 1890. Spier, p. 53.
17. Commissioner of Indian Affairs, *Report* for 1902, p. 357.
18. This account, although obtained almost twenty years later and from another informant, agrees even in detail with the one recorded by Spier on page 66.
19. *The Indian Sentinel*, 1910, p. 177.
20. Spier, pp. 67–68. I obtained the same account, except for the date.

CHAPTER THREE

1. Commissioner of Indian Affairs, *Report* for 1892, p. 499.
2. *Ibid.*, 1890, p. 126. Referring to the Ghost Dance in the Plains, the Commissioner writes, "This alleged appearance of a Messiah was not an entirely new thing. Some six or eight years ago one of the Puyallup Indians claimed that in a trance he had been to the other world. As a result of his visions a kind of society was formed, churches were built, one of the Indians claimed to be the 'Christ,' and the band became so infatuated and unmanageable that the agent was obliged to imprison the alleged 'Christ,' punish his followers, and discharge a number of Indian judges and policemen in order to regain control."

3. *Ibid.*, 1906, p. 381.

4. *American Missionary* for July, 1883, p. 211, and for May, 1884, p. 152.

5. Eells, *Ten Years of Missionary Work.*

6. *Presbyterian Home Missionary*, June, 1884, p. 135.

7. *The Indian Sentinel*, 1913, pp. 40–41.

8. Lindquist, p. 386.

9. *Ibid.*, p. 287, footnote.

10. Eells, *Ten Years of Missionary Work*, p. 174.

11. *Ibid.*, p. 174.

12. As a matter of record, the Episcopalians had made some efforts among the Makah beginning in 1883 and extending through 1888, but without the aid of a full-time resident missionary. The work was desultory, but each year they claimed a number of converts. (Commissioner of Indian Affairs, *Reports*, 1883–88.)

13. *The Indian's Friend*, XII (January, 1900), 4.

14. Commissioner of Indian Affairs, *Report* for 1899, p. 356.

15. *The Indian's Friend*, XII (January, 1900), 4.

16. *Home Mission Monthly*, XXVIII (February, 1914), 92.

17. Commissioner of Indian Affairs, *Report* for 1903, p. 334.

18. *Ibid.*, 1904, p. 356.

19. *Home Mission Monthly*, XXIX (February, 1915), 70.

20. Commission of Indian Affairs, *Report* for 1892, p. 499.

21. *Ibid.*, 1893, p. 333.

22. *Ibid.*, 1895, p. 406; 1896, p. 399.

23. *Ibid.*, 1897, p. 295; 1903, p. 334.

24. *American Missionary*, May, 1892, p. 158.

25. Shakleford, pp. 70–71.

26. *Home Mission Monthly*, XXVIII (February, 1914), 92.

27. *Presbyterian Home Missionary*, February, 1886, pp. 34–35.

28. *Ibid.*, May, 1882, p. 104.

29. *The Church at Home and Abroad*, June, 1887, p. 513.

30. *Ibid.*, April, 1888, p. 351.

31. Mooney, p. 760.

32. *The Church at Home and Abroad*, November, 1893, p. 388.

CHAPTER FOUR

1. Presumably the word means to "shake" or "tremble." In the Nisqually word list compiled by Gibbs, "o-chad-dub" is the word given for "tremble." George Gibbs, "Dictionary of the Nisqually," *Contributions to North American Ethnology* (Washington, D.C.), I (1877), 356.

2. Eells, *Ten Years of Missionary Work*, p. 165. "Mowitch Man" was a sobriquet by which Louis was sometimes known. See Commissioner of Indian Affairs, *Report* for 1904, p. 356.

3. Mooney, p. 754.

CHAPTER FIVE

1. The dances mentioned were aboriginal Yurok ceremonies. See A. L. Kroeber, *Handbook of the Indians of California* (Washington, D.C.: Bureau of American Ethnology, Bulletin 78, 1925), pp. 53–62.

2. Mooney, pp. 754–55.

3. *Ibid.*, p. 754.

4. Ober, p. 588.

5. Rakestraw, pp. 704–6.

6. Ober, p. 588

7. Mooney, p. 754.

8. Spier, p. 52.

9. Mooney, p. 754.

CHAPTER SIX

1. Mooney, pp. 753–54.

2. Ober, p. 590.

3. Spier, p. 66.

4. Olson, p. 172.

5. *Ibid.*, p. 174.

6. *The Indian Sentinel*, 1913, p. 40.

7. Olson, p. 173.

8. Spier, p. 69.

9. It was explained that Billy carried a hand bell "because he was a Catholic."

10. Spier, pp. 67–68.

11. Olson, p. 173.

12. Spier, p. 67.

CHAPTER SEVEN

1. Brown, p. 23, photograph.

2. Mooney, p. 761.

3. *Ibid.*, p. 749.

4. *Ibid.*, p. 761.

5. Rakestraw, p. 708.

6. One of the women in Rakestraw's illustration is shown with a cloth (p. 708).

7. Mooney, pp. 761–62.

8. *Ibid.*, p. 748.

9. Jean Baptiste Boulet, *Prayer Book and Catechism in the Snohomish Language* (Tulalip, Washington Territory: Tulalip Mission Press, 1879), p. 5.

10. Edward Sapir, *Wishram Texts* ("Publications of the American Ethnological Society," Vol. II [Leyden, Holland: E. J. Brill, 1909]), p. 193.

11. Mooney, pp. 755–56.

12. Ober, p. 585.

13. He also reproduced it in a published article. See Albert B. Reagan, "The Shaker Church of the Indians," *The Southern Workman* (Hampton Institute, Hampton, Va.), LVI (1927), 448.

14. Ober, p. 592.

15. Rakestraw, pp. 705, 707, and 708.

16. Spier, p. 66.

17. Mooney, p. 761.

CHAPTER EIGHT

1. Ober, pp. 590 and 592.

2. T. T. Waterman, "The 'Shake Religion' of Puget Sound," *Smithsonian Institution Annual Report for 1922* (Washington, D.C., 1924), pp. 501–2.

3. This is not a general or even an expected practice. Ordinarily the participants ignore the spectators completely, but occasionally during the handshake, as an expression of brotherly love and at times even as a solicitation to participate, the leading woman swings wide of her projected path and includes the spectators on the front row of benches if they will respond. Most Shakers do not like this, and while they will follow their leader it is obvious from their behavior that they do not relish the act of including outsiders, especially white people. The lead position is not an assigned one. Any woman may take it. Most women do not want it but there are always a few who enjoy the small measure of prominence and responsibility that it brings and they assume the function by tacit agreement.

4. This, too, was irregular. The final formation should have been two lines as at the start of the handshake.

5. O. C. Upchurch, "The Swinomish People and Their State," *Pacific Northwest Quarterly*, XXXII (1936), 294–95.

6. "Masache" is Chinook jargon for evil.

7. Rakestraw, p. 709. The "responsive exercises" that are mentioned, as well as the "litany" of the Upchurch quotation, are no doubt the concerted signs of the cross alternating with individual prayers.

8. Ober, p. 592.

9. *Ibid.*, p. 588.

10. Olson, p. 173.

11. *Ibid.*

12. *Ibid.*

13. Reagan, *Ethnological Studies.*

14. Ober, pp. 593–94.

15. This kind of a shift happens often during the course of a long shaking session. Sometimes a bell ringer initiates it himself. It always marks a change from a fast, intolerable pace to a slower one.

16. Ober, p. 586.

CHAPTER NINE

1. *Rapport sur les missions*, V (January, 1843), 66–67.

2. Mann was pleased at the response of his Nisqually congregation, "all," as he relates, "as they passed into the church shaking my hand warmly." *Presbyterian Home Missionary*, November, 1886, p. 252.

3. Eells, *Ten Years of Missionary Work*, p. 25. *Constitution of the Presbyterian Church*, p. 371.

4. Blanchet, p. 124. Ezra Meeker reports, "In looking for a plan the Vicar General imagined that by representing on a square stick, the forty centuries before Christ by 40 marks; the thirty-three years of our Lord by 33 points, followed by a cross; and the eighteen centuries and thirty-nine years since, by 18 marks and 39 points, would pretty well answer his design, in giving him a chance to show the beginning of the world, the creation, the fall of angels, of Adam, the promise of the Savior, the time of his birth, and his death upon the cross, as well as the mission of the Apostles. The plan was a great success. After eight days' explanation, the chief and his companions became masters of the subject; and, having learned to make the sign of the cross and to sing one or two canticles in Chinook jargon, they started for home well satisfied, with a square rule thus marked, which they called Sa-ha-le stick. The plan was afterward changed from a rule to a large chart containing the great epochs of the world, such as the Deluge,

the Tower of Babel, the Ten Commandments of God, the 12 Apostles, the seven sacraments and precepts of the Church; these being very useful to enable the missionary the teaching of the Indians and whites. It was called the 'Catholic Ladder.' " *Pioneer Reminiscences of Puget Sound* (Seattle, Wash.: Lowman and Hanford, 1905), p. 490.

5. In 1844 one of the missionary priests visited Whidbey Island and called upon a local headman who had come to the Cowlitz mission two years before for baptism and religious instruction. He found the Indian saying "mass." The service "consisted in explaining to the savages of his tribe the chronological history of religion (traced on a map), in teaching them to make numberless signs of the cross, and in singing a few canticles with the Kyrie Eleison." Taken from a "Letter of Mr. Bolduc, Apostolic Missionary," in Thwaites, XXIX, 53.

6. "The sign of the cross, in which we say this brief prayer, shows the spirit in which we should perform all our actions—in the name of God. This most common of all sacramentals is a beautiful prayer and a powerful weapon against evil. . . . It wins grace for its user, repels evil spirits, and wards off spiritual and temporal dangers. It is frequently used in liturgy, and there is attached to it an indulgence of 100 days, 300 days if it is made with holy water." McNeill, p. 13.

7. The issue over formalism is one, in fact, which divides the denominations. At the very time with which we are concerned a controversy was going on among the contributors to the *Presbyterian Journal* over the question of introducing more "liturgy" and other forms of group participation into Presbyterian services. The argument was touched off by a critical article submitted to the *Journal* by the eminent Presbyterian professor at Auburn Theological Seminary, Dr. Samuel Hopkins. He wrote of the existing service: "The praying is exclusively done by the minister; the singing is mostly done by a few young persons in the gallery, and with the same propriety: If the people can worship in prayer by proxy, they can equally worship by proxy in singing. Then comes usually a single short chapter of the Scripture. The long prayer, notoriously a terror, at least to the young and indifferent mind, follows. Then comes the great business of the occasion: the hearing, with more or less of critical interest, an able and carefully prepared oration from the pulpit; a short prayer ends the service. Through all this the congregation sit mute." *The Presbyterian Journal* (Presbyterian Church in the U.S.A., Philadelphia, 1880–1904), March 9, 1882, p. 2.

8. Lamps, burning fish and other oils, as well as some electric

lighting, were in use at the time around Puget Sound. See *The Washington Standard*, Friday, November, 18, 1881.

9. *The Youth's Companion*, I (May, 1881), 4.

10. *Missions de la Congregation*, III, 111.

11. See photograph of Bishop Modest Demers, an early missionary in this vicinity, in Denny, Plate XV. An anecdote which adds an amusing note to the theme of improvisation by the missionaries occurred at the time Chirouse was ordained. This ceremony took place at Fort Walla Walla under conditions of extreme urgency. An alb was not available for the priest's investment so a "chemise" or nightshirt of Mr. MacBean, the trader in charge of the fort, was borrowed for the occasion. *Missions de la Congregation*, No. 196 (March, 1912), p. 82.

12. Reporting upon the success of this undertaking, Durieu wrote to his superior on September 1, 1860: "They are proud of their short red cassocks and even more of their white dress (surplice without sleeves) which they chose themselves. I asked them one day if they preferred the alb to the surplice. 'Father,' they cried, 'we like the small white dress. The long dress (the alb) hides all, while the short allows half of the black robe to show.' " *Ibid.*, I (1862), 126.

13. *Ibid.*, p. 154.

14. Sister Mary Louise, pp. 56, 70, and 108.

15. Spier, pp. 30–49.

16. Mooney, p. 726.

17. Blanchet, p. 114.

18. *Missions de la Congregation*, VI (1867), 255, also Sister Mary Louise, p. 86–87.

19. *Rapport sur les missions*, VI (July, 1845), 28, and V (January, 1843), 28 and 43. Also Blanchet, p. 125, and *The Indian Sentinel*, 1913, p. 39.

20. Ortolan, II, 295.

21. *Missions de la Congregation*, VI (1867), 254.

22. *Rapport sur les missions*, IV (January, 1842), 54. For other references to the practice, *ibid.*, III (January, 1841), 64, and V (January, 1843), 44–45.

23. According to the Presbyterians, "The standing posture is sanctioned by Scripture," and it is recommended for a praying congregation. (*Presbyterian Rule and Form of Government*—Presbyterian Board of Publication, Philadelphia, 1898—p. 207.) The Congregationalists recommend that assembled worshipers either stand while praying or sit with bowed heads. (*Book of Church Services*—Pre-

pared by a Commission of the National Council of the Congregational Churches, Boston: Pilgrim Press, 1922—p. 84.)

24. *Rapport sur les missions*, III (January, 1841), 56.
25. Blanchet, p. 97.
26. *Ibid.*, p. 112.
27. *The Youth's Companion*, I (1881), 37.
28. A single brief passage from Archbishop Blanchet's summary of his church's activities in Oregon Territory emphasizes the importance of several of the foregoing elements in the proselytizing pattern. In March, 1841, Blanchet visited the Indians around Oregon City, and of their response to his efforts to convert them he wrote: "The sight of the altar, vestments, sacred vessels, and great ceremonies were drawing their attention a great deal more than the cold, unavailable and lay service of Brother Waller [the local Methodist missionary]. There seemed to be more attention given to the ringing of the bell, and the Mission exercises. The missionary [i.e., Blanchet] had at last the consolation to see the poor Indians make the sign of the cross, say the offering of the heart, call the seven medicines, sing a short prayer before and after meals, and also the Chinook canticles." Blanchet, p. 121.
29. Eells, *Ten Years of Missionary Work*, p. 53.
30. *American Missionary*, July, 1883, p. 211.
31. *Presbyterian Home Missionary*, February, 1885, p. 36.
32. *Ibid.*, November, 1886, p. 252. General Spot, so-called, was one of the catechists trained to encourage Catholic forms of worship at Puyallup.
33. In a letter from Durieu to his Superior General it is stated that "those who have failed in their pledge of temperance have avowed their fault before the whole assembly and have demanded public penitence." *Missions de la Congregation*, VI (1867), 40. In another place it is reported that backsliders were forced to pay two piastres fine for the poor and submit to ten lashes with a whip. *Rapport sur les missions*, XIV (March, 1861), 167.
34. Spier, pp. 13–14.
35. *Rapport sur les missions*, IV (January, 1842), 57.
36. William Fraser Tolmie, "Journal of William Fraser Tolmie—1833," *Washington Historical Quarterly*, III (July, 1912), 235–36.
37. Spier, p. 35.
38. "Occurrences at Nisqually House," p. 14.
39. *Ibid.*, p. 58.
40. *Ibid.*, pp. 40, 45, 56, and 63.

41. *Ibid.*, pp. 58 and 64.

42. In addition to the instances cited by Spier, Du Bois has collected accounts of a number of other prophets in the locality and determined their relation to Smohalla. Du Bois, pp. 8–9.

43. "Occurrences at Nisqually House," p. 42. See also pp. 27, 28, 58, and 61.

44. *Ibid.*, p. 38.

45. *Ibid.*, p. 57.

46. *Ibid.*, p. 59.

47. Du Bois, pp. 8–9.

48. *Ibid.*, pp. 11–19.

CHAPTER TEN

1. H. G. Barnett, *Innovation. The Basis of Cultural Change* (New York: McGraw, 1953), *passim.*

2. Mooney, p. 753.

3. *Ibid.*, p. 754.

4. Eells, *Ten Years of Missionary Work*, p. 180.

5. The Smohalla meeting place was simply a dwelling of the long, tunnel-like multifamily variety typical of the middle Columbia region. Later on, rectangular wooden structures were built and reserved for ceremonies.

6. "The [Catholic] church should face the east, whence light, truth, and grace of salvation have come to us." Gisler, p. 78.

7. *The Church at Home and Abroad*, November, 1893, p. 387. Ricard, the founder of the St. Joseph mission, has left a note that is pertinent at this point. In recalling his early experiences at the mission he states that he had very little success with conversions. In the beginning of his work there the Indians came in numbers at his invitation, but soon they failed to respond. Inquiring into the cause, he was told that they were disappointed that he did not provide a feast for them after his services. *Missions de la Congregation*, No. 196 (1912), p. 168.

8. Ortolan, p. 309.

9. Ober, p. 588.

10. Probably the emphasis on seven, apart from its definition of the recurring day of worship, and on twelve, can be laid more specifically to Catholic influence. See Gisler, pp. 59, 73, 85, and 87–88. In Catholicism there are seven sacraments, seven orders of the priesthood, "the seven-fold Holy Spirit, the Paraclete," "the 7 special graces called gifts of the Holy Ghost," etc. McNeill, p. 23.

11. Mooney, pp. 752–53. Aboriginally the Puget Sound area was a fusion ground with respect to ritual numbers. Both four and five were used, but the latter was by far the most prominent. It is therefore a little surprising that Slocum chose the former.

12. Eells, *Ten Years of Missionary Work*, p. 229.

13. *Ibid.*, p. 238.

14. *Rapport sur les missions*, III (January, 1841), 64.

15. *Ibid.*, IV (January, 1842), 55.

16. *Ibid.*, p. 51.

17. "In olden times everywhere, and today in some countries, the women are on the left side and the men on the right side of the church." Gisler, p. 80.

18. Thwaites, XXIX, 299.

19. *Rapport sur les missions*, II (January, 1840), 28, also Blanchet, p. 97.

20. *Rapport sur les missions*, III (January, 1841), 62.

21. Ortolan, p. 307.

22. *Rapport sur les missions*, IV (January, 1842), p. 54.

23. *Ibid.*, V (January, 1843), 66.

24. *Missions de la Congregation*, III (1864), VI (1867), 39 and 57.

25. *Rapport sur les missions*, VI (July, 1845), 56.

26. In spite of his impressive title, the Shaker bishop is still only the "headman" in Indian thinking; and all the fuss about ordaining him and other officers of the church is a formality which does not separate them from the ordinary members by any mystic barrier.

27. *Constitution of the Presbyterian Church*, p. 442.

28. *The Church at Home and Abroad*, April, 1887, p. 326.

29. Sister Mary Louise, p. 82.

30. *The Church at Home and Abroad*, June, 1887, p. 513.

31. *Presbyterian Home Missionary*, February, 1886, p. 34.

32. Mooney, p. 719.

33. Du Bois, p. 8.

34. Mooney, p. 755.

35. Melcher, pp. 70–82.

36. *Ibid.*, p. 227.

37. Andrews, pp. 144–45.

38. *Ibid.*, pp. 147–51.

CHAPTER ELEVEN

1. Mooney, p. 753.

2. Eells, *Ten Years of Missionary Work*, pp. 114–17.

3. J. B. Harrison, *The Latest Studies on Indian Reservations* (Philadelphia: Indian Rights Association, 1887), pp. 91–96.

4. Eells, *Ten Years of Missionary Work*, p. 75.

5. *Ibid.*, p. 76.

6. *The Washington Standard* for November 11 and 18, 1881; December 23, 1881; and March 3, 1882. See also Herbert Hunt and Floyd C. Kaylor, *Washington West of the Cascades* (Chicago: S. J. Clarke Publishing Co., 1917), I, 507.

7. Commissioner of Indian Affairs, *Report* for 1882, p. 166.

8. *American Missionary*, November, 1882, p. 341.

9. *Ibid.*, January, 1885, p. 14.

10. Eells, *Ten Years of Missionary Work*, pp. 163, 223–29, and 236–43.

11. *Ibid.*, p. 208.

12. *Ibid.*, pp. 158–60.

13. *Ibid.*, p. 161.

14. *Ibid.*, p. 172. See also pp. 164 and 165.

15. Mooney, pp. 751 and 746.

16. Eells, *Ten Years of Missionary Work*, p. 165.

17. *The Indian Sentinel*, 1913, p. 40.

18. *Ibid.*, January, 1920, p. 42.

19. Rakestraw, p. 706.

20. Ober, p. 584.

BIBLIOGRAPHY

American Missionary. New York: American Missionary Association. 1846–1934.

Andrews, Edward D. *The Gift To Be Simple; Songs, Dances and Rituals of the American Shakers*. New York: J. J. Augustin, 1940.

The Assembly Herald. Philadelphia: The Presbyterian Church in the U.S.A., 1894–1898.

Barnett, H. G. *Innovation. The Basis of Cultural Change*. New York: McGraw, 1953.

Blanchet, Reverend Francis N. *Historical Sketches of the Catholic Church in Oregon During the Past Forty Years (1838–1878)*. Portland, Ore., 1878.

Book of Church Services. Prepared by a Commission of the National Council of Congregational Churches. Boston: Pilgrim Press, 1922.

Boulet, Jean Baptiste *Prayer Book and Catechism in the Snohomish Language*. Tulalip, Washington Territory: Tulalip Mission Press, 1879.

Brown, DeKoven. "Indian Workers for Temperance," *Collier's, The National Weekly*. September 3, 1910, pp. 23–24.

Chalcraft, Edwin L. "The Shaker Religion of the Indians of the Northwest," *The Assembly Herald*, February, 1913, pp. 74–75.

The Church at Home and Abroad. Philadelphia: Presbyterian Church in the U.S.A., 1887–98.

Commissioner of Indian Affairs. *Report to the Secretary of the Interior*. U.S. Bureau of Indian Affairs. Washington, D.C.: U.S. Government Printing Office, 1882–1904.

Constitution of the Presbyterian Church in the United States of America. Philadelphia: Presbyterian Board of Publication and Sabbath-School Work, 1896.

Crowder, S. I. "The Dreamer Religion," *The Overland Monthly*, New Series, LXII (December, 1913), 606.

Denny, Arthur A. *Pioneer Days on Puget Sound*, ed. Alice Harriman. Seattle, Wash.: Alice Harriman Co., 1908.

Du Bois, Cora. *The Feather Cult of the Middle Columbia.* ("General Series in Anthropology," ed. Leslie Spier, No. 7.) Menasha, Wis.: Banta Publishing Co., 1938.

Eells, Reverend Myron. *History of the Congregational Association of Oregon and Washington Territory.* Portland, Oregon: The Home Missionary Society of Oregon and adjoining Territories and the Northwest Association of Congregational Ministers, 1881.

————*Ten Years of Missionary Work among the Indians at Skoko-mish, Washington Territory. 1874–1884.* Boston: Congregational Sunday-School and Publishing Society, 1886.

Gibbs, George. "Dictionary of the Nisqually," *Contributions to North American Ethnology* (Washington, D.C.,), I (1877).

Gisler, Reverend Otto. *Catholic Worship. The Sacraments, Cere-monies, and Festivals of the Church Explained in Questions and Answers. Translated from the German by Rev. Richard Brennan, LL.D.* New York: Benziger, 1888.

Good Tidings, ed. and publ. J. B. Boulet. Ferndale, Wash., 1906–12.

Gunther, Erna. "The Shaker Religion of the Northwest," *Indians of the Urban Northwest*, ed. Marian W. Smith, New York: Columbia University Press. 1949. pp. 37–76.

Harrison, J. B. *The Latest Studies on Indian Reservations.* Philadelphia: Indian Rights Association, 1887.

Henry, Rt. Rev. Msgr. Hugh T. *Catholic Customs and Symbols. Varied Forms and Figures of Catholic Usage, Ceremony and Practice Briefly Explained.* New York: Benziger, 1925.

Home Mission Monthly. New York: Woman's Executive Committee of Home Missions of the Presbyterian Church, 1886–1924.

Hunt, Herbert and Kaylor, Floyd C. *Washington West of the Cas-cades.* Chicago: S. J. Clarke Publishing Co., 1917.

The Indian's Friend. Philadelphia: National Indian Association, 1900.

The Indian Sentinel. Washington, D.C.: Bureau of Catholic Indian Missions, 1902–16.

"Indian Shakers," *Literary Digest*, XLVIII (March 7, 1914), 496.

Kroeber, A. L. *Handbook of the Indians of California.* Bulletin 78. Washington, D.C.: Bureau of American Ethnology, 1925.

Lindquist, G. E. E. *The Red Man in the United States; An Intimate Study of the Social, Economic, and Religious Life of the Ameri-can Indian, Made under the Direction of G. E. E. Lindquist, with a Foreword by Honorable Charles H. Burke.* New York: George H. Doran Company, 1923.

McNeill, Charles J. *Prayers. A Study of Prayers in Common Use in the Church . . . with an Introduction by Rev. Leon A. McNeil.* Witchita, Kan.: Catholic Action Committee, 1939.

Melcher, Mrs. Marguerite (Fellows). *The Shaker Adventure.* Princeton, N.J.: Princeton University Press, 1941.

Missions de la Congregation des Missionnaires Oblats de Marie Immaculée (Paris), I–XVI (1862–78).

——(Rome), No. 196 (March, 1912).

Mooney, James. *The Ghost-Dance Religion and the Sioux Outbreak of 1890.* "Fourteenth Annual Report, Bureau of American Ethnology, 1892–93." Part 2. Washington, D.C., 1896.

Ober, Sarah Endicott. "A New Religion Among the West Coast Indians," *The Overland Monthly.* Series 2, LVI (1910), 583–94.

"Occurrences at Nisqually House," *Told by the Pioneers. Reminiscences of Pioneer Life in Washington.* "Printed under a project directed by Secretary of State E. N. Hutchinson." I (1937[?]).

Olson, Roland L. "The Quinault Indians." *University of Washington Publications in Anthropology* (Seattle, Washington), VI (1936), 1–190.

Ortolan, R. P. Th. O.M.I. *Cent ans d'Apostolat dans des deux Hemisphères. Les Oblats de Marie Immaculée durant le premier siècle de leur existence 1841–1861.* Tome 2. Paris, 1915.

Presbyterian Home Missions (or *Missionary*). New York: Board of Home Missions, Presbyterian Church in the U.S.A., 1872–86.

The Presbyterian Journal. Philadelphia: Presbyterian Church in the U.S.A., 1880–1904.

Presbyterian Rule and Form of Government. Philadelphia: Presbyterian Board of Publication, 1898.

Puget Sound Weekly Courier. (Newspaper) Olympia, Washington Territory.

Rakestraw, Charles D. "The Shaker Indians of Puget Sound," *The Southern Workman* (Hampton Institute, Hampton, Va.), XXIX (December, 1900), 703–9.

Rapport sur les missions du Diocèse de Québec. Quebec, Canada: L'Association de la propagation de la foi, II–XIV (1840–61).

Reagan, Albert B. *Ethnological Studies of the Hoh and Quileute Indians, the Sole Survivors of the Chimakuan Linguistic Family.* Archives of Bureau of American Ethnology, Washington, D.C., MS 1802.

——. "Notes on the Shaker Church of the Indian," *Proceedings of the Indiana Academy of Science,* 1910, pp. 115–16.

——. "The Shake Dance of the Quileute Indians, With Drawings by an Indian Pupil of the Quileute Day School," *Proceeding of the Indiana Academy of Science,* 1908, pp. 71–74.

————. "The Shaker Church of the Indians," *The Southern Work-man* (Hampton Institute, Hampton, Va.), LVI (1927), 447–48.

Ricard, Reverend Pascal. "Les Origines de nos missions de l'Oregon," *Missions de la Congregation des Missionaries Oblats de Marie Imaculée* (Rome), no. 196 (March, 1912); no. 198 (June, 1912).

Sapir, Edward. *Wishram Texts.* ("Publications of the American Ethnological Society," Vol. II.) Leyden, Holland: E. J. Brill, 1909.

Shakleford, Elizabeth. "History of the Puyallup Indian Reservation." Unpublished Bachelor's thesis, The College of Puget Sound, 1918.

Sister Letitia Mary Lyons. "Francis Norbert Blanchet and the Founding of the Oregon Missions (1838–1848)." Unpublished thesis, Catholic University, Washington, D.C., 1940. Pp. 200.

Sister Mary Louise, O.P. (Nellie Sullivan). "Eugene Casimir Chirouse, O.M.I. and the Indians of Washington." Unpublished thesis, University of Washington, 1932. Pp. 131.

Smith, Marian W. "Shamanism in the Shaker Religion of Northwest America," *Man* (London), LIV (1954) 119–22.

Snowden, Clinton A. *History of Washington; the Rise and Progress of an American State.* New York: The Century History Co., 1909–11.

Spier, Leslie. *The Prophet Dance of the Northwest and Its Derivatives: The Source of the Ghost Dance.* ("General Series in Anthropology." No. 1. Leslie Spier, ed.) Menasha, Wis.: George Banta Publishing Co., 1935.

Thwaites, Reuben G. (ed.). *Early Western Travels, 1748–1846.* 32 vols. Cleveland, Ohio: The A. H. Clark Co., 1904–7.

Tolmie, William Fraser. "Journal of William Fraser Tolmie—1833," *Washington Historical Quarterly,* III (July, 1912), 229–41.

————. "Diary of Dr. W. F. Tolmie," ed. Edward Huggins, *Washington Historical Quarterly,* XXIII (1932), 205–27.

Upchurch, O. C. "The Swinomish People and Their State," *Pacific Northwest Quarterly,* XXVII (1936), 283–310.

The Youth's Companion. A Monthly Magazine for the Benefit of the Puget Sound W.T. Indian Missions. Tulalip, Washington Territory: Tulalip Mission Press, 1881–83.

The Washington Standard. (Newspaper). Olympia, Washington Territory.

Waterman, T. T. "The 'Shake Religion' of Puget Sound," *Smithsonian Institution Annual Report for 1922* (Washington, D.C., 1924), pp. 499–507.

INDEX

ABRAHAM, Enoch, 18, 62, 63, 72, 73, 74, 78, 82, 116–17, 121, 148, 179–80, 192–93, 205–6, 212–13, 215–16, 227, 231, 247, 281, 282–84

Abstention: days of, 155–56

Accusations, 137–39

Achomawi Indians, 82

Aggressiveness: and Shakerism, 142

Aiyel, 17, 69–71 passim, 74, 82, 179–80, 196–98, 234

Allen, John, 20

Allotments. See Land

Altar, 15, 43, 204–11 passim, 326. See also Prayer table

Animosities: in Shaker congregations, 137–40, 199

Articles of Incorporation of Shaker church, 13, 15, 110–12, 113–14; supplement to, 122–23

Atonement: Shaker view of, 156

BALCH, James, Lord, 61

Baptism: Shaker, 49, 51–52, 113, 133, 282–83; Christian, 49, 88, 89, 293, 295, 296, 321; Indian view of, 344

Belfries: on churches, 204, 211

Bells, 15, 33, 43, 96, 112, 123, 209–11, 293–94, 334

Benediction: sign of, 287

Bennett, Frank, 122, 123

Bible reading controversy about, 14, 15–16, 53, 115–16, 121, 122, 129, 145, 146–48

Big Bill: prophecy of, 26–27, 40, 48–49, 344–45; and John Slocum, 27, 40–41, 295, 346–47; services of, 27, 49, 101, 346; powers of, 344–45; Christian contacts of, 345

Big John, 48, 55–56, 60, 68, 92, 106, 161, 270

Bishops of Shaker church: title holders, 13, 20, 23, 78, 111; views of, 14, 16, 282; "sub-bishops," 81, 119; establishment of, 111; contentions by, 114–23

Blanchet, A. M. A., Rev., 296

Blanchet, F. N., Rev., 294, 301, 320, 322–23

Blessing: asking of by Shakers, 154. See also Thanksgiving

Blowing on patients, 242

Board of Indian Commissioners, 341

Bob, George, 29

Bois, Cora du. See Du Bois, Cora

Boston Bill, 193

Boulet, Jean Baptiste, Rev., 290, 348

Bowers, Johnny, 65

"Brushing" sins, 52, 53, 170–71. See also Hand movements

Bureau of Catholic Indian Missions, 89

Burial service, 55, 268–69

Business affairs: of Shaker church, 126–27

CALENDAR: religious, 327

Camp meetings: of Shakers, 121, 128–29; of Protestants, 328–29

Candles, 15, 33, 43, 55, 112, 123, 205–9, 289–90

Canticles, 289n, 296n, 319

Catechists: Indian, 289n, 293

Catholicism: influences on Shakerism, 48–55 *passim*, 219, 232, 233–34, 289–96, 314, 317 and n, 318, 319–20, 321, 322–25, 326; resistance to Shakerism, 65–66, 82, 87, 89; losses to Shakers, 66, 75; influence on Big Bill, 345; influence on Billy Clams, 346

Catholic Ladder, 288n, 293, 295

Celilo Falls church, 81

Cemeteries: Shaker, 321

Chalcraft, Edwin L., 95

Charley, David, 49–55 *passim*, 91

Charley, John, 79

Chehalis Shakers, 8, 20, 21, 27–28, 40, 48, 57, 60, 68–69, 81

"Chiefs," 92, 340. *See also* David Charley

Child-parent cleavages, 338

Chiloquin church, 74, 81

Chinook: jargon, 46, 106, 234, 235, 266, 295, 296n, 319; Indians, 293

Chirouse, Eugene Casimir, Rev., 291, 293, 294, 323–24, 327

Churches. *See* Shaker churches

Citizen Indians, 57–58

Civilization of Indians, 338

Clairvoyance, 17, 27, 29, 70, 82, 151, 194–203. *See also* Divination

Clallam Bay, 61

Clallam Indians, 8, 61–62, 81

Clams, Billy, 48–55 *passim*, 59, 134–35, 293, 339–40, 346–47

Clark, Helen, 95, 96, 97, 99, 102, 327

Clerk: of Shaker church, 108, 109, 110, 119, 126

Colfax, Skyler, 63, 214

Collier, Robert, 61

Color symbolism: of Shakers, 208, 212; of Society of Believers, 334

Compensation: of Shaker healers, 17, 25, 127, 173–74, 352; of Shaker officers, 111, 127

Confession: enjoined by John Slocum, 31, 144, 283; frequency of, 159; a Shaker "gift," 160; rite of, 283–84, 316; Christian, 294

Conflicts: of Slocums and Thompsons, 32–33, 351; of Eells and "Catholic set," 48–55 *passim*, 339–40; of Mud Bay Louis and Mary Slocum, 48, 59–60, 135–36, 216, 227; between bishops, 114–23; within congregations, 137–40

Congregational Church: converts to, 47, 49, 61, 344; membership of, 50, 51; attitude toward Shakerism, 86, 87, 89; influence on Shakerism, 288, 289. *See also* Myron Eells

Conscience: Shakerism as an expression of, 141

Conventions: Shaker, 127–29, 250–55, 274–75, 275–81

Conversion: public admission of, 77, 132–33, 272, 273–74; shaking as evidence of, 133, 147; relief of, 178; procedure in, 179–80; as rebirth, 181; obligations resulting from, 181–86; reasons for, 186–87; rite of, 269–82; specialists in, 270–71

Cortesa, Clara, 63

Courts of Indian Offenses, 58

Covey, Claude C., 95

Cowichan Shakers, 66, 81, 109–10

Cowlitz Shakers, 17, 69–70, 234

Cree, Sophie, 179

Cross, 53, 63, 204–5, 321–22

Crossing, 31, 53, 55, 63, 65, 68, 112, 231–32, 233–34, 289

Culture: collapse of, 338–39

Cures: by Shakers, 187–94

Cush, Lee, 116

Customs: forbidden, 5, 58, 338

DANCES: aboriginal, 312–13

Dawes Severalty Act, 57, 58, 72–73

Death: Shaker allusions to, 27, 186, 238; and resurrection concept, 299–301, 305–6

Dedication: of Shaker garments, 217; of Shaker bells, 281–82

Demers, Modest, Rev., 287, 288, 293, 322, 323

Deprivation: social consequences of, 4; among Puget Sound Indians, 4–5, 338–39

De Smet, Father, 320–21, 324

Devil, 27, 34, 147, 157, 163, 188, 205, 231
Directions: significance for Shakers, 163, 173, 218–19, 227, 314, 321
Dispossession: threat of, 341–42
Disease: Shaker theories of, 146, 164–73. *See also* Soul loss; Spirit intrusion; "Sickness"; Sin; "Pains"
Divination: Shaker rite of, 267–68. *See also* Forecasting
"Drawing" sins, 151. *See also* Hand movements
Dress: of Shakers, 240–41. *See also* Garments; Vestments
Du Bois, Cora, 304n, 330

ECONOMIC changes, 338, 340–41
Education: Indian, 5, 58, 338
Eells, Edwin: and Myron Eells, 48; and suppression of Shakerism, 55, 86, 90–94; authority of, 57–58, 91; and Cushing Eells, 90; later attitude toward Shakerism, 100; and Billy Clams, 339–40; and land survey, 340
Eells, Myron, Rev.: on John Slocum's death and resurrection, 34, 38–39, 87; as religious instructor of John Slocum, 37, 39, 49; and religious revival, 46–47, 50–51, 343; and Billy Clams, 48–55 *passim*, 339–40; on shaking, 53, 90, 100–101, 311; and information on Shakers, 102; and M. G. Mann, 102; songs composed by, 235, 319; on sins of Indians, 297; and religious instruction in Indian homes, 327; on teaching prayers to Indians, 328; and Big Bill, 345–47
Elders: of Shaker church: named, 18, 76, 78, 82, 124; appointment of, 108, 109, 119; charter for, 111, 113; acts of, 114, 116–17, 135, 138, 281, 282; duties of, 124–25; of Presbyterian church: appointment of, 104, 105
Elwha, 61
English, Johnny, 65
Epidemics, 342–43
Evangelists: Shakers specializing as, 129–31 *passim*

Evil spirits, 169
Expenses, 126–27, 128

FACIAL expressions: while shaking, 220
"Fanning" sickness. *See* Hand movements
Five: as ritual number, 20, 63, 214
Flame: candle, 207–8, 209, 223
Flowers: as ritual ornaments, 211–12
Food taboos: of Shakers, 242
Forecasting: by Shakers, 199–202. *See also* Divination
Fort Nisqually journal, 303
Four: as ritual number, 15, 20, 24, 35, 36, 42, 43, 204–5, 206, 207, 240, 276, 317–18

GARD, Paul, Rev., 183
Garments, 22, 112, 215–17, 277, 322
George, Norman, 78
Georgetown church, 81
Ghost Dance, 13, 21
Ghosts: cause of illness, 189–92
"Gifts": of Shakers: importance of for change, 9, 19; examples of, 160–62, 204–5, 207–8, 211, 212–13, 213–14, 215, 229–30, 282, 283–84; eligibility for, 162–63; nature of, 162–64; acceptance of, 163, 207–8; of Society of Believers, 334–35
Giles, Milton, 110–13 *passim*, 119
Guilt: and Shakerism, 141, 176–77
Gunyer, Frank, 74

HALL, Jacob, 61
Hall, William, 61–62, 227–28, 231, 282
Handkerchiefs: in Shaker curing rites, 217–18, 222, 223, 280
Hand movements: of Shakers, 221–24, 312, 331
Handshake: of Shakers: uses of, 17, 19, 25, 28, 31, 35, 41–42, 46, 55, 112; ritual, 228–31; origin of, 322–25; of Slocum, 287–88
Headmen: of Shakers, 108, 113–14
Healers: Shakers specializing as, 17, 129–31 *passim*
Healing: Shaker ceremony of, 256–62; instances of rites, 262–64

Heaven: in Shaker belief, 145, 149, 156–57, 215, 227, 230; in Christian belief, 296
Heck, Peter, 20, 23–27, 67–68, 78, 114–23 *passim*, 119, 120, 122, 184–86, 191–92, 282
Heck, Silas, 20–23, 67, 68
Hell, 23, 27, 47, 145, 154, 155, 157–59, 295, 296, 317
Hoffer, Homer, 70, 75
Howiatl, Charlie, 116, 118, 120
Hunaitca, 74
Hunter, David, 61
Hupa church, 80–81
Hupa Shakers, 13–16, 79–81, 138
Hymns, 318, 323

IKE, John, 20
Indian Bureau, 58–59
"Indian devils," 79–80, 137–38, 172
Individualism: in Shakerism, 9–10, 132, 134, 140, 224–25
Inheritance rules: changes in, 338
Iroquois Indians, 292, 324

JACK, George, 78, 79
Jack, Jimmy, 12–13, 75–77, 78, 79, 188, 269
Jackson, Dick, 284
Jackson, Richard, 60
Jackson (of Siletz), 76–77, 78, 138, 200, 273–74
Jacobs, Isaac, 67
James, Annie, 30–34, 167, 200, 202
James, Bob, 169
James, William (Bill), 60–61
Jamestown, 47, 61–63, 228–29, 274–75, 344
Jesuits, 320–21
Joe, Peter, 119
Johns, C. J., 17–18, 187–88, 262
Johnson, Johnny, 70, 71, 216
Johnson's Landing, 79, 81, 138, 161

KALAPA, Lans, 63–64, 96–97, 136, 161–62, 205, 213–14, 233
Karok Indians, 82
Kelso church, 69, 81
Kentucky Revival, 334
Kitsap, William, 116–23 *passim*, 147, 277, 281
Klamath Shakers, 74, 75, 76, 81, 189–91

Klickam, Bob, 65
Kneeling: Shaker practice of, 239–40; Christian practice of, 294–95
Koksilah church, 66, 81
Krise, Mary Bob, 39, 277

LAND: ceded by Puget Sound Indians, 4–5, 6–7, 340; allotment of, 57, 340; titles to, 340–41, 342
Lang, Thomas, 78
"Laying on" of hands. *See* Hand movements
Leadership: Shaker concept of, 107, 108–9, 124; legal definition of in Shaker church, 111–12, 124; informal growth of in Shaker church, 129–31; refusal of by Shakers, 139
Lee, Ann, 74, 333
Lewis, Dick, 49–55 *passim*, 59, 91, 117
Longview, 60, 69–70
Lost objects, 196–98
Lumley, David, 71
Lumley, Sarah, 70–71
Lummi Indians, 57, 81

MAKAH Indians, 62, 63–65, 81, 94–100
Mann, M. G., Rev.: and Squaxin Indians, 39, 46; and Shaker leaders, 69, 88–89, 102–6; and relations with the Eells brothers, 102–3; on Catholics, 298; in Indian homes, 327; prayer meetings of, 328–29; and Shaker fervor, 329–30
Marching movements. *See* Ritual circuits
Marriage: by Shaker officers, 113
"Medicine": of Shakers, 14, 16, 22, 23, 25, 295, 342–43; of Catholic missionaries, 295–96
Membership, 107, 131–33, 134
Messianic cults, 142. *See also* Prophet Dance; Smohalla cult; Pom Pom religion
Messiahs: appearance of, 3–4; among Indians, 86n, 100–1, 292, 304, 306, 330
Millennium: of Shakers, 24–25, 27, 31, 42–43, 51–52, 56, 88, 144, 174–75, 238–39

Ministers of Shaker church: provision for, 108, 112, 113; licensing of, 109–10; duties of, 125, 133

Minor, Edwin, 97

Miracles: in Shaker belief, 160–62

Missionaries: Christian: competition for Indian converts among, 5, 89, 104, 297–98; attitudes toward shaking, 15, 53, 87–90, 101, 102–6. *See also* A. M. A. Blanchet; F. N. Blanchet; Jean Boulet; Eugene Chirouse; Modest Demers; Myron Eells; Paul Gard; M. G. Mann; Shaker: institution of, 108, 113; duties of, 125

Mooney, James, 13, 20–21

Morality of Shakers: officers, 134–35; importance of, 146

Morse, Samuel G., 94–95

Mowitch Man, 52, 136

Muckleshoot church, 66, 81

Mud Bay church, 60, 62, 81

Mud Bay Louis (or Louie): as cult leader, 13, 15, 16–17, 18, 19, 20, 23, 28, 43, 48, 59, 68, 93, 94, 98–99, 108, 312; as convert, 47–48; in opposition to Mary Slocum, 48–59, 60, 135–36; as Presbyterian elder, 104–5; death of, 109, 119; and garments, 215–16; and handshake, 229–30; service decreed by, 244–45; curing rite initiated by, 259; and confession rite, 283–84, 316

Mud Bay Sam: as cult leader, 15, 18, 20, 68, 93; as convert, 47–48; as paramount healer, 47, 108, 136, 173; as headman, 109, 110; as bishop, 111; death, 114, 119

Musquium Indians, 66

NAME of Shakers, 108

Nanaimo Indians, 66

Nativism: and Shakerism, 142–43

Neah Bay, 63

Newton, Annie, 61

Nez Perce Indians, 83

Nisqually Indians, 8, 29, 31, 39, 46, 57, 61, 303, 322, 341

Norton, W., 188–89, 199–200, 202

BER, Sarah Endicott: on Shaker origins, 37–38, 348; as Shaker sympathizer, 99; on Shaker customs, 155, 160, 260, 265–66, 274–75; on death of John Slocum, 349

Office of Indian Affairs: policy of, 91, 100, 341–42. *See also* Dawes Severalty Act

Officers: of Shaker church. *See* Articles of Incorporation; Bishops; Clerks; Elders; Headmen; Ministers; Missionaries; Preachers

Olson, Ronald, 69, 182

Ordination, 133–34, 281

Oyster Bay church, 60, 62, 81

"PAINS": nature of, 171; cure of, 171; sources of, 172

"Patting": in Shaker curing. *See* Hand movements

Persecution. *See* Suppression of Shakers

Pictures: sacred, 318–19, 343–44

"Poisoning": by shamans, 25–26. *See also* "Indian devils"

Pom Pom religion: and Shakerism, 142, 292, 321–22. *See also* Smohalla cult

Port Angeles, 61

Port Discovery, 61

Port Gamble, 61, 62, 65–66

Postures: while shaking. *See* Facial expressions; Hand movements; Stamping; Kneeling

Potlatch: of Mud Bay Sam, 109; of Tyhee Jack, 215; and Shaker feasts, 314–15, 315n, 316

Power: Shaker concept of, 19, 27, 28, 29, 34, 36, 38, 42, 67–68, 98, 145–46; nature of, 149–50, 151; locus of, 150; effect of, 150–51; good and bad, 163–64; and white men, 174; invitation of, 221–22

Powers, John, 60

Prayer, 31, 33, 34, 36–37, 42, 68, 112, 144, 153–55, 213, 237–39, 294, 295, 328

Prayer meetings, 327–28, 343

Prayer table, 204, 206, 211–13, 290–91

Preachers: licensing of Shaker, 112

Prediction. *See* Forecasting

Presbyterians: attitude toward Shakers, 63, 82, 83, 87, 88–89, 93, 95–97, 99–100, 102–6; new congregations of, 88, 89; and Shaker ideology, 145; and influences on Shakerism, 288, 289, 327; and John Slocum, 349. *See also* M. G. Mann

Processions. *See* Ritual circuits

Prophet Dance, 292, 301, 302, 303, 304, 305, 306, 324, 330

Prophets. *See* Messiahs

Progressive-conservative splits, 338

Proselytizing: by Shakers, 183–86

Protestant influences: on Shakers: leadership structure, 107–8, 326; songs, 235, 319; on concept of sin, 297–99; after the year 1883, 325–30; on John Slocum, 296–99

Purgatory: and Shakers, 156

Puyallup Indians, 8, 39, 45, 48, 57, 58, 60, 61, 81

QUEETS Shakers, 69, 121, 122

Quileute Shakers, 65, 69, 81, 95, 97, 98, 99, 272

Quinault Shakers, 69, 81, 121, 122, 182–83, 271, 272

RAKESTRAW, Charles D., 157, 258, 349

Rank: aboriginal pattern of, 320

Reagan, Albert B., 63–64, 65, 96, 97, 98, 99–100, 161, 236, 238, 272

Religion: appeal of to Puget Sound Indians, 343–44

Reservations: establishment of, 5

Revelation: as basis of Shaker belief, 149

Revival meetings: and Shaker services, 327–28

Riddle, Joe, 63, 72, 74, 78, 179, 181, 183–84, 227–28, 230, 284

Ritual circuits: of Indian Shakers, 112, 227–28, 230–32, 239–40, 278, 312; of Smohalla cultists, 331; of Society of Believers, 335–36

Ritual numbers. *See* Three; Four; Five; Seven; Twelve

Ritual obligations, 182–86

Rules and By-Laws: of Shaker church, 13, 110, 112–13

SAINTS' days, 327

Sanders, George, 29

Sanetch Indians, 66, 81

Satus Creek church, 72, 81

"Scooping" sickness. *See* Hand movements

"Scraping" sickness. *See* Hand movements

Seven: as ritual number, 15, 16, 240, 266, 317

Sexes, separation of: by Shakers, 226–27, 320; source of idea, 320–21; by Society of Believers, 334

Shaker churches: establishment of, 59–82 *passim*; locations of, 81; construction and furnishings of, 218–19, 314

Shaker cult: spread of, 8, 59–85 *passim*; and Christianity, 8, 64, 143, 144, 148; independence of, 8–9, 143; syncretism of, 8–9, 143; changes in, 9–10; incorporation of, 13, 15, 64, 100, 110–12; as an Indian religion, 16, 141; membership of, 36, 48, 80, 83–84; anonymous statement on, 40–44, 119–21, 318, 350; legal foundation of, 59; "mother church" of, 60, 129, 314; official attitudes toward, 86–87, 89–90; conservatives, moderates, and progressives of, 144–49; puritanical code of, 297–99

Shaking: first reports of, 8, 50; religious impact of, 50, 144–45; physical consequences of, 96; as evidence of conversion, 133, 147; conservative-progressive differences on, 147–48; cures by, 187–94; movements of, 220–26; physical aspect of, 225–26; native background of, 308–16; Christian accretions of, 317–30

Shamanism: effects on Shakerism, 8, 47, 145, 166–68, 171, 308–12; antagonism of Shakers for, 25, 28, 29, 30, 31–32, 38, 142, 164, 165–66, 172–73, 193–94; abolition of, 58, 96, 338

Shamanistic contests, 138–39, 173

"Sickness," 169–70, 211

Sign of the cross. *See* Crossing
Siletz Shakers, 12, 70, 75, 76, 81
Simmons, J. W., 60
Sin: concept of, 38, 141, 144, 156, 297–99; kinds of, 99, 112–13, 177–79; cause of illness, 170–71
Singing: appeal of for Indian, 319
Sinners: exposure of by Shakers, 199
Simpson, Captain, 71–72
Skagit Indians, 81
Skokomish Indians, 8, 27, 30, 31, 38, 40, 46–47, 48, 50, 52, 57, 58, 81, 91, 100, 227, 315, 341–42, 343
Slocum, Jack, 20, 23-24, 30, 31, 60
Slocum, John: personal characteristics of, 6, 7, 21, 28, 310, 349, 350; vices of, 6, 15, 16, 24, 31–32, 39, 41, 157, 158; preaching of, 6, 17–18, 19, 22–23, 24, 25, 28, 29, 31, 39, 41–42, 296–97; second illness of, 6, 18, 19, 25, 28, 31–32; family of, 6, 23, 26, 196; backsliding of, 6, 31–32; early life of, 6, 347; alleged death and resurrection of, 6–7, 11, 13, 14, 15, 17, 18–19, 20, 21–22, 23–24, 28, 29, 30–31, 37–38, 39, 41, 49, 88, 157–59, 299–301; vision of, 6–7, 14, 15, 16, 22, 41; as proselytizer, 7, 28, 93, 349; objection to shaking by, 15, 16, 25, 29, 34, 310; threats of dying by, 22–23, 330; own account of experiences, 35–37; Catholic influence on, 37, 39, 289–96; affliction of, 41, 350–51; as cult leader, 107, 108, 349; clairvoyance of, 194–96, 238; vestment of, 214; service of, 238–39, 244; generic Christian influences on, 285–89; Protestant influences on, 296–99; native influences on, 299–307; eclipse of, 311, 349; birth and death of, 347, 348–49; hatred of shamans by, 351–52. *See also* Billy Clams
Slocum, Mary: Marriage to John Slocum, 6; and origin of shaking, 7, 14, 15, 16, 17–18, 19, 23, 25, 28–29, 33–34, 38, 43; "teachings" of, 29, 214, 227, 241; death of, 139; clairvoyance of, 194; song of,

235–36; and Smohalla cult, 330
Slocum, Tom, 23–24, 30, 31
Smet, Father de. *See* De Smet, Father
Smith, Ed, 69, 104, 108
Smith, John, 67, 68, 69, 104–5, 349
Smohalla cult: color symbolism of, 209; messianic character of, 292–93, 304; and Shakerism, 301, 313, 314, 321–22, 330–32; ritual movements of, 331
Snohomish Indians, 81
Songish Indians, 66, 81
Songs of Shakers: importance of, 15, 43, 49, 76, 93–94, 112, 152; good and bad, 152–53; "gift" of, 162; characteristics of, 235–38, 239; Christian sources of, 319
Soul in Shaker belief: destiny of, 146, 156–57; loss of, 151, 165–66, 189–93; nature, 165, 166, 192
Specialization, 129–31
Spier, Leslie, 69n, 71n, 82n, 168, 197, 291–92, 300, 301, 302, 303, 306, 331
Spirit intrusion, 166–69, 193–94
Spirit possession, 313
Spott, Robert, 77, 199, 272–73
Squamish Indians, 66–67
Squaxin Indians, 5, 9, 39, 55, 57, 91, 104, 341
Stamping: while shaking, 220–21, 313
Stanley, Pedro, 74
Stanup, Peter, 89
Steve, Johnny, 65, 94
Stick bundles: as mnemonic devices, 283–84, 316
Sunday: as day of rest for Shakers. *See* Abstention
Suppression of Shakers, 9, 15, 20, 43–44, 55–56, 59, 63–64, 65, 90–106 *passim*, 145
Swinomish Indians, 57, 81
Systematization: of Shaker belief, 143–44

"TEACHINGS" of Shakers. *See* "Gifts"
Teio, Alex, 71, 72, 74, 82, 114, 197, 212–13, 217, 247, 268
Teio, Harry, 74, 116
Teio, Mabel, 71, 178, 197, 201–2

Temperance: of Shakers, 298–99
Temptation: Shaker view of, 159–60
Testimonials, 176–77, 328
Thanksgiving: Shaker rite of, 264–67, 319–20
Thompson, Isaac, 1~~ 28. 20. 32, 33, 34, 43,
Thompson, Mary. S
Three: as ritual num~ 21, 43, 54, 213, 24
Tobacco habit, 188–8
Tobin, James, 60
Tolmie, William Fra~ 303, 304, 305
Tolowa Indians, 78, 81
Tom, Isadore, 277–80 *pa*
Treaty, 4–5, 57, 340
Tulalip church, 206, 219, 2~ 82
Tulalip Shakers, 57, 65–66, ~ 94, 100, 275–81
Turner, Ery, 78, 79
Twelve: as a ritual number, ~ 207, 219, 240, 276, 317

UMATILLA Indians, 82–83
Unbelievers, 23, 27, 51, 330
Underwood, Burt, 119
United Society of Believers in Christ's Second Appearing (or "Society of Believers" or "Ann Lee Shakers"), 333–36
Upchurch, O. C., 255, 258n
"Ushers": at Shaker meetings, 315

VERBAL expressions: in Shaker ritual, 233–35
Vestments: Shaker, 182–83, 214–17, 291, 292–93. *See also* Garments
Vices: introduced by whites, 5, 338–39; Indian's weakness for, 6, 177; Shaker rejection of, 20, 22, 28, 29, 31, 41, 99, 112, 142, 159–60

Visionaries: as Shaker leaders, 129, 131, 151
Visions: of Shakers, 52, 53, 79–80, 92, 144, 215, 217; aboriginal background of, 299; of Society of Believers, 333; of Big Bill, 345,

See Aiyel
~69, 93, 104
~342
~rs, 74, 81
~46
~1, 72

~uoting John
~oting Mud
~court case,
~rs, 59, 60,
~ganizer of
~oducer of
~, 332–34

~nts, 163,
~52, 335
~of, 17,
~, 155–
~327;
~er of,

~of,
~26;
~7
~5,

Ya~ 8
Yuct~ 32,
Yucto~
Yurok 199

ZACK, William, 70